'Alas! the love of Women!'

BYRON'S LETTERS AND JOURNALS
VOLUME 3
1813–1814

Alas! the love of Women! it is known
   To be a lovely and a fearful thing;
For all of theirs upon that die is thrown,
   And if 't is lost, Life hath no more to bring
To them but mockeries of the past alone,
   And their revenge is as the tiger's spring,
Deadly, and quick, and crushing; yet, as real
Torture is theirs—what they inflict they feel.
                DON JUAN, 2, 199

BYRON
From a portrait by
Thomas Phillips, RA, 1814

'Alas! the love of Women!'

BYRON'S LETTERS AND JOURNALS

Edited by
LESLIE A. MARCHAND

VOLUME 3
1813–1814

*The complete and unexpurgated text of
all the letters available in manuscript and
the full printed version of all others*

THE BELKNAP PRESS OF
HARVARD UNIVERSITY PRESS
CAMBRIDGE, MASSACHUSETTS
1974

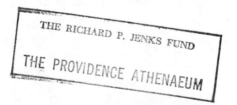

CONTENTS

Editorial Note   vii

Byron Chronology   xiii

TEXT OF THE LETTERS   3
(January 1, 1813—December 31, 1813)

JOURNAL
(November 14, 1813—April 19, 1814.)   204

Appendix   I   List of Letters and Sources   259

          II   List of Forgeries of Byron's Letters   269

         III   Bibliography for Volume 3   270

         IV   Biographical Sketches for Volume 3   271

Index of proper names   275

EDITORIAL NOTE

It is my intention in this volume and all succeeding ones to follow the editorial principles set forth in the first volume (*In My Hot Youth*), but for convenience they are repeated at the end of this editorial note and will be repeated in future volumes. To make each as self-contained as possible, the Byron chronology, the list of letters and sources, the list of forgeries, and the bibliography are added as they pertain to the letters in the volume. This applies also to the acknowledgments and the index of proper names. Biographical sketches of chief correspondents and persons frequently mentioned are added as they first appear in the text. The final volume will contain a subject index and a cumulative index of all the volumes. It is planned also to include there all letters discovered too late to place in their proper chronological sequence in earlier volumes.

ACKNOWLEDGMENTS. (Volume 3). I owe a continuing debt of gratitude to John G. Murray for his inestimable assistance and encouragement to me in the editing of this volume as of previous ones. A Research Grant from the National Endowment for the Humanities enabled me to travel to libraries while I was working on the notes, and to make an extensive tour in England, Italy, and Greece to search for new letters and get photocopies of them. Mr. John S. Borden, Program Specialist, Division of Research Grants of the National Endowment, deserves my special thanks for his help. I wish to thank the Earl of Lytton for his permission to print letters of Byron to Annabella Milbanke before their marriage, parts of which are hitherto unpublished and which are under his control. Mrs. Doris Langley Moore has furnished me with much valuable information from her extensive study of Byron's accounts.

For permission to get photocopies of letters in their possession and to use them in this volume I wish to thank the following libraries and individuals: Beinecke Rare Book and Manuscript Library, Yale University; Henry E. and Albert A. Berg Collection, New York Public Library; Bodleian Library, Oxford; British Museum (Department of Manuscripts); Waverley B. Cameron; Clark Library, University of California at Los Angeles; Houghton Library, Harvard University; Henry E. Huntington Library; The Earl of Lytton;

John S. Mayfield Library, Syracuse University; Mrs. C. Earle Miller; Pierpont Morgan Library; Mr. John Murray; National Library of Scotland; Nottingham Public Libraries; Carl H. Pforzheimer Library; Meyer Davis Collection, University of Pennsylvania Library; Robert H. Taylor Collection, Princeton University Library; Francis Lewis Randolph; Gordon N. Ray; Roe-Byron Collection, Newstead Abbey; Royal College of Surgeons Library; Stark Library, University of Texas; Trinity College Library, Cambridge; Victoria and Albert Museum (John Forster Collection); D. M. S. Watson Library, University College London.

For assistance of various kinds I wish to thank the following: Dott. Domenico Berardi, Director of Historical Archives and Acting Director of the Biblioteca Classense, Ravenna; John Buxton; Vera Cacciatore; Contessa Emmy Calderara-Gamba; John Clubbe; Miss Lucy Edwards; Malcolm Elwin; Paul Fussell, Jr.; Professor Ian Greenlees, Director of the British Institute, Florence; Piero Innocenti, Department of Manuscripts, Biblioteca Nazionale Centrale, Florence; E. D. H. Johnson, M. K. Joseph; John S. Mayfield; Panagiotis G. Nicolopoulos, Curator of Manuscripts of the National Library of Greece, Athens; Professor E. S. Pearson, University College, London; Mrs. Percival, University College, London; M. Byron Raizis; Gordon N. Ray; Theodore Reff; Donald H. Reiman; William St. Clair; T. G. Steffan; Paul Sykes; Nassos Tzartzanos; Carl Woodring.

* * * * * *

EDITORIAL PRINCIPLES. With minor exceptions, herein noted, I have tried to reproduce Byron's letters as they were written. The letters are arranged consecutively in chronological order. The name of the addressee is given at the top left in brackets. The source of the text is indicated in the list of letters in the Appendix. If it is a printed text, it is taken from the first printed form of the letter known or presumed to be copied from the original manuscript, or from a more reliable editor, such as Prothero, when he also had access to the manuscript. In this case, as with handwritten or typed copies, or quotations in sale catalogues, the text of this source is given precisely.

When the text is taken from the autograph letter or a photo copy or facsimile of it, the present whereabouts or ownership is given, whether it is in a library or a private collection. When the manuscript

viii

is the source, no attempt is made to indicate previous publication, if any. Here I have been faithful to the manuscript with the following exceptions:

1. The place and date of writing is invariably placed at the top right in one line if possible to save space, and to follow Byron's general practice. Fortunately Byron dated most of his letters in this way, but occasionally he put the date at the end. Byron's usual custom of putting no punctuation after the year is followed throughout.

2. Superior letters such as S^r or 30th have been lowered to Sr. and 30th. The & has been retained, but &^{c} has been printed &c.

3. Byron's spelling has been followed (and generally his spelling is good, though not always consistent), and *sic* has been avoided except in a few instances when an inadvertent misspelling might change the meaning or be ambiguous, as for instance when he spells *there* t-h-e-i-r.

4. Although, like many of his contemporaries, Byron was inconsistent and eccentric in his capitalization, I have felt it was better to let him have his way, to preserve the flavour of his personality and his times. With him the capital letter sometimes indicates the importance he gives to a word in a particular context; but in the very next line it might not be capitalized. If clarity has seemed to demand a modification, I have used square brackets to indicate any departure from the manuscript.

5. Obvious slips of the pen crossed out by the writer have been silently omitted. But crossed out words of any significance to the meaning or emphasis are enclosed in angled brackets ⟨ ⟩.

6. Letters undated, or dated with the day of the week only, have been dated, when possible, in square brackets. If the date is conjectural, it is given with a question mark in brackets. The same practice is followed for letters from printed sources. The post mark date is given, to indicate an approximate date, only when the letter itself is undated.

7. The salutation is put on the same line as the text, separated from it by a dash. The complimentary closing, often on several lines in the manuscript, is given in one line if possible. The P.S., wherever it may be written in the manuscript, follows the signature.

8. Byron's punctuation follows no rules of his own or others' making. He used dashes and commas freely, but for no apparent reason, other than possibly for natural pause between phrases, or sometimes for emphasis. He is guilty of the "comma splice", and one can seldom be sure where he intended to end a sentence, or whether

ix

he recognized the sentence as a unit of expression. He did at certain intervals place a period and a dash, beginning again with a capital letter. These larger divisions sometimes, though not always, represented what in other writers, particularly in writers of today, correspond to paragraphs. He sometimes used semicolons, but often where we would use commas. Byron himself recognized his lack of knowledge of the logic or the rules of punctuation. He wrote to his publisher John Murray on August 26, 1813: "Do you know anybody who can *stop*—I mean point—commas and so forth, for I am I fear a sad hand at your punctuation." It is not without reason then that most editors, including R. E. Prothero, have imposed sentences and paragraphs on him in line with their interpretation of his intended meaning. It is my feeling, however, that this detracts from the impression of Byronic spontaneity and the onrush of ideas in his letters, without a compensating gain in clarity. In fact, it may often arbitrarily impose a meaning or an emphasis not intended by the writer. I feel that there is less danger of distortion if the reader may see exactly how he punctuated and then determine whether a phrase between commas or dashes belongs to one sentence or another. Byron's punctuation seldom if ever makes the reading difficult or the meaning unclear. In rare instances I have inserted a period, a comma, or a semicolon, but have enclosed it in square brackets to indicate it was mine and not his.

9. Words missing but obvious from the context, such as those lacunae caused by holes in the manuscript, are supplied within square brackets. If they are wholly conjectural, they are followed by a question mark. The same is true of doubtful readings in the manuscript.

Undated letters have been placed within the chronological sequence when from internal or external evidence there are reasonable grounds for a conjectural date. This has seemed more useful than putting them together at the end of the volumes. Where a more precise date cannot be established from the context, these letters are placed at the beginning of the month or year in which they seem most likely to have been written.

ANNOTATION. I have tried to make the footnotes as brief and informative as possible, eschewing, sometimes with reluctance, the leisurely expansiveness of R. E. Prothero, who in his admirable edition of the *Letters and Journals* often gave pages of supplementary biographical information and whole letters *to* Byron, which was possible at a time when book publishing was less expensive, and when the extant and available Byron letters numbered scarcely more than a third of those in the present edition. Needless to say, I have found Prothero's notes of inestimable assistance in the identification of persons and quotations in the letters which he edited, though where possible I have double checked them. And I must say that while I have found some errors, they are rare. With this general acknowledgment I have left the reader to assume that where a source of information in the notes is not given, it comes from Prothero's edition, where additional details may be found.

The footnotes are numbered for each letter. Where the numbers are repeated on a page, the sequence of the letters will make the reference clear.

In an appendix in each volume I have given brief biographical sketches of Byron's principal correspondents first appearing in that volume. These are necessarily very short, and the stress is always on Byron's relations with the subject of the sketch. Identification of less frequent correspondents and other persons mentioned in the letters are given in footnotes as they appear, and the location of these, as well as the biographical sketches in the appendix, will be indicated by italic numbers in the index. Similarly italic indications will refer the reader to the principal biographical notes on persons mentioned in the text of the letters.

With respect to the annotation of literary allusions and quotations in the letters, I have tried to identify all quotations in the text, but have not always been successful in locating Byron's sources in obscure dramas whose phrases, serious or ridiculous, haunted his memory. When I have failed to identify either a quotation or a name, I have frankly said so, instead of letting the reader suppose that I merely passed it by as unimportant or overlooked it. No doubt readers with special knowledge in various fields may be able to enlighten me. If so, I shall try to make amends with notes in later volumes.

I have sometimes omitted the identification of familiar quotations. But since this work will be read on both sides of the Atlantic, I have explained some things that would be perfectly clear to a British reader but not to an American. I trust that English readers will make allowance for this. As Johnson said in the Preface to his edition of Shakespeare: "It is impossible for an expositor not to write too little for some, and too much for others . . . how long soever he may deliberate, [he] will at last explain many lines which the learned will think impossible to be mistaken, and omit many for which the ignorant will want his help. These are censures merely relative, and must be quietly endured."

I have occasionally given cross references, but in the main have left it to the reader to consult the index for names which have been identified in earlier notes.

SPECIAL NOTE, The letters to Thomas Moore, first published by him in his *Letters and Journals of Lord Byron* (1830), were printed with many omissions and the manuscripts have since disappeared. Moore generally indicated omissions by asterisks, here reproduced as in his text. The same is true of the Journal of 1813-1814, the manuscript of which was no longer extant when Prothero published it from Moore.

BYRON CHRONOLOGY

1813 Jan. 1–17—At Eywood Presteign, with Lady Oxford.

Jan. 19—Returned to London—at lodgings, 4 Bennet St., St. James's.

Jan.–Feb.—Frequent visits to Princess Caroline with Lady Oxford.

March—Schemes for going abroad with Oxfords or others.

—First version of *The Giaour* written—private printing of *The Waltz*.

March 28—Accompanied Oxfords to Eywood.

April 24—Back in London.

May 20—Accompanied Moore on visit to Leigh Hunt in jail.

June 1—Last speech in House of Lords, presenting Cartwright's petition.

June 5—First edition of *Giaour* published.

June 20—Met Madame de Staël.

June 27—Took his sister Augusta to see Madame de Staël at Lady Davy's.

July 1—Preparations to go abroad.

—Much in society—intimate with Sheridan, Rogers, Moore, Colman.

Aug.—deeply involved in liaison with his half-sister Augusta.

—correspondence with Miss Milbanke begun.

Sept.—visit to Wedderburn Webster.

Oct.—"Platonic" love for Lady Frances Webster.

—Wrote amusing account of affair to Lady Melbourne.

Oct. 19—Byron "spared" Lady Frances and returned to London.

Nov.—Wrote *Bride of Abydos*.

Nov. 14—Began Journal (continued to April 19, 1814).

Dec. 2—*Bride of Abydos* published.

Dec.—Love affair with Lady Frances Webster degenerating.

Dec. 18—Began *The Corsair*.

1814 Jan. 17—Set out for Newstead with Augusta.

Feb. 1—*Corsair* sold 10,000 copies on day of publication.

Feb. 6—Left Newstead for London.

Feb.—Attacked in Tory press for "Lines to a Lady Weeping".

March—Sat to Phillips for portrait.
March 28—Took apartment in Albany.
April 2—With Augusta at Six-Mile-Bottom.
April—"Ode to Napoleon Buonaparte."

BYRON'S LETTERS AND JOURNALS

[TO LADY MELBOURNE (*a*)]   *Monday.* [*1813?*]

My dear Ly. M[elbourn]e,—Your letter is quite a *relief* & all I hope is, that she[1] may fall into what she calls love at the fête, or into anything that may keep her in some order. When you get the picture I will send her request & you may promise whatever you please or she requires—except a conference.

Blake[2] in the course of [a] month will perform the part of a Gnome better than even your dexterous La–ship.

All these fooleries are very well at the beginning—but I don't understand them at the winding up of these concerns. Her letter is burnt according to order. The seclusion from your society is one and not the least weighty of the 500 reasons I have for wishing her safe in the country or quiet in town. Adieu for the present. I wish you well through *her* & all your approaching fatigues.

Believe me Yrs. ever, Dear Ly. M., B.

[TO LADY MELBOURNE (*b*)]   [*1813?*]

Dear Ly. M.—I send you four brace of *grouse* from my Moors.— just arrived from Rochdale & I hope fresh.—I have been signing the N[ewstea]d contracts today, & that business is happily terminated.—

ever yrs.

[TO LADY MELBOURNE. (*c*)]   *Monday Even.* [*1813?*]

A "person of the least consequence"! you wrong yourself there my dear Ly. M—& so far *she* is right—you know very well, & so do I—that you can make me do whatever you please *without reluctance*— I am sure there exists no one to whom I feel half so much obliged—& for whom (gratitude apart) I entertain a greater regard.——With regard to *her*[1]—I certainly *love*—& in that case it has always been my

---

[1] Lady Caroline Lamb. Byron was pestered by her when he wanted to be quiet with his new mistress, Lady Oxford.

[2] Blake was a famous barber who cut the locks of the aristocracy. Byron mentioned him in a letter to his sister. March 25, 1817, and again on Nov. 18, 1820, in a letter to Murray. Byron thought highly of him as a person as well as a barber as is indicated in the letter to Murray and in a note to line 476 of *Hints from Horace*. The reference here is not clear.

[1] Lady Oxford.

lot to be entirely at the disposal of "la regnante" their caprices I cannot reason upon—& only obey them.—In favour of my acquaintance with you there is however a *special clause*—& nothing shall make me cancel it I promise you.—I meant to have paid you a visit on Saturday in your box—but I thought it possible C[aroline] might be there—from her I find 2 epistles—in the last the old story of the interview to which if she still harps upon it I have no objection—she desires me not to go to Ly. Ossulstone's—I was not asked—she was there—I presume—for she talks of going away if *I* came.—But I can't help laughing at the *coincidence* of objections in the *late* & *present* to my going there—both unnecessary—for the presence of the one or the absence of the other would operate sufficiently as a dissuasive.—I am just returned from Harrow—where I managed to get a headache which that I may not communicate I will close this sheet—ever dr. Ly. M.

yrs. most truly
B

P.S.—C[aroline]'s letter is half in rhyme—an additional proof that she is not in earnest—at least I know from experience—one may *begin* with it—or *end*—when the subject is dead or changed and indifferent—but during the *meridian*—it is impossible—all is happiness & nonsense—

[TO JOHN MURRAY?]   [*1813?*]

Is the enclosed fit or unfit for publication?———Let me know—if you choose only to make extracts for the further review of B.s in the J.[1]—you may use it in that way.—Or (if *good*)—you may publish it entire,—but pray—let it first be read with attention.—

[TO MATTHEW GREGORY LEWIS]   [*1813?*]

My dear L[ewi]s—I will call about 6—we have *both* an offer of places from Ly. M[elbourn]e in Ld. Egremont's[1] box—but I think

[1] Unidentified.
[1] The 3rd Earl of Egremont (1751–1837), for many years a leading figure in London society, was an art patron and one of the first to appreciate Turner. Horace Walpole had once arranged a match for Egremont and Lady Charlotte Maria Waldegrave (Walpole's great niece), but the match was broken off. According to the D.N.B. "Mrs Delaney attributes Egremont's conduct to his being under the dominion of a great lady (Lady M-l-b-e)" [Lady Melbourne].

we shall have more of the audience (always more amusing than the performers on a *first* night) in the seats you have taken. . . .

BIRON

[TO ANNA MARIA BARROW?]   *Thursday Noon [1813?]*

Ld. Byron will have the Honour of accepting Mrs. Barrow's[1] polite Invitation for Tuesday next.

[TO THE EARL OF CLARE ?]   *[January 1813?]*

I hope—and indeed am not aware—that any *harm* has been or can be done on the subject which alarms you—but if any does exist the blame & the punishment (no slight one self reproach) both must be mine—for I cannot perceive how you can participate in either—unless you regret having wished in common with all the connections & even acquaintances of these untoward personages—that it could be made up between them if only for the comfort of their sisters & cousins to say nothing of themselves.[1]—If in my eagerness upon a topic which has been a *Dragon* to me these last 7 years—I have by word or letter said or caused you to say anything which has given you a moment's uneasiness I shall not soon forgive myself—though I hope you will—and now My dearest C I lay aside all my plans & imaginations—& drop the subject altogether—trusting that time or chance will bring about a reconciliation between them.—My wish to have seen you before you went to Paris arose first because I don't see you very often and next because you are one of the few people with whom I could talk on the subject—& some other reasons not worth mentioning.——

[TO CHARLES HANSON]   *[January, 1813?]*

My dear Charles—When your father returns and my presence is necessary a letter to Eywood will find me. In the meantime I press strongly upon your mind and his the necessity of making some

---

1 Probably Anna Maria Barrow, wife of John Barrow, then second secretary of the Admiralty under John Wilson Croker. He was known as a wit and was one of Murray's literary advisers. He was a contributor to Murray's *Quarterly Review* on scientific and geographic subjects.

1 There is no clue to the identity of the "untoward personages".

arrangement about Rochdale—as I go in May—I will not hazard a long lawsuit—. . . .

January 2d. 1813

Dear Hobhouse,—Will you execute a commission for me & receive my best thanks by anticipation.—Get the enclosed draft *cashed* yourself, as I do not wish it to pass through other hands—& pay Mrs. Mee Upper Berkeley St. *66*—for a picture of Ly. O[xford] which the enclosed note will authorize you to receive.—Pray favour me by doing this immediately—& let the picture carefully *packed* & *out of sight* be sent to Murray's in Albemarle St. there to wait my directions.——Excuse this trouble dear H. & believe me

ever yrs.

B

P.S.—Pray send me an answer.—If there is any demur about the draft I will send you one on Hoares where I have certain monies.— Ly. O[xford] & Ly. Jane send their best remembrances. I would not trouble you but I have no other friend in town.——

[TO JOHN HANSON] *January 2d. 1813*

Dear Sir—I am in some surprise at not having heard one word from you since I left town—particularly as I must be very anxious to hear how C[laughto]n means to proceed.——I now write principally to apprize you of my having drawn on you for £105—a draft will be presented by Mr. Hobhouse & if the Credit is inadequate now in yr. hands I authorise you to take from the £2000 now in Hoare's.— Pray present all the compts. of the Season to Mrs. H. &c. & accept them yourself—believe me dr. Sir

Yrs. truly

B

P.S. Pray do not let there be any delay about the draft as it is for a particular purpose!——

[TO FRANCIS HODGSON] *February [January] 3, 1813.*

My dear Hodgson,—I will join you in any bond for the money you require, be it that or a larger sum. With regard to security, as

Newstead is in a sort of abeyance between sale and purchase, and my Lancashire property very unsettled, I do not know how far I can give more than personal security, but what I can I will. At any rate you can try, and as the sum is not very considerable, the chances are favourable. I hear nothing of my own concerns, but expect a letter daily. Let me hear from you where you are and will be this month. I am a great admirer of the *R. A.* [*Rejected Addresses*],[1] though I have had so great a share in the cause of their publication, and I like the *C. H.* [*Childe Harold*] imitation one of the best. Lady Oxford has heard me talk much of you as a relative of the Cokes,[2] etc., and desires me to say she would be happy to have the pleasure of your acquaintance. You must come and see me at K[insham]. I am sure you would like *all* here if you knew them.

The "Agnus"[3] is furious. You can have no idea of the horrible and absurd things she has said and done since (really from the best motives) I withdrew my homage. "Great pleasure" is, certes, my object, but *"why brief,* Mr. Wild?"[4] I cannot answer for the future, but the past is pretty secure; and in it I can number the last two months as worthy of the gods in *Lucretius.* I cannot review in the *"Monthly;"*[5] in fact I can just now do nothing, at least with a pen; and I really think the days of Authorship are over with me altogether. I hear and rejoice in Bland's and Merivale's intentions.[6] Murray has grown great, and has got him new premises in the fashionable part of town. We live here so shut out of the *monde* that I have nothing of general import to communicate, and fill this up with a "happy new year," and drink to you and Drury.

Ever yours, dear H.,

B.

---

[1] The *Rejected Addresses*, by James and Horace Smith, parodied the styles of the authors who submitted addresses for the opening of Drury Lane Theatre in 1812. *Cui Bono* was a parody of the style of *Childe Harold.*

[2] Hodgson's uncle, the Rev. Richard Coke, lived at Lower Moor, Herefordshire, and therefore was a near neighbour of the Oxfords.

[3] Lady Caroline Lamb.

[4] An adaptation of a passage in Fielding's *Life of Mr. Jonathan Wild* (Book III, chapter viii), which Byron was fond of quoting in various contexts: Laetitia asks her husband: "But pray, Mr. Wild, why b—ch? Why did you suffer such a word to escape you?"

[5] Hodgson reviewed frequently for the *Monthly Review.* Despite his protest, however, Byron did write one review for the *Monthly* in 1813: *Neglected Genius,* by W. H. Ireland (Vol. 70, 1813, pp. 203–205).

[6] The Rev. Robert Bland and J. Herman Merivale collaborated in *Collections from the Greek Anthology* and *A Collection of the most Beautiful Poems of the Minor Poets of Greece,* both published in 1813.

I have no intention of continuing *"Childe Harold."* There are a few additions in the "body of the book" of description, which will merely add to the number of pages in the next edition. I have taken Kinsham Court. The business of last summer I broke off, and now the amusement of the gentle fair is writing letters literally threatening my life, and much in the style of "Miss Matthews" in *"Amelia,"* or "Lucy" in the *"Beggar's Opera."* Such is the reward of restoring a woman to her family, who are treating her with the greatest kindness, and with whom I am on good terms. I am still in *palatia Circes*, and, being no Ulysses, cannot tell into what animal I may be converted; as you are aware of the turn of both parties, your conjectures will be very correct, I daresay, and, seriously, I am very much *attached*. She [Lady Oxford] has had her share of the denunciations of the brilliant Phryne,[7] and regards them as much as I do. I hope you will visit me at K[insham] which will not be ready before spring, and I am very sure you would like my neighbours if you knew them. If you come down now to Kington.[8] pray come and see me.

[TO LADY MELBOURNE]   *January 4th. 1813*

My dear Ly, M.——The passage I allude to contains these words at the end of a long tirade "which—God forgive me—I solemnly denied"—on looking again I find it is "denied with a solemn oath."— I am now tolerably aware from herself & others of her late proceedings —her [Lady Caroline Lamb's] last epistle was really not in ye. language of a Gentlewoman on the subject of my resumption of my picture after however restoring her *own*.——I should esteem it as a great favour if you would once more speak to her from *me*—again & again I repeat that I have no wish to disturb her, nor am at all conscious of having misrepresented her or indeed mentioned her name but to those to whom she had already committed herself, once more I beseach her for her own sake to remain quiet,—& having done this for the *last* time I must add that if this is disregarded it will be out of my *power* to prevent consequences *fatal* to her perhaps to others also, & which I must sincerely wish to avoid.—She forgets that *all* does not depend upon me—& she is not aware that I have done my utmost to silence

---

7 One of Caroline Lamb's fanciful signatures.
8 Kington was the home of Hodgson's relations not far from Eywood.

some whose narratives would not be very pleasing.—Remind her that the same man she is now trying by every serious & petty means to exasperate is the same who received the warmest thanks from herself & Ly. B[essborough] on the occasion of her *Kensington* excursion, one with whose conduct she has repeatedly professed herself perfectly satisfied, & who did not give her up till he was assured that he was not abandoning a woman to her fate but restoring her to her family.—I have particular reasons for wishing her to be once more *warned*—if this is not attended to, I shall remain *passive*— & interfere no further between her & her destiny—however disagreeable to myself, the effects I fear will be worse for her. She is perfectly at liberty to dispose of her necklaces &c. to "Grimaldi" if she pleases, & to put whatever motto she may devise on her *"livery buttons"* this last she will understand but as you probably may not— it is as well to say that one of her amusements by her own account has been engraving on the said "buttons" *Ne* "Crede Byron" an interesting addition to the motto of my family which thus atones for it's degradation in my acquaintance with her.——I however do not think it very creditable to *yours* to have the above proclaimed to every lacquey who meets her Ladyship's couriers in their respectable vocations & fear that the appearance of the *name* may lead to errors in the translation of the *learned* of the *livery*.——This is her own account & may therefore probably be false which you will not regret.— We shall leave this about the 15th, we have had no Sir Rd. *any body* here (I can't read the name) but I am glad to hear of C[aroline]'s reconciliation with the *Bart*—his second blunder will not be so lucky as the first I fear—that is their concern.——Her "real good spirits" I rejoice to hear notwithstanding her efforts to spoil mine—her own would have been tolerably dashed very lately had it not been for my *interposition*—I do not mean *here* however for the *Enchantress* [Lady Oxford] looks upon her with great coolness since her late epistles, & I do not believe thinks of C[aroline] as anything formidable—besides the contrast is all in her favour.—We all go on without any interruptions or disagreeables—very few guests & no inmates—books music &c. all the amusements without the *rigidity* of Middleton.—I shall be very *qualmish* at the thought of returning to town—it is an accursed abode for people who wish to be quiet.—I am not sure that I shall not take a journey into Notts before I proceed to town but this depends on circumstances. So you dislike the Secretary's definition of *"Permanency"* pray how does *everyone else* like it?——Why should I not believe in all sorts of *"Innocence?"* assure yourself that my creed

9

on that subject is exactly *your own*.—"Virtue my dear Ly. Blarney Virtue"[1] &c. &c. see the Vicar of Wakefield.

ever yrs.

B.—

[TO LADY MELBOURNE]   *January 5th. 1813*

My dear Ly. M.—I wrote you a long letter yesterday respecting C[aroline] & as I did not quite explain what may appear to you a little singular, I will just write this much in addition.—I have reason to imagine that since she has been making this business so public that it will appear perhaps still more publicly if she is not more prudent— which is the more provoking as the least circumspection on her part would prevent people from thinking of it at all.—You will easily imagine that this would be most disagreeable to me, but how can I prevent it if she persists in talking on the subject to every one— *writing* to *Sanders* the Painter &c. &c.?—However unpleasant this is to me it must be more so to the other parties—I believe Ly. B[essborough] & C[aroline] would hardly survive it—it would distress me beyond everything—& destroy all done in her favour.—Prevail upon her if possible to consider the probable consequences of her buffooneries.—

ever yrs.

B

P.S. Conceive of my having heard of it in this *wilderness*—Ld. O[xford] had a long sermon upon it from his Mother & *maiden* Sisters yesterday—who are all as old as Owen Glendower & have lived out of the world since Henry 4th's reign.—

[TO JOHN MURRAY]   *Eywood Presteign.-January 8th. 1813*

Dear Sir—You have been imposed upon by a letter forged in my name to obtain the picture left in your possession.—This I know by the confession of the culprit, & as she is a woman (& of rank) with whom I have unfortunately been too much connected you will for the present say little about it, but if you have the letter *retain* it—& write to me the particulars. You will also be more cautious in future & not allow anything of mine to pass from your hands without my *seal* as

---

[1] In Chapter XI of the *Vicar of Wakefield* Miss Skeggs said: "Virtue, my dear Lady Blarney, virtue is worth any price; but where is that to be found?"

10

well as signature.—I have not been in town—nor have written to you since I left it—so I presume the forgery was a skilful performance.[1]— I shall endeavour to get back the picture by fair means if possible.—

ever yrs

BYRON

P.S. Keep the letter if you have it.—I did not receive your parcel & it is now too late to send it as I shall be in town on the 17th.— The *delinquent* is of one of the first families in this kingdom—but as Dogberry says this "is flat burglary"—Favour me with an answer— I hear I am scolded in the Quarterly[2]—but you & it are already forgiven—I suppose that made you bashful about sending it.—

[TO LADY MELBOURNE]   *January 9th. 1813*

Dear Ly. M.—C[aroline] by her own confession has *forged* a *letter* in my *name* (the hand she imitates to perfection)[1] & thus obtained from Mr. Murray in Albemarle Street the picture for which I had restored her own.——This fact needs no comment from me—but I wish you could reobtain it for me—otherwise I very much fear an unpleasant exposure will transpire upon this subject.——She shall have a copy & all her *own* gifts if she will restore it to *you* for the present.—This picture I must have again for several weighty reasons —if not—as she has shown an utter disregard for all *consequences*—I shall follow her example.—I am hurried now as we are all going out but will write tomorrow dear Ly. M.

yrs. ever

B

[TO LADY MELBOURNE]   *January 10th. 1813*

Dear Ly. M.—This morning I heard from town (inclosed a letter from C[aroline] to the person in A[lbemarle] Street) that it was in

---

[1] A facsimile of the forgery is given in *Lord Byron's Correspondence*, ed. Murray, 1922, Vol. II, 130–131. It is not a very skilful forgery and should not have fooled anyone who knew Byron's hand, though the signature was close enough to fool everyone at a glance. Apparently, however Caroline Lamb did not use the forged letter to get the picture, but seized it in person. See Jan. 10, 1813, to Lady Melbourne.

[2] *The Quarterly Review* (Sept. 1812, pp. 172–181) in an article on *The Rejected Addresses* by James and Horace Smith says that the parody of Byron in that volume "exceeds the ennui and carelessness of *Childe Harold*".

[1] See Jan. 8, 1813, to Murray, note 1.

person she seized upon the picture.—Why she should herself say that she *forged* my *name* &c. to obtain it—I cannot tell—but by her letter of yesterday (which I shall keep for the present) she expressly avows this in her wild way and *Delphine* language—It is singular that she not only calumniates others but even *herself*, for no earthly purpose. I wrote to you yesterday in a perilous passion about it—& am still very anxious to recover the picture with which she will certainly commit some foolery.——Murray is in amaze at the whole transaction & writes in a laughable consternation—I presume she got it by flinging his own best bound folios at his head.—I am sure since the days of the Dove in the Ark no animal has had such a time of it as *I*—no *rest* any where.—As Dogberry says "this is flat Burglary"—will you recover my *effigy* if you can—it is very unfair after the restoration of her own—to be *ravished* in this way.—I wanted to scribble to you a long letter—but I am called away again—for which *you* will not be sorry—remember C[aroline] is responsible for any *errata* in my letter of yesterday—for I sent you her *own* statement in fewer words.—

Dear Ly. M. ever yrs.

B

[TO LADY MELBOURNE]   *January 11th. 1813*

My dear Ly. M.—So you cannot understand *"everybody"*—well—I thought *anybody* would but as *somebody* can't *Nobody* will be the wiser.—And my *"Cheltenham speeches"*—blessings on your memory!—what were they?—they were very sincere I will swear—& if not—you have heard I doubt not the ancient & approved saying—viz—that "the most *artful* man is not a match for the most *sincere* woman" now *we* are just the reverse, & I am used accordingly—I am still in a prodigious pucker about this picture of which I sent you details yesterday & the day before.—The *worthy* C[aroline] tells me in her last letter that she has now broken all but the 6th & 9th Commandments & threatens to omit the *"Not"* in them also unless I submit to her late larceny;—I have enquired after your Sir R. F. but *we* know no such person—she has changed her opinion about Ly. B. A. for Annabella but has no idea (at least expresses none) that my *proxy* succeeded no better than if I had done it in *person*, nor who this said *Proxy* was.——I shall wait your "story about A". till it suits

12

your pleasure—I suppose it is a good one, & will at all events have the advantage of being well told. I dont understand you about "what I found fault with at M[iddleton] I should have wished at E[ywood]". —Your Ladyship is enigmatical—a perfect *Sphinx*—& I am not Œdipus.—It is now snowing perfect Avalanches, & when we shall get away Jove knows—Ld. O[xford] is in town & on the 17th we mean to attempt it with the permission of the skies & roads.—— C[aroline] may think what she pleases—whether *I* am afraid of *her* Time may show—but Ly. O[xford] is not I am very certain.—I rejoice to hear you will be in town but you don't say whether you will patronize me any further—I am sure you have found me the most submissive of slaves. Don't get *ill*—I see by the papers that poor Ly. C. Rawdon is dead—a pretty encouragement to fall sick—Bessy will be in black, which does not become her, & will add considerably to the dear Soul's affliction, if she at all resembles the rest of what Mrs. Slipslop[1] terms the "frail sect".——We are all in tolerable plight—I have been looking over my Kinsham premises which are close to a church & churchyard full of the most facetious Epitaphs I ever read—"*Adue*"! (a new orthography taken from one of them) I commend me to your orisons and am ever Dear Ly. M.

yrs. most truly
B

[TO JOHN HANSON]   *January 12th. 1813*

Dear Sir—I spoke to you some time ago about taking me a lodging in Albemarle[,] Dover Street or any in that part of town.—Will you look out for me as I shall be in London by the 18th.

yrs ever
B

Best remembrances to *all*.

[TO LADY MELBOURNE]   *Jy. 13th. 1813*

My dear Ly. M.—Tell *her* to *show* you my letters from *Cheltenham*— if *you* are once mentioned otherwise than with praise I will not only eat my words but the paper & seal included.—My *kind* epistle was

---

[1] Mrs. Slipslop, Lady Booby's maid in Fielding's *Joseph Andrews*, was adept at the kind of Malapropisms which Byron admired.

13

written before I either heard of her *folly* or her *felony*—the Advertisements I have never seen.—That one so perverted with every wrong feeling should mistake forbearance for fear is to be expected—but if that picture is not restored & speedily too, the mistake will be unravelled.—I confess I look upon the thing in a more serious light than you do—I have seen the forged billet—the hand very like[1]—now what is to prevent her from the same imitation for any less worthy purpose she may choose to adopt?—M[urray] does not know her name nor have I *yet* informed him of it—if known she will have the credit of being the authoress of all the letters *anonymous* & *synonimous*, written for the next ten years & the last five.———For aught I know she may have forged 50 such to *herself*—& I do not feel very much refreshed by the supposition.—I shall not write to *her* again—but I request once more as respectfully as I can that she will restore the picture—if not—as nothing but a scene will satisfy her—she shall have one performed which will be more edifying than entertaining.—*You know* how anxious I have been to preserve quiet; *what* I have borne from her—I have done this it should seem in vain—& henceforth be the consequence what it may to *me* to *her* & *hers* I leave no measures to keep with any but yourself.—I am sick of the suspense & one way of the other it shall soon be over. My offer to recover the things was in consequence of a foolish but conciliatory letter of her own—this I now revoke—Ly. B[essborough]'s letter is very amusing—I had no idea that Ly. O[xford] & *suite* were of such consequence—but how far the *assurer* was right—I cannot say —at least more than I did to *you* already—the voyage does not depend on me.—that they have such an intention is true—how it transpired I know not but "dont know" & "haven't heard" will make a very pretty response from you on being catechised.—I shall be in town in a few days & hope to see you there—*and the picture.*—

dear Ly. M. ever yrs.

B

[TO JOHN CAM HOBHOUSE]   [*Ledbury*] *January 17th. 1813*

Dear H.—I am on my way to town—writing from my sordid Inn—many thanks for your successful diplomacy with Ma-Mee[1]—& now "Grant him one favour & he'll ask you two".—I have written to Batt for rooms—would it hurt your dignity to order me some at any

1 See Jan. 8, 1813, to Murray, note 1.
1 See Jan. 2, 1813, to Hobhouse.

14

other hotel (by a note) in case he should not have them? for I have no opportunity of receiving your or his answer before I reach London, & if he has not any to spare & I arrive late I shall be as bewildered as Whittington—I rejoice in your good understanding with Murray—through him you will become a *"staple author".*—D[allas?] is a *damned* nincom—assuredly—he has bored me into getting young Fox to recommend his further *damnation* to the Manager Whitbread—God (& the Gods) knows & know what will become of his *"25 acts & some odd scenes".*—I am at Ledbury—Ly. O[xford] & famille I left at Hereford—as I hate travelling with Children unless they have gotten a Stranguary.—However I wait here for her tomorrow like a dutiful Cortejo—O[xford] has been in town these ten days.—Car[oline] L[amb] has been *forging letters* in my name & hath thereby pilfered the best picture of *me* the Newstead Miniature!!!—Murray was the imposed upon.—The Devil, & Medea, & her Dragons to boot, are possessed of that little maniac. Bankes[2] is gone or going to tourify—I gave him a few letters.——I expect & hope you will have a marvellous run & trust you have not forgotten *"monogamy* my dr. boy"—if the "learned world are not in arms against your paradoxes"[3] I shall despise these coster-monger days when Merit availeth not.—Excuse my buffoonery for I write under the influence of a solitary nipperkin of Grog such as the Salsette afforded "us youth" in the Arches.—

ever yrs. dr. H.

B

[TO [LADY MELBOURNE?]]

Sunday Morn—[January 19, 1813?][1]

I fully intended calling yesterday but business—the consequence of being longer from town than I intended—prevented me.—I am obliged to leave it again for 2 days—but on Tuesday or Wednesday at farthest I hope to find you well—& myself *wel*come.—Any hour that suits you after *two*—I will take my chance and if you are out I shall not be discouraged but try again.—

ever yrs. obliged & truly

BYRON

[2] William Bankes, a Cambridge friend of Byron, later travelled extensively in the Near East.

[3] These are some of Byron's favourite quotations from the *Vicar of Wakefield.*

[1] For a discussion of the conjectural date of this letter, see *The Journal of the Byron Society*, No. 1, Philadelphia, 1972, pp. 7–8.

Dear Ly. M.—I see nothing but the prospect of an endless correspondence in answering Ly. C[aroline]'s letters;—assure her of my good wishes & let it end.—Ly. B[essborough] was at home this morning & after *mutually* premising that neither *"would believe one word the other had to say"* much civil upbraiding took place.—She lectured pleasantly upon "Soothing", complained that I had deceived *you* & Mrs. L[amb] &c. into a belief that I was a "sober quiet Platonic well disposed person"—added that you was "the best & cleverest of all possible women", which was very lucky, inasmuch if she had said you was ye. worst, you would probably have heard it again.—She was a good deal horrified at my deficiency in *Romance*—& quite petrified at my behaviour altogether, more especially the affair of that never sufficiently to be confounded necklace, which ought not to have been given away a second time, (for want of *precedent* I presume) & which certainly has been more celebrated than any similar collar since the famous one of the "Cardinal de Rohans".[1]——The result of all this is that I shall restore the brilliant epistles, & get back the baubles, which (God knows) I was most unwilling to receive.—To Ly. C[aroline]'s good resolutions I have nothing to say, but my fervent prayer to Asmodeus that they may continue.—That my opinion upon her character should alter, is neither to be *desired* nor expected, I will *forbear* as much as possible, but——I have already sent her the requested absolutions & remissions—why must I repeat them?——In short I wish to hear no more of the matter—to be on good terms with *"you*, by *yourself, you"*—& to remain as quiet as Medea & her Dragons will allow me.—I wish to see you—but do not let me intrude—I fear I did yesterday——Today I am twenty five years of age, & *yours* for as many centuries dear Ly. M.

&c. &c.

B

P.S. Ly. B[essborough] says *you* fear a renewal—now this is impossible—& that *you* should think so—still more incomprehensible.[2]—

[1] The scandal of the diamond necklace presented to Marie Antoinette was a well known anecdote of pre-Revolutionary France, which Carlyle later made more famous by his essay.

[2] Following this letter there should be here, if it were extant, a letter from Byron to Robert Southey, dated Jan. 26, 1813. The cover only, addressed: R[ober]t Southey, Esqre. Keswick, is in the Nottingham Public Libraries. A letter written thus early, before he had quarrelled violently with Southey, should be interesting. The manuscript may yet turn up.

[TO JOHN HANSON]   [*February 3, 1813 post mark*]

Dear Sir—Will you forward the inclosed immediately to Corbet whose address I do not exactly remember.—It is of consequence— relative to a foolish woman I never saw who fancies I want to marry her.—[1]

yrs. ever
B

P.S. I wish you would see Corbet & talk to him about it—for she plagues my soul out with her d----d letters.—

[TO LADY MELBOURNE]   *Fy. 7th. 1813—*

My dear Ly. M.—You perhaps do not know that your amiable charge has at last thought proper to expose herself to Murray— Yesterday to my utter astonishment—in marches Miss W.[1]—(I was present) & says in a tone more audible than requisite—"Mr. M[urray] Ly. C[aroline] L[amb] desires you will call tomorrow at—God knows when—"—The man bowed & promised acquiescence—he did not know that she was the picture woman[2]—What was I to do?—if I said "*don't go*" to a person who knew nothing of *her*—& who dreamed only of an order for books &c. he would have thought it very singular that I should forbid the banns between him & his anticipated profits— & inevitably have found out the fact twenty four hours before the sight of C[aroline] confirmed it.—The room being full I thought it best to say nothing.—This morning he saw her & of course recognized the respectable pilferer.—She gave him some *designs* for a certain book—the which I have asked him to return not only because I have no intention of having drawings for the thing—but (though I did not state to him the last reason) because certainly C[aroline]'s are the performances of all others I would rather decline. This is the statement of her last *scene.*—What a pity she had no *fête* nor occupation for this *day* as well as the three last!—I am going out of town for a day— *tomorrow*—I regret this last blunder since she has been so quiet & silent since her arrival that I trusted our cares were over.—I hear also she behaved to admiration last night—pray Heaven it may be

---

[1] See March 6, 1809, to his Mother, and March 5, 1813, to Corbet. The lady was the widow of Lord Falkland, whom Byron had given £500 to sustain her and her children after her husband, Byron's friend, had been killed in a duel. See Marchand, *Byron: A Biography*, I, 346–47.
[1] Unidentified.
[2] See Jan. 8, 1813, to Murray.

permanent.——You were at the Opera tonight—so was I—but the ⟨Istmuhus⟩ Isthmus (curse the word I *can't spell it*) of *2 boxes* between us was impassable—& prevented our *two seas* from uniting.

Ever dr. Ly. M. yrs.

B

[TO CAROLINE, PRINCESS OF WALES]   *Fy. 10th. 1813—*

Madam—I had the honour of complying with your R[oya]l Highness's commands[1] in a letter to Sir F[rancis] B[urdett] which I forwarded early this morning.—In this I stated to the best of my memory the substance of the conversation with which I was last night honoured.—From *myself* I presumed to offer no opinion whatever, conceiving that your R[oyal] H[ighness]'s wishes neither required nor could derive weight from any suggestions of mine.—If Sir F. B. condescends to consult me on the subject I shall undoubtedly state my sentiments in the same manner in which they were expressed to yr. R[oya]l Highness.—Of this for the present I have no opportunity —as Sir F. B. left town early this morning.—Your R[oya]l H[ighness]'s letter is forwarded by this Evening's post to Oxford.—I shall ever feel proud & happy in obeying any commands with which I may be honoured.—It is the smallest return I can make for many most obliging marks of your condescension.——I have the honour to be with the highest respect

yr. Royal Highness's most dutiful & humble St.

BYRON

To Her Rl. Hs.
The Princess of Wales &c. &c. &c.

[TO LADY MELBOURNE]   *Fy. 12th. 1813*

My dear Ly. Melbourne——I shall be very happy to encounter A[nnabella] in such a manner as to convince her that I feel no *pique* nor diminution of the *respect* I have always felt for her—the latter is perhaps rather increased than otherwise—I do not know whether I really am above the common prejudices which the *Animal* Man entertains on such occasions but I trust I am above showing them.— All I hope is that whatever my manner may be—she will neither

[1] The Princess had apparently asked for some advice in political matters which Byron put into the hands of Sir Francis Burdett, as more politically experienced.

18

think me *cold* nor *confident*—I do not wish to seem piqued at the past, nor as a future *aspirant.*—With regard to the P's [Princess?][1]—why the thing is to be secret I cannot see—I have never denied it—if anyone is a sufferer it must be myself—& it is one of those afflictions which made me smile when Bankes cried—I shall neither poison nor lampoon her—& am very sure that if she does not misunderstand me nor my views—we shall be very good friends—& "live happy ever after"—in that state of life to which it may "please God to call us".—So—you have seen Mrs. C.[2]—this is excellent.—She sent me an Opera ticket, which I returned, being already engaged—& having paid part of another man's subscription last year I was the less inclined to add my own for this. I was also invited to her house— for which at present I have no pressing occasion—but I dare say her *friends* will find *it* (and all it's furniture) convenient as ever should circumstances render that respectable mansion a pleasant place of conference.—I only hope it may never cost any one more than the segment of a *predecessor's* Opera ticket.——I saw you last night—but I was literally jammed in between a cursed card-table & an elbow chair—so that I could not rise but in the most ungainly of all possible postures—& you are the last person before whom I would appear more akward in my devoirs than I *naturally* am.——I trust that Mrs. C. & the *C.* of *Cs.*[3] will not break—it would be an infinite loss to both—on *my* account they certainly shall not.—I fear C[aroline] will find some further method of exposing herself—I mean in this last affair—any *future* one would be too great a blessing for *me*—& I rather think *you* will leave the *next* entirely to herself.—*We* have great ideas of going abroad—in which you will heartily concur—I wish I had never left a country with more quiet & fewer clouds— Everything is so roundabout here—there every thing is to be *got* or *got rid* of sans circumlocution—& much *cheaper.*——Ever my dear Ly. M.

yrs most truly

B

[TO — — — — — — — — — —.]   *Fy. 20th. 1813*

My dear Sir—With my best thanks I return your friend's letters— He is indeed a traveller—& I wish him the success he deserves.—I

[1] The reference is not clear, but it may be that the Princess of Wales was curious about Byron's proposal and had inquired of Lady Melbourne?
[2] Unidentified.
[3] Unidentified.

send you the copy of the thing you wanted—it is my own & the only one left of *nine* the whole number circulated.[1]—I am very glad to get rid of it.—Believe me dear Sir—

ever yr. obliged & faithful St.

BYRON

[TO JOHN MURRAY]   *Fy. 20th. 1813*

Dear Sir—In "Horace in London" I perceive some stanzas on Ld. E[lgin][1]—in which (waving the kind compliment to myself) I heartily concur.—I wish I had the pleasure of Mr. S[mith]'s acquaintance as I could communicate the curious anecdote you read in Mr. T's letter[2]—if he would like it he can have the *substance* for his second Edition—if not I shall add it to *our* next—though I think *we* already have enough of Ld. E[lgin].—What I have read of this work seems admirably done—my praise however is not much worth the Author's having—but you may thank him in my name for *his*.—The idea is new—we have excellent imitations of the Satires &c. by Pope but I remember but one imitative ode in his works & *none* anywhere else.— I can hardly suppose that *they* have lost any fame by the fate of the Farce,[3] but even should this be the case—the present publication will again place them on their pinnacle.—

yrs. truly

B

[TO ROBERT RUSHTON]

4 *Bennet Street St. James's Fy. 24th. 1813*

I feel rather surprised to have heard nothing from you or your father in answer to Fletcher's last letter.—I wish to know whether

[1] Some privately printed poem? Perhaps the Drury Lane Address, of which Murray struck off some copies?

[1] *Horace in London; consisting of Imitations of the First Two Books of the Odes of Horace*, by James and Horace Smith (1813) contains an imitation called "The Parthenon" in which Minerva says

All who behold my mutilated pile
Shall brand its ravager with classic rage,
And soon a titled bard from Britain's Isle,
Thy country's praise and suffrage shall engage,
And fire with Athens' wrongs an angry age!

[2] Unidentified.

[3] Horace Smith's *First Impressions; or, Trade in the West*, was a failure when performed at Drury Lane.

20

you intend taking a share in a farm with your brother—or chuse to wait for some other situation in Lancashire—the first will be best because at your time of life it is highly improper to remain idle.—If this *marriage* which is spoken of for you is at all advantageous I can have no objection—but I should suppose after being in my service from your infancy, you will at least let me know the name of your *intended*, & her expectations.—If at all respectable nothing can be better for your settlement in life—& a proper provision will be made for you—at all events let me hear something on the subject—for as I have some intention of leaving England in the Summer—I wish to make my arrangements with regard to yourself before that period.———As you & Mr. [Joe] Murray have not received any money for some time—if you will draw on *me* for *fifty* pounds (payable at Messrs. Hoare's Bankers Fleet Street) & tell Mr. J. Murray to draw for the *same sum* on his *own* account—both will be paid by me.—

&c. &c.

B

[TO THE EDITOR OF *The Day*.[1]]   [*February 24, 1813?*]

Sir—The garbled & ill-connected extracts from an unpublished poem which appeared in your paper of Fy. 23d.—were communicated by some unreflecting correspondent without the knowledge or consent of the author.—Besides other more weighty objections to their publication there is hardly one *line* in the copy you have inserted without a gross mistake—it is not the intention of the author to publish any corrected copy & it is requested that the Editor of the Day will not admit into his journal any extracts whatever whether correct or otherwise—from a production never intended to be obtruded on the public.—

[TO LADY MELBOURNE]   *Fy. 25th.* [*1813*]

My dear Ly. M—Her [Caroline's] letter is "melancholy & gentle*man*like"—you know she does not write like a *gentle-woman* & the contents of no great importance—the interview is put off for

---

[1] Unidentified. Founded in 1809 by a committee of London merchants, *The Day* set out to rival *The Times*, but it expired in 1817 and was transformed into *The New Times*.

certain weeks & I shall not hasten it—however much I may wish to regain my letters & other fooleries.—The idea of meeting you was a great *temptation* to Ly. Cowper's the other night but—I resist temptation better than I used to do which you will be glad to hear.— I am just from the H[ouse] of C[ommons] where Plunket made the best speech *I* ever heard[1]—& one Master Tomlin[2] the worst which I did not hear—having had recourse (after patiently listening to a very common place beginning) to supper for a pleasanter conclusion.— As you are a bitter politician you won't dislike this parliamentary gossip—Good night—

ever yrs. most truly
B

[TO JOHN HANSON] *Fy. 27th. 1813*

Dear Sir—I have called several times & you may suppose am very anxious to hear some thing from or of Mr. Claughton.—It is my determination on account of a malady to which I am subject & for other weighty reasons to go abroad again almost immediately.—To this you will object—but as my intention cannot be altered I have only to request that you will assist me as far as in yr. power to make ye. necessary arrangements.—I have every confidence in you & will leave the fullest powers to act in my absence—if this man still hesitates I must sell my part of Rochdale for what it will bring—even at a loss—& fight him out about Newstead—without this I have no funds to go on with & I do not wish to incur further debts if possible.— Pray favour me with a short reply to this—& say when I can see you— excuse me to Mrs. H. for my non-appearance last night—I was detained in the H[ouse] of C[ommons] till too late to dress for her party.—Compts to all—

ever yrs.
BN

1 William Conyngham Plunket (1764–1854), later created Baron Plunket, an eloquent Irish lawyer, who sat in the House of Commons from 1812, made a great impression by his speeches in favour of the Roman Catholic claims, which Byron had supported in his second speech in the House of Lords.
2 Probably Sir George Pretyman Tomline (1750–1827), tutor and friend of the younger Pitt. He became Bishop of Lincoln and Dean of St. Paul's, London, and was later Bishop of Winchester. He published *A Refutation of Calvinism* in 1811.

My dear Ly. M.—I shall probably leave town in less than a fort-night—& in all probability shall not return but for a day or two before my purposed voyage.—To *you* I may say that I see no good that can result from this eternal conference—& if possible I shall avoid it. I have given up all expectation of the letters—or anything like fair dealing from such a quarter.—In my answer it was hinted that a little reflection might probably induce her to give up the idea— if we are to meet only with indifference or hatred (& I know no other alternative at least in *our* case) why meet at all?—& then my Lady Bl[arney] with her eternal tremors—she is foolish in this respect— The requested "forgiveness" you & I have both *said* forty times at least—there is something to forgive & a little to forget on both sides— I am not very apt at either—but as the remembrance is not very pleasing I shall try to dismiss it—& as for the *forgiveness* I am willing to *say* it as often as she pleases—but I have not the wish—& sincerely hope I may never have the opportunity to put it to the trial—for my feelings are not I fear thoroughly *English* as to the charities—& I should be loath to trust my *magnanimity*—the least durable of all mortal qualities.——"Resist the devil & he will flee from you" says some pious person who if he had known more of the world would have found out that we can't "resist him" & that the best way is to anticipate his flight by our own.—I am not afraid of the *charms* of the fair Phryne—but I do dread by some word or inadvertancy discovering a *dislike* (to term it gently) which were better concealed—for after all I am no actor.—

ever yrs. dr. Ly. M.

B

P.S. The Opera box is given up—which I do not much regret—& I go out nowhere—so that you & I are not likely to encounter during the remnant of my sojourn in town.—I shall however pay my parting devoirs at Whitehall—& you will now & then write to me in ye. country—& perhaps even to one more distant.—If your Son has left Sicily any other *branch* of the family he may have left to flourish there I shall value in proportion to its lawful or unlawful resemblance to yourself.———

[TO JOHN HANSON]   *March 1st. 1813*

Dear Sir—I am sorry that I could not call today but will tomorrow —Your objections I anticipated & can only repeat that I cannot act otherwise—so pray hasten some arrangement—for with or without I must go.—A person told me yesterday there was one who would give within 10000 of C[laughton]'s price & take the title as it was— C[laughton] is a fool or is shuffling—Think of what I said about *Rochdale*[1] for I will sell it for what I can get—and will not stay three months longer in this country—I again repeat I will leave all with full powers to you—I commend your objection which is a proof of an honourable mind—which however I did not need to convince me of your character.——If you have any news send a few lines———

ever yrs.

BN

[TO ———CORBET.[1]]   *Mh. 5th. 1813*

Dear Sir—Ly. F[alkland] has returned by Mr. Hanson the only two letters I ever wrote her[2]—both some time ago—& neither containing the least allusion which could make any person suppose that I had any intention further than regards the children of her husband.——My servant returned the packet & letter of yesterday at the moment of receiving them—by her letter to Mr. H[anson] it should seem they have not been *re*delivered—I am sorry for this— but it is not my fault—& they ought never to have been sent.—After her Ly.ship's mistakes so often repeated—you will not blame me for declining all further interference in her affairs—& I rely much upon your word in contradicting her foolish assertions & most absurd imaginations.—She now says that "I need not leave the *country* on her account"—how the devil she knew that I was about to leave it at all I cannot guess—but however for the first time she has *dreamed* right.—But *her* being the cause is still more ludicrous than the rest— first she would have it that I returned here for love of a woman I *never saw*—& now that I am going, for the same whom I *have never seen* & certainly never wished nor wish to see!—the maddest *consistency* I ever heard of.—I trust she has regained her senses—as she tells Mr. H[anson] she will not scribble any more—which will also save *You* from the troublesome correspondence of your obliged & obedt. Servt.

BYRON

[1] Byron's estate in Lancashire.
[1] Corbet was a relative of Lady Falkland, to whom Byron returned her foolish letters.
[2] See Feb. 3, 1813, to Hanson, note 1.

24

Dear Sir—I must be ready in April at whatever risk—at whatever loss—you will therefore advertize Rochdale—if you decline this—I will sell it for what it will bring even though but a few thousand pounds. —With regard to Claughton I shall only say that if he knew the ruin—the misery he occasions by his delay he would be sorry for his conduct—& I only hope that he & I may not meet or I shall say something he will not like to hear.—I have called often—I shall call today at three or between three & four—again & again I can only beg of you to forward my plans—for here no power on earth shall make me remain six weeks longer.—

ever yrs.
B.—

Dear Ly. M.—Will you have ye. goodness to forward the enclosed? —it contains a request for the picture—& a *hint* at ye. letters.—I wish to make this one more effort—which may succeed.—I shall make you blush by asking you if you have read the *perjuries* in the Morning Post—with the immaculate deposition of the Lady Douglas[1] —much good will the publication add to the rising marriageables of this innocent metropolis—& I doubt not that for the rest of ye. 19th. Century every body will be "satisfied with *only* Sir John."[2]— It is rather hard however on the poor knight that he should be transmitted down to all posterity as the very type of insufficiency—& byeword of bad evidence.—"Laud we the Gods! these be truths"[3] as one Shakespeare says.—Pray forgive me—or rather the Morning's Post & Herald.—You are well again—at least I won't suppose you otherwise—

ever Dear Ly. M. yr. obliged servitor
B

---

[1] In 1806 Sir John and Lady Douglas deposed that in 1802 the Princess of Wales had a child by Sir Sidney Smith, but a formal commission of enquiry pronounced the accusation false. The accusation was revived by the Tory *Morning Post*, in support of the Prince Regent's efforts to discredit his wife.

[2] Quotation unidentified

[3] "Laud we the gods" is from Shakespeare's *Cymbeline* (V, 5, 475) Byron has added "these be truths", perhaps from *Macbeth*, II, 1, 181: "here be truths".

My dear Ly. M.—It has not been well managed—she wrote a submissive & *denying* letter to Ly. O[xford] who at first seemed disposed to agree to the interview—but on further consideration—& having in the interim heard more of her abuse (which I think you are not unacquainted with) she answered shortly & not uncivilly in ye. negative.——My wish that Ly. O[xford] should be the third person was to save you a scene—& I confess also—odd as it may seem—that it would have been less awkward for me—you will wonder why—& I can't tell you more than that she might make some brilliant harangue to which——[Lady Oxford] would be a less embarrassed listener than you could possibly be.—The letter you may read & put in the fire or keep as you please—I did & do want the picture—but if she will adhere to her present silence—I shall not tempt her into further scribbling.—You will at least allow I have gained one point—I shall get away without seeing her at all—no bad thing for the original whatever may become of the copy.——I have no pretensions to *"diplomacy"*—possessing only one requisite—viz adhering closely to my instructions.—You are quite right—as *usual*—upon ye. subject of being *governed*—in that respect I consider myself a *competent* witness.— It will be very cruel if Sir Sidney[1] turns Regent-evidence—after the compliment to his prowess in Ly. D's[2] deposition.——Poor Sir John[3] seems in a pretty dilemma—as the matter now stands—he is perjured if he publishes such a letter as you describe—methinks he will resemble one Sir Pandarus of Troy of convenient memory— except in betraying his trust.—The Smith family must also be uneasy —for if Sir Sidney's head is taken off—it may be doubted how far the remainder may be useful at home or abroad.——So—you won't get well—you must—or what is to become of me? I am very selfish about you.—

ever yrs. dr. Ly. M
B

P.S. [at top of first page] She wrote to Ly. O[xford] desiring to see *her*—& I thought it as well to *lump* the interviews into one—& cut you out as the *third*—for reasons below mentioned.—

[1] Sir Sidney Smith. See March 13, 1813, to Lady Melbourne, note 1.
[2] Lady Douglas.
[3] Sir John Douglas.

My dear Ly. M.—I read the note (for letter it was not) in which there was *no mention* nor *allusion* to any females of any family whatever —I would not have allowed such an epistle to go—besides—whatever Ly. O[xford] may have thought I am certain she entertains no such notions at present.—The last sentence in it I erased—because it expressed *pity* for C[aroline] & I wished to spare her that humiliation. —This assertion then is a gross & malignant falsehood of your correspondent's to make more mischief.—Pray—burn my letter—at any rate do not send it—I now recall my intention of complying with her request—& will *not meet her*—her *depositions* will rival Ly. D's.[1]— ——I am so provoked at this last piece of malice—that I really am not fit to write a line—I will call soon—& hope to find you well— believe me—If Ly. O[xford] entertained or expressed such opinions of you or yours—we should quickly quarrel—I would not hear those who have treated me with forbearance & kindness traduced even by her—& I certainly like her better than anything on earth.—

ever yrs. dr. Ly. M
B

My dear Ly. M.—If I had gone to Mrs. Hope's[1] I should have found the only *"novelty"* that would give me any pleasure in yourself— & lately I am sorry to say you have become quite a *rarity*—even more so than the subsidiary viands which you mention & which are not amiss in their way as additions to supper conversation.—But then I should have been checkmated by the Ly. Blarney who ranks next to a breast of Veal, an earwig, & her own offspring, amongst my antipathies.—"After all there is a charm in Novelty" is there indeed? it is very wicked in you to say so to a person who is so bigoted to the opposite system.——I believe I leave town next week—in the meantime I am in the agonies of three different schemes—the first you know—the 2d. is Sligo's Persian plan—he wants me to wait till Septr. set off & winter at Athens (our old headquarters) & then in the Spring to Constantinople (as of old) & Bagdad & Tahiran.—This has its charms too & recalls one's predilections for gadding,—then

---

[1] Lady Douglas. See March 13, 1813, to Lady Melbourne, note 1.
[1] Wife of Thomas Hope (1770?–1831). Hope later (1819) published a novel *Anastasius*, with a Greek setting, which Byron much admired.

there is Hobhouse with a Muscovite & Eastern proposal also—so that I am worse off than ever Ass was before to which bundle of hay I shall address myself.—However I am going somewhere though my[2] agents want me to stay where I am—an additional reason for desiring to get away. I am hiring doctors, painters, and two or three stray Greeks, now here, and as tired of England as myself, and I have found a trusty vassal in one of Buonaparte's Mamaluke Guard, who will go with Sligo or myself. These I am measuring for uniforms, shoes, and inexpressibles without number, and quite overwhelmed with preparations of all sorts. As soon as I get me to the country, I shall cherish once more my dear[3] mustachios—with whom I parted in tears—& trust they will now have the good manners to grow blacker than they did formerly—& assume the true Ottoman twist—of which your *hussars* are deplorably ignorant.———I now recollect C[aroline]'s letter—let it come—if it will come—& let her stay which will be still better.—

ever dear Ly. M yrs.

[TO CHARLES HANSON] *4 Bennett St. March 18th. 1813—*

My dear Charles—If I write to this man[1] I shall only say something that will answer no purpose.—I have then to request that you will *do so* stating that you write at my desire to know—why he has not kept his appointment in town, & if he *will* or *will not.*—Pray do this immediately,—& believe me

ever yrs.

B

[TO JOHN MURRAY] *Mh. 24th. 1813*

Dear Sir—Let the 15 copies be struck off[1]—& will you have the goodness to attend to the *few* alterations without sending me another

---

2 One page missing from MS, here supplied from *Lord Byron's Correspondence*, I, 143.

3 The manuscript resumes with this word.

1 Thomas Claughton, who was reluctant to fulfil his contract in the purchase of Newstead Abbey.

1 Byron had completed the first draft of *The Giaour* in March 12. While he was debating with himself whether to publish it under his name, he asked Murray to run off some copies to give to friends.

revise.—I want them as soon as possible.—The picture will be in town today—sent by the waggon to the *White bear* in Basinghall Street.—

yrs. ever

2

[TO CHARLES HANSON] *March 24th. 1813*

My dear Charles,—This is very evasive & dissatisfactory—what is to be done I cannot tell but your father had better see his letter & this of mine.[1]—A long litigation neither suits my inclination nor circumstances—it were better to take back the estate & raise it[2] to what it will bear which must be at least double—to dismantle the house & sell the materials—& sell Rochdale—Something I must determine on & that quickly—I want to go abroad immediately—it is utterly impossible for me to remain here—every thing I have done to extricate myself has been useless—Your father said *"sell"* I have sold—& see what has become of it!—If I go to Law with this fellow—after five years litigation at the present depreciation of money—the *price* will not be worth the *property*—besides how much of it will be spent in the contest! & how am I to live in the interim?——Every day land rises and money falls—I shall tell Mr. C[laughto]n he is a *scoundrel* & have done with him—& I only hope he will have spirit enough to resent the appellation & defend his own rascally conduct.—In the interim of his delay in his journey—I shall leave town—on Sunday I shall set out for Herefordshire[3] from whence when wanted I will return.—Pray tell your father—to get the money on Rochdale—or I must sell it directly—I must be ready by the last week in *May*—& am consequently pressed for time.—I go first to Cagliari in Sardinia— & on to the Levant.—

Believe me dear Charles, yrs truly

B

[TO SAMUEL ROGERS] *March 25th, 1813*

My dear Rogers—I enclose you a draft for the usurious interest due to Lord B[oringdon]'s[1] protege—I also could wish you would

---

[1] See March 18, 1813, to Charles Hanson, note 1.
[2] That is, raise the rents.
[3] To Eywood, the home of the Oxfords.
[1] The name is supplied from a letter of Rogers to Byron (*LJ*, II, 195n). Rogers replied that he would not execute Byron's commission to pay any more than the legal interest.

state thus much for me to his Lordship.—Though the transaction speaks plainly in itself for the borrower's folly and the lender's usury—it never was my intention to *quash* the demand as I *legally* might—nor to withhold payment of principal or perhaps even *unlawful* interest.—You know what my situation has been—& what it is—I have parted with an estate (which has been in my family for nearly three hundred years & was never disgraced by being in possession of a *lawyer*—a *churchman*—or a *woman*—during that period) to liquidate this & similar demands—& the payment of the purchaser is still withheld—& may be perhaps for years.—If therefore I am under the necessity of making these persons *wait* for their money (which considering the *terms*, they can afford to suffer) it is my misfortune. When I arrived at majority in 1809—I offered my own security on *legal* interest—& it was refused—*now* I will not accede to this.—This man I may have seen—but I have no recollection of the names of any parties but the *agents* & securities.—The moment I can —it is assuredly my intention to pay my debts—this person's case may be a hard one—but under all circumstances what is mine? I could not foresee that the purchaser of my estate was to demur in paying for it. I am glad it happens to be in my power so far to accommodate my Israelite—& only wish I could do as much for the rest of the twelve tribes.—

ever yrs. dear R.

B<small>N</small>.

[TO LORD HOLLAND]   *March 25th. 1813*

My dear Lord—I regret very much the *cause* of my yesterday's loss —& trust that it exists no longer.—I leave town on Sunday—it will not therefore be in my power to have the pleasure of meeting you on Wednesday next—but I will not leave this country without taking you by the hand & thanking you for many kindnesses.—The fact is I can do no good anywhere—& am too patriotic—not to prefer doing ill in any country rather than my own.—Where I am going—I cannot positively say—& it is no great matter—"there is a world beyond Rome" and all parts of it are much the same to a personage with few friendships & no connections.—My affairs are also not in the most brilliant order—& the sins of my nonage sit heavy upon my majority—I thought the sale of Newstead would relieve these— but it has merely led me within gunshot of a lawsuit.—I have neither the verve nor the "copia fandi" to rival Ld. Ellenborough in Moloch-like declamation in the house [of Lords]—& without occupation of some kind I cannot exist—travel therefore is the only pursuit left me —though I have some notion of taking orders.—*"Naxos"* I may perhaps visit—but *"Cyprus"*—is an Island I have long been sick of.— I heard today that Ly. Holland is much better & need not say that I hope my information was correct—pray make my best respects acceptable to her.—Believe me

yr. ever obliged & sincere St.

BYRON

[TO LADY MELBOURNE]   *March 26th. 1813—*

My dear Ly. M[elbourn]e—It becomes you wonderfully to reproach me for *fussing* about *trifles*—after the lectures of last summer about things of no great importance—I send you nevertheless the precious addition—though I already gave you enough to make a peruque— and now pray let me lay hands upon the picture immediately. It is too bad in C[aroline] to raise up the Ghosts of my departed vows against me—She made me sign I know not what or how many *bonds*—& now like a Jew she exacts usurious interest for an illegal transaction— Pray promise anything—& I will promise you anything—copies— originals—what you please—but let me have the picture forthwith. —I leave town on Sunday—I believe & shall not write to her again without some further epistle arrives requiring response.—As I can't go to Lady Spencer's[1]—would you make some *decent* excuse there for me? but that would not be proper now I think of it—& yet she is one of very few people from whom I don't like to exclude myself altogether—I must say I am ill.—I shall call tomorrow or Saturday to take a temporary leave of you—I must return to town on business— perhaps very soon.———I certainly am indebted to C[aroline] for the continuance of your *countenance*—& this cancels all her libels & larcenies—& makes me even hear Ly. B[essborough]'s name without being very sick—besides making me admire Mrs. G[eorge] L[amb] & all the rest of the family.—

ever yrs. dear Ly. M.

---

[1] Wife of the 2nd Earl Spencer and maternal grandmother of Lady Caroline Lamb.

4 *Bennet Street St. James's. March 26th. 1813—*

My dearest Augusta—I did not answer your letter—because I could not answer as I wished but expected that every week would bring me some tidings that might enable me to reply better than by apologies.—But Claughton has not—will not—& I think cannot pay his money—& though luckily it was stipulated that he should never have possession till the whole was paid—the estate is still on my hands—& your brother consequently not less embarrassed than ever. —This is the truth & is all the excuse I can offer for inability but not unwillingness to serve you[1]—I am going abroad again in June— but should wish to see you before my departure—you have perhaps heard that I have been fooling away my time with different *"regnantes"* but what better can be expected from me?—I have but one *relative* & her I never see—I have no connections to domesticate with—& for marriage I have neither the talent nor the inclination—I cannot fortune-hunt nor afford to marry without a fortune—my parliamentary schemes are not much to my taste—I spoke twice last Session—& was told it was well enough—but I hate the thing altogether—& have no intention to "strut another hour" on that stage.—I am thus wasting the best part of life daily repenting & never amending.—On Sunday I set off for a fortnight for Eywood—near Presteign—in Herefordshire—with the *Oxfords*—I see you put on a *demure* look at the name—which is very becoming & matronly in you—but you wont be sorry to hear that I am quite out of a more serious scrape with another singular personage[2] which threatened me last year—& trouble enough I had to steer clear of it I assure you.—I hope all my nieces are well & increasing in growth & number—but I wish you were not always buried in that bleak common near Newmarket.— I am very well in health—but not happy nor even comfortable—but I will not bore you with complaints—I am a fool & deserve all the ills I have met or may meet with—but nevertheless very *sensibly* dearest Augusta

yr. most affec[tionat]e brother
BYRON

---

[1] Augusta was in financial difficulties because of the debts of her gambling husband.
[2] Lady Caroline Lamb.

[TO SAMUEL ROGERS]   *M[arc]h 27th. 1813*[1]

Dear Rogers—I send you some of my obscurities—one of which I
should like to give to Moore & the other to Mr. R. P. K²—I *dare*
not write his name at length.—The others to any of your fair or
bearded acquaintance you think proper.—If you think the picture
you saw at Murrays worth your acceptance it is yours³—& you can
put a *glove* or a *masque* on it if you like.

ever yrs
B

[TO CHARLES HANSON]   *March 28, 1813*

My dear Charles.—When your father returns & my presence is
necessary a letter to Eywood—Presteign—will find me.—In the
meantime I press strongly upon your mind & his the necessity of
making some arrangement about Rochdale as I go in *May*.—I have
no dependence upon Claughton whatever—therefore it is useless to
wait for him—& I will not hazard a long lawsuit for the reasons I
mentioned before.

Yrs. truly
BYRON

[TO JOHN MURRAY]   *March 29th. 1813—*

Dear Sir—Westall has I believe agreed to illustrate your book—&
I fancy one of the engravings will be from the pretty little girl you
saw the other day—though without her name¹—& merely as a
model for some sketch connected with the subject.—I would also
have the portrait (which you saw today) of the friend who is mentioned

---

¹ The month is not clear in the manuscript. It might be Mh for March, or Jul.
for July. But since the context seems to refer to the privately printed version of
The Giaour which Byron was distributing to friends at the end of March, the former
seems probable.
² Unidentified.
³ Probably the miniature by Sanders mentioned by Moore (I, 379n.)
¹ At Byron's request Richard Westall painted a portrait of Lady Charlotte
Harley, Lady Oxford's daughter, then 11 years old, to whom he later wrote some
dedicatory stanzas for the opening of the seventh edition of *Childe Harold*, the
stanzas "To Ianthe".

in the text at the close of Canto 1st. & in the notes[2]—which are subjects sufficient to authorise that addition.—

Believe me yrs truly

[TO ———————.]   *March 29th. 1813*

Sir—I will thank you to send down immediately a bottle of "Adam's Solvent for the Stone" with the directions—it is prepared by Perry a Surgeon.——My address is *Eywood* Presteigne—Herefordshire— let it be sent immediately by the *Leominster* Coach.

Yr. obedt. Sert.

BYRON

[TO LORD HOLLAND]   *Eywood. April 3d. 1813*

My dear Lord—As I must be in town (perhaps in a short time) to make many arrangements before my voyage I yet hope to see you before I go & trouble you with "more last words".—The causes of my going I explained to you—indeed—they were of too little consequence to anyone but myself—for me to wish them to be kept secret.—There are also other reasons not worth mentioning that may induce me to hasten my expedition—in the meantime the snows of an English *Spring* now falling around me add one more inducement to reconcile me to expatriation.—I feel not less sensible to the kindness of your letter than to every part of your conduct which preceded it— to thank you would be endless.—It pleases me much that you like "the Giaour" of which I had great doubts—the measure is by no means after my own heart but perhaps the fittest for such a thing— & if I erred in the adoption of it—it was the meeting between Cortes & Pizarro in the beautiful fragment in Rogers's notes to Columbus— which led me astray—& it is an unfortunate propensity of the rhyming genus to wish to imitate what they despair of equalling.——The story was too long in all it's details to make anything of but the disjointed fragments you saw & I have neither the time nor the impetus to make a poem of it—the incidents are founded I believe on facts—& made an impression on my memory when I heard them—

[2] Stanza XCI, referring to John Wingfield, his Harrow friend, who died at Coimbra in 1811.

34

which at last in an idle evening broke forth into that rhapsody with all their Turkish & Arabesque accompaniments which crept in to the puzzlement I doubt not of the reader—for these I can offer no excuse—if they can be *pronounced* it is more than my due.—If I push forward to Greece or Persia it is not improbable that the want of better employment may lead me on to further scribbling—if so your wishes for my success will be a spur to my Pegasus "where giant Kaff protrudes his granite toes". But I think my migrations will be more circumscribed & of no long duration—& I am sufficiently grateful for the favour already shewn without drawing further on the purse & patience of the "gentle reader". With the hope of soon seeing Lady Holland & yourself as well as I wish you—believe me my dear Lord

ever truly your obliged & affectionate &c.

BYRON

[TO LADY MELBOURNE] *April 5th. 1813*

My dear Ly. M.—If in town at all I shall only remain a few days—& it will not be in my power to see Ly. C[aroline]—she has fairly worn out every wish to please or displease her—if she sends you the picture—keep it—but for the love of quiet let me hear no more of or *from* her—I shall not open any letter from her in future therefore do not send me the Sunday's dispatch or any future packet—unless from *yourself.*—The charm of the ring exists only in her own malignant imagination—every *ring* was *English*—I recollect something of a Comboloio or Turkish rosary of amber beads which I gave to her—to which she attached some absurd mystery—but the rings (among others a *wedding* one which she *bestowed* upon *herself* & insisted on my placing it on her finger) were all the manufacture of a Bondstreet Artist who certainly was no Conjuror.———I cannot break my *promise*—pray say at once & once for all—that I have nothing more to say to see or to do on the subject—& nothing but a wish to make her act right in giving up what she ought not to retain would have induced me to submit so long to the *fragments* of her yoke—& hear the clanking of the last links of a chain forever broken.—I have much to do & little time to do it in—certainly not an instant to spare to a person for whom the iron (to use her own metaphor) retains all the *heat* but none of the flexibility.—I give up pictures letters &c. to her tender mercies—let that satisfy her—the detestation —the utter abhorrence I feel at part of her conduct—I will neither

35

shock you with nor trust myself to express.—That feeling has become a part of my nature—it has poisoned my future existence—I know not whom I may love but to the latest hour of my life I shall hate that woman.—*Now* you know my sentiments—they will be the same on my deathbed.——To her I do not express this because I have no desire to make her uncomfortable—but such is the state of my mind towards her for reasons I shall not recur to & I beg to be spared from meeting her until we may be chained together in Dante's Inferno.——————The *date* ring you shall have if you like it—the others have been transferred to Charlotte Harley whom I should love forever if she could always be only eleven years old—& whom I shall probably marry when she is old enough & bad enough to be made into a modern wife.——We have had as yet very few fine days & these I have passed on the water & in the woods—scrambling and splashing about with the children—or by myself—I always feel happier here or at Newstead than elsewhere—& all my plagues are at least 150 miles off a distance unfortunately not quite sufficient to exempt me from their persecution.—But I am writing to you at greater length than I ought for your pleasure.—I shall endeavour to get a glimpse of you before I go——but for C[aroline] you have my ultimatum.———The thing you mention reminds me of the *Nun* (Ly. Heathcote told me last year I ran away with) & a Mr. Landor's tragedy[1]—the *reputation* of which I was obliged to bear this winter—

> "And then for mine obligingly mistakes
> The first lampoon Sir Will or Bubo [makes] ["][2]

so said the poet whom I resemble in nothing but the destiny expressed in the above couplet.——Could I have kept such a secret from you? or any secret?—I suppose there is somebody I like abused in it that I am charged with the authorship—& then the *character* you send is such an inducement to wear his bays——I presume it is anony[mous] [remainder torn off]

[TO LADY MELBOURNE] *April 7th. 1813*

My dear Ly. M[elbourn]e—"You have gotten ye picture"!![1]— now—do not on any account allow it to be taken out of your hands

---

[1] Walter Savage Landor's tragedy *Count Julian* was published by Murray in February 1813, anonymously, and was for a time credited to Byron.

[2] Pope, *Epistle to Dr. Arbuthnot*, lines 279–280.

[1] This was the portrait of Byron which Caroline Lamb had seized at John Murray's.

where it will remain very much to the refreshment of the original—copies &c. I leave to your discretion. The *double* hair amuses you[2]—she will never discover the difference—& of *course you* cannot know it or tell it—it was a lucky coincidence of colour & shape for my purpose—& may never happen again—& surely it is a very innocent revenge for some very scurvy behaviour.—It grieves me however that Ly. Blarney will never be able to lift up her eyes & hands on ye. occasion—as heretofore—it is worthy of her own school—in which had I been earlier initiated I should have been an adept. I believe you are right about C[aroline] & the "Giaour" but Mrs. L[amb] astonishes me—*"pale"* what has that to do with it?—it is merely the distinction of all Europeans comparatively speaking from an Asiatic—it is rather hard upon me that all my poetical personages must be identified with the writer—& just as fair as if Dr. Moore must be Zeluco—or Milton (begging pardon for mentioning such men in the same sentence with myself) the Devil.——I have received her letter—& but for a circumstance not worth relating should have returned it—after a good deal of flattery & something of abuse she concludes by terming me "the greatest villain that ever existed".—My opinion of her I expressed in my last—& the *effect* of her conduct upon my feelings—this I cannot revoke—but will not repeat.———The Duchess of M!![3] by the blessing of Diana all *our* footmen & Gardeners are frightful.—I write with m'amie very near me—if she looks over my shoulder the foregoing paragraph will be a proper reward for peeping—& I scribble it on purpose.—I still adhere to my resolution of not conferring with your *"Scorpion"*——but do not let this induce you to part with my property—I am by no means sure that I shall be in town—at all—but if so—incog.—to embrace you & Ly. *Holland* before my voyage.——Your letters are delightful—particularly the parts *not* about Caroline but Carol*us*—I wish he had exchanged heads with your Regent *Log* with all my heart—or that they were *stitched together*—what an admirable Janus of a fool & a knave!—I take C[harles] 1st. to be the greatest *king* (that is—villain) that ever lived.—Our family got a peerage & lost every thing else for the Stuarts—& my mother was their lineal descendant (from James 2d.

[2] Caroline Lamb had requested through Lady Melbourne a lock of Byron's hair, presumably as a price for returning the picture. He sent her a lock of Lady Oxford's hair instead.

[3] The Duchess of Manchester (1774–1828) was married off by her mother, the Duchess of Gordon, to William (Montagu), 5th Duke of Manchester, but she ran off with her footman.

of Scotland's daughter) all the bad blood in my own composition I derive from those bastards of Banquo.———

Believe me dear Ly. M. ever yrs. most truly

P.S. on the other side see some *mild* verses
To the *discoverer* of the bodies of
Charles 1st. & Henry 8th.
Famed for their civil & domestic quarrels
See heartless Henry lies by headless Charles!
Between them stands another sceptred *thing*
It lives—it reigns "aye every inch a king!"
Charles to his people—Henry to his wife
The double tyrant starts at once to life,
Justice & Death have mixed their dust in vain
Each royal vampire quits his vault again!
Curst be the tomb that could so soon disgorge
Two such to make a Janus or a George"[4]

Will you give Ld. Holland or anybody you like or dislike a copy of this—but I suppose you will be *tender* or *afraid*—you need not mind any *harm* it will do me.—

[TO JOHN HANSON] *Eywood—Presteigne—April 11th. 1813*

Dear Sir—It is with regret rather than surprise that I have in vain expected tidings on the subject of Mr. Claughton. I have determined not to go to law with him—before the suit was concluded the price would not be worth the purchase independent of the loss—expence & uncertainty attending the procedure.—Already at the present depreciation of money—it is some thousands less than last year—we must therefore do the best we can with Newstead & other concerns.— Before I left town I wrote to you—repeating my intention of leaving England in May & expressing in the strongest terms my wish that something should be done about Rochdale—to enable me to carry that intention into effect.—I shall go in three weeks—be the consequences as they may.—but I do wish much to hear from you & immediately.—

yrs. ever

B

[4] The Prince Regent had been present at the opening of the tomb at Windsor which contained the bodies of Charles I and Henry VIII. Byron wrote several versions of this poem. Copies were circulated privately, and one was published in a Paris edition of Byron's *Poetical Works* in 1819. See *Poetry*, VII, 35–36.

P.S. My best respects to Mrs. H.—& all the family.——If I have no letter—I must write to Claughton.—

[Presteigne] April 15th. 1813

Dear Sir—I wrote to you requesting an answer last week—& again apprising you of my determination of leaving England early in May—& proceeding no further with Claughton—Now having arrived—I shall write to that person immediately—to give up the whole business—I am sick of delays attending it—& can wait no longer—& I have had too much of *law* already at Rochdale to place Newstead in ye. same predicament.—I shall only be able to see you for a few days in town—as I shall sail before the 20th of May—

Believe me yrs. ever

B

P.S. My best compts to Mrs. H & the family.—

[Presteigne] April 17th. 1813

Dear Sir—I shall follow your advice & say nothing to our shuffling purchaser but leave him to you & the fullest powers of *Attorney* which I hope you will have ready on my arrival in town early next week.——I wish if possible the arrangement with Hoare to be made immediately as I must set off forthwith—I mean to remain *incog* in London for the short time previous to my embarkation.—I have not written to Claughton—nor shall of course after your counsel on the subject.—I wish you would turn in your mind the expediency of selling Rochdale—I shall never make any thing of it as it is.—I beg you will provide (as before my last voyage) the fullest powers to act in my absence & bring my cursed concerns into some kind of order—you must at least allow that I have acted according to your advice about Newstead—& I shall take no step without your being previously consulted.————I hope I shall find you & Mrs. H. &c. well in London—& that you have heard something from this dilatory gentleman.—

Believe me ever yrs. truly

B

My dear Ly. M[elbourn]e—I rejoice to hear for the fiftieth time of C[aroline]'s reformation & am inclined to think it permanent from the silence in that quarter whence I have not been disturbed for the last fortnight.—In a few weeks I shall be beyond her correspondence & in the mean time shall take care not to renew it.————I leave this place in a day or two for London where I shall remain in obscurity for a week or two.—*We* are at present in a slight perplexity owing to an event which certainly did not enter into my calculation—what it is—I leave to your own ingenious imagination which will not let me off for a little I am sure.[1]—I am not quite certain that I shall embark in the same ship—but I shall sail nearly at the same time—& join them—unless the vicinity of Greece should be too tempting for so vagrant a personage.—The approbation of your Duchess is very obliging—if she really wants your copy—I will give you another with pleasure.—As for C[aroline] I do not know to what she alludes—the thing in question "the Giaour" was written some time ago & printed when you had it—lately—I have had neither time nor inclination to scribble —far less publish.——I asked Ly. O[xford] if she had seen your satire & she tells me she has neither seen nor heard of it—I wonder that any of these *young* ladies you mention should be attacked & still more that I should be presumed the assailant[2]—the mention of any of their names might preserve me from the charge.—If C[aroline] gets hold of "the Giaour" she will bring it in wilful murder against the author—& if she discovers that the hair was that of her "dearest Aspasia" I question whether Medusa's would not be more agreeable.[3] —I have a long arrear of mischief to be even with that amiable daughter of Ly. B[essborough]'s—& in the long run I shall pay it off— by instalments.—I consider this as payment the first for the bonfire[4]—a debt too heavy to discharge all at once.—After all—if from this hour I were never to hear her name mentioned—at least from herself—I should be too happy to let her off with all her laurels—but if she recommences hostilities—I have no protection against her madness but my own foolery—& I shall avail myself of my cap & bells accordingly————How is the Ly. Blarney? [Bessborough]—if that

---

[1] Byron seems clearly hinting that he has fathered another member of the "Harleian Miscellany" on Lady Oxford, but since nothing more is said about it, the "perplexity" was probably caused by a false alarm.
[2] Unidentified. Byron was liable to be accused of the authorship of any anonymous satire.   [3] See April 7, 1813, to Lady Melbourne, note 2.
[4] See Dec. 23, 1812, note 2 (vol. 2, p. 260).

sagacious person knew how matters stand just at present I think her alarms would be at rest forever—if ever I were again smitten in that family it would be with herself & not C[aroline]—but hatred is a much more delightful passion—& never cloys—it will make us all happy for the rest of our lives.

Believe me dear Ly. M. ever yrs

B

[TO JOHN MURRAY]

April 21st. 1813

Dear Sir—I shall be in town by Sunday next & will call & have some conversation on the subject of Westall's proposed designs.—I am to sit to him for a picture at the request of a friend of mine[1] &—as Sanders's is not a good one you will probably prefer the other.—I wish you to have Sanders's taken down & sent to my lodgings immediately—before my arrival.——I hear that a certain malicious publication on Waltzing is attributed to me.—This report I suppose you will take care to contradict—as the Author I am sure will not like that I should wear his cap & bells.[2]—Hobhouse's quarto will be out immediately[3]—pray send to the author for an early copy which I wish to take abroad with me.

Dr. Sir. I am yrs. very truly

B

P.S. I see the Examiner threatens some observations upon you next week—what can you have done to share the wrath which has heretofore been principally expended upon the Prince? I presume all your Scribblers will be drawn up in battle array in defence of the modern Tonson—Mr. Bucke for instance.[4]—Send in my account to Bennet Street as I wish to settle it before sailing.

---

[1] Probably for Lady Oxford.

[2] The *Waltz* was published anonymously in the spring of 1813, not by Murray, to whom Byron had offered it, but by Sherwood, Neely, and Jones, Paternoster Row. Perhaps Murray was afraid of it because of the *lèse majesté* in the references to the Prince Regent.

[3] Hobhouse's *Journey through Albania*. . . .

[4] Charles Bucke (1781–1846), one of Murray's authors, published in 1813 his *Philosophy of Nature; or, the Influence of Scenery on the Mind and Heart.*

My dear Lady M[elbourn]e—I thought the silence would not last— it has been broken & in an epistle somewhat longer than a maiden speech or a matron's letter ought to be.—However the tone is less harsh & consequently it grieves me "who pleads so well should ever plead in vain".—It is the particular request of "several persons of distinction" that this plaguy conference should not take place—& just at present it is highly expedient that their wishes should meet a ready compliance—& my inclination being luckily on the same side I am glad to have this excuse for following it.—"A bird in the hand is worth two in the bush" says the approved saw—if so—two birds in hand are probably worth more than any given bird in a bush particularly if the said bird has been in hand already & has pecked one's fingers into the bargain.——I am directed by C[aroline] to send my answer to you—pray—fight off this interview for me if you can—as I am pledged to avoid it—& surely you all agree with me how much better it is to allow me to depart in peace.——C[aroline] is coming to town—I am glad of it as far as regards myself—she will immediately take a new turn—& I think there is no chance of our encountering during my stay there.—She tells me they want 90 guineas for copying the picture[1]—the original cost but 75—& that was fifty too much—it is rather hard that *you* must pay for her pilferings nevertheless.—On Sunday I expect to be in London—but as privately & quietly as I can[.] I have a good deal of business to get through during the ensuing fortnight—The rest of our family go to Cheltenham till the vessel is ready—mine will be a separate embarkation.———I see no use in answering her letter—having lately lived with commonsensible people—these heroics are too *Devonshire* for me.[2]—Besides I am very busy educating my future wife[3]—& look upon the epistle of another's spouse with a prophetic twinge that makes me feel like Moody in the Country Girl.—[4]I leave you to deal with C[aroline]—or *double*-deal

[1] Probably the picture Caroline had taken from Murray and which she finally returned to Lady Melbourne, through whom Byron had given permission for a copy to be made if Caroline wished it.

[2] A reference to the wildness of Caroline's mother Lady Bessborough and her sister the Duchess of Devonshire, who in their youth were almost as "heroic" as Caroline herself.

[3] Lady Charlotte Harley, Lady Oxford's daughter. See April 5, 1813, to Lady Melbourne.

[4] In *The Country Girl*, a comedy by Garrick, altered from Wycherley, Moody brings up his ward, Peggy Thrift, in the country in perfect seclusion. When Moody is 50 and Peggy 19, he wants to marry her but she outwits him and marries a young man.

with her—she has no right to anything like candour from anyone—&
from me the most she can desire & more than she deserves is—
silence. Believe me dear Ly. M[elbourn]e

ever yrs.

[TO LADY CAROLINE LAMB]

4 Bennet Street April 29th. 1813

If you still persist in your intention of meeting me in opposition to
the wishes of your own friends & of mine—it must even be so—I
regret it & acquiesce with reluctance.———I am not ignorant of the
very extraordinary language you have held not only to me but others
—& your avowal of your determination to obtain what you are
pleased to call "revenge"—nor have I now to learn that an incensed
woman is a dangerous enemy.—Undoubtedly those against whom we
can make no defence—whatever they say or do—must be formidable—
your words & actions have lately been tolerably portentous—&
might justify me in avoiding the demanded interview—more especially
as I believe you fully capable of performing all your menaces—but as
I once hazarded every thing *for* you—I will not shrink *from* you—
perhaps I deserve punishment—if so—you are quite as proper a
person to inflict it as any other. You say you will *"ruin me"*—I
thank you—but I have done that for myself already—you say you will
"destroy me" perhaps you will only save me the trouble.—It is
useless to reason with you—to repeat what you already know—
that I have in reality saved you from utter & impending destruction.—
Every one who knows you—knows this also—but they do not know
as yet what you may & will tell them as I now tell you—that it is in a
great measure owing to this persecution—to the accursed things you
have said—to the extravagances you have committed—that I again
adopt the resolution of quitting this country—In your assertions—
you have either *belied* or *betrayed* me—take your choice—in your
actions—you have hurt only yourself—but is that nothing to one who
wished you well?——I have only one request to make—which is not
to attempt to see Ly. O[xford]—on her you have no claim.—You will
settle—as you please—the arrangement of this conference—I do not
leave England till June—but the sooner it is over the better—I once
wished for your own sake Ly. M[elbourne] to be present—but if you

43

are to fulfil any of your threats in word or deed—we had better be alone—

yrs. ever

[signature]

[TO LADY DAVY.[1]]   *Thursday Eve. [May, 1813]*

Dear Ly. Davy—I am but too happy to be of your party without Princesses or Patriots to deprive myself of that pleasure when they are present.[2]—I fear nobody but Miss Edgeworth.[3]—Next year I hope we shall all dine together with a Pasha—in the meantime I will have the honour of accepting your invitation.—

I am ever yr. obliged Sert.

BYRON

[TO SAMUEL ROGERS]   [*May, 1813?*]

My dear Rogers—Will you allow me to come in *after* dinner tomorrow instead of before—for I have so bedevilled my digestion— that your *light* supper—the other night—half killed me.—And will you have any objection to my inscribing to you "the Giaour" in the next E[ditio]n of C[hilde] H[arol]d where it will be published for the 1st. time.[1]—

ever yrs.

BN

[TO LADY MELBOURNE]   *April—May 2d. 1813*

My dear Ly M[elbourn]e—The illness of Mr. Hobhouse's step-mother has spoiled our party.—Your invitation is tempting—in

---

[1] Lady Davy was a rich widow, Jane Apreece, née Kerr, when she married in 1812 the famous chemical scientist, Sir Humphry Davy, later inventor of the Safety Lamp. Her social ambitions made her hostess to the most famous people of her day. Byron was fond of the Davys. Sir Humphry visited him in Ravenna in 1820.

[2] Miss Berry (*Journal*, Vol. II, p. 535) supped with Lady Davy in May, 1813, to meet the Princess of Wales. She noted that Byron was among the guests.

[3] See May 15, 1813, to Lady Davy.

[1] Byron's first intention was to publish *The Giaour* with *Childe Harold*, but he finally allowed Murray to publish it separately. The first edition of 41 pages and 685 lines was published on June 5, 1813. It was dedicated to Samuel Rogers.

various ways—firstly—I never yet dined at M[elbourne] House—
there is *novelty*—2dly.—I never expected that Lord M[elbourne] at
all events would be my inviter—there is *surprise*—3dly. the pleasure
of meeting you which is neither novel nor surprising but something
better than both—& 4thly. I am rather hungry having lived on tea &
bread & butter ever since I left E[ywoo]d (where I was under the
necessity of conforming to a less Eremitical regimen) & should do
justice to your viands.—Yet I must resist all these—though I can't
very well say why—unless it be that I am in a very solitary mood &
quite unfit for so much good company—will you therefore make my
most humble apologies to your lord & *master*—I wont say excuse me
to *you*—for you will do that very readily.——Ly. ——————[Oxford]
at last thinks it as well to allow the conference—for fear I believe of
being dragged herself into some scene & put in peril by the scissors
or bodkin of the enemy.—And here hath been in the city of London a
female cousin of mine going for her health (& a husband which is the
same thing) to the Bermudas[1]—wanting to have last words with all
her relatives—& me amongst the number—which I have declined—
it is very odd the fuss people make about partings—when I went
abroad last time it was without any of these things—which are much
better avoided if they like one another—& if they do not what
purpose can they answer?——Your friend *Kolfkovsky*[2] was with me
yesterday—complaining of the English husbands & the restrictions
upon their wives—with whom he appears to have made little progress
—but lays it all upon the *husbands*—I was obliged to comfort him
with the assurance that the fault was all his own—& that husbands
& wives are much the same here as elsewhere—it was impossible to
hear them so traduced with patience.—Talking of patience puts me in
mind of the thing you asked for which I send but remember you asked
me for it *this* time—& don't accuse me of inflicting my rimé upon you
without compassion—believe me

ever yrs. most truly

[1] Julia Byron (see August 27, 1811, to Dallas) later (in 1817) married Robert
Heath. She was probably the cousin here referred to.

[2] Prince Kozlovsky was a Russian diplomat who was visiting in England. The
Biographie Universelle lists a Prince Feodor Alexeivitch Koslofski, a Russian
literary man and general who knew Voltaire. He died in 1770. The Kozlovsky
mentioned here and elsewhere in Byron's letters, may have been a descendant,
perhaps a grandson, since he bore the title of Prince.

[On cover.]

Dr. Ly. M—Will you read—wafer or seal—& send the inclosed answer to an epistle of Your Agnus[3]—in which she menaces me with her "ghost"—which I long to see—if she is but half as fractious *there* (where you please) as *here* they will be glad to remit her to this world

ever yrs—

[TO LADY MELBOURNE] *May 7th. 1813—*

Dear Ly. M[elbourn]e—I passed your house with ye. intention of calling—but seeing a carriage I would not disturb you & possibly drive away some of your near & dear relations—as generally happens upon my intrusion.——It is impossible for me to guess "the long story" about the picture—but it is doubtless some new foolery of C[aroline]'s—you need not take ye trouble to tell it—let her amuse herself. I wished to have had it again—because another *paramount* personage has taken a fancy to have *that* picture at all events—but I meant the one now in *their* possession for you—indeed it is the best of the two—for it was done some years before.—As to C[aroline] she is so far out of the question—that I would rather throw it into the fire & the original after—than leave it in her possession—if it could be avoided.—I *must* see you at Sir *Joshua's*[1]—though I don't much like venturing on the sight of *seventeen*—it is bad enough *now*—& must have been *worse then*—the painter was not so much to blame as you seem to imagine by adding a few years—he foresaw you would lose nothing by them.—On Wednesday I leave town—it is exactly the same to me morning or evening—the less light the better— either for quarrels or reconciliations—but I once more enter my protest against C[aroline]'s meeting me at all—it will end in some ludicrous scene—you must be present—it will make you laugh which will be some consolation.——————I am asked to Ly. Spencer's tonight—but have doubts about going—for I have an invitation to a

[3] Byron's answer to the epistle of Lady Caroline Lamb ("Your Agnus") is not extant.

[1] Byron probably refers to Sir Joshua Reynolds' portrait "Lady Melbourne and Child" (Graves and Kronin, catalogue of Reynolds' works, No. 637). It was included in the British Institution's exhibition of 1813 (No. 14). Lady Melbourne had married, before she was 17, Sir Peniston Lamb who became the 1st Viscount Melbourne. Her first child, Peniston, was born in 1770.

city or rather *citizen's* ball where I wish to see the young people unmuzzled—& as Hobhouse is going—who is a Cynic after my own heart—I shall be regaled with his observations—which may be safely made as we are both mere spectators—I *can't* dance—& he *wont.*————I shall contrive to be at Ly. S[pencer]'s first if possible—solely & entirely to see you—& *not* to hear about C[aroline] if you can help it—I am sure it is a sickening subject to both.—

ever dr. Ly. M[elbourn]e yrs.

[TO LADY MELBOURNE]   *May 9th. 1813*

My dear Ly. M[elbourn]e—At nine be it then—but I still retain my opinion & act entirely on the judgment of others.—I have been so often the dupe of everyone with whom I ever was connected———& have so little reason to credit the asertions of Ly. C[aroline]—that I hear of her indisposition with some degree of scepticism.—If she really is unwell *all* that Ly. C[aroline] has done to destroy my regard will not prevent my feeling much regret—& sincerely wishing her recovery.—

Believe me my dear Ly. M[elbourn]e

[TO LADY MELBOURNE]   *May 14th. 1813*

My dear Ly. M[elbourn]e—Say whatever you please in answer to the letter addressed to us—it is all very well.—————I am in some anxiety—in consequence of a letter from C[heltenha]m this morning—*she*[1] has burst a small bloodvessel—& is weak & ill—all which she attributes to "me & my *friends* in town"!!—I presume it will end in an indisposition which however unpleasant for a time—would eventually be a great *relief* to both.—It is very odd that all the women of my acquaintance abuse *R[oge]rs*—C[aroline]'s letter is *full* of it—& Ly. —————[Oxford's] *fuller.*—The malady is perhaps a "ruse" but at all events it will probably take me from town next week—very much to the detriment of my temporal & *spiritual* concerns.—I shan't have spirits to tell you my stories this Even—unless seeing

[1] Lady Oxford.

47

you restores them—your conversation is really *Champaigne* to them.—
C[aroline]'s *platonic* speculations are all nonsense—we began in that
way before—& they ended in—all this uproar.—I can't help being
amused at "your permission to *see me* on my return"—I suppose you
trust in the plague—or a tempest—or Ly. O[xford] to sweep me from
the earth before that occurs.

ever dr. Ly. M[elbourn]e yrs.

℘

[TO LADY DAVY]   *May 15th. 1813*

Dear Ly. Davy—I will be punctual to the hour on Monday
morn[in]g but I fear I shall not be in town on ye 23d. which will
deprive me of a great pleasure.———My nerves will I trust be adequate
to encounter this awful introduction—I have no apprehensions of the
temper of "Griselda"[1] but I confess myself rather appalled by the
wit of "Ly. Delacour"[2] & the sense of "Miss Nugent"[3]—though it is
some consolation that in such company I shall at all events run no
risk of "Ennui".[4]—With my best compliments to Sir Humphry I have
the honour to be

yr. obliged & faithful Svt.

BYRON

[TO JOHN MURRAY]   *May 16th. 1813*

Dear Sir—I send you back "the Giaour"—& about 160 lines in
addition—I have marked in page 27—the place of insertion.—The

[1] The invitation was to meet Maria Edgeworth, the Irish novelist, who was
visiting London with her father at the time. She had published her novel *The
Modern Griselda: A Tale* in 1804. Annabella Milbanke had reminded Byron of
Emma in that novel. See Sept. 18, 1812, to Lady Melbourne.

[2] Lady Delacour was the most important character in Miss Edgeworth's novel
Belinda (1801). She was witty and intelligent, but also cunning, hypocritical and
scheming.

[3] Miss Grace Nugent was the heroine of one of Miss Edgeworth's Tales of
Fashionable Life, *The Absentee* (1812).

[4] *Ennui* was another tale of fashionable life. It was published in 1809. The
Davys had arranged this breakfast for Maria to meet Byron. He respected the
talents of Maria but thought her father a great bore. See Nov. 4, 1820, to Murray,
and "Detached Thoughts", Nos. 61–64.

copy (printed) is all wrong—& mixed up in the most blundering way by the printer with extra & misplaced sheets.—

yrs. truly

P.S. I want a *proof*—& a few more complete copies *soon*.———

[TO JOHN MURRAY] *May 17th, 1813*

Dr. Sir—I send a corrected & I hope amended copy of the lines for the "fragment" already sent this evening—Let the enclosed be the copy that is sent to the Devil (the printer's) and burn the other.

yrs. &c.

[TO THOMAS MOORE] *May 19th, 1813*

Oh you, who in all names can tickle the town,
Anacreon, Tom Little, Tom Moore, or Tom Brown,[1]—
For hang me if I know of which you may most brag,
Your Quarto two-pounds, or your Twopenny Post Bag;[2]
    * * * * * * * * * * * * * * * *
But now to my letter—to *yours* 'tis an answer—
To-morrow be with me, as soon as you can, sir,
All ready and dress'd for proceeding to spunge on
(According to compact) the wit in the dungeon[3]—
Pray Phœbus at length our political malice
May not get us lodgings within the same palace!
I suppose that to-night you're engaged with some codgers,
And for Sotheby's Blues have deserted Sam Rogers;
And I, though with cold I have nearly my death got,
Must put on my breeches, and wait on the Heathcote.

---

[1] These are the names under which Moore published his various volumes of poetry.

[2] Moore had just published his *Intercepted Letters, or the Twopenny Post-bag*, by Thomas Brown the Younger.

[3] Leigh Hunt, then serving a two-year sentence in the Surrey Gaol for "libelling" the Prince Regent.

But to-morrow, at four, we will both play the *Scurra*,
And you'll be Catullus, the R[egen]t Mamurra.[4]

Dear M.—having got thus far, I am interrupted by * * * *
10 o'clock.

Half-past 11. * * * * is gone. I must dress for Lady Heathcote's.—
Addio.

[TO JOHN HERMAN MERIVALE]   [*May 20, 1813?*]

Dear Merivale—What is this news?[1] if anything will you send me
your paper for 2 minutes?

B.

[TO LADY MELBOURNE]   *May 21st. 1813*

Dear Ly. M[elbourn]e—I shall be with you at Ly. C[owper?]'s
(to whom I request you will present my inexcusable excuses) before
seven—that we may form a compact body for ye. expedition.——I
have unfortunately dined for the week yesterday—& if Kovlov[sky][1]
would follow my example—in that respect—we should be less squeezed
in our respective positions this Evening.—

ever yrs.

[TO JOHN MURRAY]   *May 22d. 1813*

Dear Sir—I return the "C[uriosities] of Literature"[1]—pray is it
fair to ask if the "twopenny Postbag" is to be reviewed in *this*

---

[4] Catullus, xxix, 3:

> Quis hoc potest videre, quis potest pati, etc.
> Who can see this, or who can bear
> That it should be Mamurra's share
> To have what long-haired Gaul can give,
> Or the far land, where Britons live,
> Unless indeed a glutton he,
> Gambler or shameless wretch should be!

[1] Merivale was a friend of Hodgson and of Byron's friend Henry Drury, whose
sister he married. There is no clue to the "news" mentioned here.

[1] See May 2, 1813, to Lady Melbourne, note 2.

[1] The six volumes of Isaac D'Israeli's *Curiosities of Literature* were published at
intervals from 1791 to 1834. Two volumes had already appeared. D'Israeli was
a close friend of John Murray. Byron became a great admirer of the *Curiosities* and
later wrote some comments in the margins of a volume that got back to D'Israeli,
who then reproduced the marginalia in a later volume.

*No.?*² because if not I should be glad to undertake it—& leave it to Chance & the Editor for a reception into your pages.—

yrs. truly
B

P.S. You have not sent me Eustace Travels³—

[TO JOHN MURRAY]   *May 23d. 1813*

Dear Sir—I question whether ever author before received such a compliment from his *master*—I am glad you think the thing is tolerably *vamped* & will be *vendible.*—Pray look over the proof again—I am but a careless reviser—& let me have *12* struck off & one or two for yourself to serve as M.S. for the thing when published in the body of the volume.¹ If Ly. -----[Caroline Lamb] sends for it—do *not* let her have it—till the copies are all ready & then you can send her one.—

yrs. truly
Μπαίρων

P.S. H[obhouse]'s book is out at last²—I have my copy—which I have lent already.

[TO LADY MELBOURNE]   *May 24th. 1813*

My dear Ly. M[elbourn]e—I had a card for ye. Ly. S. Sh's¹ this evening—but I was engaged in taking leave of Mr. Hobhouse who quits us for ye. Continent tomorrow—& whom it is not very probable I shall see again—he is ye. oldest—indeed—ye. only friend I have—& my regrets are equally *social* & *selfish*—for if I have[sic] had attended to his advice—I should have been anything but what I am—& in parting with him I lose "a guide philosopher & friend" I neither *can*

² It is interesting that Byron wanted to review Moore's volume for, apparently, the *Quarterly Review* which Murray published. It would have been a "friendly" review, but no review of Moore's poem appeared in the *Quarterly.*
³ John Chetwode Eustace (1762?–1815) published his *Tour through Italy* in 1815. Murray may have had the manuscript at this time.
¹ Byron was still at work on revisions and extensions of *The Giaour.*
² Hobhouse's *Journey through Albania* . . . was published in a large quarto with many plates in colour in May, 1813.
¹ Possibly Lady Sarah Shannon (1780–1820), wife of the Earl of Shannon of the Irish Peerage.

nor *wish* to replace.———Now for our everlasting theme.—I think *terror* must be ye. order of ye. day—*suspicion* on your part will maintain discipline—& believe me it will not be misplaced—you know my situation—I have no excuse which could be offered in a court of law or even of honour—but if a woman will force her way in defiance of every thing—even against ye. remonstrance & request of her *fool*— the said fool has no chance but running away—which at present does not happen to suit the springs of her puppet.—I am not ye. dupe of her pretended passion—I see it is totally selfish—she is a right woman with all the courage to dare but not to suffer—the hardihood of guilt united to the *fear* of shame—the passions of an *Oriental* without her spirit—in short the oddest antithesis of *pipe-* & common-clay that ever was compounded since the first husband betook himself to stealing apples—& begetting heirs to his own vexations in this world—and (I hope for his pains & the truth of ye. Pentateuch) his utter d – mnation in ye. next. —————My own situation at this moment is such that without a boast I may say—that perhaps the present *suspense* would be alleviated by the worst *positive* event that could happen—I am utterly ruined in fortune—not very brilliant in reputation—sans plan—or prospect of any kind—but of getting out of ye. country— with nothing to *hope*—but (by the peculiar patronage of Beelzebub) —with little to *fear*.—

> "My greatest comfort is, that now,
> My dubbolt fortune is so low,
> That either it must quickly end—
> Or turn about again & mend—["]

you will pardon a quotation from Hudibras.[2] If she is at all in her senses—she will now pause—if not—neither the patience of Job nor the wisdom of Solomon (neither very remarkable by ye. bye) could bear or accomplish more than you have long ago done for ye. salvation of a thing not worth saving.—

I am dr. Ly. M. yrs.

P.S. All my epistles to ye. C[aroline] must go for nothing—you know there is but one way in which a man can write to ladies afflicted

---

[2] Byron made his own adaptation of the lines from *Hudibras* (Second Part, Canto I, lines 39–42):

> His only Solace was, That now
> His dog-bolt Fortune was so low,
> That either it must quickly end.
> Or turn about again, and mend.

with these phantasies—& to her above all others—I must say *yes*—
yes—*yes*—(like a crier in a country town) to keep her quiet—& to
prove to Ly. B[essborough] how *admirably* her *"soothing"* system
succeeds.—*Silence* C[aroline] for *"3 days"*—& *I* am *dumb* forever.—

My dear Ly. M[elbourn]e—By the *"worst possible"* I doubtless
meant the event which for aught I know may be very probable—as to
her remaining with me—that were out of the question—I would not
stir a furlong—but patiently wait the wrath of the Blarneys—whom
I unfortunately detest too cordially—to give them a chance of putting
me out of my *then* misery—without doing my best to obtain a fellow
passenger in Charon's hoy.—I only expressed the fact—that the
difficulties in which I am steeped are such as to render any step of hers
or any other female or male—a matter next to indifference—believe
me the idea of our *living together*—never entered into my calculation
for a moment.—I have no attachment—within these two thousand
miles—but I feel some old ones reviving—& I hope I shall yet pray
for your prosperity with my face towards Mecca.———In the meantime
—Ly. O[xford] arrives in town tomorrow—which I regret—when
people have once fairly parted—how do I abhor those partings!—
I know them to be of no use—& yet as painful at the time as the first
plunge into purgatory.————All you say upon *Law* is Gospel—
but I am perdu—I don't know what you call temporary—Law is
eternal.—I shall soon I trust be where there is none—& where even
the wreck of my shattered fortunes will be affluence.—I now heartily
rejoice in the escape of your niece [Annabella Milbanke]—at the time
I could not foresee this—any more than I could imagine that the
means I adopted to extricate myself would have plunged me into that
same morass (to prolong your metaphor) in which I am now chin-
deep.—I trust you will believe that I did not wish to put the Lady's
philosophy to such a proof—I did not think her wrong then—still less
now.———I believe I shall sell Rochdale—for ye. sake of another
lawsuit—& at a certain loss—it would quite disappoint me to meet
with anything like profit—& as to pleasure—that was all over with
me before I was eighteen.———I shall be very sorry not to go as soon
as you wish—but I assure you——never did Prudery long more for a
lover—than I to be out of a country in which I certainly was not

born with my own consent.—If therefore I am here a month beyond your hopes—& an age beyond my own—pardon me.

ever yrs.

P.S. C[aroline] tells you I said &c. &c. &c.!—to be sure I did—& will say as much more——& as much more to that—to any woman whatever who puts the same questions—who would dare to say *No* within arm's-length?———

[TO JOHN MURRAY. (*a*)]   [*June, 1813?*]

Dear Sir—Can you keep the proofs standing a day for the G[iaou]r? if so—I will send you a few more lines—

ever yrs
B

[TO JOHN MURRAY. (*b*)]   [*June, 1813?*]

Add these two lines to paragraph 3d. sent this M[ornin]g
————————"tomb;
Expression's bright departing ray—
A Halo gilding round decay!——"[1]

[TO THOMAS MOORE]   [*June, 1813?*]

My dear Moore,—"When Rogers"[1] must not see the enclosed, which I send for your perusal. I am ready to fix any day you like for our visit. Was not Sheridan good upon the whole? The "Poulterer"[2] was the first and best.

Ever yours, &c.

[1] For the final version of *The Giaour*. But the lines were later changed to read: Expression's last receding ray,/A gilded halo hovering round decay.

[1] A humourous reference to a poem to Rogers by Lord Thurlow beginning with those words. When Byron read the verses aloud to Moore and Rogers, they all three broke down with laughter. Byron sent these lines to Moore a few days later. For more details see *LJ*, II, 211–212.

[2] Many of the contestants in the Drury Lane address competition introduced the Phœnix. Samuel Whitbread, of the Drury Lane Committee, sent in his contribution, also using the Phœnix. Sheridan, at dinner with Byron and Moore at Rogers' house, said: "But Whitbread made more of this bird than any of them:-he entered into particulars, and described its wings, beak, tail, &c.; in short, it was a *poulterer's* description of a Phenix!" (Moore, *Memoirs of the Life of the Right Hon. Richard Brinsley Sheridan*, Chapter XXI.)

1.

When T * * [Thurlow] this damn'd nonsense sent,
(I hope I am not violent)
Nor men nor gods knew what he meant.

2.

And since not ev'n our Rogers' praise
To common sense his thoughts could raise—
Why *would* they let him print his lays?

3.

* * * * * * * * * * * * * * *

4.

* * * * * * * * * * * * * * *

5.

To me, divine Apollo, grant—O!
Hermilda's first and second canto,
I'm fitting up a new portmanteau;

6.

And thus to furnish decent lining,
My own and others' bays I'm twining—
So, gentle T[hurlow], throw me thine in.

[TO JOHN MURRAY]   *June 2—1813*

Dear Sir—I presented a petition to the house yesterday[1]—which gave rise to some debate—& I wish you to favour me for a few minutes with the *Times* & Herald to look on their *hostile* report—You will find if you like to look at my *prose*—all my words nearly verbatim in the M[orning] Chronicle.

[TO JOHN HANSON. (*a*)]   *June 3d. 1813*

Dear Sir—When you receive this I shall have left town for a week—& it is perfectly right we should understand each other—I

[1] Byron spoke in the House of Lords on June 1, 1813, in support of Major Cartwright's petition protesting at the interruption by civil and military forces of his peaceful circulation of a petition for the reform of representation in Parliament. He then presented Major Cartwright's petition for the right to petition. This was Byron's last speech in the House of Lords. Byron's only defender in the House was the pariah Earl Stanhope, disowned by all parties for his "Jacobinism". Byron later wrote: ". . . Stanhope and I stood against the whole House, and mouthed it valiantly—and had some fun and a little abuse for our opposition." (Journal, Dec. 1, 1813.)

think you will not be surprised at my persisting in my intention of going abroad.—If the Suit can be carried on in my absence—*well*—if not—it must be given up—one word—one letter to C[laughto]n would put an end to it—but this I shall not do—at all events without acquainting you before hand—nor at all—provided I am enabled to go abroad again—but at all hazards at all losses—on this last point I am as determined as I have been for the last six months—& you have always told me that you would endeavour to assist me in that intention—every thing is ordered & ready—now—do not trifle with me—for I am in very solid serious earnest—& if utter ruin *were* or *is* before me—on the one hand—& wealth at home on the other—I have made my choice—& go I will—If you wish to write address a line before Saturday to Salthill[1]—Post office—Maidenhead I believe but am not sure is the Post town—but I shall not be in London till Wednesday next. Believe me

yrs. ever
B<small>N</small>

P.S. Let all the books go to Mr. Murray's immediately—& let the plate linen &c. which I find *excepted* by the *contract*—be sold—particularly a large silver vase—with the *contents* not removed as they are curious—& a silver cup—(not the skull) be sold also—both are of value.———

The Pictures also—& every moveable that is mine & can be converted into cash[2]—all I want is a few thousand pounds—& then adieu —you shan't be troubled with me these ten years—if ever.———

[TO JOHN HANSON. (*b*)]   *June 3d.* [*1813*]

Dear Sir—I have to request (if not done already) that our money now in Mr. V's[1] name be placed to my account—as soon as possible with Messrs Hoare.—

ever yrs.
B<small>YRON</small>

P.S.—I told the *Lady*[2] yesterday that you had a great curiosity to see her from your admiration of her figure—at a distance—& the

---

[1] Where he was to meet the Oxfords before their departure for the Continent.
[2] The contents of Newstead not contracted to Claughton Byron wished to sell to raise money for his intended trip abroad with the Oxfords.
[1] Unidentified.
[2] Lady Oxford.

vanity of the sex prevailed for she leaned forward without her veil to the window—so that you had a full view.————

June 6, 1813.

My dear Hodgson.—I write to you a few lines on business. Murray has thought proper at his own risk, and peril, and profit (if there be any) to publish the "Giaour";[1] and it may possibly come under your ordeal in the "Monthly." I merely wish to state that in the published copies there are additions to the amount of ten pages, *text* and *margin* (*chiefly* the last), which render it a little less unfinished (but more unintelligible) than before. If, therefore, you review it, let it be from the published copies and not from the first sketch. I shall not sail for this month, and shall be in town again next week, when I shall be happy to hear from but more glad to see you. You know I have no time or turn for correspondence(!) But you also know, I hope, that I am not the less

Yours ever

Μπαίρων

[TO JOHN GALT]   *4 Bennet St. St. James's June 8th. 1813*

My dear Sir—I have to thank you for a most agreeable present[1]— which has in no respect disappointed expectations which had been raised very high by the account of my friend Hobhouse—the rarity of whose praise may perhaps render it acceptable—more particularly as he is a rival writer—& in some opinions an adversary. I am no critic—& if I were inclined to cavil it would not be at the volume before me—but I wish you had given us *more*—as I trust you will—no one has yet treated the subject in so pleasing a manner.—If there is any page where your readers may be inclined to think you have said too much—it will probably be that in which you have honoured me

[1] Byron had circulated privately printed copies of *The Giaour* to friends for some weeks before Murray persuaded him to publish it. In the meantime he had added some three hundred lines. Hodgson did not review it for the *Monthly Review*. The review appeared in the June, 1813, issue (N. S. LXXI, p. 202). In the Editor's copy it is ascribed to "Den." (*LJ*, II, 215n.)

[1] John Galt's present to Byron was no doubt his *Letters from the Levant* (published in 1813) in which he made some references to his meeting with Byron on the voyage from Gibraltar to Malta and in Athens.

with a notice far too favourable—I thank you nevertheless & feel much more flattered than I could possibly be by the praise of any one who has not been on the spot—or indeed who has—as far as I am acquainted with the works of contemporary travellers.———I know nothing more attractive in *poetry* than your description of the Romaika[2] —which I confess appeared to me the most *prosaic* of dances—on my second voyage I shall endeavour to view it with your eyes—& in the mean time am obliged to you for setting me right on that & many other points—& if you will prove to me that Ld. E[lgin]'s "*is* the error of a liberal mind" the "Muse" shall forthwith eat her own words although they choak her—& me into the bargain.——Can you tell me anything of the history of Soliman the Renegade[3]— Bairactor's *co*-reformist? H[obhouse] has not mentioned him in his narrative—I thought Seid Ali was the next in command—& may I ask if the verse translations are your own—or from Pope—where you quote the "blind old man that dwelt in rocky Scio"?—But I am pestering you with a long letter—when all I have any business with— is to thank you for a volume on the subject of Greece—which has not yet been equalled—& will with difficulty be surpassed.—

Believe me truly yr. obliged & faithl. Sert.

BYRON

P.S. Ly. O[xford] is very much delighted with your work—I am not an impartial judge of her attainments—but you know she is a Grecian—& a clever woman—& as far as petticoat praise can go hers is quite as well worth having as that of any other she that ever wore Coronet above—& blue beneath.———

[2] The Romaika, as Byron called the traditional Greek dance, was described by Galt in his *Letters from the Levant* (pp. 194–95), as "very like the Highland-reel . . . The dancers arrange themselves in opposite parties and the music commencing with a cheerful strain, they mutually advance, eying each other askance, as they pass to opposite sides . . . The music growing more and more impetuous, the rage of the dancers kindles into fury. They snap their fingers in one another's faces; they spurn at the earth; their hands are tossed towards the heavens; they wheel, and howl the war-whoop of the Celts; and they jostle with such violence backward, that . . . it is unsafe [as Milton says] to come within the wind of such concussion."

[3] Byron possibly referred to Soliman, Pasha of Bagdad (1720–1802) who had a reputation for justice and gentleness which was unusual at the time. He was tolerant of the Christians and during a war with the French he protected the French Consul. Bairaktar (or Beirakdar) (1755–1808) was Pasha of Rouschouk when the revolt of the Janissaries overthrew Selim III and gave the throne to Mustapha, who had his rival strangled. Bairaktar marched on Constantinople, avenged the death of his benefactor, overthrew Mustapha, and placed Selim's brother Mahmoud on the throne. He was named grand vizier and undertook some reforms, but died soon after in a new revolt of the Janissaries.

My dear Hodgson—In town for a night I find your card—I had written to you at Cambridge merely to say that Murray has thought it expedient to publish ye. Giaour at his own risk (& reimbursement if he can) & that as it will probably be in yr. department in ye. Monthly[1] —I wished to state that in the published copies there are additions to the tune of 300 lines or so towards the end—& if reviewed it should *not* be from the privately printed copy—So much for scribbling.—I shall manage to see you somewhere before I sail which will be next month—till then I am yours here—& afterwards any where & every where

dear H[odgson] tutto tuo

Dear Ly. M[elbourn]e—On my arrival in town about half an hour ago (which I leave again tomorrow) I found your letter—I was determined not to plague you without.—Ly. – – – – [Oxford] has been in town—& we left it on Thursday for Salthill where she now is on her way to Portsmouth.—*I* expect to get away sometime next month—C[aroline] has been quiet to a degree of *awful* calmness— which was fortunate for God knows what I should have done—had she acted otherwise—she does not know that I am in town but was equally decorous ever since the arrival of Ly. [Oxford]—a very lucky accident—in that quarter we go on as usual—I do not know when she sails—I shall be with them till they embark—*he* is I believe with the ship—or in the sea—I saw him but once in town—& then it was to dispute about a stupid blunder on the subject of Kinsham—& other farming concerns.———Ly [Oxford] agrees with you perfectly that there must be no more interviews—but we have such a turbulent *minority* to deal with—that you must allow me to set off quietly—& even without weeping over you—for which I had prepared several pocket Handkerchiefs.—I shall now be but little in London—as I must see my sister &c.—& it is not impossible I may embark finally without taking leave of you—if so—I leave everything about pictures & all such frivolities to the entire disposal of C[aroline]—whom I pray heartily I may not see before my departure—nor after.—If

[1] See June 6, 1813, to Hodgson, note 1.

you wish to say anything you would have me do or not do—a line before three tomorrow will reach me here.—I am in the most robust health—have been eating & drinking—& fatten upon ill fortune.—

ever yrs. my dear Ly. M[elbourn]e

P.S. I have just this moment had letters from the Levant where every thing is going on in the old way—& well enough.—

[TO JOHN MURRAY]   *J[un]e 9th. 1813*

Dear Sir—I regret much that I have no profane garment to array you with for ye. masquerade.—As my motions will be uncertain—you need not write nor send the proofs till my return.—

yrs. truly

P.S. My wardrobe is out of town—or I could have dressed you as an Albanian—or a Turk—or an officer—or a waggoner.—

[TO JOHN MURRAY]   *June 12th. 1813*

Dear Sir—Having occasion to send a servant to London—I will thank you to inform me whether I left with the other things—3 miniatures in your care—(if not—I know where to find them) & also to "report progress" in unpacking the books?——The bearer returns this evening.———How does Hobhouse's work go on or rather off—for that is the essential part?—In yesterday's paper immediately under an advertisement on *"Strictures in the Urethra"* I see most appropriately consequent—a poem with *"strictures* on Ld. B. Mr. Southey & others"[1]—though I am afraid neither "Mr. S's" poetical distemper nor "mine" nor "others" is of the *suppressive* or stranguary kind—you may send me the prescription of this kill or

---

[1] In the *Morning Chronicle* of June 10, 1813, appeared advertisements for *Practical Observations on the best mode of curing Strictures* . . . by William Wadd, and *Modern Poets; a Dialogue in Verse, containing some Strictures on the Poetry of Lord Byron, Mr. Southey, and Others.* In the latter the author takes Byron to task for using "incongruous forms" such as "Northern Wolves", "Harpies", and "Bloodhounds", in referring to the Edinburgh reviewers in *English Bards and Scotch Reviewers* (lines 429–437), and criticises *Childe Harold* as "uncouth" and lacking in "plot . . . action and fable, interest, order, end." (See *LJ*, II, 216–217n)

cure physician—the medicine is compounded at White & Cochrane's Fleet Street.—As I have nothing else to do—I may enjoy it like Sir Fretful or the Archbishop of Grenada or any other personage in like predicament.—Recollect that my lacquey returns in the Evening—& that I set out for Portsmouth tomorrow.—All here are very well—& much pleased with your politeness & attention during their stay in town.—

Believe me yrs. truly

P.S.—Are there anything but books? if so—let those *extras* remain untouched for the present—I trust you have not stumbled on any more "Aphrodites" & have burnt those.————I send you *both* the Advertisements but don't send me the first treatise—as I have no occasion for *caustic* in that quarter.————

[TO JOHN MURRAY]   [*Maidenhead*] *June 13th. 1813*

Dear Sir—Amongst the books from B[enne]t St. is a small vol. of abominable poems by the Earl of Haddington[1]—which must *not* be in ye. catalogue or sale—also—a vol. of French Epigrams in the same predicament. On the title page of Meletius is an inscription in writing which must be *erased*[2]—& made illegible.————I have read the strictures which are just enough—& not grossly abusive—in very fair couplets—there is a note against Massinger near the end—& one cannot quarrel with one's company at any rate.————The author detects some incongruous figures in a passage of E[nglish] B[ar]ds page 23—but which edition I do not know—in the *sole* copy in your possession—I mean the *5th*. E[ditio]n you may make these alterations —that I may profit (though a little too late) by his remarks.——For "*hellish* instinct"—substitute "*brutal* instinct"—for "*harpies*"—alter to "*felons*" & for "bloodhounds" write "hell-hounds".[3]—Those be "very bitter words by my troth" & the alterations not much sweeter— but as I shall not publish the thing—they can do no harm—but are a satisfaction to me in the way of amendment.—The passage is only 12 lines————You do not answer me about H[obhouse]'s book—I

---

[1] Thomas Hamilton, 6th Earl of Haddington (1680–1735) had a reputation for buffoonery and raillery. But there is no record of the "abominable poems".

[2] Probably the inscription which noted that it was stolen from the Bishop of Chrisso. See July 7, 1811, to Drury; and July 15, 1811, to Hobhouse.

[3] Byron apparently took to heart some of the "Strictures" in the book referred to in the previous letter. See June 12, 1813, to Murray, note 1.

want to write to him—& not to say anything unpleasing.—If you direct to Post Office Portsmouth till *called* for—I will send & receive your letter.——You never told me of the forthcoming critique on Columbus—which is not *too* fair[4]—& I do not think justice quite done to the "Pleasures"[5]—which surely entitle the author to a higher rank than that assigned him in ye. Quarterly.—But I must not cavil at the decisions of the *invisible infallibles*—& the Article is very well written.—The general horror of *fragments* makes me tremulous for the "Giaour"[6]—but you would publish it—I presume by this time to your repentance—but as I consented—whatever be it's fate I won't now quarrel with you—even though I detect it in my pastry—but I shall not open a pye without apprehension for some weeks.[7]—The books which may be wanted by Ly. O[xford] I will carry out.——Do you know Clarke's Naufragia?[8]—I am told that he asserts the *first* vol. of R[obinso]n Crusoe was written by the first Ld. Oxford—when in the Tower—& given by him to Defoe—if true—it is a curious anecdote.—Have you got back Ld. Brooke's M.S.?[9] & what does Heber say of it?—Write to me at P[ortsmout]h.—

ever yrs. &c.

[TO EDWARD DANIEL CLARKE]

4 Bennet Street St. James's—June 17th. 1813

My dear Sir—On my return to town from Portsmouth I found your very kind letter.—If you knew how *very* vain your praise renders me—

[4] The reviewer of Roger's *Columbus* (J. W. Ward) in the *Quarterly Review* for March, 1813, found "evident marks of haste" in the poem.

[5] *The Pleasures of Memory* (1792) by Rogers, also mentioned in the review in the *Quarterly*.

[6] Both *Columbus* and *The Giaour* were written in "fragments". Byron later referred to his disjointed work as "this snake of a poem."

[7] Byron was fond of this stale joke based on the assumption that unsalable works found their way to pastry cooks who used them to wrap their wares, or were used to line trunks.

[8] James Stanier Clarke in his *Naufragia, or Historical Memoirs of Shipwrecks* (1805) quoted a letter to the *Gentleman's Magazine* for 1788 (Vol. LVIII, part 1, p. 208) which asserted that *Robinson Crusoe* was really written by the first Earl of Oxford and given to Defoe. (See *LJ.*, II, 219n.)

[9] See Nov. 22, 1812, to Murray, Murray apparently had referred the matter to Richard Heber, the bibliophile and book collector, instead of to Gifford as Byron requested. It may be that Gifford was too busy to look over the lengthy manuscript. Fulke Greville, first Baron Brooke (1554–1628), poet and statesman of the time of Elizabeth, was a close friend of Sir Philip Sidney.

I believe you would be less liberal of it—much less than you have said were enough (from *you*) to turn my head.—Ecce signum—I have ordered M[urra]y to send you *three* copies in which you will find an addition towards the end of nearly 300 lines—M[urra]y has thought proper at his own peril (& profit if there be any) to publish it—contrary to my original intention—the copy sent to you was the first sketch printed off like "the Curse" merely for the "benevolent few"[;] the present copies are as published—two for yourself & any friend—& the other for Mr. Smyth[1]—whatever his judgment may be —it will in no way detract from my esteem for his character & talents. —I trust *your third* will be out before I sail next month—can I say or do anything for you in the Levant? I am now in all the agonies of equipment—& full of schemes some impracticable & most of them improbable—but I mean to fly "freely to the green earth's end" though not quite so fast as Milton's sprite.[2]——My companion is a gentleman whom I should regard were it for nothing else but bearing your name[3]—so auspicious to travel—a name for which you have done as much though in a different department as the great *suspected* Arian who refused Archbishoprics.[4]——Believe me ever most truly yr. obliged & faithful St.

BYRON

[TO WILLIAM GIFFORD] *June 18th. 1813*

My dear Sir—I feel greatly at a loss how to write to you at all— still more to thank you as I ought.—If you knew the veneration with which I have ever regarded you long before I had the most distant prospect of becoming your acquaintance literary or personal—my

---

[1] Probably William Smyth, Professor of Modern History at Cambridge, whom Byron may have met through Clarke or other Cambridge friends.

[2] *Comus*, line 1014: "Quickly to the green earth's end."

[3] Dr. William Clark of Cambridge had agreed to accompany Byron on his projected journey to the East. There was considerable correspondence between them during the summer when the journey seemed imminent, but was put off repeatedly and finally abandoned. Dr. Clark, who had taken his B.A. at Trinity College in 1808, studied medicine in London and was from 1809 a fellow in anatomy at Cambridge. He was often confused with his "namesake", Dr. Edward Daniel Clarke, the traveller, who was Professor of Mineralogy at Cambridge.

[4] Samuel Clarke (1675–1729), a disciple of Newton, was a free-thinking clergyman, rector of St. James's, Westminster, from 1709. He was the founder of the "intellectual" school, who "deduced the moral law from a logical necessity". In 1714 he was accused of Arianism.

embarrassment would not surprize you.—Any suggestion of yours even were it conveyed in the less tender shape of the text of the Baviad or a Monk Mason note in Massinger would have been obeyed —I should have endeavoured to improve myself by your censure—judge then—if I shall be less willing to profit by your kindness.—It is not for me to bandy compliments with my elders & my betters—I receive your approbation with gratitude—& will not return my brass for your Gold by expressing more fully those sentiments of admiration which however sincere would I know be unwelcome.———To your advice on Religious topics I shall equally attend—perhaps the best way will be by avoiding them altogether—the already published objectionable passages have been much commented upon—but certainly have been rather *strongly* interpreted—I am no Bigot to Infidelity—& did not expect that because I doubted the immortality of Man—I should be charged with denying ye. existence of a God.—It was the comparative insignificance of ourselves & *our world* when placed in competition with the mighty whole of which it is an atom that first led me to imagine that our pretensions to eternity might be overrated.——This—& being early disgusted with a Calvinistic Scotch School where I was cudgelled to Church for the first ten years of my life—afflicted me with this malady—for after all it is I believe a disease of the mind as much as other kinds of Hypochondria. ————I regret to hear you talk of ill health—may you long exist! not only to enjoy your own fame but outlive that of fifty such ephemeral adventurers as myself.—As I do not sail quite so soon as Murray may have led you to expect (not till July) I trust I have some chance of taking you by the hand before my departure—& repeating in person how sincerely & affectionately I am

yr. obliged Sert.
BYRON

[TO JOHN MURRAY] *June 18th. — 1813*

Dear Sir—Will you forward the enclosed answer to the kindest letter I ever received in my life—my sense of which I can neither express to Mr. G[ifford] himself nor to any one else.—

ever yrs.

Dear Sir—You will perceive by the 4 first lines of the enclosed of what part of the text it is a continuation—the 4th line is also altered from the published copy—the rest are all new—& will be printed accordingly[1]

yrs. ever

[TO LADY MELBOURNE] *June 21st. 1813*

My dear Ly. M[elbourn]e—The Devil—who ought to be civil on such occasions has at last persuaded Ld. ————[Oxford] to be so too—for on *her* threatening to fill up my "carte blanche" in her own way—he quietly ate his own words & intentions—& now they are to "live happy ever after"—& to sail in the pleasing hope of seeing or not seeing me again.—So that the very letter in which I most committed myself to her—has by Good fortune turned out the most successful of peremptory papers.——But on the other hand—your plague & mine has according to her own account been in "excellent fooling"[.] Mr. L[amb] on his return found her in tears—& was (no wonder) wroth to a degree—& wanted to know if I (the most inoffensive of men) had affronted her &c.—now this is really laughable—if I *speak* to her *he* is insulted—If I *don't* speak to her—*she* is insulted—now if he is to be equally offended at both—I shall not be long in choosing——I had much rather differ about *something* than *nothing.*—All this I only know from her—& probably it is not true—I however must say that it is not to be expected that I shall throw myself *in* or *out* of the way of either—let them amuse themselves in their own way—I may *shut* myself out of society for my own pleasure—but I will not be *put* out of it by any couple in Christendom. With regard to the miseries of this *"correct* & *animated* Waltzer" as the M[orning] Post entitles her—I wish she would not call in the aid of so many compassionate Countesses—there is Ly. W[estmorland] (with a tongue too) conceives me to be the greatest Barbarian since the days of Bacchus & Ariadne—and all who hate Ly. O[xford]—consisting of *one half* the world—and all who abominate me—that is the *other*

---

[1] These were additions and alterations for the second edition of *The Giaour*, which appeared at the end of June or the beginning of July. It contained 47 pages and 816 lines.

half—will tear the last rag of my tattered reputation into shreds—
threads—filaments & atoms.————Where is my ticket?—that I
may personify Ld. M[elbourne]—a gentleman whom I should like to
have represented for the last—let me see—how many years has he
been your proprietor?——Why wont *you* go off with me?—I am
sure our elopement would have greater effect—cause a "greater
sensation" as our Orators say—than any event of the kind—since
Eve ran away with the Apple. Believe me

ever yrs. most truly—

[TO JOHN MURRAY]   *June 22d. 1813*

Dear Sir—I send you a *corrected copy* of the lines with several
important alterations—so many that this had better be sent for proof
rather than subject the other to so many blots.—You will excuse the
eternal trouble I inflict upon you—as you will see I have attended to
your Criticism & softened a passage you proscribed this morning[1]—

yrs. veritably,—

[TO THOMAS MOORE]   *June 22d, 1813*

* * * * * * * * * * * * * * * *

Yesterday I dined in company with "* * [Mme. de Staël], the
Epicene"[1] whose politics are sadly changed. She is for the Lord of
Israel and the Lord of Liverpool—a vile antithesis of a Methodist and
a Tory—talks of nothing but devotion and the ministry, and, I
presume, expects that God and the government will help her to a
pension.

* * * * * * * * * * * * * * * *

Murray, the αναξ of publishers, the Anac of stationers, has a
design upon you in the paper line. He wants you to become the

---

[1] These were alterations for the second edition of *The Giaour*.

[1] The phrase originally appeared in the *Anti-Jacobin*, in a poem called "Canning's
New Morality". The line "Neckar's fair daughter, Staël the Epicene" was based
on the accusation of Quatremer, who questioned her sex in the Council of Five
Hundred and was deported to Guyana. (See *LJ*, II, 223n.) Madame de Staël
came to London in June, 1813, for a stay of several months. Byron saw her a
number of times in various social gatherings.

staple and stipendiary Editor of a periodical work. What say you? Will you be bound, like "Kit Smart, to write for ninety-nine years in the Universal Visitor?"[2] Seriously, he talks of hundreds a year, and —though I hate prating of the beggarly elements—his proposal may be to your honour and profit, and, I am very sure, will be to our pleasure.

I don't know what to say about "friendship." I never was in friendship but once, in my nineteenth year, and then it gave me as much trouble as love. I am afraid, as Whitbread's sire said to the king, when he wanted to knight him, that I am "too old:" but, nevertheless, no one wishes you more friends, fame, and felicity than

Yours, &c.

[TO THE COUNTESS OF WESTMORLAND]   *June 23, 1813.*

I have several times been upon the point of calling upon you—but an unwillingness to disturb you by the unavoidable egotism of the subject has prevented me—But I am too anxious for your good opinion to pass it over altogether. I can assure you most sincerely that during the whole evening at Lady J[ersey]'s I was never in the same part of the room with B [Ly.?] C[aroline] L[amb] that neither in word look nor gesture was it in my power nor inclination to molest her— and that I am at this moment as ignorant of my offense as I then was of having offended—I saw her for one instant at a distance as she entered the room but she neither saw nor appeared to see me—I can say no more—& would not have said so much were I not desirous to vindicate myself to you (as her friend) from the imputation of affronts I did not offer & offences I do not understand.

[TO AUGUSTA LEIGH]   *4 Bennet Street June 26th. 1813*

My dearest Augusta—Let me know when you arrive—& when & where & how you would like to see me—any where in short—but at *dinner*—I have put off going into ye. country on purpose to *waylay* you—

ever yrs.

BN

[2] Christopher Smart, according to Dr. Johnson, was employed by Gardner the bookseller to write a monthly miscellany called the *Universal Visitor*. The written contract was for a period of ninety-nine years. (Boswell, April 6, 1775)

[TO JOHN MURRAY]   *June 26. 1813*

Dear Sir—I am sorry to say that it will not be in my power to
sit to Mr. P[hillips] this day—but (if he can) tomorrow or Monday I
will be disengaged[1]—later in the week I fear I shall have left town—
so that perhaps you had better give it up altogether.

                                                           ever yrs.

                                                           B--

[TO AUGUSTA LEIGH]   [*June 26–27, 1813?*]

My dearest Augusta—And if you knew *whom* I had put off besides
my journey—you would think me grown strangely fraternal—
However I won't overwhelm you with my *own praises.*—Between
one & two be it.—I shall in course prefer seeing you all to myself
without the incumbrance of third persons even of *your* (for I won't
own the relationship) fair cousin[1] of *eleven page* memory—who by
the bye makes one of the finest busts I have seen in ye. Exhibition or
out of it.—Good night

                                                           ever yrs.

                                                           BYRON

P.S. Your writing is grown like my Attorney's—& you gave me a
qualm—till I found the remedy in your signature.

[TO AUGUSTA LEIGH]   *June 27th. 1813*

My dearest Augusta—If you like to go with me to ye. Lady Davy's
tonight I *have* an invitation for you—There you will see the *Stael*—
some people whom you know—& *me* whom you do *not* know—&
you can talk to which you please—& I will watch over you as if you
were unmarried & in danger of always being so—Now do as you like
—but if you chuse to array yourself before or after half past ten I will
call for you—I think our being together before 3d. people will be a
new *sensation* to *both*.—

                                                           ever yrs.

                                                           B.

---

1 Byron sat for several portraits by Phillips. The famous one with the open
collar, of which Phillips made several copies, is now in the Byron room at John
Murray's. The one in Albanian costume, of which there are also several copies,
is in the British Embassy at Athens.
1 Lady Gertrude Howard. See Vol. 1, p. 68.

Dear Ly. M[elbourn]e—I am just returned from Ld. Eardley's[1] whence seeing nobody—I came away without entering—which is quite as well—if C[aroline] & her mamma are there—I never look upon the latter without an idea of *hartshorn*.—My lacquey I believe announced me which is awkward—but no matter—here I am safe & solitary.——Ly. ————[Oxford] sailed yesterday—& now my dear Ly. M[elbourn]e without pretending to *affect* or *effect*—will you not mention her name to me for the remainder of my weeks in England? to tell you the truth—I feel more *Carolinish* about her than I expected —they went at last so suddenly the very day I was to have met her on the coast—all the fault of my Sister's arrival—the last letter was written on board the diabolical ship.——I am doing all I can to be ready to go with your Russian[2]—depend upon it I shall be *either* out of the country or nothing—very soon—all I like is now gone—& all I abhor (with some few exceptions) remains—viz—the R[egent]— his government—& most of his subjects—what a fool I was to come back—I shall be wiser next time—unless there is a prospect of alteration in the whole system.———I shall see you somewhere soon I trust—& in the meantime if you could convince Ly. B[essborough] that—whatever may happen—neither love of *her* nor *hers* will have any thing to do with it you will set the poor soul at ease.—

ever yrs.

Dear Sir—There is an error in my dedication—the word *"my"* must be struck out "my" admiration &c.—it is a false construction & disagrees with the signature. I hope this will arrive in time to prevent a *cancel* & serve for a proof—recollect it is only the *"my"* to be erased throughout.—There is a critique in the Satirist[1]—which

---

[1] Sampson Eardley, formerly Gideon, was the son of a wealthy Portuguese stockbroker. He married a daughter of Sir John Eardley Wilmot, Chief Justice of the Common Pleas. On the recommendation of Pitt in 1789 he was made Baron Eardley of Spalding.

[2] Prince Kozlovsky. See May 2, 1813, to Lady Melbourne, note 2.

[1] *The Satirist*, July 1, 1813, pp. 70–78, reviewed *The Giaour*, not unfairly, saying that the poem "abounds with proofs of genius", but criticising its fragmentary character and obscurity. It blamed Byron for overpricing it, a criticism which he passed on to Murray, who was responsible.

I have read—fairly written & though *vituperative*—very fair in judgement.—One part belongs to you viz—the 4S. & 6d. charge—it is unconscionable—but you have *no conscience*.—

yrs. truly

[TO LADY MELBOURNE] *July 1st. 1813*

Dear Ly. M[elbourn]e—I will endeavour to be precise as if I were to meet a more than friend or an enemy.———At last (at a pretty time you will say) I declared to C[aroline] my real sentiments about Ly. [Oxford]—& I think they had a good effect.—Do you know I am Constancy in the abstract—& am much more faithful to people on the "high seas" than if they were on shore—I suppose from my natural love of contradiction & paradox.—Tomorrow the Newstead Cause comes on in Chancery—but I shall not embarrass myself about such trifles—for I have got to stand for my picture[1]—& to sit with my Sister—& to drive to you—all which are matters more to my taste & equally to my profit.——I missed you last night—our party had all the refuse of the Regent & the Red book—Bedfords—Jerseys—Ossulstones—Greys & the like—but the sexes separated—the women were tied back to back upon half a dozen woolsacks in the middle of the room hating each other & talking—& the Men were sprinkled round the corners in dull duets—Rogers fell to my share—& we abused every body—Your Frederick[2] (by the bye your introduction has done wonders for we never speak) followed the degenerate example—every body seemed to have lost an acquaintance—I never saw anything like it but a print from a scene in Dante's Inferno—*which* I leave you to guess.————I want a *she* voucher for a ticket to the A[lmack's] Masque tomorrow—it is for my Sister who I hope will go with me—I wish she were not married for—(now I have no house to keep) she would have been so good a housekeeper. Pour soul—she likes her husband—I think her thanking you for your abetment of her abominable marriage (7 *years* after the event!!) is the only instance of similar gratitude upon record.—However now she is married I trust she will remain so.——

ever yrs. dear Ly. M[elbourn]e

---

1 Byron was then sitting for his portrait by Thomas Phillips.
2 Probably Frederick Lamb, 3rd son of Lady Melbourne.

My dear Ly. M[elbourn]e—God knows what has happened—but at 4 in the morning Ly. Ossulstone looking angry (& at that moment ugly) delivered to me a confused kind of message from you of some scene—this is all I know—except that with laudable logic she drew the usual feminine deduction that I *"must* have behaved very ill".——
If Ly. C[aroline] is offended it really must be anger at my *not* affronting her—for one of the few things I said was a request to know her will & pleasure—if there was anything I could say do or not do to give her the least gratification—she walked away without answering—& after leaving me in this not very dignified situation— & showing her independence to twenty people near—I only saw her dancing—& in the doorway for a moment—where she said something so very violent—that I was in distress lest Ld. Y. or Ly. Rancliffe[1] overheard her—I went to Supper—& saw & heard no more till Ly. Ossulstone told me your words & her own opinion—& here I am in stupid innocence & ignorance of my offence or her proceedings.—— If I am to be haunted with hysterics wherever I go—& whatever I do— I think she is not the only person to be pitied.—I should have returned to her after her *doorway whisper*—but I could not with any kind of politeness leave Ly. Rancliffe to drown herself in wine & water or be suffocated in a Jelly-dish—without a spoon or a hand to help her— besides—if there was & I foresaw there would be something ridiculous —surely I was better absent than present.—This is really insanity— & every body seems inoculated with the same distemper—Ly. W[estmorland] says "you must have done something—you know between people in your situation—a word or a look goes a great way" &c. &c.—so it seems indeed—but I never knew that *neither* words nor looks—in short—downright—innocent—vacant—indefinable *Nothing* had the same precious power of producing this perpetual worry. I wait to hear from you—in case I have to answer you—I trust nothing has occurred to spoil your breakfast—for which the Regent has got a fine day.—

---

[1] Lord Y, was probably the Earl of Hertford and Yarmouth (1777–1842), styled Earl of Yarmouth until 1822. He was a person of importance at the Court of the Prince Regent and was used as a model by Thackeray for the Marquis of Steyne in *Vanity Fair* and also as the Monmouth of Disraeli's *Coningsby*. Lady Rancliffe was the wife of the second Baron Rancliffe [George Augustus Henry Anne (Parkyns)], Equerry to the Prince of Wales and a Whig M.P. He married in 1807 Mary Theresa, first daughter of George (Forbes), 6th Earl of Granard by Selina Frances, daughter of the first Earl of Moira.

Dear Ly. M[elbourn]e—Since I wrote ye. enclosed I have heard a strange story of C[aroline]'s scratching herself with glass—& I know not what besides—of all this I was ignorant till this Evening.— What I did or said to provoke her—I know not—I told her it was better to *waltze*—"because she danced well—& it would be imputed to *me*—if she did not"—but I see nothing in this to produce cutting & maiming—besides before supper I saw her—& though she said & did even then a foolish thing—I could not suppose her so frantic as to be in earnest.—She took hold of my hand as I passed & pressed it against some sharp instrument—& said—"I mean to use this"—I answered— ["]against me I presume["]—& passed on with Ly. R[ancliffe] trembling lest Ld. Y. & Ly. R[ancliffe] should overhear her—though not believing it possible that this was more than one of her not uncommon *bravadoes*—for *real feeling* does not disclose its intentions— & always shuns display.—I thought little more of this—& leaving the table in search of her would have appeared more particuar than proper —though of course had I guessed her to be serious or had I been conscious of offending I should have done every thing to pacify or prevent her.———I know not what to say or do—I am quite unaware of what I did to displease—& useless regret is all I can feel on the subject—Can she be in her senses?—yet—I would rather think myself to blame—than that she were so silly without cause.—I really remained at Ly. H[eathcote]'s till 5 totally ignorant of all that passed—nor do I now know where this cursed scarification took place—nor when—I mean the room—& the hour.[1]————

[TO THOMAS MOORE]

4, Benedictine-street[1], *St. James's, July 8th, 1813*

I presume by your silence that I have blundered into something noxious in my reply to your letter, for the which I beg leave to send,

---

[1] Various accounts of this episode have been told. According to Lady Melbourne, Lady Caroline Lamb came to the party at Lady Heathcote's determined to pique Byron by her waltzing (Airlie, p. 156). When he showed his indifference a little sarcastically, she lost all control and enacted the scene Byron described at second hand. Caroline gave her own account to Medwin (*LJ*, II, 453). Byron kept a curious memento of this party, Lady Heathcote's card on which she had written "At home—Monday July 5th—A small Waltzing Party—10 o'clock". Byron wrote on the card: "This Card I keep as a curiosity—since it was at that Ball (to which it is an invitation) that Ly. Caroline L. performed ye. dagger Scene of indifferent memory." (Clark Library, University of California, Los Angeles)
[1] *i.e.*, Bennet Street.

beforehand, a sweeping apology, which you may apply to any, or all, parts of that unfortunate epistle. If I err in my conjecture, I expect the like from you, in putting our correspondence so long in quarantine. God he knows what I have said; but he also knows (if he is not as indifferent to mortals as the *nonchalent* deities of Lucretius), that you are the last person I want to offend. So, if I have,—why the devil don't you say it at once, and expectorate your spleen?

Rogers is out of town with Madame de Staël, who hath published an Essay against Suicide, which, I presume, will make somebody shoot himself;—as a sermon by Blinkensop,[2] in *proof* of Christianity, sent a hitherto most orthodox acquaintance of mine out of a chapel of ease a perfect atheist. Have you found or founded a residence yet? and have you begun or finished a Poem? If you won't tell me what *I* have done, pray say what you have done, or left undone, yourself. I am still in equipment for voyaging, and anxious to hear from, or of, you *before* I go, which anxiety you should remove more readily, as you think I sha'n't cogitate about you afterwards. I shall give the lie to that calumny by fifty foreign letters, particularly from any place where the plague is rife,—without a drop of vinegar or a whiff of sulphur to save you from infection. Pray write: I am sorry to say that * * * *.

The Oxfords have sailed almost a fortnight, and my sister is in town, which is a great comfort—for, never having been much together, we are naturally more attached to each other. I presume the illuminations have conflagrated to Derby (or wherever you are) by this time. We are just recovering from tumult and train oil, and transparent fripperies, and all the noise and nonsense of victory.[3] Drury-lane had a large *M. W.* which some thought was Marshal Wellington; others, that it might be translated into Manager Whitbread; while the ladies of the vicinity and the saloon conceived the last letter to be complimentary to themselves. I leave this to the commentators to illuminate. If you don't answer this, I sha'n't say what *you* deserve, but I think *I* deserve a reply. Do you conceive there is no Post-Bag but the Twopenny?[4] Sunburn me, if you are not too bad.

---

[2] Unidentified.

[3] The illuminations in honour of the victory of Wellington's armies at Vittoria (June 21, 1813) which took place on July 7, caused a great fire at Woolwich, which Byron suggests might spread as far as Mayfield Cottage near Ashbourne in Derbyshire, where Moore was living at the time.

[4] Moore's *Intercepted Letters, or the Twopenny Post-bag,* a gay lampoon with some political and social bite, was published anonymously in 1813.

My dear Ly. Melbourne—I do not know how she will make out any duplicity on my part towards you—for she is eternally asking if I am not in *love* with you—which at least shows that no *abuse* can have fallen from me on ye. subject. Who or what the persons may be who suppose me to blame——because a woman falls into a fury in public—I know not nor am anxious to know—they may as well be quiet—for although I neither have nor shall attempt to vindicate myself to any but you & her from the truly absurd reasons she has adduced for her conduct—I have borne too much already to submit even to explanation.—I shall be under way in a few weeks—having nearly indeed quite arranged my business—& in the mean time—they shall not have far to hunt for me.—Do you know that I look upon myself as the aggrieved person in this instance—as far as regards *her* & *her* own family (not yours of course for they cannot be blamed do what they will) & with this conviction I defy them in any & every manner.—I do not understand her "sometimes cruel" & "sometimes kind" but her notions of kindness are not very well adapted for a public display—was it not in complying with the request of all her connections that I incurred this ebullition of selfish anger & distempered vanity?—I have never from the moment the connection ended last year—encouraged her in any of her absurdities— but if she absolutely of her own accord committed herself at any time—how could I betray or ill-treat her? you see what my *not* objecting to her waltzing (for I did & said nothing more) has produced.—Let them begin at once instead of talking about it—do they suppose there is anything so terrific in the Devonshire hive— *bees* or *drones?*—they shall find me a wasp.————As to taking care of myself—that I must leave to Providence—there is no guarding against her—I have done my best.—To you I have now & ever to return my best thanks—if I am either angry or ungrateful it neither is nor shall be to yourself.

ever yrs. most affectionately,
BYRON

[TO DR. WILLIAM CLARK] *July 11th. 1813*

Dear Sir—Our sailing day is the 30th. & it will be proper we should be quite ready to leave London on the 25th. Pray let me see you as soon as convenient or I will call if it suits you better.—

ever yrs.
B.—

* * * * * * * * * * * * * * *

Your letter set me at ease; for I really thought (as I hear of your susceptibility) that I had said—I know not what—but something I should have been very sorry for, had it, or I, offended you;—though I don't see how a man with a beautiful wife—*his own* children—quiet—fame—competency and friends (I will vouch for a thousand, which is more than I will for a unit in my own behalf), can be offended with any thing.

Do you know, Moore, I am amazingly inclined—remember I say but *inclined*—to be seriously enamoured with Lady A. F. [Adelaide Forbes][1]—but this * * has ruined all my prospects. However, you know her;—is she *clever*, or sensible, or good-tempered? either *would* do—I scratch out the *will*. I don't ask as to her beauty—that I see; but my circumstances are mending, and were not my other prospects blackening, I would take a wife, and that should be the woman, had I a chance. I do not yet know her much, but better than I did. * * * * *

I want to get away, but find difficulty in compassing a passage in a ship of war. They had better let me go; if I cannot, patriotism is the word—"nay, an' they'll mouth, I'll rant as well as they."[2] Now, what are you doing?—writing, we all hope, for our own sakes. Remember you must edite my posthumous works, with a Life of the Author, for which I will send you Confessions, dated "Lazaretto," Smyrna, Malta, or Palermo—one can die any where.

There is to be a thing on Tuesday ycleped a national fete. The Regent and * * * are to be there, and every body else, who has shillings enough for what was once a guinea. Vauxhall is the scene[3]—there are six tickets issued for the modest women, and it is supposed that there will be three to spare. The passports for the lax are beyond my arithmetic.

[1] Lady Adelaide Forbes was the daughter of George, 6th Earl of Granard, and his wife, Lady Selina Rawdon, daughter of the first Earl of Moira. Since Lord Moira was Moore's patron, Moore was acquainted with her and praised her good qualities to Byron. She was born in 1789 and died in 1858 unmarried. In Rome in 1817 Byron compared the Apollo Belvedere to Lady Adelaide Forbes (May 12, 1817, to Moore).

[2] See *Hamlet*, Act V, scene i. In his *The Twopenny Post bag*, in attacking the Prince Regent, Moore wrote:
Nay, an thou'lt mouth, I'll rant as well as thou.

[3] The Grand National Fête celebrating the victory of Vittoria was held at Vauxhall Gardens on July 20, beginning with a banquet at which Wellington was toasted. The Fête was sponsored by the Regent.

P.S. The Staël last night attacked me most furiously—said that I had "no right to make love—that I had used * * [Caroline] barbarously —that I had no feeling, and was totally *in*sensible to *la belle passion*, and *had* been all my life." I am very glad to hear it, but did not know it before. Let me hear from you anon.

[TO JOHN WILSON CROKER]   *4 Bennet Street July 13th.—1813*

Sir,—Prince Koslovsky informed me a few days ago—that he had reason to think by a proper application to you—I should obtain a passage in the ship which is to convey him to the Mediterranean.—I confess that I did not foresee any impropriety or difficulty in this—as it had already been my good fortune to obtain the same favour several times during my last absence from England—by the kindness of some whose influence was much inferior to your own.—But as I had not the honour of your acquaintance—& certainly not the slightest pretension to intrude upon you for the mere purpose of serving myself —I thought the application would come with a better grace from one whom you would have greater pleasure in obliging.——Though he has failed—which does not make my own prospect of success very promising—may I now venture to say that by obtaining for me a passage in any ship of war bound to the Mediterranean at or nearly at the same time with the Boyne—you will confer upon me the last— indeed I might add—the only favour which can be rendered me in this country.—If I am wrong or informal in the present application you will excuse an unintentional offence. I have the honour to be Sir—

yr. most obedt. humble Servt.

Byron

[TO T. [J?] CLARKE]   *July 15, 1813*

If Mr. S. thinks proper to wait till the Purchaser of Newstead has fulfilled his contract his demand will be liquidated, if not—he must pursue his own remedy—Mr. T. [J.] Hanson—65 [6] Chancery Lane is the address of my attorney, I shall forward your letter to him this day.

[TO JOHN HANSON]   *Sunday July 18th. 1813*

Dear Sir—A Report is in general circulation (which has distressed my friends & is not very pleasing to me—)that the Purchaser of

N[ewstea]d is a *young* man—who has been overreached—ill treated—
& ruined—by me in this transaction of the sale—& that I take an
unfair advantage of the *law* to enforce the contract.—This must be
contradicted by a true & open statement of the circumstances attending
& subsequent to the sale & that immediately & publicly—surely—if
anyone is ill treated it is myself—He bid his own price—he took
time before he bid at all—& now when I am actually granting him
further time as a favour—I hear from all quarters that I have acted
unfairly.—Pray do not delay on this point—see him—& let a proper
& true statement be drawn up of the sale &c. & inserted in the
papers.—

ever yrs.

B

P.S. Mr. C[laughton] himself if he has either honour or feeling will
be the first to vindicate me from so unfounded an implication.——it
is surely not for his credit to be supposed *ruined* or *overreached.*———

[TO LADY MELBOURNE]   *July 18th. 1813*

My dear Ly. M[elbourn]e—The purchaser of Newstead is not a
young Man—it was supposed that the purchase was for a Mr. Leigh[1]—
& I wish it were—for that Gentleman could make 50 such without
injury to himself.——Of Mr. Claughton's circumstances I know
little or nothing—he bought the estate *not* at the public auction—but
after a *fortnight's* deliberation after the public biddings—the price was
certainly his own offer.—He himself has never made such a representation to me or my agents—& till this moment I never heard the
report—he declared & declares himself willing to complete when a
title is made out—this we of course are prepared to provide—I do
not it is true consider him a willing purchaser—he evaded & at last
drove me into Chancery—but if he is ruined by this contract or has
been ill treated by me or mine—on that subject he has hitherto been
silent—at least to me.—If any one is injured in this transaction in
circumstances or unfair treatment—it is myself—the title to my
estate (of 300 years standing) has been doubted—my hopes & my
arrangements overthrown & confused—& it should now seem—
my character called in question.—I have no time now to expatiate
further on a subject which I feel persuaded will not require explanation

[1] See Feb. 1, 1814, to Hanson, note 1.

to those who know me—besides I am not very fond of defending myself—I shall however have an immediate explanation with the interesting *youth* (a *lawyer* of forty five years) who is so much over-reached by the dreadful chicane & wily experience of that mercenary & litigious person who is

yrs. most truly

P.S. You will make my best acknowledgements to Miss M[ilbanke] —& say what is most proper—I have not the skill—you are an adept— you may defend me if it amuses you—not else—let them say anything but what is true & I forgive your prattlers against me.—

[TO JOHN MURRAY]   *July 22d. 1813*

Dear Sir—I have great pleasure in accepting your invitation to meet anybody or nobody as you like best.—Pray what should you suppose the book in the inclosed advertisement to be? is it anything relating to Buonaparte or Continental concerns—if so it may be worth looking after particularly if [it] should turn out to be your purchase—Lucien's Epic.[1]—Believe me very truly yrs.

BYRON

[TO HENRY FOX]   *July 22d. 1813*

Dear Fox[1]—Will you part with one of your Toledos? if so—pray tell me *when* & *which*—& *what?*—

ever yrs.
BN

[TO THOMAS MOORE]   *July 25th, 1813*

I am not well versed enough in the ways of single woman to make much matrimonial progress. * * * * *

[1] Lucien Buonaparte's poem *Charlemagne* was published in an English translation by Murray in 1815. Byron apparently suspected that it had been pirated by another publisher.
[1] Henry Fox was the young son of Lord Holland of whom Byron was fond, in part because, like himself, Fox was lame. See July 29, to Henry Fox.

78

I have been dining like the dragon of Wantley[1] for this last week. My head aches with the vintage of various cellars, and my brains are muddled as their dregs. I met your friends, the D * *s [Daltons]:—[2] she sung one of your best songs so well, that, but for the appearance of affectation, I could have cried; he reminds me of Hunt, but handsomer, and more musical in soul, perhaps. I wish to God he may conquer his horrible anomalous complaint. The upper part of her face is beautiful, and she seems much attached to her husband. He is right, nevertheless, in leaving this nauseous town. The first winter would infallibly destroy her complexion,—and the second, very probably, every thing else.

I must tell you a story. M * * [Morris][3] (of indifferent memory) was dining out the other day, and complaining of the P[rinc]e's coldness to his old wassailers. D' * * [D' Israeli] (a learned Jew) bored him with questions—why this? and why that? "Why did the P[rinc]e act thus?"—"Why, sir, on account of Lord * *, who ought to be ashamed of himself." "And why ought Lord * * to be ashamed of himself?"—"Because the P[rinc]e, sir, * * * * * * * *." "And why, sir, did the P[rinc]e cut *you*?"—"Because, G–d d– –mme, sir, I stuck to my principles." "And *why* did you stick to your principles?"

Is not this last question the best that ever was put, when you consider to whom? It nearly killed M * * [Morris]. Perhaps you may think it stupid, but, as Goldsmith said about the peas,[4] it was a very

---

[1] *The Dragon of Wantley, a Burlesque Opera* was performed at Covent Garden. The libretto was by "Sig. Carini" (*i.e.* Henry Carey):

> All sorts of Cattle this Dragon did eat,
> Some say he eat up Trees,
> And that the Forest shure he would
> Devour by degrees.
> For Houses and Churches were to him Geese and Turkies;
> He eat all, and left none behind,
> But some Stones, dear Jack, which he could not crack,
> Which on the Hills you'll find.

[2] Edward T. Dalton, an Irish musician who was long a friend of Moore. At one time he competed with Sir John Stevenson for the musical arrangement of some of Moore's songs. His wife was godmother to one of Moore's children.

[3] Charles Morris (1745–1838) was laureate and punch-maker to the Beefsteak Club, founded in 1735 by John Rich, patentee of Covent Garden Theatre. The Prince of Wales became a member of the Club in 1785, and Morris wrote political songs for his party and against Pitt, but his political friends failed to reward him and he turned his talents against them in an ode, "The Old Whig Poet to his Old Buff Waistcoat".

[4] Goldsmith told Reynolds that "a handful of grey peas, given him by a girl at a wake (after fasting for twenty-four hours) the most comfortable repast he had ever made." (Forster, *Life of Goldsmith*, Vol. 1, p. 34) Prothero suggests that Byron meant it was a good joke to one who had not heard one for some time.

good joke when I heard it—as I did from an earwitness—and is only spoilt in my narration.

The season has closed with a Dandy Ball;—but I have dinners with the Harrowbys, Rogers, and Frere[5] and Mackintosh,[6] where I shall drink your health in a silent bumper, and regret your absence till "too much canaries" wash away my memory, or render it superfluous by a vision of you at the opposite side of the table. Canning has disbanded his party by a speech from his * * * *—the true throne of a Tory. Conceive his turning them off in a formal harangue, and bidding them think for themselves. "I have led my ragamuffins where they are well peppered. There are but three of the 150 left alive, and they are for the *Town's-end* (*query*, might not Falstaff mean the Bow-street officer? I dare say Malone's posthumous edition[7] will have it so) for life."

Since I wrote last, I have been into the country. I journeyed by night—no incident or accident, but an alarm on the part of my valet on the outside, who, in crossing Epping Forest, actually, I believe, flung down his purse before a mile-stone, with a glow-worm in the second figure of number XIX—mistaking it for a footpad and dark lantern. I can only attribute his fears to a pair of new pistols, wherewith I had armed him; and he thought it necessary to display his vigilance by calling out to me whenever we passed any thing—no matter whether moving or stationary. Conceive ten miles, with a tremor every furlong. I have scribbled you a fearfully long letter. This sheet must be blank, and is merely a wrapper, to preclude the tabellarians of the post from peeping. You once complained of my *not* writing;—I will heap "coals of fire upon your head" by *not* complaining of your *not* reading. Ever, my dear Moore, your'n (isn't that the Staffordshire termination?)

BYRON

---

5 John Hookham Frere, the author of "Whistlecraft", which Byron later much admired and which gave him the first ideas for the burlesque style of *Beppo*.

6 Sir James Mackintosh (1765–1832), philosopher and historian, had answered Burke on the French Revolution, but later changed his views, though he continued to be a liberal Whig. He then represented Nairn in Parliament. Byron admired him for his great intellectual powers.

7 Edmund Malone (1741–1812), the Shakespearean scholar, had published an edition of Shakespeare in 1790. He gathered material for a new edition which he left to James Boswell the younger, who published it in 21 volumes in 1821 (the "third variorum" edition).

4 Bennet Street, St. James's July 25th. 1813

My dear Webster,—I have just heard of your present residence.[1]— Rushton tells me that you offered him a situation last Spring on your Agricultural establishment for which he is well adapted having been educated for that purpose.—If you still wish to have him—though it is eventually my intention to provide for him—it would be a very good thing for him for a few years—as I am now going abroad almost immediately—& having parted with Newstead—& not quite arranged my Rochdale concerns, I am rather at a loss for his present employment. On this of course you will act as you think proper—his own statement led me to write to you on this subject.—He is honest— good tempered & has had a very fair education—as far as a country school could give. Will you favour me with an answer when conveni- ent.——I have been very little in town this year & [am?] quite ignorant of all your movements—I hope however that L[ad]y F[rances] has increased your happiness & family & have little doubt of your welfare which I wish you sincerely. If I prolonged this letter I should only talk to you of myself a topic not very interesting & of which you have had too much already—my Egotism therefore shall briefly end in my begging you to believe that I ever am

yours very truly & affect[ionate]ly.

Byron

July 27th, 1813

When you next imitate the style of "Tacitus," pray add, "de moribus Germanorum;"—this last was a piece of barbarous silence, and could only be taken from the *Woods*, and, as such, I attribute it entirely to your sylvan sequestration at Mayfield Cottage.[1] You will find, on casting up accounts, that you are my debtor by several sheets and one epistle. I shall bring my action;—if you don't discharge, expect to hear from my attorney. I have forwarded your letter to Ruggiero;[2] but don't make a postman of me again, for fear I should be tempted to violate your sanctity of wax or wafer.

Believe me ever yours *indignantly*,

BN.

[1] Webster had leased Aston Hall in Yorkshire, where, as Byron later told Moore, Captain John Byron, his father, had "adulterated" with Lady Carmarthen after they eloped.

[1] Moore's house near Ashbourne in Derbyshire.

[2] *i.e.* Samuel Rogers.

Can't you be satisfied with the pangs of my jealousy of Rogers, without actually making me the pander of your epistolary intrigue? This is the second letter you have enclosed to my address, notwithstanding a miraculous long answer, and a subsequent short one or two of your own. If you do so again, I can't tell to what pitch my fury may soar. I shall send you verse or arsenic, as likely as any thing,— four thousand couplets on sheets beyond the privilege of franking; that privilege, sir, of which you take an undue advantage over a too susceptible senator, by forwarding your lucubrations to every one but himself. I won't frank *from* you, or *for* you, or *to* you—may I be curst if I do, unless you mend your manners. I disown you—I disclaim you—and by all the powers of Eulogy, I will write a panegyric upon you—or dedicate a quarto—if you don't make me ample amends.

P.S. I am in training to dine with Sheridan[1] and Rogers this evening. I have a little spite against R[ogers] and will shed his "Clary wines pottle-deep."[2] This is nearly my ultimate or penultimate letter; for I am quite equipped, and only wait a passage. Perhaps I may wait a few weeks for Sligo; but not if I can help it.

My dear Fox—I must not take advantage of your munificence.— Pray tell me the pretium—or if that shocks you—allow me at all events to have the pleasure of easing my conscience by some exchange —you have perhaps Manton's pistols—if not I have some excellent— & an Albanian dress—& other sundries wherewithal I shall endeavour to rob you as little as possible.—I have kept one & return the other— but you really must allow me either to pay or exchange—you are too royal in your gifts[1]—& I have done nothing to deserve them though always

truly yrs.
BYRON

---

[1] For an account of Byron's relations with Sheridan, see the biographical sketch of Sheridan in Appendix IV.

[2] *Othello*, Act. II, Scene 3, line 54.

[1] See July 22, 1813, to Henry Fox. Byron had expected to buy the Toledo swords.

[TO JOHN MURRAY]   *July 30, 1813*

Dear Sir—Could you send me a copy of *that* [magazine?] tonight or early tomorrow if possible—

yrs. &c.
Bₙ

[TO LADY MELBOURNE]   *[July 30th. 1813]*

My dear Ly. M[elbourn]e,—There is Karlovsky's[1] farewell for you.—She charges me with making my valet read her [Caroline Lamb's] letters to me when in a *hurry* (as if that would not be the time for a man to read them himself) on the report of somebody whom I suspect by the brilliancy of the invention to be some of the she-Blarneys—pray tell her that it is false (now let me beg you to do so or she will never be quiet) & that I don't think the man *could* if I wished him decypher her dispatches—but would resign rather [than] undertake unravelling her hieroglyphics.—"I dont tell you anything!" —very good—every body rates me about my confidences with you— Augusta for example writes today & the last thing she says—is *"this* must not go to Ly. M[elbourn]e"—& to punish you it *shant.*——I commit you to the care of Providence—& am ever my dear Ly. M.

most affectionately yr. obliged St.
Byron

[To Dr. William Clark]   *July 31st. 1813*

Dear Sir—I am going out of town for a week (near Cambridge)[1] we shall wait for Sligo—& if he returns within the period of my absence & you are still in town will you be good enough to tell him in answer to his proposal that we will join him & take part of his storeship.—Perhaps you may be down at Cambridge if so I will come over from Six Mile Bot[to]m where I shall be for some days.— Hudson[2] called here on you—I don't know what he wants but I hope he don't plague you—you cannot regret any delay in our

---

[1] Prince Kozlovsky. See May 2, 1813, to Lady Melbourne.
[1] He was going to visit his half-sister, Augusta Leigh, at Six Mile Bottom, near Newmarket.
[2] Unidentified.

departure more than I do but a few days or weeks for a comfortable passage will not I trust be thrown away.—

Believe me truly yours

BYRON

P.S. I have [E. D.] Clarke's letter safe & will return it to you when we meet.—

[TO JOHN MURRAY]   [*July 31, 1813*]

Dear Sir—As I leave town early tomorrow the proof must be sent tonight—or many days will be lost.—If you have any *reviews* of the G[*iaou*]r to send—let me have them now—I am not very well today—I thank you for the Sat[irist][1]—which is short but savage on this unlucky affair—& *personally* facetious on me which is much more to the purpose than a tirade upon other people's concerns.—

ever yrs.

B

[TO JOHN WILSON CROKER]   B[*enne*]t Str. *August 2d, 1813*

Dear Sir,—I was honoured with your unexpected and very obliging letter when on the point of leaving London, which prevented me from acknowledging my obligation as quickly as I felt it sincerely. I am endeavouring all in my power to be ready before Saturday[1]—and even if I should not succeed, I can only blame my own tardiness, which will not the less enhance the benefit I have lost. I have only to add my hope of forgiveness for all my trespasses on your time and patience, and with my best wishes for your public and private welfare, I have the honour to be, most truly,

Your obliged and most obedient servant,

BYRON

[TO DR. WILLIAM CLARK]   [*August 2, 1813*]

Dear Sir,—We sail on board the Boyne,[1]—& must be at Portsmouth on Saturday next.—I have only just heard this—could I see you now?

Ever yrs.

BYRON

[1] *The Satirist* (Vol. XIII, pp. 150–151) gave a facetious and distorted account of the affair at Lady Heathcote's, naming Lord B———n and Lady C. L——b.

[1] See [Aug. 2, 1813] to Dr. Clark.

[1] See July 13, 1813, to Croker. Croker was successful in getting passage for Byron on the *Boyne*, but it was only for himself and one servant, and he gave it up and waited for a better passage. See Aug. 11, 1813, to Lady Melbourne.

My dear Ly. M[elbourn]e—My sister who is going abroad with me is now in town where she returned with me from New[mar]ket— under the existing circumstances of her lord's embarrassments—she could not well do otherwise—& she appears to have still less reluctance at leaving this country than even myself.—Ly. C[aroline] may do as she pleases—if Augusta likes to take her she may—but in that case she will travel by *herself*.—Nugent[1] does not know I am in town—& if he did—I could not at present accept his invitation— though your presence is a strong temptation—indeed much stronger for not being a new one.——So Me. de Stael says my visit was *"justificatory"*—this is not very justifiable in her—if she asserts that I said what I really did not—I shall revenge myself by repeating what she really did say—this she would not like—although our conversation was neither *amatory* nor *political*.—I called because she said by not visiting her "I treated her with contempt"—an *impression* of which Common Politeness required the removal—I am always delighted to visit you at your own hour—but I am never myself in a morning—or rather I am myself or Lord Stair[2] (I doubt which very often) my dullness is so very ineffable.—We have an event in our family—a female cousin going to *Mouros* for religion[3]—could not you send *one* of your family to join her—she is to have a *spare* waistcoat—that will fit the *other* I dare say.—If not I believe I must try it myself.—

ever yrs. dr. Ly. M.

B

My dear Fox—You must pardon me for letting you go so abruptly —but the Gentleman who interrupted us was engaged in a *quarrel*

[1] Nugent was a friend of Henry Luttrell, the Irish wit and poet of society. Byron mentions him several times in his letters and journals.

[2] John William Henry (Dalrymple), 7th Earl of Stair (1784–1840), a liberal in politics, married in 1804, Johanna, 1st. daughter of Charles Gordon of Cluny. Not considering such a marriage to be valid (it was a matter of simple promises), he married in 1808 by special licence Laura, youngest daughter of John Manners by Louisa, afterward Countess of Dysart. The last marriage was, however, set aside by the Consistorial Court of London, July 16, 1811. But the marriage of 1804 was terminated by divorce in 1820.

[3] The cousin who was apparently going out as a missionary has not been identified.

with a *friend* of mine[1] & I was acting the part of present peacemaker or future second—the business is now luckily settled.—

ever yrs.

B

P.S. This must be my excuse—you know we could not discuss before a third person.—

August 8th. 1813

My dear Ly. M[elbourn]e—I wrote ye. annexed note 3 days ago—& as it contains a "direct" answer to some of your queries—I shall even let it go as it is—I put it in my drawer & forgot it—for I have been occupied to weariness with various somethings & nothings ever since—amongst others in preventing two men (one an old friend) from cutting one another's throats after a quarrel in which I was called in to mediate & succeeded in reserving them for a different fate[1]—& I humbly hope a better.——I rather plume myself upon this—being the first decent deed I have done since my acquaintance with the most celebrated personage of your illustrious house—whose fault it is not —that I have not had the obligation returned.—I have not broken in upon your grief for the departure of your diplomatic progeny[2] to cope with Buonaparte—I think Ly. Ay.[3] might be an useful appendage to his suite—as by all late accounts the Emperor is rather more frail than becomes a hero.——Me. de Stael's favourite son has had his head cleft by a vile Adjutant who knew the broadsword exercise better than piquet—for *that* was ye. cause of carnage.[4] I thought *that* game had been only dangerous to your sex.—Corinne is doubtless very much affected—yet methinks—I should conjecture—she will want some spectators to testify how graceful her grief will be—& to relate what fine things she can say on a subject where common-

1 The friend was Scrope Davies, who had a gambling quarrel with Lord Foley. See Aug. 21, 1813, to Lady Melbourne, and Aug. 22, 1813, to Moore.

1 See Aug. 6, 1813, to Henry Fox, note 1.

2 Frederick Lamb, Lady Melbourne's third son, had entered the diplomatic service and was Secretary of Legation under Lord William Bentinck in Sicily, and later Minister Plenipotentiary to the Court of the Two Sicilies.

3 Lady Ay. may have been the widow of the 5th Earl of Aylesford (1786–1812).

4 Mme de Staël's favourite son, Albert de Staël, was killed in a gambling duel at Doberan, a small city in the duchy of Mecklenburg-Schwerin, on the coast of the Baltic Sea.

place mourners would be silent.——Do I err in my judgment of the woman think you?—She is in many things—a sort of C[arolin]e in her senses—for *she is sane*.—

ever yrs truly

B

[TO JOHN MURRAY]

Half past two—in the Morn. August 10th. 1813

If you send more proofs I shall never finish this infernal story— "Ecce signum"—thirty three more lines enclosed!—to the utter discomfiture of the printer—& I fear—not to your advantage.[1]—

B

[TO LADY MELBOURNE]   *August 11th. 1813*

My dear Ly. M[elbourn]e—I ought to have called on you—& I ought—all kinds of *oughts*—for omitting which I can only plead many excuses which will not amount to one apology.—As this is the case I shall omit them altogether—having already written & destroyed two ineffectual notes upon that & other subjects.——From C[aroline] after a long (for her) interval of silence—I have received a most rational letter full of good resolves—& a most tempting basket full of excellent fruit—the grapes & gooseberries I have returned having no great appetite that way—but I keep the letter—which might do me more good—were it written by a grave character & signed by the Abbess of Quedlinburg.[1]————C[aroline] I assure you—I have not seen—& I do really believe she has determined to leave me in quiet— God knows I want it.—The few things—I wished to have said to you —did not at all concern her nor hers—nor you nor yours [——] daughters nor *nieces*——I should have been glad of your advice how to untie two or three "*Gordion* knots" tied round me[2]—I shall cut them without consulting anyone—though some are rather closely twisted round

---

[1] During the first half of August several issues of the third edition of *The Giaour* were published, each with additions and emendations.

[1] The Abbess of Quedlinberg was a "grave character" in Sterne's *Tristram Shandy*.

[2] At this time Byron's letters to Lady Melbourne are full of hints of his liaison with his half-sister Augusta, an affair against which he was struggling ineffectually. He was torn between the desire to take Augusta abroad with him and the feeling that he ought to escape by going alone or with Lord Sligo.

my *heart* (if you will allow me to *wear* one).———I suppose you will think I shall never go—I almost think so myself—though every day renders it more necessary in all but a worldly point of view—I don't know whether to be glad or sorry that I separated from the O[xford] party—though I have no great disposition to rejoin them.———Perhaps I shall not see you again—if not—forgive my follies & like as much of me as you can—it is odd that I should begin by liking all of your house but *you* & end by the reverse—with one exception.—But you must recollect that I thought you my *enemy*—& my dislike was merely *defensive*.—

ever yrs.

B

P.S. I had a passage in ye. Boyne—but it was for *one* servant only & myself—this would not do[3]—I am now casting throws for a store-ship—I have since I last saw you found out about 50 better reasons than ever for migrating—"he says farewell & yet he goes not" so say I—but I will go nevertheless.—

[TO JAMES WEDDERBURN WEBSTER]   *August 12th. 1813*

My dear Webster—I am you know a detestable correspondent—& write to no one person whatever—you therefore cannot attribute my silence to anything but want of good breeding or good taste—& not to any more atrocious cause—& as I confess the fault to be entirely mine—why—you will pardon it.———I have ordered a copy of ye. Giaour (which is nearly doubled in quantity in this Edition)[1] to be sent—& I will first scribble my name on the title page.—many & sincere thanks for your good opinion of book—& (I hope to add) author.———Rushton shall attend you whenever you please[2]—though I should like him to stay a few weeks—& help my other people in forwarding my chattels—your taking him is no less a favour to me than him—& I trust he will behave well—if not—your remedy is very simple—only don't let him be idle—honest I am sure he is—& I believe very good hearted & quiet.——No pains has been spared—& a good deal of expence been incurred in his education—

[3] See Aug. 2, 1813, to Dr. Clark, note 1.

[1] In the first issue of the 3rd edition of *The Giaour* the poem had grown to 53 pages and 950 lines, and more was added in subsequent issues.

[2] Byron had been anxious to find a place for Robert Rushton and Webster agreed to take him into his service.

accounts & mensuration &c. he ought to know & I believe he does.——
————I write this *near* London but your answer will reach me better
in Bennet Street 4 (as before)—I am going very soon—& if you
would do the same thing—as far as Sicily—I am sure you would not
be sorry—my Sister, Mrs. L[eigh] goes with me³—her spouse is
obliged to retrench for a few years (but *he* stays at home) so that his
link-boy prophecy (if ever he made it) *recoils* upon himself.—I am
truly glad to hear of Ly. F[rances]'s good health—have you added to
your family?—pray make my best respects acceptable to her
Ladyship.⁴————Nothing will give me more pleasure than to hear
from you as soon & as fully as you please.—

ever most truly yrs.
BYRON

[TO SAMUEL JACKSON PRATT.¹]   *August 15th. 1813*

Sir—In reply to ye. letter with which I was yesterday honoured I
am sorry to say that my own involvements are at present of such a
description as to put it entirely out of my power to be of ye. smallest
service to my neighbors—& to these I have to add ye. similar
embarrassment of some near relations.—Your situation is certainly a
hard one particularly after a life replete I believe with proofs of
worth & certainly of talent—but I will not occupy your time with
useless words since I cannot offer more than my wishes for your
welfare—You have however a consolation—which I cannot boast—
that your difficulties are neither to be imputed to vice nor imprudence.
——Your friend Mr. Dallas I have not seen very recently—but I
fear that his circumstances also are unequal to his merits—I return
your friend's letter with your annexed production—both are well
worth preserving. I have ye. honour to be

very sincerely yr. wellwisher & Svt.
BYRON

P.S. Your former letter would have received an earlier answer but
I left England almost immediately on attaining majority & my affairs
have since been yearly assuming a more poetical posture—& rendered
a satisfactory reply impracticable.

---

³ See Aug. 11, 1813, to Lady Melbourne, note 2.
⁴ See Biographical Sketch of Webster, Vol. 2, p. 287.
¹ Samuel Jackson Pratt (1749–1814) was a miscellaneous writer and one-time
actor. He had been the discoverer and patron of the cobbler-poet Blacket.

My dear Ly. M[elbourn]e—I *am* "a very weak person" & can only answer—your letter—I have already written & *torn three* to you—& probably may finish in the same way with ye. present.—Ld. S[ligo] is in town & we are much embarrassed with ye. plague which is it seems all over ye. Levant—but having been both at a prodigious expenditure in large trunks—small clothes—& small arms for ourselves—snuff boxes & Telescopes for the Mussulman gentry—& gewgaws for such of the Pagan women as may be inclined to give us trinkets in exchange—why—lest so much good preparation should be thrown away—we are determined to go—God knows where—for he is bewildered & so am I.—His Balarina has presented him with a babe—& Malice says that he divides the honours of paternity with the Editor of the Courier—who—I suppose—published his trial & tried his fortune with the Lady—much about the time that Sir Wm. Scott passed sentence of matrimony upon his mother[1]—He is going to part with her—& is right—those Opera house connections are not very creditable—besides the eternal chaldron of boiling *suspicion* into which a man must be plunged if he likes one of those women must be insufferable—at least for a permanency.———Who is your *pencil* correspondent?—*her* query (for it looks like a female's) is too lively for Mrs George—has too few words for Ly. Jersey—is not starch enough for your niece—nor patient enough for C[aroline]—it is not Ly. Blarney's for it is legible—it is not ill-natured—so it can't be Ly. Holland's—I have already named more people than I believe care where I am or what I am doing—or at any rate that would ask you the question—tell me & in return I will tell—no I wont.—Of C[aroline] I know nothing—I hear very seldom from her—& then she sends me sermons & fruit—that if one don't make me sick the other may—I have a letter (not from her) today—in which there is an enquiry—"tell me when *did* you see Ly. M"—I will answer it—when my correspondent can reply to me "when I *shall* see Ly. M."———I have scribbled on without saying a single thing I wished to say—this victory![2]—sad work—nothing but Conquest abroad & High health at home—only think what a disappointment—the Wapping Plague—has turned out to be merely a vulgar low—common place

[1] Sir William Scott, the brother of John Scott, 1st Earl of Eldon, was Judge of the Consistory Court (1788–1821). Daniel Stuart, who owned the Tory *Morning Post*, was also proprietor of *The Courier*. The editor was Thomas G. Street, a high liver whose escapades furnished much gossip at the time.

[2] Byron probably refers to the victory at Vittoria in Spain, or possibly Wellington's victories around San Sebastian in late July and early August.

Typhus fever & wont kill one of our acquaintance unless they go to Gravesend to smuggle.—Then the Congress—Ld. A[3]—is to my conception as empty a piece of Caledonian Coxcombry as ever wore a Thistle—& as fit to negotiate as I to dance a Bolero—or C[aroline] to *sit* still—or Ly. O[xford] to *lie* still—or Ly. Anybody to be still—I don't know him but merely judge from an air of pretension about him which is generally the solemn cloak of Shallowness—I have heard him speak badly—on Spanish affairs—very likely he may do better with our own.——Write to me soon—& believe me ever

yrs. most explicitly

B

[TO LADY MELBOURNE]   *August 20th. 1813*

My dear Ly. M[elbourn]e—When I don't write to you or see you for some time you may be very certain I am about no good—& vice versa—I have sent you a long scrawl & here be a second—which may convince you that I am not ashamed of myself—or else I should keep out of the way of one for whom I have so much regard.—C[aroline] has been a perfect Lake—a mirror of quiet—& I have answered her last 2 letters.—I hope they will neither ruffle the Lake nor crack the Mirror—but when she really & truly has been behaving prettily—I could not write ferociously—besides I happened just then to be in exquisite good humour with myself and two or three other people.—

"Perhaps Prosperity becalmed his breast—
Perhaps the Wind just shifted from the East."[1]

Everything in this life depends upon the weather & the state of one's digestion—I have been eating & drinking—which I always do when wretched for then I grow fat & don't show it—& now that I am in very good plight & Spirits—I can't leave off the custom though I have no further occasion for it—& shan't have till—the next change of Weather—I suppose or some other atmospherical reason.——And now what are you doing? in this place we can only say what we are not doing—Town is empty but not the worse for that—it is a delight of a place now there's no one in it—I am totally & unutterably possessed by the ineffable power of Indolence—I see no one—I say nothing—I do nothing—and I wish for noth—oh yes—I wish to see you—& next to that—to hear from you—I have great hopes of

3 Lord Aberdeen, who was Ambassador Extraordinary at Vienna in 1813.
1 Pope, *Moral Essays*, I, 111–112.

91

sailing soon—for Cadiz I believe first—& thence wherever the Gods permit—I shan't be sorry to see that best & whitest of Sea port towns again—but all this depends upon the weather—or my own caprices which are much more whimsical.———How is your sole companion the Countess of Panshanger?[2]—I have now been a retainer of your house one year & sundry months & I know rather less of that illustrious Lady than I did the first moment of my introduction—yet I have thought as much about her as any of you—not the Gods know with any but the most profound reverence—but she puzzled me—(which is very easy) & furnished me with many an entertaining soliloquy upon a variety of topics—do you know I am an observer but my observations upon man—or rather womankind like deep metaphysical researches lead only to doubt—& then I leave them—or they me.— Is not this a laudable spirit of enquiry into things that don't concern myself? make my best respects—& don't be angry with me—which you will however—first for some things I have said—& then for others I have not said—you would not have me always talking *Egotism* though it is said to be allowable in a letter & only in a letter.—I am now going to dine—where I shall be obliged to drink more than is prudent—& I congratulate myself & you on having written this before dinner instead of after—though it is stupid enough to make you believe that I have anticipated my Claret—yours ever my dear Ly. M. in *sober sadness*—or as a winebibber ought to say—in *sad sobriety*—

B

[TO LADY MELBOURNE] *August 21st. 1813*

My dear Ly. M[elbourn]e—We are sadly bewildered—I ask you who was so good as to enquire after me—& you send me in reply some speculations upon a note in *pencil* you once saw—which came from a person you certainly never saw in your life—& who I am almost sure was never in London but once & then only for two months. From or of that personage I have not heard since last March.—I do not know that anyone ever reproached me for illtreating C[aroline] as far as regarded my acquaintance with you———Oh yes—there was one— but I know as little where she is as I do of the other—& we never

2 Countess of Panshanger was a facetious name Byron gave to Lady Melbourne's daughter, Lady Cowper. Panshanger was the Hertfordshire seat of the 5th Earl Cowper.

were nor—I dare swear—ever will be in the least intimate. I have not said that any person objected at present to the magical influence I will not deny that you possess not only over me but any one on whom you please to exert it—I never knew but three people who did object to it—& much good it did them.————I am "sick & serious" am I?—then you must cure the one & laugh away the other—but I equally deny the malady & the melancholy.—Of C[aroline]'s parcel & it's contents I am in utter ignorance—to the picture I plead guilty— I thought I had already said to you as I did to C[aroline] that it was for Augusta—who took it with her I believe into the country.—She wants to go with me to Sicily or elsewhere—& I wish it also—but the intelligence of the progress of the plague is really too serious— & she would take one of the children[1]—now Ly. O[xford] sickened me of *every body's* children—besides it is so superfluous to carry such things with people—if they want them can't they get them on the Spot?—After all I shall probably go alone—S[ligo] wants to go to Russia—only to see a *worse* London at St. Petersburg—he prefers— (as anyone in their senses would) the Mediterranean but is staggered by the pestilence.——He is not I believe the least jealous of his precious appendage but *tired* of her—& I don't much wonder—poor fellow—why should his *"figure"* prevent him from jealousy—I think it would be a very good cause—though he is less than the Prince— who I fancy did not find his *figure* in his way—Heaven knows what is to become of any or at least most of our Sex—if our masculine ugliness is to be an obstacle—it is fortunate that the caprice of your gender generally gets the better of their taste.——I am delighted to hear of your return to town—I shall then see you— you don't know how much good your conversation does me—you must promise me—if I stay away two years—to send me an invitation to Brocket on my return—I hope there will then be no alarm—it is very hard to live in perpetual Quarantine—

ever dear Ly. M[elbourn]e
B

P.S. Scrope Davies & Ld. Foley were the Quarrelers you mention[2]— & I was called in by the former—a second's is a most inglorious & ungrateful office—& having as little desire to make others play the fool—as to quarrel myself—with a little management I made it up between them—as might be done nine times in ten if the Mediator

---

[1] Byron was still planning to take Augusta abroad with him. See Aug. 11, 1813, to Lady Melbourne, note 2.

[2] See Aug. 6, 1813, to Henry Fox, note 1.

is not a bully or a butcher.—You say my handwriting is altered—I fear not for the better—it depends upon my pens & my humours—*both* as you know none of the best.

* * * * * * * * * * * * * * * *

As our late—I might say, deceased—correspondence had too much of the town-life leaven in it, we will now, "paulo majora." prattle a little of literature in all its branches; and first of the first—criticism. The Prince is at Brighton, and Jackson, the boxer, gone to Margate, having, I believe, decoyed Yarmouth to see a milling in that polite neighborhood.[1] Made. de Staël Holstein has lost one of her young barons, who has been carbonadoed by a vile Teutonic adjutant,—kilt & killed in a coffee-house at Scrawsenhawsen.[2] Corinne is, of course, what all mothers must be,—but will, I venture to prophesy, do what few mothers could—and write an Essay upon it. She cannot exist without a grievance—and somebody to see, or read, how much grief becomes her. I have not seen her since the event; but merely judge (not very charitably) from prior observation.

In a "mail-coach copy" of the Edinburgh, I perceive the Giaour is 2d article.[3] The numbers are still in the Leith smack—*pray, which way is the wind?* The said article is so very mild and sentimental, that it must be written by Jeffrey *in love*;—you know he is gone to America to marry some fair one, of whom he has been, for several *quarters*, *éperdument amoureux*. Seriously—as Winifred Jenkins says of Lismahago—Mr. Jeffrey (or his deputy) "has done the handsome thing by me,"[4] and I say *nothing*. But this I will say,—If you and I

---

[1] On Aug. 23, 1813, Harry Harmer, "the Coppersmith" beat Jack Ford in a boxing match at St. Nicholas, near Margate. Prothero has some interesting details about the Earl of Yarmouth, who like Byron was a friend of "Gentleman" Jackson and a patron of prize fights. He was also an intimate friend of the Regent and a patrician libertine, the model of "Monmouth" in *Coningsby*, and of "Steyne" in *Vanity Fair*. He occupied 13 Piccadilly Terrace, the house of the Duchess of Devonshire, before the Byrons moved there in April, 1815. There is no indication that Byron knew him, but he made a slighting allusion to his red whiskers in a note to *The Waltz*, (line 142n.)

[2] See Aug. 8, 1813, to Lady Melbourne, note 4.

[3] The *Edinburgh Review* for July, 1813, reviewed *The Giaour*, praising its poetic power, but deprecating the "worthlessness and guilt" of the leading characters and lamenting Byron's devotion to gloomy and revolting subjects.

[4] In Winifred Jenkyns's last letter in *Humphry Clinker*.

had knocked one another on the head in his quarrel, how he would have laughed, and what a mighty bad figure we should have cut in our posthumous works. By the by, I was called *in* the other day to mediate between two gentlemen bent upon carnage, and,—after a long struggle between the natural desire of destroying one's fellow-creatures, and the dislike of seeing men play the fool for nothing,—I got one to make an apology, and the other to take it, and left them to live happy ever after. One was a peer, the other a friend untitled, and both fond of high play;—and one, I can swear for, though very mild, "not fearful," and so dead a shot, that, though the other is the thinnest of men, he would have split him like a cane. They both conducted themselves very well, and I put them out of *pain* as soon as I could.[5]

* * * * * * * * * * * * * * * *

There is an American Life of G. F. Cooke,[6] *Scurra* deceased, lately published. Such a book!—I believe, since Drunken Barnaby's Journal,[7] nothing like it has drenched the press. All green-room and tap-room —drams and the drama—brandy, whisky-punch, and, *latterly*, toddy, overflow every page. Two things are rather marvelous—first, that a man should live so long drunk, and, next, that he should have found a sober biographer. There are some very laughable things in it. nevertheless;—but the pints he swallowed and the parts he performed are too regularly registered.

All this time you wonder I am not gone: so do I; but the accounts of the plague are very perplexing—not so much for the thing itself as the quarantine established in all ports, and from all places, even from England. It is true the forty or sixty days would, in all probability, be as foolishly spent on shore as in the ship; but one likes to have one's choice, nevertheless. Town is awfully empty; but not the worse for that. I am really puzzled with my perfect ignorance of what I mean to do;—not stay, if I can help it, but where to go? Sligo is for the North,—a pleasant place, Petersburgh, in September, with one's ears and nose in a muff, or else tumbling into one's neckcloth or pocket-handkerchief! If the winter treated Buonaparte with so little ceremony, what would it inflict upon your solitary traveller?—Give me a *sun*, I care not how hot, and sherbet, I care not how cool, and

[5] See Aug. 6, 1813, to Henry Fox, note 1.
[6] *Memoirs of George Frederick Cooke, late of the Theatre Royal, Covent Garden*, by W. Dunlap, 2 Vols., 1813. Cooke had been the idol of the Dublin stage before he came to Covent Garden in 1800, where he had a great success in Shakespearean parts. He died in 1812 in New York of excess drinking.
[7] Printed anonymously about 1650, supposed to be by Barnaby Harrington of Queen's College, Oxford; also ascribed to Richard Braithwait.

my Heaven is as easily made as your Persian's.[8] The Giaour is now 1000 and odd lines. "Lord Fanny spins a thousand such a day,"[9] eh, Moore?—thou wilt needs be a wag, but I forgive it.

Yours ever,

Bn.

P.S. I perceive I have written a flippant and rather cold-hearted letter; let it go, however. I have said nothing, either, of the brilliant sex; but the fact is, I am, at this moment, in a far more serious, and entirely new, scrape than any of the last twelvemonths,[10]—and that is saying a good deal. * * * It is unlucky we can neither live with nor without these women.

I am now thinking and regretting that, just as I have left Newstead, you reside near it. Did you ever see it? *do*—but don't tell me that you like it. If I had known of such intellectual neighbourhood, I don't think I should have quitted it. You could have come over so often, as a bachelor.—for it was a thorough bachelor's mansion— plenty of wine and such sordid sensualities—with books enough, room enough, and an air of antiquity about all (except the lasses) that would have suited you, when pensive, and served you to laugh at when in glee. I had built myself a bath and a *vault*—and now I sha'n't even be buried in it. It is odd that we can't even be certain of a *grave*, at least a particular one. I remember, when about fifteen, reading your poems there,—which I can repeat almost now,[11]— and asking all kinds of questions about the author, when I heard that he was not dead according to the preface; wondering if I should ever see him—and though, at that time, without the smallest poetical propensity myself, very much taken, as you may imagine, with that volume. Adieu—I commit you to the care of the gods—Hindoo, Scandinavian, and Hellenic!

P.S. 2d. There is an excellent review of Grimm's Correspondence and Made. de Staël in this No. of the E[dinburgh] R[eview][12] * * * * * Jeffrey, himself, was my critic last year; but this is, I believe, by another

[8]   A Persian's Heav'n is easily made —
               'Tis but black eyes and lemonade

[9] Pope's *Imitations of Horace*, Satire I, line 6.

[10] Byron hinted to Moore of his liaison with Augusta Leigh. That he told him more is suggested by the asterisks.

[11] Byron was fifteen in 1803. He must then have first come across Moore's early erotic verses in *The Poems of the Late Thomas Little*, first published in 1801.

[12] Madame de Staël's *Germany* was reviewed in the *Edinburgh Review* for July, 1813, by Sir James Mackintosh, and in the same number was a long review of Grimm's *Correspondance Littéraire et Philosophique*.

hand. I hope you are going on with your *grand coup*—pray do—or that damned Lucien Buonaparte will beat us all. I have seen much of his poem in MS., and he really surpasses every thing beneath Tasso. Hodgson is translating him *against* another bard.[13] You and (I believe, Rogers) Scott, Gifford and myself, are to be referred to as judges between the twain,—that is, if you accept the office. Conceive our different opinions! I think we, most of us (I am talking very impudently, you will think—*us*, indeed!) have a way of our own,—at least, you and Scott certainly have.

[TO LADY MELBOURNE]   *August 23d. 1813*

My dear Ly. M[elbourn]e—Would that Luttrel had travelled—or that one could provide him with a mattress stuffed with peachstones to teach him more philosophy in such petty calamities[1]—I remember my friend Hobhouse used to say in Turkey that I had no notion of comfort because I could sleep where none but a *brute* could—& certainly where *brutes did* for often have the *Cows* turned out of their apartment *butted* at the door all night extremely discomposed with the unaccountable ejectment.—Thus we lived—one day in the palace of the Pacha & the next perhaps in the most miserable hut of the Mountains—I confess I preferred the former but never quarrelled with the latter—& as to eating (by the bye I have lately stuffed like Count Staremberg)[2] you know I am easily victualled.————A pretty panegyric you have passed upon the Countess—"honourable & amiable"—God knows I have no reason to doubt either & never did—but methinks this is a marvellous insipid eulogium—"amiable" she must be because she reminds us very much of yourself—& "honourable" because she reminds one of nobody else—the fact is you love her better than anything in existence—& for that reason you don't know how to praise her properly—so you must confine yourself

---

[13] Hodgson and Dr. Samuel Butler translated Lucien Buonaparte's poem *Charlemagne*. It was published in 1815.

[1] Henry Luttrell (1765?–1851) was a natural son of Henry Lawes Luttrell, 2nd Earl of Carhampton (Irish Peerage). He had been in the Irish parliament before he was introduced to London society by the Duchess of Devonshire. He was a wit and poet and a famous conversationalist and diner-out. He later published "Advice to Julia, a Letter in Rhyme" (1820).

[2] Count Staremberg is referred to in Lady Holland's *Journal* (II, 236) as Prince Staremberg. He was the Austrian ambassador in London. He is mentioned frequently in Miss Berry's diary.

97

to abusing me in which if you don't succeed it is no fault of mine.——
You tell me I don't know women—did I ever pretend to be an
unraveller of riddles?—& was there ever any one more easily deceived
& led by anyone who will take the trouble than myself?—"Know
them"—not I indeed—& I heartily hope I never may.—"Was my
good humour from deceiving or being duped" the *last* of course—
or how could I be so happy as you seem to think me.—My head is a
little disturbed today—I have to write—first—a soothing letter to
C[aroline] a sentimental one to X Y Z.—a sincere one to T. Moore—
and one a mixture of all three to yourself with as much of the ludicrous
as you like to find in it.—I ought to have said this in ye. beginning
for now I must end it.—

Adieu ever yrs.

B

[TO ANNABELLA MILBANKE] *4 Bennet Street August 25th 1813*

I am honoured with your letter which I wish to acknowledge
immediately.—Before I endeavour to answer it—allow me—briefly
if possible—to advert to the circumstances which occurred last
Autumn.—Many years had [occurred?] since I had seen any woman
with whom there appeared to me a prospect of rational happiness—
I now saw but one—to whom however I had no pretentions—or
at least too slight for even the hope of success.—It was however
said that your heart was disengaged—& it was on that ground that
Ly. M. undertook to ascertain how far I might be permitted to
cultivate your acquaintance on the chance (a slender one I allow) of
improving it into friendship and ultimately to a still kinder sentiment.
—In her zeal in my behalf—friendly and pardonable as it was—she
in some degree exceeded my intentions when she made the more
direct proposal—which yet I do not regret except as far as it appeared
presumptuous on my part.—That is the truth you will allow when I
tell you that it was not till lately I mentioned to her that I thought
she had unwittingly committed me a little too far in the expectation
that so abrupt an overture would be received—but I stated this
casually in conversation & without the least feeling of irritation towards
her or pique against yourself.—Such was the result of my *first* &
nearest approach to that altar—to which in the state of your feelings—

I should only have led another victim.—When I say the *first* it may perhaps appear irreconcileable with some circumstances in my life to which I conceive you allude in part of your letter—but such is the fact—I was then too young to marry though not to love[1]—but this was the *first direct* or *indirect* approach ever made on my part to a permanent union with any woman & in all probability it will be the last. Ly. M. was perfectly correct in her statement that I preferred you to all others—it was then the fact—it is so still—but it was no disappointment—because it is impossible to impart one drop more to a cup which already overflows with the waters of bitterness.—We do not know ourselves—yet I do not think that self love was much wounded by this event—on the contrary I feel a kind of pride even in *your rejection*—more I believe than I could derive from the attachment of another—for it reminds me that I once thought myself worthy of the affection of almost the only one of your sex I ever truly respected.—To your letter—the first part surprises me—not that you should feel attachment—but that such attachment should be "without hope" may you recover that hope with it's object!—To the part of your letter regarding myself—I could say much—but I must be brief—if you hear ill of me it is probably not untrue though perhaps exaggerated—on any point in which you may honour me with an interest I shall be glad to satisfy you—to confess the truth or refute the calumny.—I must be candid with you on the score of Friendship—it is a feeling towards you with which I cannot trust myself—I doubt whether I could help loving you—but I trust I may appeal to my conduct since our eclaircissement for the proof—that whatever my feelings may be—they will exempt you from persecution—but I cannot yet profess indifference—and I fear that must be the first step—at least in some points—from what I feel to that which you wish me to feel.—You must pardon me & recollect that if anything displeases you in this letter—it is a difficult task for me to write to you at all—I have left many things unsaid—& have said others I did not mean to utter.—My intended departure from this country is a little retarded by accounts of Plague &c. in the part of the world to which I was returning, & I must bend my course to some more accessible region—probably to Russia.—I have only left myself space to sign myself

ever your obliged Sert.
BYRON

[1] A reference to his love for Mary Chaworth when he was 15.

Dear Sir—I have looked over & corrected one proof but not so carefully (God knows if you can read it through but I can't) as to preclude your eye from discovering some omission of mine or commission of ye. Printer.—If you have patience look it over—do you know any body who can *stop*—I mean *point*—commas & so forth—for I am I fear a sad hand at your punctuation. I have but with some difficulty *not* added any more to this snake of a poem[1]—which has been lengthening its rattles every month—it is now fearfully long—being more than a Canto & a half of C[hilde] H[arold]—which contains but 882 lines per book—with all late additions inclusive.———The last lines Hodgson likes—& it is not often he does—& when he don't—he tells me with great energy—& then I fret & alter—I have thrown them in to soften the ferocity of our Infidel—& for a dying man have given him a good deal to say for himself—Do you think you shall get hold of the *female* M.S. you spoke of today[2]—if so—you will let me have a glimpse—but don't tell our *master* (not W's) or we shall be buffeted.—I was quite sorry to hear you say you staid in town on my account—& I hope sincerely you did not mean so superfluous a piece of politeness.———Our *6* critiques!—they would have made half a quarterly by themselves—but this is the age of Criticism.—

Ever yrs.

B

Ay, my dear Moore, "there *was* a time"—I have heard of your tricks, when "you was campaigning at the King of Bohemy."[1] I am much mistaken if, some fine London spring, about the year 1815, that time does not come again. After all, we must end in marriage; and I can conceive nothing more delightful than such a state in the country,

---

1 Before the end of August a 4th edition of *The Giaour* containing 58 pages and 1048 lines appeared, and shortly after a 5th edition with 66 pages and 1215 lines. The additions, however, did not make the narrative less disjointed and snake-like in its twistings and turnings.

2 The *"female"* manuscript has not been identified. The reference to "our *master*" may mean Gifford, who would normally read manuscripts for Murray and pass on them. "W." is unidentified.

1 Jerry Sneak, in Foote's *Mayor of Garratt* (Act. II) says to Major Sturgeon, "I heard of your tricks at the King of Bohemy."

reading the county newspaper, &c. and kissing one's wife's maid. Seriously, I would incorporate with any woman of decent demeanor to-morrow—that is, I would a month ago, but, at present, * * * * *

Why don't you "parody that Ode?"[2]—Do you think I should be *tetchy*? or have you done it, & won't tell me?—You are quite right about Giamschid, and I have reduced it to a dissyllable within this half hour.[3] I am glad to hear you talk of Richardson, because it tells me what you won't—that you are going to beat Lucien.[4] At least, tell me how far you have proceeded. Do you think me less interested about your works, or less sincere than our friend Ruggiero [Rogers]? I am not—and never was. In that thing of mine, the "English Bards," at the time when I was angry with all the world, I never "disparaged your parts," although I did not know you personally;—and have always regretted that you don't give us an *entire* work and not sprinkle yourself in detached pieces—beautiful, I allow, and quite *alone* in our language, but still giving us a right to expect a *Shah Nameh* (is that the name?) as well as Gazels.[5] Stick to the East;—the oracle, Staël, told me it was the only poetical policy. The North, South, and West, have all been exhausted; but from the East, we have nothing but S * *'s [Southey's] unsaleables,—and these he has contrived to spoil, by adopting only their most outrageous fictions. His personages don't interest us, and yours will. You have no competitor; and, if you had, you ought to be glad of it. The little I have done in that way is merely a "voice in the wilderness" for you; and, if it has had any success, that also will prove that the public are orientalizing, and pave the path for you.

I have been thinking of a story, grafted on the amours of a Peri and a mortal—something like, only more *philanthropical* than, Cazotte's Diable Amoureux.[6] It would require a good deal of poesy, and tenderness is not my forte. For that, and other reasons, I have given up the idea, and merely suggest it to you, because, in intervals of your

---

[2] Moore had suggested that Horace's Ode beginning:- Natis in usum lætitiæ "might be parodied, in allusion to some of his late adventures." (Moore, I, 423n.) See Horace's *Odes and Epodes*, I, 27.

[3] Moore, on the authority of Richardson's *Persian Dictionary*, made the suggestion that caused Byron to change the line from "Bright as the gem of Giamschid." to "Bright as the jewel of Giamschid."

[4] Moore's reference to Richardson's *Persian Dictionary* suggests to Byron that Moore was already at work on an Oriental poem (which he was—*Lalla Rookh*) that would surpass Lucien Buonaparte's *Charlemagne*.

[5] *The Sháh Námeh* by Abul Kásim Firdausí (c. 950–1030) was a rhymed history of Persia.

[6] Jacques Cazotte (1720–1792) published *Le Diable Amoureux* in 1772.

101

greater work, I think it a subject you might make much of.[7] If you want any more books, there is "Castellan's Moeurs des Ottomans,"[8] the best compendium of the kind I ever met with, in six small tomes. I am really taking a liberty by talking in this style to my "elders and my betters;"—pardon it, and don't *Rochefoucault* my motives.[9]

[TO LADY MELBOURNE]   *August 31st. 1813*

My dear Ly. M[elbourn]e—Your kind letter is unanswerable—no one but yourself would have taken the trouble—no one but me would have been in a situation to require it.——I am still in town so that it has as yet had all the effect you wish.[1]———I enclose you a letter from Sligo with *his Giaour*[2]—which differs from our friend C[aroline]'s as much as from mine—for that reason I send it you.—The part I have erased merely contained some barbarous Turkish names of no consequence—& [one line blotted out] some circumstances not immediately relevant to the story.——When you have read it I will thank you for it again—I think it will make you laugh when you consider all the poetry & prose which has grown out of it.——

ever my dear Ly. M. yrs.

B—

P.S. Do you go to Ly. Le De[spenser]'s[3] tonight—I am asked.—

[7] Byron gave up the idea of using a Peri, in deference to Moore, who was already contemplating it (see Moore, I, 424n.), but he did use the theme of the love of women and angels in his *Heaven and Earth*, published in *The Liberal* in 1824. Moore had published his *Loves of the Angels* in 1823.

[8] A. L. Castellan, *Mœurs, usages costumes des Othomans*, et abrégé de leur histoire, Paris, 1812.

[9] Rochefoucault, Maxime 85: "Nous nous persuadons souvent d'aimer les gens plus puissans que nous, et néanmoins c'est l'interêt seul qui produit notre amitié; nous ne nous donnons pas à eux pour le bien que nous leur voulons faire, mais pour celui que nous en voulons recevoir."

[1] It seems apparent that Byron had by this time confessed his passion for Augusta to Lady Melbourne, who had warned him of the dangers to himself and to her of the relationship, and he had for the time being resisted the temptation to see her again.

[2] This was the letter Lord Sligo had written at Byron's request telling what he knew of the episode in which Byron was involved that had been the basis of the story of *The Giaour*. After carefully inking out ten lines Byron used it to counter some stories that Lady Caroline Lamb and others were spreading concerning his activities in the East. Sligo's letter is printed in *LJ*, II, 257–258n.

[3] Lady Le Despenser was the illegitimate daughter of the last (14th) Lord Le Despenser (1774?–1829?). Her name was Rachel Fanny Antonina, but she called herself Baroness Le Despenser. Her discreditable adventures are recounted in DeQuincey's *Autobiographical Sketches*. See also *Annual Register* for 1804.

4 Bennet Street St. J's London
August 31st 1813

It is not my wish to draw you into a correspondence—yet I must say a few words on your last letter or rather on my own reply to your first.—Neither Ly. M. nor yourself could possibly be to blame —if any one was wrong it was myself—and after all she (Ly. M[elbourn]e.) merely saved me from a personal repulse.—My intention was too plain to admit of misrepresentation—though under existing—or perhaps any circumstances—it was presumptuous—& certainly precipitate.—I never did nor ever can deny that I aspired to the honour which I failed in obtaining.—That I never even sought to conceal my ill success—the following circumstance will convince you—and may at least afford you a moment's amusement.—My equally unlucky friend W. Bankes—whom I have known many years— paid me a visit one evening last Winter with an aspect so utterly disconsolate that I could not resist enquiring into the cause.—After much hesitation on his part—& a little guessing on mine—out it came—with tears in his eyes almost—that he had added another name to our unfortunate list.—The coincidence appeared to me so ludicrous that not to laugh was impossible—when I told him that a few weeks before a similar proposal had left me in the same situation.—In short we were the Heraclitus & Democritus of your Suitors—with this exception—that our crying and laughing was excited not by the folly of others but our own—or at least mine—for I had not even the common place excuse of a shadow of encouragement to console me.— Do not suppose because I laughed then—that I had no feeling for him or for myself—the coincidence of our common grievance—and not the circumstance itself provoked my mirth—& I trust I need not add that want of respect to you made no part of the feelings or expressions of either—nor had I mentioned this at all could it place *him* in an unfavourable point of view.—For myself—I must also beg you to believe that whatever might be my momentary levity—your answer to me had been received with respect and admiration rather encreased than diminished by the dignified good sense which dictated your decision & appeared in your reply.—There is not the least occasion for any concealment of the rejection of my proposal—it is a subject I have never sought nor shunned—I certainly have nothing to boast of—but it would be meaness on my part to deny it.————I hope I did not accuse Ly. M. of misrepresentation—it certainly was not my intention—I thought my overture was too abrupt—but in

the proposal itself—and indeed in every thing else the fault was &
must be mine only.—Your friendship I did not reject—though in
speaking of mine I expressed some doubts on the subject of my own
feelings—whatever they may be I shall merely repeat that if possible
they shall be subdued—at all events—silent.————If you regret a
single expression in your late 2 letters—they shall be destroyed or
returned—do not imagine that I mistake your kindness or hope for
more.—I am too proud of the portion of regard you have bestowed
upon me to hazard the loss of it by vain attempts to engage your
Affection—I am willing to obey you—and if you will mark out the
limits of our future correspondence & intercourse they shall not be
infringed.—Believe me with the most profound respect—

ever gratefully yrs.

BYRON

P.S.—I perceive that I *begin* my letter with saying "I do not wish to
draw you into a correspondence" and *end* by almost soliciting it—
admirably consistent!—but it is human nature—& you will forgive it—
if not you can punish.———

[TO THOMAS MOORE]   *August—September, I mean—1st, 1813*

I send you, begging your acceptance, Castellan, and three vols.
on Turkish Literature, not yet looked into.[1] The *last* I will thank
you to read, extract what you want, and return in a week, as they are
lent to me by that brightest of Northern constellations, Mackintosh,—
amongst many other kind things into which India has warmed him,
for I am sure your *home* Scotsman is of a less genial description.[2]

Your Peri, my dear M., is sacred and inviolable; I have no idea of
touching the hem of her petticoat.[3] Your affectation of dislike to
encounter me is so flattering, that I begin to think myself a very fine
fellow. But you are laughing at me—"stap my vitals, Tam! thou art
a very impudent person;"[4] and, if you are not laughing at me, you

---

[1] For Castellan, see Aug. 28, 1813, to Moore, note 8. The three volumes on
Turkish literature were by Giovanni Battista Toderini (1728–1799), *Della
Letteratura Turchesca*, 1787. It was translated into French as *De la Littérature des
Turcs*, 1789.

[2] From 1803 to 1812 Sir James Mackintosh was Recorder of Bombay.

[3] See Aug. 28, 1813, to Moore, note 7.

[4] Byron remembered Sheridan's *Trip to Scarborough* (Act. V, Scene 2) an
adaptation of Vanbrugh's *The Relapse* (Act IV, Scene 6), in which Lord Foppington
says, "Strike me dumb, Tam, thou art a very impudent fellow."

deserve to be laughed at. Seriously, what on earth can you, or have you, to dread from any poetical flesh breathing? It really puts me out of humour to hear you talk thus.

* * * * * * * * * * * * * * *

The "Giaour" I have added to a good deal; but still in foolish fragments. It contains about 1200 lines, or rather more—now printing.[5] You will allow me to send you a copy. You delight me much by telling me that I am in your good graces, and more particularly as to temper; for, unluckily, I have the reputation of a very bad one. But they say the devil is amusing when pleased, and I must have been more venomous than the old serpent, to have hissed or stung in your company. It may be, and would appear to a third person, an incredible thing, but I know *you* will believe me when I say that I am as anxious for your success as one human being can be for another's, —as much as if I had never scribbled a line. Surely the field of fame is wide enough for all; and if it were not, I would not willingly rob my neighbor of a rood of it. Now you have a pretty property of some thousand acres there, and when you have passed your present Inclosure Bill, your income will be doubled (there's a metaphor, worthy of a Templar, namely, pert and low), while my wild common is too remote to incommode you, and quite incapable of such fertility. I send you (which return per post, as the printer would say) a curious letter from a friend of mine, which will let you into the origin of "the Giaour."[6] Write soon.

Ever, dear Moore, yours most entirely, &c.

P.S. This letter was written to me on account of a *different story* circulated by some gentlewomen of our acquaintance, a little too close to the text. The part erased contained merely some Turkish names, and circumstantial evidence of the girl's detection, not very important or decorous.

[TO JAMES WEDDERBURN WEBSTER]   *Sept. 2d. 1813*

My dear Webster—You are just ye same generous and I fear— careless gentleman of the years of indifferent memory 1806–7—but I must not burthen you with my entire household.—Joe[1] is I believe necessary for the present as a fixture to keep possession till every

[5] This must have been the 5th edition, which contained 1215 lines.
[6] See Aug. 31, 1813, to Lady Melbourne, note 2.
[1] Joe Murray, the old servant at Newstead.

thing is arranged—& were it otherwise—you don't know what a perplexity he would prove—honest & faithful but fearfully super-annuated—now *this I* ought & do bear—but as he has not been 50 years in your family—it would be rather hard to convert your mansion into a hospital for decayed domestics.——Rushton is or may be made useful & I am less *compunctious* on his account.—"Will I be Godfather?"[2] yea—verily—I believe it is the only species of parentage I shall ever encounter—for all my acquaintance—Powerscourt[3]—Jocelyn[4]—yourself—Delawarr—Stanhope[5]—with a long list of happy &c. are married—most of them my Juniors too—and I as single & likely to remain so as—nay—more than if I were seventy.———If it is a *Girl* why not also?—Georgina—or even *Byron* will make a classical name for a spinster—if Mr. Richardson's Sir Charles Grandison is any authority in your estimation.———My ship is not settled—my passage in the Boyne was only for *one* servant—& would not do of course—you ask after the expence—a question no less interesting to the married than the single—unless things are much altered no establishment in the Mediterranean countries could amount to a quarter of the expenditure requisite in England for the same or an inferior household.—I am interrupted—& have only time to offer my best thanks for all your good wishes and intentions—& to beg you will believe me equally

yours ever
B

P.S. Rushton shall be sent on Saturday next.—

[TO THOMAS MOORE]   *Sept. 5, 1813*

You need not tie yourself down to a day with Toderini,[1] but send him at your leisure, having anatomized him into such annotations as

---

[2] In a manuscript note on this letter Webster later wrote: "My eldest son—now dead! was christened "Byron Wedderburn" and when I afterward mentioned the loss to Lord Byron he almost chuckled with Joy—or Irony—& said "Well—I cautioned you—& told you that my name would almost damn any thing or creature"!!

[3] Richard Wingfield, Lord Powerscourt, was the brother of Byron's friend John Wingfield, who died in 1811, and to whom Byron paid tribute in *Childe Harold*.

[4] Lord Jocelyn was at Harrow with Byron.

[5] See Sept. 21, 1813, to Lady Melbourne, note 1.

[1] See Sept. 1, 1813, to Moore, note 1.

you want; I do not believe that he has ever undergone that process before, which is the best reasons for not sparing him now.

* * [Rogers] has returned to town, but not yet recovered of the Quarterly.[2] What fellows these reviewers are! "these bugs do fear us all."[3] They made you fight, and me (the milkiest of men) a satirist, and will end making * * [Rogers] madder than Ajax. I have been reading Memory again, the other day, and Hope together, and retain all my preference of the former.[4] His elegance is really wonderful— there is no such thing as a vulgar line in his book. * * * * * * * *

What say you to Buonaparte? I back him against the field barring Catalepsy and the Elements. Nay, I almost wish him success against all countries but this,—were it only to choke the Morning Post, and his undutiful father-in-law, with that rebellious bastard of Scandinavian adoption, Bernadotte.[5] Rogers wants me to go with him on a crusade to the Lakes, and to besiege you on our way. This last is a great temptation, but I fear it will not be in my power, unless you would go on with one of us somewhere—no matter where. It is too late for Matlock, but we might hit upon some scheme, high life or low,—the last would be much the best for amusement. I am so sick of the other, that I quite sigh for a cider-cellar,[6] or a cruise in a smuggler's sloop.

You cannot wish more than I do that the Fates were a little more accommodating to our parallel lines, which prolong ad infinitum without coming a jot the nearer. I almost wish I were married, too— which is saying much. All my friends, seniors and juniors, are in for it, and ask me to be godfather,—the only species of parentage which, I believe, will ever come to my share in a lawful way; and, in an unlawful one, by the blessing of Lucina, we can never be certain,— though the parish may. I suppose I shall hear from you to-morrow.

[2] The *Quarterly Review*, of March, 1813 (IX, 207) had a review of Rogers' *Poems*. It was by J. W. Ward. Although it was balanced, its censure disturbed Rogers for some months.

[3] Henry VI, Part 3, Act. V. Scene 2 . . .: "Warwick was a bug that feared us all."

[4] Rogers published *The Pleasures of Memory* in 1792, and Campbell produced his best known poem, *The Pleasures of Hope* when he was only 21 in 1799. Byron was a great admirer of both. Rogers and Campbell were two of the very few contemporaries whom Byron praised in *English Bards and Scotch Reviewers*.

[5] Bernadotte, Crown Prince of Sweden, once a general of Napoleon, had been adopted by the King of Sweden. He turned against Napoleon and helped the Dutch in their revolution in 1813.

[6] A cider-cellar was a tavern where comic songs were sung and where a general informality reigned. Such a tavern was the *Cider Cellars* at 20 Maiden Lane, Covent Garden, frequented by the famous Greek scholar Porson.

If not, this goes as it is; but I leave room for a P.S., in case any thing requires an answer. Ever, &c.

No letter—*n'importe*. R[ogers] thinks the Quarterly will be at *me* this time: if so, it shall be a war of extermination—no *quarter*. From the youngest devil down to the oldest woman of that Review, all shall perish by one fatal lampoon. The ties of nature shall be torn asunder, for I will not even spare my bookseller; nay, if one were to include readers also, all the better.

[TO LADY MELBOURNE] *Septr. 5th. 1813*

Dear Lady Melbourne—I return you the plan of A[nnabella]'s spouse elect of which I shall say nothing because I do not understand it[1]—though I dare say it is exactly what it ought to be.—Neither do I know why I am writing this note as I mean to call on you—unless it be to try your "new patent pens" which delight me infinitely with their colours—I have pitched upon a yellow one to begin with—Very likely you will be out—& I must return you the annexed epistles—I would rather have seen your answer—she seems to have been spoiled—not as children usually are—but systematically Clarissa Harlowed into an awkward kind of correctness—with a dependence upon her own infallibility which will or may lead her into some egregious blunder—I don't mean the usual error of young gentlewomen—but she will find exactly what she wants—& then discover that it is much more dignified than entertaining.—[two pages torn away] . . . in town—. . . .

[TO ANNABELLA MILBANKE] *Septr 6th 1813*

Agreed—I will write to you occasionally & you shall answer at your leisure & discretion.—You must have deemed me very vain & selfish to imagine that your candour could offend—I see nothing that "could hurt my feelings" in your correspondence—you told me you declined me as a lover but wished to retain me as a friend—now as one may meet with a good deal of what is called love in this best of all possible worlds—& very rarely with friendship I could not find fault

---

[1] Annabella Milbanke had sent her aunt, Lady Melbourne, a statement of her requirements for a husband, which she sent on to Byron.

—upon calculation at least.—I am afraid my first letter was written during some of those moments which have induced your belief in my *general despondency*—now in common I believe with most of mankind— I have in the course of a very useless & ill regulated life encountered events which have left a deep *impression*—perhaps something at the time recalled *this* so forcibly as to make it apparent in my answer— but I am not conscious of any habitual or at least long continued pressure on my spirits.—On the contrary—with the exception of an occasional spasm—I look upon myself as a very facetious personage— & may safely appeal to most of my acquaintance (Ly. M. for instance) in proof of my assertion.—Nobody laughs more—& though your friend Joanna Baillie says somewhere that "Laughter is the *child* of Misery" yet I don't believe her—(unless indeed in a hysteric)— though I think it is sometimes the *Parent*.—Nothing would do me more honour than the acquaintance of that Lady—who does not possess a more enthusiastic admirer than myself—she is our only dramatist since Otway & Southerne—I don't except Home[1]—With all my presumed prejudice against your sex or rather the perversion of manners & principle in many which you admit in some circles— I think the worst woman that ever existed would have made a *man* of very passable reputation—they are all better than us—& their faults such as they are must originate with ourselves.—Your sweeping sentence "in the circles where we have met" amuses me much when I recollect some of those who constituted that society—after all bad as it is it has it's agremens.—The great object of life is Sensation—to feel that we exist—even though in pain—it is this "craving void" which drives us to Gaming—to Battle—to Travel—to intemperate but keenly felt pursuits of every description whose principal attraction is the agitation inseparable from their accomplishment.——I am but an awkward dissembler—as my friend you will bear with my faults— I shall have the less constraint in what I say to you—firstly because I may derive some benefit from your observations—& next because I am very sure *you* can never be perverted by any paradoxes of mine.— You have said a good deal & very well too—on the subject of Benevolence *systematically* exerted—two lines of Pope will explain mine (if I have any) and that of half mankind—

[1] John Home (1722–1808) made his first success as a dramatist in Edinburgh with the historical drama *Douglas*. He was for a time tutor to the Prince of Wales and was pensioned by George III. From 1778 he settled in Edinburgh among a brilliant circle of literary men. He supported the claims of Macpherson to be the translator of Ossian.

'Perhaps Prosperity becalmed his breast
'Perhaps the Wind just shifted from ye. East.[2]—

By the bye you are a *bard* also—have you quite given up that pursuit?
—is your friend Pratt[3] one of your critics?—or merely one of your
"systematic benevolents? ["] You were very kind to poor Blackett
which he requited by falling in love rather presumptuously to be
sure[4] like Metastasio with the Empress Maria Theresa.—When you
can spare an instant I shall of course be delighted to hear from or of
you—but do not let me encroach a moment on better avocations—
Adieu

ever yrs.
B

[TO JAMES WEDDERBURN WEBSTER]   *Septr. 6th 1813*

My dear Webster—This will be delivered to you by Rushton who
sets off tomorrow, & I have directed him to make the best of his way
to your mansion.—As I wrote to you recently at some length I will
not now further encroach upon your time than to say I shall always
be glad to hear from or of you & ever am

very faithfully yrs.
BIRON

P.S. Have you ever [heard of?] a mansion untenanted in a decent
situation within ten miles of your neighborhood?—————

[TO LADY MELBOURNE]   *Septr. 7th. 1813*—

My dear Ly. M[elbourn]e—A letter from *A[nnabella]*—from you—
& from Ali Pacha by Dr. Holland[1] just arrived in which that amiable
potentate styles me his "most excellent & dearest friend."—What do
you think was "dearest friend's" last exploit?—Forty two years ago
the inhabitants of a hostile city seized his mother & 2 sisters &

---

[2] Pope, *Moral Essays*, I, 111–112. Byron quoted the same lines in a letter to
Lady Melbourne, Aug. 20, 1813.
[3] Samuel Jackson Pratt, was the patron of the cobbler-poet, Joseph Blacket, who
was also patronized by Miss Milbanke.
[4] This is a rather interesting revelation if true, that Blacket should have become
romantically interested in his patroness.
[1] Dr., afterward Sir Henry, Holland (1788–1873) published his *Travels in the
Ionian Islands, Albania . . .* in 1815.

treated them as Miss Cunegonde was used by the Bulgarian cavalry. Well—this year he at last becomes master of the aforesaid city—selects all the persons living in the remotest degree akin to this outrage (in *Turkey* these are affronts) their children grand children—cousins &c. to the amount of 600—& has them put to death in his presence.—I don't wonder at it—but the interval of 42 years is rather singular.—this H[ollan]d tells me occurred in the present spring.—He writes to me to get him a gun made—& assures me of his tender remembrance & profound respect.—I dine out & am afraid I shall hardly be in time—but I will doubtless endeavour to have the pleasure of seeing you—I have a great many things to say—& some very good things to *hear* at any rate—

ever yrs.
B

[TO THOMAS MOORE]   *Sept. 8, 1813*

I am sorry to see Tod[erini][1] again so soon, for fear your scrupulous conscience should have prevented you from fully availing yourself of his spoils. By this coach I send you a copy of that awful pamphlet "the Giaour," which has never procured me half so high a compliment as your modest alarm. You will (if inclined in an evening) perceive that I have added much in quantity,—a circumstance which may truly diminish your modesty upon the subject.

You stand certainly in great need of a "lift" with Mackintosh. My dear Moore, you strangely underrate yourself. I should conceive it an affectation in any other; but I think I know you well enough to believe that you don't know your own value. However, 'tis a fault that generally mends; and, in your case, it really ought. I have heard him speak of you as highly as your wife could wish; and enough to give all your friends the jaundice.

Yesterday I had a letter from *Ali Pacha!* brought by Doctor Holland, who is just returned from Albania.[2] It is in Latin, and begins "Excellentissime, *nec non* Carissime," and ends about a gun he wants made for him;—it is signed "Ali Vizir." What do you think he has been about? H[olland] tells me that, last spring, he took a hostile town, where, forty-two years ago, his mother and sisters were treated as Miss Cunigunde was by the Bulgarian cavalry. He takes

---

[1] See Sept. 1, 1813, to Moore, note 1.
[2] Byron told the same story to Lady Melbourne the day before.

the town, selects all the survivors of this exploit—children, grand-children, &c. to the tune of six hundred, and has them shot before his face. Recollect, he spared the rest of the city, and confined himself to the Tarquin pedigree,—which is more than I would. So much for "dearest friend."

[TO LADY MELBOURNE]   *Septr. 8th. 1813*

My dear Ly. M[elbourn]e—I leave town tomorrow for a few days—come what may—and as I am sure you would get the better of my resolution—I shall not venture to encounter you.[1]—If nothing very particular occurs you will allow me to write as usual—if there does—you will probably hear *of* but not *from* me (of course) again.— Adieu—whatever I am—whatever & wherever I may be—believe me most truly your obliged

& faithful
B

[TO THOMAS MOORE]   *Sept. 9, 1813*

I write to you from Murray's, and I may say, from Murray, who, if you are not predisposed in favour of any other publisher, would be happy to treat with you, at a fitting time, for your work.[1] I can safely recommend him, as fair, liberal, and attentive, and certainly, in point of reputation, he stands among the first of "the trade." I am sure he would do you justice. I have written to you so much lately, that you will be glad to see so little now. Ever, &c. &c.

[TO LADY MELBOURNE]   *Septr. 9th. 1813*

My dear Ly. M[elbourn]e—I did not receive your note till Midnight —having gone out immediately on writing my own—or you may feel assured that I could have as little resisted your *conjuration*—as any

[1] Byron was going to visit Augusta, and he was sure that Lady Melbourne, who had already warned him of the danger of his liaison with his sister, would try to dissuade him.

[1] Moore cast his lot with Longman, who paid him £3,000 for *Lalla Rookh.* After Byron's death Murray became the publisher of Moore's *Letters and Journals of Lord Byron*, 2. vols, 1830.

other spell you may think proper to cast over me.—Something has occurred which prevents my leaving town till Saturday perhaps till Sunday—later than that day I cannot well remain.—Without as A[nnabella] says being in a state of *despondency*—I am nevertheless very much perplexed—however that must end one way or the other—. You say "write to me at all events" depend upon it I will—till the moment arrives (if it does arrive) when I feel that you ought not to acknowledge me as a correspondent[1]—in that case a sense of what is due to yourself—& a very grateful remembrance of all you have done to save one not worth preserving—will of course close our correspondence and acquaintance at once—the sincerest & only proof I could then afford of the value I set upon your friendship.—

ever yrs.
B.

[TO THOMAS PHILLIPS]   *Septr. 9th. 1813*

Dear Sir—I send you the biography of one of your Sitters & I hope you will derive some amusement from the singular anecdotes contained in the volume.—When you can spare time and inclination I confess it would gratify me to see the half-length finished as M[urray] wants it for an engraving—I dont care what becomes of the arms so that *pens* [&] *books* are *not* upon ye. canvas [ha]ving left every thing else to your own better judgment with which [I] have every reason to be more than satisfied—I shall only beg you to follow your own taste as before.— When ye. copy or ye. Original is finished have ye. goodness to let me know—if I leave town it will be only for a few days—and I do not expect to sail before October.—

yrs. very truly
BIRON

[TO GEORGE THOMSON[1]]   *Septr. 10th. 1813*

Sir—Mr. Murray informs me that you have again addressed him on ye. subject of some songs which I ought long ago to have contri-

---

[1] Byron felt that if he took some desperate step with Augusta, such as going abroad with her alone, he ought not to expect Lady Melbourne to continue to correspond with him, for fear she would share in his disgrace.

[1] George Thomson was a collector of Scottish music, and publisher of Scottish, Welsh, and Irish airs. He had published Moore's *Irish Melodies* (1807).

buted.—The fact is—I have repeatedly tried since you favoured me with your first letter (and ye. valuable musical present which accompanied it) without being able to satisfy myself—judge then if I should be able to gratify you or others.———A bad song would only disgrace beautiful music—I know that I could rhyme for you—but not produce anything worthy of your publication.—It is not a species of writing which I undervalue—on the contrary Burns in your country—& my friend Moore in this—have shewn that even their splendid talents may acquire additional reputation from this exercise of their powers.—You will not wonder that I decline writing after men whom it were difficult to imitate—& impossible to equal.—I wish you every success—& I have only declined complying with your request—because I would not impede your popularity.—Believe me your wellwisher

& very obedt. Sert.
BIRON

P.S.—You will not suspect me of caprice nor want of inclination—it is true you may say I have already made attempts apparently as hazardous—but believe me I have again & again endeavoured to fulfil my promise without success.—nothing but my most decided conviction that both you & I would regret it could have prevented me from long ago contributing to your volume.———

[TO AUGUSTA LEIGH] *Septr. 15th. 1813*

My dear Augusta—I joined my friend Scrope about 8 & before eleven we had swallowed six bottles of his burgundy & Claret—which left him very unwell & me rather feverish[1]—we were tete a tete. I remained with him next day & set off last night for London which I reached at three in the morning—tonight I shall leave it again—perhaps for Aston[2]—or Newstead—I have not yet determined—nor does it much matter—as you perhaps care more on the subject than I do—I will tell you when I know myself.— When my departure is arranged—& I can get this long-evaded passage—you will be able to

---

[1] The implication seems to be that Byron's conference with Augusta resulted in an impasse. His letters contain no more references to her going abroad with him.
[2] The home of Wedderburn Webster.

tell me whether I am to expect a visit or not—I can come for or meet you as you think best—if you write address to Bennet Street.—

yrs. very truly
B

[TO JOHN MURRAY] *Sep. 15th. 1813*

Dear Sir—Will you pray enquire after any ship with a convoy *taking passengers* & get me one if possible—I mean not a ship of war—but anything that may be *paid for*—I have a friend & 3 servants.[1]— Gibraltar—or Minorca—or *Zante*.—

[TO JAMES WEDDERBURN WEBSTER] *Septr. 15th. 1813*

My dear Webster—I shall not resist your second invitation & shortly after the receipt of this you may expect me.—You will excuse me from ye. races—as a guest I have no "antipathies" & few preferences—you won't mind however my *not dining* with you—every day at least.—When we meet we can talk over our respective plans—mine is very short & simple—viz—to sail when I can get a passage—if I remained in England—I should live in ye country—& of course in the vicinity of those whom I know would be most agreeable.— I did not know that Jack's graven image[1] was at Newstead—if it be—pray transfer it to Aston.——It is my hope to see you so shortly—tomorrow or the next day—that I will not now trouble you with my speculations.—

ever yrs. very faithfully
BYRON

P.S.—I don't know how I came to sign myself with ye. "i" it is the old spelling—& I sometimes slip into it.—When I say I can't *dine* with you—I mean that sometimes I don't dine at all—of course when I do—I conform to all hours & domestic arrangements.———

[TO LADY MELBOURNE] *Aston Hall Rotherham—Septr. 21st. 1813*

My dear Ly. M[elbourn]e—My stay at Cambridge was very short—but feeling feverish & restless in town I flew off & here I am on a visit

---

[1] The friend was Dr. William Clark, though he talked also of going abroad with Lord Sligo.

[1] Jack's graven image was a portrait of John "Gentlemen" Jackson.

to my friend Webster now married—& (according to ye. Duke of Buckingham's curse—) "settled in ye. country."—His bride Lady Frances is a pretty pleasing woman—but in delicate health & I fear going—if not gone—into a decline—Stanhope & his wife[1]—pretty & pleasant too but not at all consumptive—left us today—leaving only ye. family—another single gentleman & your slave.—The sister Ly. Catherine is here too—& looks very pale from a *cross* in her love for Lord Bury (Ld. Alb[emarl]e's son)[2] in short we are a society of happy wives & unfortunate maidens.—The place is very well & quiet & the children only scream in a low voice—so that I am not much disturbed & shall stay a few days in tolerable repose.—W[ebster] don't want sense nor good nature but both are occasionally obscured by his suspicions & absurdities of all descriptions—he is passionately fond of having his wife admired—& at the same time jealous to jaundice of every thing & every body—I have hit upon the medium of praising her to him perpetually behind her back—& never looking at her before his face—as for her I believe she is disposed to be very faithful—& I don't think any one now here is inclined to put her to the test.— W[ebster] himself is with all his jealousy & admiration a little tired— he has been lately at Newstead—& wants to go again—I suspected this sudden penchant & soon discovered that a foolish nymph of the Abbey—about whom fortunately I care not—was the attraction—now if I wanted to make mischief—I could extract much good perplexity from a proper management of such events—but I am grown so good or so indolent—that I shall not avail myself of so pleasant an opportunity of tormenting mine host—though he deserves it for poaching.—I believe he has hitherto been unsuccessful—or rather it is too astonishing to be believed.—He proposed to me with great gravity to carry him over there—& I replied with equal candour that *he* might set out when he pleased but that I should remain here to take care of his household in the interim—a proposition which I thought very much to the purpose—but which did not seem at all to his satisfaction—by way of opiate he preached me a sermon on his wife's good qualities concluding by an assertion that in all moral & mortal qualities she was very like "*Christ*!!![*"*] I think the virgin Mary would have been a more appropriate typification—but it was the first comparison of the kind I

---

[1] Philip Henry (Stanhope), 4th Earl Stanhope (1781-1855) married in 1803 Catherine Lucy, daughter of the 1st Baron Carrington.

[2] Lord Bury must have been a son of the 4th Earl of Albemarle. The Earl's son and heir, styled Viscount Bury, died in 1804 at age 11, but the title could have passed to another son.

ever heard & made me laugh till he was angry—& then I got out of humour too—which pacified him & shortened his panegyric—Ld. Petersham[3] is coming here in a day or two—who will certainly flirt furiously with Ly. F[rances]—& I shall have some comic Iagoism with our little Othello—I should have no chance with his Desdemona myself—but a more lively & better dressed & formed personage might in an innocent way—for I really believe the girl is a very good well disposed wife & will do very well if she lives & he himself don't tease her into some dislike of her lawful owner.——I passed through Hatfield the night of your *ball*—suppose we had jostled at a turnpike!!—At Bugden I blundered on a Bishop—the Bishop put me in mind of ye Government—the Government of the Governed—& the governed of their *indifference* towards their governors which you must have remarked as to all *parties*—these reflections expectorated as follows—you know I *never* send you my scribblings & when you read these you will wish I never may.—

Tis said—*Indifference* marks the present time
Then hear the reason—though 'tis told in rhyme—
A King who *can't*—a Prince of Wales who *don't*—
Patriots who *shan't*—Ministers who *won't*—
What matters who are *in* or *out* of place
The *Mad*—the *Bad*—the *Useless*—or the *Base*?

---

you may read the 2d. couplet *so* if you like—

"A King who *cannot*—& a Prince who don't—
Patriots who *would not*—ministers who won't—"

I am asked to stay for the Doncaster races but I am not in plight—& am a miserable beau at the best of times—so I shall even return to town or elsewhere—and in the mean time ever am

yrs. dear Ly. M[elbourn]e

B

P.S.—If you write address to B[enne]t Street, were I once gone—I should not wish my letters to travel *here* after me for fear of *accidents*.————There is a delightful epitaph on Voltaire in Grimm—I read it coming down—the French I should probably misspell so take

---

[3] Charles Stanhope, later (1829), 4th Earl of Harrington, was styled Lord Petersham. He was Lord of the Bedchamber in 1812, and was apparently a ladies' man. He was also a notorious dandy, who had a famous collection of snuff boxes. (See *LJ*, II, 268-269n.)

it only in bad English—"Here lies the spoilt child of *the*/*a* world which he spoiled."[4]—It is good short & true.————

Aston Hall—Rotherham
Septr. 23rd. 1813

You had not answered my last letter when I left London from which I infer—not that you were displeased with it—for that I think you would at once tell me—but that you have been better employed—a reflection which would console me for greater disappointments. As it is possible however that a letter from you may now be with my other epistles in London—I venture to write these few lines—lest my silence in that case should look like neglect—as I have not the plea of better avocations for delaying my reply.—I shall return to town in a few days—in the hope that you are well & happy believe me ever

yr. obliged & sincere
B

[TO JAMES WEDDERBURN WEBSTER] *Stilton Septr. 25th. 1813*

My dear W[ebste]r—Thus far can I "report progress"—& as a solid token of my remembrance I send you a *cheese* of 13 lbs. to enable your digestion to go through ye. race week.—It will go tonight—pray let your retainers enquire after it—the *date* of this letter will account for so homely a present.—On my arrival in town I will write more at length on our different concerns—in ye. mean time I wish you & yours all the gratification at Doncaster you can wish for yourselves. —My love to ye. faithless *Nettle*[1] (who I dare say is *wronging* me during my absence) & my best compts. to all in your house who will receive them.—

ever dear W. yrs. truly
B

P.S.—I fully intend to rejoin you on Saturday if nothing very particular occurs to prevent me.—

---

[4] Byron may have been reading the lengthy review of Baron De Grimm's *Correspondance Littéraire, Philosophique et Critique* which was the leading article in the *Edinburgh Review* for July, 1813. This epitaph, ascribed to a lady of Lausanne, is quoted from Grimm on page 274 of the *Edinburgh*: "Ci gît l'enfant gaté du monde qu'il gata." Byron was fond of quoting Grimm frequently later and probably read the book itself.

[1] Nettle was a poodle which Webster gave to Byron. See Sept. 27, 1813, to Moore.

My dear friend—for such you will permit me to call you—on my
return to town I find some consolation for having left a number of
pleasant people—in your letter—the more so as I [had] begun to doubt if
I should ever receive another.— — You ask me some questions—& as
thay are about myself—you must pardon ye Egotism into which my
answers must betray me.—I am glad that you know any "good deed"
that I am supposed ever to have blundered upon—simply—because
it proves that you have not heard me *invariably* ill spoken of—if
true—I am sufficiently rewarded by a short step towards your good
opinion.—You don't like my "restless" doctrines[1]—I should be very
sorry if *you* did—but *I* can't *stagnate* nevertheless—if I must sail let
it be on the ocean no matter how stormy—anything but a dull cruise
on a level lake without ever losing sight of the same insipid shores by
which it is surrounded.— —"Gay" but not "content" very true.— —
You say I never attempt to "justify" myself. you are right—at times
I can't & occasionally I wont defend by explanations—life is not worth
having on such terms—the only attempt I ever made at defence was in
a poetical point of view—& what did it end in? not an exculpation of
me but an attack on all other persons whatsoever—I should make a
pretty scene indeed if I went on defending—besides by proving myself
(supposing it possible) a good sort of quiet country gentleman—to
how many people should I give more pain than pleasure?—do you
think accusers like one the better for being confuted?— —You have
detected a laughter "false to the heart"—allowed—yet I have been
tolerably sincere with you—& I fear sometimes troublesome.—To the
charge of Pride—I suspect I must plead guilty—because when a boy
& a very young one it was the constant reproach of schoolfellows &
tutors—since I grew up I have heard less about it—probably because
I have now neither schoolfellows nor Tutor—it was however originally
*de*fensive—for at that time my hand like Ishmael's was against every
one's & every one's against mine.—I now come to a subject of your
enquiry which you must have perceived I always hitherto avoided—an
awful one "Religion"— —I was bred in Scotland among Calvinists in
the first part of my life—which gave me a dislike to that persuasion—
since that period I have visited the most bigotted & credulous of
countries—Spain—Greece—Turkey—as a spectacle the Catholic is
more fascinating than the Greek or ye. Moslem—but the *last* is the

---

[1] See Sept. 6, 1813, to Annabella Milbanke where Byron speaks of the "craving
void" which drives men to gaming, battle, and travel.

only believer who practices the precepts of his Prophet to the last chapter of his creed.—My opinions are quite undecided—I may say so sincerely—since when given over at Patras in 1810—I rejected & ejected three Priest-loads of spiritual consolation by threatening to turn Mussulman if they did not leave me in quiet—I was in great pain & looked upon death as in that respect a relief—without much regret of the past—& few speculations on the future—indeed so indifferent was I to my *bodily* situation—that though I was without any attendant but a young Frenchman as ill as myself—two barbarous Arn[a]outs—and a deaf & desperate Greek Quack—and my English servant (a man now with me) within 2 days journey—I would not allow the last to be sent for—worth all the rest as he would have been in attendance at such a time because—I really don't know why—unless it was an indifference to which I am certainly not subject when in good health. —I believe doubtless in God—& should be happy to be convinced of much more—if I do not at present place implicit faith on tradition & revelation of any human creed I hope it is not from a want of reverence for the Creator but the created—& when I see a man publishing a pamphlet to prove that Mr. *Pitt* is risen from the dead (as was done a week ago) perfectly positive in the truth of his assertion—I must be permitted to doubt more miracles equally well attested—but the *moral* of Christianity is perfectly beautiful—& the very sublime of Virtue— yet even there we find some of its finer precepts in earlier axioms of the Greeks.—particularly "do unto others as you would they should do unto you."—the forgiveness of injuries—& more which I do not remember.—Good Night—I have sent you a long prose—I hope your answer will be equal in length—I am sure it will be more amusing.— You write remarkably well—which you won't like to hear so I shall say no more about it—

ever yrs. most sincerely
Biron

P.S.—I shall post-scribble this half sheet.—When at Aston I sent you a short note—for I began to feel a little nervous about the reception of my last letter.—I shall be down there again next week & merely left them to escape from ye Doncaster races—being very ill-adapted for provincial festivities—but I shall rejoin ye party when they are over.—This letter was written last night after a two day's journey with little rest & no refreshment (eating on the road throws me into a fever directly) you will therefore not wonder if it is a meagre performance.—When you honour me with an answer address to London

—present my invariable respects to Sir R. & Ly. Mil[bank]e & once more receive them for yourself—Good Morning.—

Septr. 27th. 1813

Sir—My absence from London prevented till yesterday the receipt & acknowledgement of ye. volume of poems for which I now thank you.—I have derived considerable pleasure from ye. perusal of parts of the book—to the whole I have not yet had time to do justice by more than a slight inspection.—Poetry has always been so unprofitable a pursuit—& the fame of our present race of bards depends so much upon the caprice of ye. public & ye. fashion of ye. day—that I hardly know if it be not injurious to a young man to encourage him to proceed—many however have succeeded with less claim to talent than your work indicates—but on this point you must judge for yourself [.] I like your D[rury] L[ane] Address very much (excepting the *Phœnix*) & see no reason why with a very little alteration it might not have been spoken. You are not perhaps aware that *I* was *not* one of the candidates—the spoken address was written at the subsequent request of ye. committee (which decided on the rejection of the poems transmitted—) on a very short & unexpected notice & certainly without any interference or wish on my part to undertake the task—with ye. consequent *uproar* you are doubtless well acquainted & I hope amused. —I will give orders to my bookseller to transmit the publication you favour me by requesting—& wishing you every success with many thanks for yr. volume I remain—Sir—

yr. obliged & humble Sert.
BIRON

[TO SIR JAMES MACKINTOSH] *Sept. 27th. 1813*

Dear Sir James,—I was to have left London on Friday, but will certainly remain a day longer (and believe I *would* a *year*) to have the honour of meeting you. My best respects to Lady Mackintosh.

Ever your obliged and faithful servant,
BIRON.

[1] Unidentified. Thomson must have written again, for Byron recorded in his journal on Dec. 6, 1813: "A Mr. Thomson has sent me a song, which I must applaud. I hate annoying them with censure or silence;—and yet I hate *lettering*."

Thomas Moore,—(Thou wilt never be called *"true* Thomas," like He of Ercildoune),[1] why don't you write to me?—as you won't, I must. I was near you at Aston the other day, and hope I soon shall be again. If so, you must and shall meet me, and go to Matlock and elsewhere, and take what, in *flash* dialect,[2] is poetically termed "a lark," with Rogers and me for accomplices. Yesterday, at Holland-house, I was introduced to Southey—the best looking bard I have seen for some time. To have that poet's head and shoulders, I would almost have written his Sapphics. He is certainly a prepossessing person to look on, and a man of talent, and all that, and—*there* is his eulogy.

* * read me *part* of a letter from you. By the foot of Pharaoh, I believe there was abuse, for he stopped short, so he did, after a fine saying about our correspondence, and *looked*—I wish I could revenge myself by attacking you, or by telling you that I have *had* to defend you—an agreeable way which one's friends have of recommending themselves by saying—"Ay, ay, *I* gave it Mr. Such-a-one for what he said about your being a plagiary and a rake, and so on." But do you know that you are one of the very few whom I never have the satisfaction of hearing abused, but the reverse;—and do you suppose I will forgive *that?*

I have been in the country, and ran away from the Doncaster races. It is odd,—I was a visitor in the same house which came to my sire as a residence[3] with Lady Carmarthen (with whom he adulterated before his majority—by the by, remember, *she* was not my mamma)—and they thrust me into an old room, with a nauseous picture over the chimney, which I should suppose my papa regarded with due respect, and which, inheriting the family taste, I looked upon with great satisfaction. I staid a week with the family, and behaved very well— though the lady of the house is young and religious, and pretty, and the master is my particular friend. I felt no wish for anything but a poodle dog, which they kindly gave me.[4] Now, for a man of my courses, not even to have *coveted* is a sign of great amendment.

---

[1] Thomas Learmont of Ercildoune, called "Thomas the Rhymer", was the seer and poet who predicted the battle of Bannockburn. As an oracle he was said to be *"true* Thomas".

[2] A thieves' or underworld language which Byron liked to display his knowledge of on occasion. He introduced some of it into *Don Juan* (Canto XI, stanzas 16–19).

[3] Aston Hall, which Webster was renting.

[4] See Sept. 25, 1813, to Webster, note 1.

Pray pardon all this nonsense, and don't "snub me when i'm in spirits."[5]

Ever yours,
Bn.

Here's an impromptu for you by a "person of quality," written last week, on being reproached for low spirits.

> When from the heart where Sorrow sits,
>   Her dusky shadow mounts too high,
> And o'er the changing aspect flits,
>   And clouds the brow, or fills the eye:
> Heed not that gloom, which soon shall sink;
>   My Thoughts their dungeon know too well—
> Back to my breast the wanderers shrink,
>   And bleed within their silent cell.

[TO LADY MELBOURNE]   *Septr. 28th. 1813*

My dear Lady Melbourne—I sent you a long letter from Aston last week which I hope has been received at *Brocket*.—The Doncaster races (as I *foretold* you) drove me to town but I have an invitation to go down again this week upon which I am pondering—I had reasons of my own some bad & others good for not accompanying the party to D[oncaste]r[1]—my time was passed pleasantly enough—& as innocently at *Aston*—as during the *"week"* of immaculate memory last autumn at Middleton.—If you received my letter you will remember my sketch of the *Astonian* family—when I return I shall complete it— at present I doubt about the colours—I have been observing & have made out one conclusion which is that my friend W[ebster] will run his head against a wall of his own building.—There are a Count & Countess—somebody—(I forget the name of the exiles)—the last of whom made a desperate attack on W. at Ld. Waterpark's[2] a few weeks ago—& W. in gratitude invited them to his house—there I suppose they now are—(they had not arrived when I set out) to me it appears from W's own narrative—that he will be detected & bullied by the

---

[5] In *She Stoops to Conquer* (Act 2) Tony Lumpkin says, "I wish you would let me and my good alone, then—snubbing this way when I'm in spirits." Byron later used this quotation against his friends who wanted to curb his spirits in *Don Juan*.

[1] Byron was pondering going to see Augusta again. His reasons are given in more detail in his letter of Oct. 1, 1813, to Lady Melbourne.

[2] Richard Cavendish, 2nd Baron Waterpark (in the Irish Peerage).

husband into some infernal compromise—& I told him as much—but like *others* of our acquaintance he is deaf as an adder.—I have known him several years & really wish him well—for which reason I overlooked his interference in some concerns of my own where he had no business—perhaps because also they had ceased to interest me—(for we are all selfish & I no more trust myself than others with a good motive) but be that as it may—I wish he would not indulge in such freaks—for which *he* can have no excuse—& the example will turn out none of the best for Ly. F[ann]y.—She seems pretty & intelligent—as far as I observed which was very little—I had & have other things to reflect upon.—Your opinion of ye. Giaour or rather ye. *additions* honours me highly—you who know how my thoughts were occupied when these last were written—will perhaps perceive in parts a coincidence in my own state of mind with that of my hero[3]—if so you will give me credit for feeling—though on the other hand I lose in your esteem.—I have tried & hardly too to vanquish my demon—but to very little purpose—for a resource that seldom failed me before—did in this instance—I mean *transferring* my regards to another—of which I had a very fair & not *discouraging* opportunity at one time—I willingly would—but the feeling that it was an effort spoiled all again—& *here* I am—*what* I am you know already.[4]—As I have never been accustomed to parade my thoughts before you in a larmoyante strain I shall not begin now.—The epistles of your mathematician (*A* would now be ambiguous)[5] continue—& the last concludes with a repetition of a desire that none but Papa & Mamma should know it—why *you* should not seems to me quite ludicrous & is now past praying for—but—observe—here is the strictest of St. Ursula's 11000 what do you call 'ems?[6]—a wit—a moralist—& religionist—enters into a clandestine correspondence with a personage generally presumed a great Roué—& drags her aged parents into this secret treaty—it is I believe not usual for single ladies to risk such brilliant adventures—but this comes

---

[3] Byron was aware that Lady Melbourne knew enough of his present quandaries to read the meaning of some of his additions to *The Giaour*.

[4] Byron knew that Lady Melbourne would be disappointed that he had not transferred his regards to Lady Frances Webster or another as an escape from his more dangerous attachment to Augusta.

[5] Since Byron in his letters to Lady Melbourne used the initial A. to refer to Augusta, he had to find some other way of referring to Annabella Milbanke. He sometimes referred to "your A" (Annabella), and "my A." (Augusta).

[6] A reference to the legend of St. Ursula and her 11,000 virgins. Byron saw their supposed bones in Cologne in his passage up the Rhine in 1816, and he gave a couplet to them in *Don Juan* (Canto X, stanza 62):
Eleven thousand maiden heads of bone./The greatest number flesh hath ever known.

of *infallibility*—not that she ever says anything that might not be said by the Town cryer—still it is imprudent—if I were rascal enough to take an unfair advantage.—Alas! poor human nature—here is your niece writing—& doing a foolish thing—*I lecturing* Webster!—& forgetting the tremendous "beam in my own eye" no—I *do* feel but cannot pluck it out.—These various absurdities & inconsistencies may amuse you—but there is a fate in such small as well as great concerns or how came Moreau by his loss of legs?[7] I saw an extract from his last letter to his wife (in M.S. not published) he says—that *"Coquin de Bonaparte est toujours heureux!"* Good night.

ever yrs.
B

[TO JOHN MURRAY]   *Sep. 29th. 1813*

Dear Sir—Pray suspend the *proofs* for I am *bitten* again & have *quantities* for other parts of ye. Giaour.—

yrs. ever
B

P.S.—You shall have these in the course of the day.—

[TO LADY MELBOURNE]   *Septr. 29th. 1813*

My dear Ly. M[elbourn]e—I have written you a long letter which I don't know whether to send or not—since I came to town—which I leave again on Sunday.—C[aroline]'s communication to ye. Lady who *inherits your eyes* is quite a mistake or what do I *here?*—in my way through Southwell (where I passed a year when eighteen—) I might have been liable to what she calls a "new attachment" or at any rate an old one or two[1]—but the letter I have written you will not please you—as I think you will perceive from it's tone that I have *no newer* attachment.[2]————I am asked again to Aston—& I think I shall

---

[7] Jean Victor Marie Moreau, French general under Napoleon, was mortally wounded at the battle of Dresden. Both his legs were amputated in an attempt to save his life, but he died a few days later.

[1] Caroline Lamb was making guesses as to Byron's "new attachment" but had not guessed right. The lady who inherits Lady Melbourne's eyes is probably her daughter, Lady Cowper. The old attachment in Southwell could be one of the Southwell girls in whom he was briefly interested in 1806.

[2] See Sept. 28, 1813, to Lady Melbourne, note 4.

go because—you shan't have the real because (though it has nothing to do with W[ebster]'s family)³ but instead of *it because*—they gave me a poodle dog which I left there & want to bring away with me— Ly. Blarney [Bessborough]'s *anomaly* delights me beyond every thing —I think I can guess C[aroline]'s question—might it not be how far such a production was independent of "new attachments"⁴—depend upon it she will never rest till she has obtained in a philosophical way all the information which can be seen or heard of such a phenomenon.— How Lady B[essborough] must delight in my being in the secret— though I really don't see any thing so astonishing—in C[aroline]'s telling it to me—unless her Ladyship—but no matter—and Grand-mamma too—I suppose she will certainly found an hospital for the species—& appoint C[aroline] Canoness thereof.—If I write much more I shall run into repetition of my last letter—many thanks for all your own—I suppose the Sultan's communication was about the L[amb]'s & G[eorge] L[amb]'s embarrassments—I don't think Ward is the reviewer of Fox⁵—though he was certain to be suspected— Rogers will never recover *his*—he harps on it yet.—Heigh ho—I have been signing my will today⁶—& must do the same for this letter—

ever yrs. most affectly.

B

[TO JAMES WEDDERBURN WEBSTER]   *Septr. 30th. 1813*

My dear Webster—Thanks for your letter—I had answered it by *anticipation* last night—& this is but a *postscript* to my reply—my yesterdays contains some advice which I now see you dont want—& hope you never will—So—Petersham has not joined you—I pity the poor women—no one can properly repair such a deficiency—but rather than such a chasm should be left utterly unfathomable—I—even I—the most awkward of attendants—& deplorable of danglers would have been of your forlorn hope—on this expedition—nothing but business & the notion of my being utterly superfluous in so numerous a

³ The "real because" was that he had asked Lady Frances Webster to invite Augusta to Aston. See Sept. 30, 1813, to Webster, note 2.

⁴ Caroline was hoping that some of the passages on love in *The Giaour* referred to her.

⁵ In the *Quarterly Review* (Vol. IX, pp. 313–328) for July, 1813, was a critique of *Correspondence of the late Gilbert Wakefield, B.A. with the late Right Hon. Charles James Fox in the Years 1796–1801, chiefly on the Subjects of Classical Literature.* J. W. Ward was the reviewer.

⁶ In his will of 1813 Byron left half his property to Augusta. See Marchand, *Byron: A Biography*, I, 412.

party would have induced me to resign so soon my quiet apartments—never interrupted but by the sound of your swearing or the more harmonious barking of Nettle[1] & clashing of billiard balls.—On Sunday I shall leave town & mean to join you immediately—I have not yet had my sister's answer to Lady Frances's very kind invitation[2]—but expect it tomorrow.—Pray assure Lady Frances that I never can forget the obligation conferred upon me in this respect—and I trust that even Ly. Catherine[3] will in this instance not question my *"stability"*.—I yesterday wrote you rather a long tirade about La Comtesse[4]—but you seem in no immediate peril I will therefore burn it—yet I don't know why I should—as you may relapse—it shall een go.———I have been passing my time with Rogers & Sir James Mackintosh—& once at Holland house I met Southey—he is a person of very *epic* appearance—& has a fine head as far as the outside goes—and wants nothing but taste to make the inside equally attractive.——

ever my dear W. yours
BIRON

P.S.—I read your letter thus "the Countess is *miserable*"—instead of which it is *"inexorable"*—a very different thing—the best way is to let her alone—she must be a *diablesse* by what you told me—you have probably not *bid* high enough—now you are not perhaps of my opinion—but I would not give the tithe of a Birmingham farthing for a woman who could or would be purchased—nor indeed for any woman *quoad mere woman*—that is to say unless I loved her for something more than her sex.—If she *loves*—a little *pique* is not amiss—nor even if she dont—the next thing to a woman's *love* in a man's favour is her *hatred*—a seeming paradox but true—get them once out of *indifference*—and circumstance & their passions will do wonders for a *dasher* which I suppose you are—though I seldom had the impudence or patience to follow them up.

[TO LADY MELBOURNE]   *Septr.—Octr. 1st. 1813*

My dear Ly. M[elbourn]e—You will have received two letters of mine to atone for my late portentous silence & this is intended as a further expiation—I have just been dining at Holland house—the Queen is grown thin & gracious both of which become her royalty—

---

[1] The poodle given to Byron by the Websters.
[2] Lady Frances had invited Augusta to Aston but she could not come.
[3] Lady Frances Webster's sister, Lady Catherine Annesley.
[4] See Sept. 28, 1813, to Lady Melbourne.

I met Curran[1] there who electrified me with his imagination—& delighted me with his humour—he is a man of a million—the Irish *when* good are perfect—the little I have seen of him has less *leaven* than any mortal compound I have lately looked into.—Today I heard from my friend W[ebster] again—his *Countess* is he says "inexorable" what a lucky fellow! happy in his obstacles—in his case I should think them very pleasant—but I don't lay this down as a general proposition.

———All my prospect of amusement is clouded—for Petersham has sent an excuse—& there will be no one to make him jealous of but the Curate & the Butler—& I have no thoughts of setting up for myself—I am not exactly cut out for the Lady of the mansion—but I think a stray Dandy would have a chance of preferment—she evidently expects to be attacked—& seems prepared for a brilliant defence—my character as a Roué had gone before me—& my careless & quiet behaviour astonished her so much that I believe she began to think herself ugly—or me blind—if not worse.—They seemed surprised at my declining the races in particular—but for this I had good reasons—firstly—I wanted to go elsewhere—secondly—if I had gone I must have paid some attention to some of them—which is troublesome unless one has something in memory or hope to induce it—& then mine host is so marvelous greeneyed that he might have included me in his Calenture—which I don't deserve—& probably should not like it a bit the better if I did—I have also reason for returning there on Sunday—with which they have nothing to do[2]—but if C[aroline] takes a suspicious twist *that way*—let her—it will keep her in darkness—but I hope however she won't take a fit of scribbling as she did to Ly. Oxford last year—though Webster's face on the occasion would be quite a Comet—& delight me infinitely more than O[xford]'s which was comic enough.—

Friday Morn.

Yours arrived I will answer on the next page.—

So Ly. H[ollan]d says I am *fattening*—& you say I talk *"nonsense"* well—I must fast & unfool again if possible. But as Curran told me last night that he had been assured upon oath by half the Court that "the Prince was *not* at all *corpulant*—that he was stout certainly but by no means protuberant—or obese—['] "there's comfort yet" as to folly—that's incurable.—"See C[aroline]!—*if* I should see C!"—I hope not—

---

[1] John Philpot Curran (1750–1817) had been Master of the Rolls in Ireland, but he was chiefly noted for his brilliant conversation, which made him a popular guest in Whig society in London. Byron wrote enthusiastically of him in his "Detached Thoughts" (Numbers 24 and 41), and he spoke of him in a similar manner to Lady Blessington (*Conversations*, Lovell ed., p. 107).

[2] See Sept. 30, 1813, to Lady Melbourne, note 2.

though I am not sure a visit would be so disagreeable as it ought to be—"I pique myself on Constancy" but it is but a sensitive plant & thrives best by itself.——Then there is the story of Ly. B[ess-borough]'s novelty—which I am sure she longs to unravel—how your passage on "the kneeling in the *middle* of the room" made me laugh this morning—it certainly was not the centre of gravity—pardon a wretched quibble which I don't often hazard.—I did not kneel in the middle of the room—but the first time I saw her this year—she thought proper to fix herself there & turn away her head—& as one does not kneel exactly for one's own convenience—my genuflexions would have been all lost upon her if she did not perceive them.——To return to the W[ebster]'s—I am glad they amuse you—anything that confirms or extends one's observations on life & character delights me even when I don't know people—for this reason—I would give the world to pass a month with Sheridan or any lady or gentleman of the old school—& hear them talk every day & all day of themselves & acquaintance —& all they have heard & seen in their lives.——W[eb-ster] seems in no present peril—I believe the woman is mercenary—& I happen to know that he can't at present bribe her—I told him that it would be known—& that he must expect reprisals—& what do you think was his answer?—"I think any woman fair game—because I can *depend* upon Ly. F[rances]'s principles—she can't go wrong—& there-fore I may["]—["]then why are you jealous of her?["]——["]because —because—zounds I am not jealous—why the devil do you suppose I am?—["]I then enumerated some very gross symptons which he had displayed even before her face—& his servants—which he could not deny—but persisted in his determination to add to his "bonnes fortunes"—it is a strange being—when I came home in 1811—he was always saying—["]B—do marry—it is the happiest &c.—["] the first thing he said on my arrival at A[ston] was "B—whatever you do *don't marry*" which considering he had an unmarried sister in law in the house was a very *un*necessary precaution.————Every now & then he has a fit of fondness—& kisses her hand before his guests—which she receives with the most lifeless indifference—which struck me more than if she had appeared pleased or annoyed—her brother told me last year that she married to get rid of her family—(who are ill tempered) —& had not been *out* two months so that to use a foxhunting phrase she was "killed in covert".—You have enough of them & me for ye present.

yrs. ever
B

P.S.—I do not wish to know ye. person's name—but to whom is the likeness—to *me* or to *her?*—

[TO FRANCIS HODGSON]   *October 1, 1813*

My dear H.—I leave town again for Aston on Sunday, but have messages for you. Lord Holland desired me repeatedly to bring you; he wants to know you much, and begged me to say so; you will like him. I had an invitation for you to dinner there this last Sunday, and Rogers is perpetually screaming because you don't call, and wanted you also to dine with him on Wednesday last. Yesterday we had Curran there—who is beyond all conception!—and Mackintosh and the wits are to be seen at H[olland] H[ouse] constantly, so that I think you would like their society. I will be a judge between you and the attorneo. So B[utler] may mention me to Lucien if he still adheres to his opinion.[1] Pray let Rogers be one; he has the best taste extant. Bland's nuptials delight me; if I had the least hand in bringing them about it will be a subject of selfish satisfaction to me these three weeks.[2] Desire Drury— if he loves me—to kick Dwyer thrice for frightening my horses with his flame-coloured whiskers last July. Let the kicks be hard, etc.

[TO THOMAS MOORE]   *October [1]–2, 1813*

You have not answered some six letters of mine. This, therefore, is my penultimate. I will write to you once more, but, after that—I swear by all the saints—I am silent and supercilious. I have met Curran at Holland-house[1]—he beats every body;—his imagination is beyond human, and his humour (it is difficult to define what is wit) perfect. Then he has fifty faces, and twice as many voices, when he mimics;— I never met his equal. Now, were I a woman, and eke a virgin, that is

---

[1] Dr. Samuel Butler, Headmaster of Shrewsbury, was translating, in collaboration with Hodgson, Lucien Buonaparte's poem *Charlemagne*. Byron was eager to meet him (Lucien), partly because he was a brother of the Emperor, and partly because he admired the poem which he had seen.

[2] Robert Bland, Hodgson's friend. There is a suggestion in a note of Hodgson to this letter that Byron gave financial assistance to Bland, as he did to Hodgson, that enabled him to marry. Hodgson wrote: "Were it possible to state *all* he [Byron] has done for numerous friends, he would appear amiable indeed. For myself, I am bound to acknowledge, in the fullest and warmest manner, his most generous and well-timed aid; and, were my poor friend Bland alive [he died in 1825], he would as gladly bear the like testimony. (Moore, I, 195)

[1] See Oct. 1, 1813, to Lady Melbourne, note 1.

the man I should make my Scamander. He is quite fascinating. Remember, I have met him but once; and you, who have known him long, may probably deduct from my panegyric. I almost fear to meet him again, lest the impression should be lowered. He talked a great deal about you—a theme never tiresome to me, nor any body else that I know. What a variety of expression he conjures into that naturally not very fine countenance of his! He absolutely changes it entirely. I have done—for I can't describe him, and you know him. On Sunday I return to * * [Aston], where I shall not be far from you. Perhaps I shall hear from you in the mean time. Good night.

Saturday Morn.—Your letter has cancelled all my anxieties. I did *not suspect* you in *earnest*. Modest again! Because I don't do a very shabby thing, it seems, I "don't fear your competition." If it were reduced to an alternative of preference, I *should* dread you, as much as Satan does Michael. But is there not room enough in our respective regions? Go on—it will soon be my turn to forgive. To-day I dine with Mackintosh and Mrs. *Stale* [de Staël]—as John Bull may be pleased to denominate Corinne—whom I saw last night, at Covent-garden, yawning over the humour of Falstaff.

The reputation of "gloom," if one's friends are not included in the *reputants*, is of great service; as it saves one from a legion of impertinents, in the shape of common-place acquaintance. But thou know'st I can be a right merry and conceited fellow, and rarely "larmoyant." Murray shall reinstate your line forthwith. I believe the blunder in the motto was mine;[2]—and yet I have, in general, a memory for *you*, and am sure it was rightly printed at first.

I do "blush" very often, if I may believe Ladies H[olland?] and M[elbourne?]—but luckily, at present, no one sees me. Adieu.

[TO JOHN MURRAY]   *Oct. 2 1813*

Dear Sir—The lines are certainly *lost* there is no proof of them whatever.

yrs. *B.*

There were 82—sent on Wednesday.

---

[2] Byron had misquoted a passage from one of Moore's *Irish Melodies*, "As a beam o'er the face," in the early editions of *The Giaour*, but corrected it in later editions.

Dear Sir—I have just recollected an alteration you may make in the proof to be sent to Aston—among the lines on Hassan's Serai not far from the beginning is this—

"Unmeet for Solitude to share"

now to share implies more than *one*—& Solitude is a single gentleman —it must be thus—

"For many a gilded chamber's there
Which Solitude might well forbear["]

& so on.—My address is Aston Hall Rotherham. Will you adopt this correction—& pray accept a *cheese* from me for your trouble.—

ever yrs.

B

P.S.—I leave this to your discretion if anybody thinks the old line a good one—or the cheese a bad one don't accept either.—but in that case—the word *share* is repeated soon after in the line "to *share* the Master's 'bread & salt'" & must be altered to—"to break the Master's" bread & salt[;] this is not so well though—confound it.—If the old line stands let the other run thus

"Nor there will weary stranger halt
To bless the sacred 'bread & salt'"

Note—To partake of food—to break bread & taste salt with your host—ensures the safety of the guest even though an enemy—his person from that moment becomes sacred. There is another additional note sent yesterday—on the Priest in the Confessional.—

[TO JOHN MURRAY]   *Aston Hall, Rotherham   Oct. 4, 1813*

In the proof from the "Curse" alter this line "Whose arts and arms but live in poet's lore" to "Whose arts revive, whose arms avenge no more."[1] Remember this.

[TO LADY MELBOURNE]   *Aston Hall, Rotherham   Octr. 5th. 1813*

My dear Ly. M[elbourn]e—W[ebster] has lost his Countess—his time—& his temper—(I would advise anyone who finds the *last* to

---

[1] This correction in *The Curse of Minerva*, which was privately printed in a few quarto copies for Byron by Murray's printer, T. Davison, in 1812, was not made, probably because the revised printing which he apparently contemplated was not accomplished.

return it immediately—it is of no use to any but the owner—) Ly. F[rances] has lost Petersham for the present at least—the other sister as I said before has lost Ld. Bury—& I—have nobody to lose—*here* at least—& am not very anxious to find one.—Here be two friends of the family—besides your slave—a Mr. Westcombe[1] very handsome but silly—& a Mr. Agar[2] frightful but facetious—the whole party are out in carriages—a species of amusement from which I always *avert*— & consequently declined it today—it is very well with two—but not beyond a *duet*—I think being bumped about between two or more of one's acquaintance intolerable.—W[ebster] grows rather intolerable too—he is out of humour with my *Italian* books—(Dante & Alfieri & some others as harmless as ever wrote) & requests that sa femme may not see them—because forsooth it is a language which doth infinite damage!! & because I enquired after the Stanhopes our mutual acquaintance—he *answers* me by another *question*—"pray do you enquire after *my* wife of others in the same way?—so that you see my Virtue is it's own reward—for never in word or deed—did I speculate upon his spouse—nor did I ever see much in her to encourage either hope or much fulfilment of hope—supposing I had any.—She is pretty but not surpassing—too thin—& not very animated—but good tempered—& a something interesting enough in her manner & figure—but I never should think of her nor anyone else—if left to my own cogitations—as I have neither the patience nor presumption to advance till met half-way.—The other two pay her ten times more attention—& of course are more attended to—I really believe he is bilious & suspects something extraordinary from my nonchalance—at all events he has hit upon the wrong person.—I can't help laughing to you—but he will soon make me very serious with him—& then he will come to his senses again—the oddest thing is that he wants me to stay with him some time—which I am not much inclined to do—unless the gentleman transfers his fretfulness to some one else.—I have written to you so much lately—you will be glad to be spared from any further account of the "Blunderhead family".

ever yrs. my dear Ly. Me.
B

[TO LADY MELBOURNE]   *Octr 8th. 1813*

My dear Ly. M[elbourn]e—I have volumes—but neither time nor space—I have already trusted too deeply to hesitate now—besides for

---

[1] Unidentified.
[2] Unidentified.

certain reasons you will not be sorry to hear that I am anything but what I was.—Well then—to begin—& first a word of mine host—he has lately been talking *at* rather than *to* me before the party (with the exception of the women) in a tone—which as I never use it myself I am not particularly disposed to tolerate in others—what *he* may do with impunity—it seems—but not suffer—till at last I told him that the whole of his argument involved the interesting contradiction that "he might love where he liked but that no one else might like what he ever thought proper to love" a doctrine which as the learned Partridge observed[1]—contains a "non sequitur" from which I for one begged leave as a general proposition to dissent.—This nearly produced a scene—with me as well as another guest who seemed to admire my sophistry the most of the two—& as it was after dinner & debating time—might have ended in more than wineshed—but that the Devil for some wise purpose of his own thought proper to restore good humour—which has not as yet been further infringed.—————In these last few days I have had a good deal of conversation with an amiable persion—whom (as we deal in *letters*—& initials only) we will denominate *Ph.*[Frances]—well—these things are dull in detail—take it once—I have made love—& if I am to believe mere *words* (for there we have hitherto stopped) it is returned.—I must tell you the place of declaration however—a billiard room!—I did not as C[aroline] says "kneel in the middle of the room" but like Corporal Trim to the Nun—"I made a speech"[2]—which as you might not listen to it with the same patience—I shall not transcribe.—We were before on very amiable terms—& I remembered being asked an odd question—"how a woman who liked a man could inform him of it—when he did not perceive it"—I also observed that we went on with our game (of billiards) without *counting* the *hazards*—& supposed that—as mine certainly were not—the thoughts of the other party also were not exactly occupied by what was our ostensible pursuit.—Not quite though pretty well satisfied with my progress—I took a very im-

[1] Partridge, the learned schoolmaster in Fielding's *Tom Jones*, replied to the sergeant who said, ". . . every man who curses the cloth would curse the king if he durst," "Excuse me there, Mr. Sergeant, that's a *non sequitur*." (Book IX, Chapter 6.)

[2] Corporal Trim, in telling his story of how the Beguine roused his passions by rubbing his wounded knee, ended by saying "I seized her hand—" and Uncle Toby interposed, "And then thou clapped'st it to thy lips, Trim, . . . and madest a speech." Tristram commented: "Whether the corporal's amour terminated precisely in the way my uncle Toby described it is immaterial . . ." (Sterne, *Tristram Shandy*, Book VIII, Chapter 22.) Byron may have wanted Lady Melbourne to think the same.

prudent step—with pen & paper—in tender & tolerably turned *prose* periods (no *poetry* even when in earnest) here were risks certainly—first how to convey—then how it would be received—it was received however & deposited not very far from the heart which I wished it to reach—when who should enter the room but the person who ought at that moment to have been in the Red sea if Satan had any civility—but *she* kept her countenance & the paper—& I my composure as well as I could.—It was a risk—& *all* had been lost by failure—but then re-collect—how much more I had to gain by the reception—if not de-clined—& how much one always hazards to obtain anything worth having.—My billet prospered—it did more—it even (I am this moment interrupted by the *Marito*—& write this before him—he has brought me a political pamphlet in M.S. to decypher & applaud—I shall content myself with the last—Oh—he is gone again)—my billet produced an *answer*—a very unequivocal one too—but a little too much about virtue—& indulgence of attachment in some sort of etherial process in which the soul is principally concerned—which I don't very well understand—being a bad metaphysician—but one generally *ends* & *begins* with Platonism—& as my proselyte is only twenty—there is time enough to materialize—I hope nevertheless this spiritual system won't last long—& at any rate must make the experiment.—I remem-ber my last case was the reverse—as Major O'Flaherty recommends "we fought first & explained afterwards."—This is the present state of things—much mutual profession—a good deal of melancholy—which I am sorry to say was remarked by "the Moor" & as much love as could well be made considering the time place & circumstances.——I need not say that the folly & petulance of —— [Webster] have tended to all this—if a man is not contented with a pretty woman & not only runs after any little country girl he meets with but absolutely boasts of it—he must not be surprised if others admire that which he knows not how to value—besides he literally provoked & goaded me into it—by something not unlike bullying—*indirect* to be sure—but tolerably obvious—"he *would* do this—& he would do that—if any man["] &c. &c.—& *he* thought that every woman "was *his* lawful prize nevertheless["]—Oons! who is this strange monopolist?—it is odd enough but on other subjects he is like other people but on this he seems infatuated—if he had been rational—& not prated of his pursuits —I should have gone on very well—as I did at Middleton—even now I shan't quarrel with him—if I can help it—but one or two of his speeches has blackened the blood about my heart—& curdled the milk of kindness—if put to the proof—I shall behave like other people I

135

presume.—I have heard from A[nnabella]—but her letter to me is *melancholy*—about her old friend Miss M[ontgomer]y's[3] departure &c. —&c.—I wonder who will have her at last—her letter to you is *gay*— you say—that to me must have been written at the same time—the little demure Nonjuror!————I wrote to C[aroline] the other day— for I was afraid she might repeat the last year's epistle—& make it *circular* among my friends.————Good evening—I am now going to *billiards.*—

P.S. 6 o'clock—This business is growing serious—& I think *Platonism* in some peril—There has been very nearly a scene—almost an *hysteric* & really without cause for I was conducting myself with (to me) very irksome decorum—her *expressions* astonish me—so young & cold as she appeared—but these professions must end as usual—& *would*— I think—*now*—had "l'occasion" been *not* wanting—had any one come in during the *tears* & consequent consolation all had been spoiled—we must be more cautious or less larmoyante.———

P.S. second—10 o'clock—I write to you just escaped from Claret & vociferation—on G–d knows what paper—my Landlord is a rare gentleman—he has just proposed to me a bet "that *he* for a certain sum wins any given *woman*—against any given *homme* including *all friends* present["]—which I declined with becoming deference to him & the rest of the company—is not this at this moment a perfect comedy?— I forgot to mention that on his entrance yesterday during the letter scene—it reminded me so much of an awkward passage in "the Way to keep him"[4] between Lovemore—Sir Bashful—& my Lady—that embarrassing as it was I could hardly help laughing—I hear his voice in the passage—he wants me to go to a ball at Sheffield—& is talking to me as I write—Good Night. I am in the act of praising his pamphlet.— I don't half like your story of *Corinne*—some day I will tell you why— If I can—but at present—Good Night.

[TO LADY MELBOURNE]   *Newstead Abbey Octr. 10th. 1813*

My dear Ly. M[elbourn]e—I write to you from the melancholy mansion of my fathers—where I am dull as the longest deceased of my

[3] Mary Milicent Montgomery, an invalid, had been Annabella's friend from girlhood. Her brother, Hugh Montgomery, was one of Annabella's early suitors, as she later confessed to Byron.
[4] *The Way to Keep Him*, a comedy by Arthur Murphy (1760). The "awkward passage" occurs in Act V, scene 1, when Lovemore's love letter to another woman is discovered to his wife.

progenitors—I hate reflection on irrevocable things & won't now turn sentimentalist. W[ebster] alone accompanied me here (I return tomorrow to Aston) he is now sitting opposite—& between us are Red & white Champ[agn]e—Burgundy—two sorts of Claret—& lighter vintages—the relics of my youthful cellar which is yet in formidable number & famous order—but I leave the wine to him—& prefer conversing soberly with you.—Ah! if you knew what a quiet Mussulman life (except in wine) I led here for a few years—but no matter.—Yesterday I sent you a long letter & must now recur to the same subject which is uppermost in my thoughts.—I am as much astonished but I hope not so much mistaken as Lord Ogleby[1] at the denouement or rather commencement of the last week—it has changed my views—my wishes—my hopes—my everything—& will furnish you with additional proof of my weakness.—Mine guest (late host) has just been congratulating himself on possessing a partner without *passion*—I don't know—& cannot yet speak with certainty—but I never yet saw more decisive preliminary symptoms.————As I am apt to take people at their word—on receiving my answer—that whatever the weakness of her heart might be—I should never derive further proof of it than the confession—instead of pressing the point—I told her that I was willing to be hers on her own terms & should never attempt to infringe upon the conditions—I said this without pique—& believing her perfectly in earnest for the time—but in the midst of our mutual professions or to use her own expression "more than mutual" she burst into an agony of crying—& at such a time & in such a place as rendered such a scene particularly perilous to both—her sister in the next room—& —— [Webster] not far off—of course I said & did almost everything proper on the occasion—& fortunately we restored sunshine in time to prevent anyone from perceiving the cloud that had darkened our horizon.—She says—she is convinced that my own declaration was produced solely because I perceived her previous penchant—which by the bye—as I think I said to you before—I neither perceived nor expected—I really did not suspect her of a predilection for anyone—& even now in public with the exception of those little indirect yet mutually understood—I don't know how & it is unnecessary to name or describe them—her conduct is as coldly correct as her still—fair—Mrs. L[amb] like aspect.—She however managed to give me a note—& to receive another & a ring before —— [Webster]'s very face—& yet she is a thorough devotee—& takes prayers morning

---

[1] Lord Ogleby is a superannuated peer who affects the manners of a youth in *The Clandestine Marriage* by Garrick and the elder Colman.

and evening—besides being measured for a new bible once a quarter.—
The only alarming thing—is that —— [Webster] complains of her
aversion from being beneficial to population & posterity—if this is an
invariable maxim—I shall lose my labour.—Be this as it may—she
owns to more—than I ever heard from any woman within the time—&
I shan't take —— [Webster]'s word any more for her feelings than I
did for that celestial comparison which I once mentioned.—I think her
eye—her change of colour—& the trembling of her hand—& above all
her devotion tell a different tale.—Good night—we return tomorrow
—& now I drink your health—you are my only correspondent & I
believe friend—

ever yrs.

B

[TO AUGUSTA LEIGH]   *October 10th. 1813*

My dearest Augusta—I have only time to say that I am not in the
least angry—& that my silence has merely arisen from several circumstances which I cannot now detail—I trust you are better—& will
continue *best*—ever my dearest

yrs.

B

[TO JOHN HANSON (*a*)]   *Octr. 10th. 1813*

Dear Sir—Claughton has *broken* open the *cellar*!—You must talk to
him of this—I trust he has no more than a temporary possession—till
he pays up the price—I enclose you a letter & have time for no more.—
Pray address to Aston Hall—Rotherham.—

ever yrs.

B

[TO JOHN HANSON (*b*)]   *Octr. 10th. 1813*

Dear Sir—I am disposed to advance a loan of 1000 £ to James
Webster Wedderburne Webster Esqre. of Aston Hall York County—
& request you will address to me *there* a *bond* & *judgement* to be signed
by the said as soon as possible.—Of Claughton's payments I know
nothing further—and the demands on myself I know also—but

W[ebster] is a very old friend of mine—& a man of property—& as I can command the money he shall have it—I do not at all wish to inconvenience you—& I also know that when we balance accounts it will be much in your favour—but if you could replace the sum at Hoares from my advance of two thousand eight hundred in July—it would be a favour—or still better if C[laughton] makes further payments—which will render it unnecessary.—Don't let the first part of the last sentence embarrass you at all—the last part about Claughton I could wish you to attend to—I have written this day—about his opening the cellar.—Pray send the bond & judgement to Aston as directed—

ever dr. Sir
B

P.S.—Many many thanks for your kind invitation—but it was too late—I was in this county before it arrived—My best remembrances to Mrs. H. & all the family.———

[TO LADY MELBOURNE]   *Octr. 11th. 1813*

My dear Ly. M[elbourn]e—C[aroline] is angry with me for having written by the *post* not a *very cold* letter—but below (it seems) her freezing point—pray—say something—anything to prevent any of the old absurdities—her letter arrived during my absence at N[ewstead] with a never sufficiently to be confounded seal—with C—at full length on the malignant wax—this must have been to answer the purpose it effected—at any rate—the person who opened the *bag* was the last I wished to see the *impression*—and it is not yet *effaced*—but it shall be—this is not to be endured—that my "chienne of a Star" as Captain Ragaddo says[1]—should have produced such an incident—& at such a time!————I have written to you so much—& so frequently that you must be sick of the sight of my scrawls——I believe all the *Stars* are no better than they should be —— [Webster] is on the verge of a precious scrape—his quondam *tutor*! & ally who has done him some not very reputable services since his marriage—writing I believe his billets—& assisting him to those to whom they were addressed—being now discarded—threatens a development &c.— —— [Webster] consults me on the subject!—of this I shall take no advantage in another quarter however convenient—if I gain my point it shall be as fairly—

[1] Unidentified.

as such things will admit—it is odd enough that his name has never hitherto been taken in vain by her or me.———I have told him that if the discovery is inevitable—*his* best way is to anticipate it & sue for an act of indemnity—if she likes him she will forgive—& if she don't like him it don't matter whether she does or no.———From me she shall never hear of it.———It is three in the morning—& I cannot rest but I must try—I have been at N[ewstead] & between that & this—my mind is in a state of chaotic inaction—but you won't pity & I don't deserve it—was there ever such a slave to impulse? as

yrs. ever

B

Monday—Afternoon—

I am better today—but not much advanced—I began the week so well that I thought the conclusion would have been more decisive— but the topography of this house is not the most favourable—I wonder how my father managed—but he had it not till Ly. Carmarthen came with it too—we shall be at N[ewstead] again the whole party for a week in a few days and there the Genii of the place will be perhaps more propitious—*he* haunts me—here he is again—and here are a party of purple stockings come to dine—Oh that accursed pamphlet! I have not read it what shall I say to the author now in the room? thank the Stars which I yesterday abused he is diverted by the Mirror opposite—& is now surveying himself with great complacency—he is gone—Your letter has arrived—but is evidently written before my last three have been delivered.—Adieu for the present—I must dress— & have got to *sheer* one of those precious curls on which you say I set so high a value—& I cannot & *would* not play the same pass you may laughingly remember on a similar occasion with C[aroline].[2]—My proselyte is so young a beginner—that you must wonder at these exchanges & mummeries—you are right—she is "very pretty"—& not so inanimate as I imagined—& must at least be allowed an excellent taste!!———

10 o'clock—

Nearly a scene—(always *nearly*) at dinner—there is a Lady Sitwell[3] a wit & blue—& what is more to the purpose a dark tall fine looking

[2] Byron had sent a lock of Lady Oxford's hair instead of his own to Caroline Lamb.

[3] Sarah Caroline, daughter of James Stovin of Whitgift Hall, Yorkshire, married Sir Sitwell Sitwell (created a baronet in 1808). It was at a party at her house in Seymour Road in 1814 that Byron saw Mrs. Wilmot in a spangled dress and was inspired to write "She walks in Beauty like the Night". (See *LJ*, III, 92n.)

conversable personage—as it is usual to separate the women at table I was under the necessity of placing myself between her & the sister— & was seated & in the agonies of conjecture whether the dish before me required carving—when my little Platonist exclaimed "Ld. B— *this* is your place" I stared—& before I had time to reply she repeated looking like C[aroline] when *gentle* (for she is very unlike that fair creature when angry) "Ld. B—change places with Catherine" I did & very willingly—though awkwardly—but "the Moor" (mine host) roared out "B—that is the most ungallant thing I ever beheld"—and Lady Catherine by way of mending matters answered—"did not you hear Frances ask him?"—*he* has looked like the Board of *Green* Cloth ever since—& is now mustering wine & spirits for a lecture to her—& a squabble with me—he had better let it alone—for I am in a pestilent humour at this present writing—& shall certainly disparage his eternal "*pamphlet*".—Good Even—I solicit your good wishes in all good deeds—& your occasional remembrance.—

[TO JOHN MURRAY] *Octr. 12th. 1813*

Dear Sir—You must look the Giaour again over carefully—there are a few lapses particularly in the last page—'I *know* 'twas false— she could not die"—it was & ought to be I *knew* pray observe this & similar mistakes.——I have received & read the British Review[1]— I really think the writer in most parts very right—the only mortifying thing is the assertion of imitation—*Crabbes'* passage I never saw—& Scott I no further meant to follow than in his *Lyric* measure—which is Gray's—Milton's & any one's who likes it.—The Giaour is certainly a bad character—but not dangerous—& I think his fate & his feelings will meet with few proselytes.—I shall be very glad to hear from or of you when you please—but don't put yourself out of your way on my account—

yrs. ever
B

[TO LADY MELBOURNE] *Octr. 13th. 1813*

My dear Ly. M[elbourn]e— You must pardon the quantity of my letters & much of the *quality* also—but I have really no other *confiden*-

[1] The *British Review* (No. IX, pp. 132–135) said that Byron "had the bad taste to imitate Mr. Walter Scott", and it accused him of borrowing from Crabbe's *Resentment*.

tial correspondent on earth—& much to say which may call forth that advice which has so often been to me of essential service.—Any thing you will allow is better than the *last*[1]—& I cannot exist without some object of attachment—you will laugh at my perpetual *changes*—but recollect the circumstances which have broken off the last three[2]—& don't exactly attribute their conclusion to caprice—I think you will at least admit whatever C[aroline] may assert that I did not use her ill—though I find *her own* story even in this part of the world to be the *genuine* narrative—as to Ly. O[xford] that I did to please you—& luckily finding it pleasant to myself also & very useful to C[aroline] it might have lasted longer but for the voyage—I spare you the third.— I am so spoilt by intellectual *drams*—that I begin to believe that *danger* & *difficulty* render these things more piquant to my taste—as far as the *former* goes—C[aroline] might have suited me very well—but though we may admire *drams*—nobody is particularly fond of Aqua fortis—at least I should have liked it a *little diluted*—the liquid I believe which is now slowly mingling in my cup.—In the mean time let us laugh while we can—for I see no reason why you should be tormented with sentimental or solid sorrows of your acquaintance—I think you will allow that I have as little of that affectation as any person of similar pursuits.———I mentioned to you yesterday a laughable occurrence at dinner—this morning *he* [Webster] burst forth with a homily upon the subject to the *two*—& myself—instead of taking us separately (like the last of the *Horatii* with the *Curiatii*) you will easily suppose with such odds he had the worst of it, and the satisfaction of being laughed at into the bargain.—Serious as I am—or seem—I really cannot frequently keep my countenance—yesterday—*before my face*—they disputed about their apartments at N[ewstead]—*she* insisting that her sister should share her room—& he very properly—but heinously out of place—maintaining & proving to his own satisfaction that none but husbands have any legal claim to divide their spouses' pillow—you may suppose notwithstanding the ludicrous effect of the scene I felt & looked a little uncomfortable—this she must have seen for of course I said not a word & turning round at the close of the dialogue—she whispered "N'importe—this is all nothing" an am- biguous sentence which I am puzzled to translate—but as it was meant to console me I was very glad to hear it, though quite unintelligible.— As far as I can pretend to judge of her disposition & character—I will say—of course I am partial.—She is—you know—very handsome—&

[1] With Augusta.
[2] Caroline Lamb, Lady Oxford, and Augusta.

very gentle though sometimes decisive—fearfully romantic—& singularly warm in her *affections* but I should think—of a *cold* temperament —yet I have my doubts on that point too—accomplished (as all decently educated women are) & clever though her style a little too *German*—no dashing nor desperate talker—but never—and I have watched in *mixed* conversation—saying a silly thing—(*duet dialogues* in course between young & Platonic people must be varied with a little checquered absurdity) good tempered—(always excepting Ly O[x-ford]'s—which was outwardly the *best* I ever beheld) and jealous as *myself*—the ne plus ultra of green eyed Monstrosity—seldom abusing other people but listening to it with great patience—these qualifications with an unassuming and sweet voice & very soft manner constitute the *bust* (all I can yet pretend to model) of my present Idol.——

You who know me & my weakness so well—will not be surprised when I say that I am totally absorbed in this passion—that I am even ready to take a *flight* if necessary—& as she says—"we *cannot* part"—it is no impossible denouement—though as yet *one* of us at least does not think of it—W[ebster] will probably want to cut my throat— which would not be a difficult task—for I trust I should not return the fire of a man I had injured though I could not refuse him the pleasure of trying me as a target.—But I am not sure I shall not have more work in that way—there is a friend in the house—who looks a little suspicious—he can only conjecture—but if he *Iagonizes* or finds or makes mischief—let him look to it.——To W[ebster] I am decidedly wrong —yet—he almost provoked me into it—*he* loves other women—at least he follows them—*she* evidently did not love him even before—I came here with no plan—no intention of the kind—(as my former letters will prove to *you* the only person to whom I care about proving it) & I have not yet been here *ten* days—a week yesterday on recollection—you cannot be more astonished than I am how & why all this has happened.———All my correspondences—& every other business are at a stand still—I have not answered A[ugusta]—no—nor B—nor C[aroline] nor any *initial* except your own.—you will wish me to be less troublesome to *that one*—& I shall now begin to draw at longer dates upon yr. patience

ever yrs.
B

P.S.—*Always P.S.*—I begged you to pacify C[aroline] who is pettish about what she calls a *cold* letter—it was not so—but she evidently has been too long quiet—she threatens me with growing very bad—& says that if so "I am the sole cause" this I should regret but she is in no danger—no one in his senses will run the risk till her late exploits are forgotten. Her last I shall not answer—it was very silly in me to write at all—but I did it with the best intention like the Wiseacre in "the Rovers"—"let us by a song conceal our purposes" you remember it in "the Antijacobin".———I have gone through a catechism about her without abusing or betraying her—which is not exactly the way to recommend myself—I have generally found that the *successor* likes to hear both of the last regnante. But I really did not—notwithstanding the temptation.———

[TO LADY MELBOURNE]   *Octr. 14th. 1813*

But this is "le premier pas" my dear Ly. M[elbourn]e at least I think so & perhaps you will be of my opinion—when you consider the *age*—the *country*—& the short time since such a *pas* became probable.— I believe little but "l'occasion manque" & to that many things are tending.—He [Webster] is a little *indirect* blunderer—who neither knows what he would have nor what he deserves—today at breakfast (I was too late for the scene) he attacked *both* the girls in such a manner—no one knew why or wherefore—that on my arrival I found one had left the room—& the other had half a mind to leave the house —this too before servants & the other guest! on my appearance the storm blew over—but the narrative was detailed to me subsequently by one of the sufferers.—You may be sure that I shall not "consider *self*" nor create a squabble while it can be avoided—on the contrary I have been endeavouring to serve him essentially—(except on the *one* point & there I was goaded into it by his own absurdity) & extricate him from some difficulties of various descriptions[1]—of course all obligations are cancelled between two persons in our circumstances— but that I shall not dwell upon—of the other I shall try to make an "affaire reglee" if that don't succeed we shall probably go off together —but *she* only shall make me resign the hope—as for him he may convert his Antlers into *powder-horns*—& welcome—& such he has announced as his intention when "*any* man—at *any time* &c. &c[,"] "*he* would not give *him* a chance but exterminate *him* without suffering defence["] do you know—I was fool enough to lose my temper at this circuitous specimen of Bobadil jealousy—& tell him & the other (there are a brace—Lion & Jackall) that *I*—not their roundabout *he*—desired

---

[1] Byron had offered to lend Webster £1,000. See Oct. 10, 1813, to Hanson (*b*).

no better than to put these "epithets of war" with which their sentences were "horribly stuffed" to the proof—this was silly & suspicious but my liver could bear it no longer. My poor little *Helen* tells me that there never was such a *temper* & *talents*—that the marriage was *not* one of attachment—that—in short *my* descriptions fade before hers—all foolish fellows are alike—but this has a patent for his cap & bells. ——The scene between Sir B[ashful] & Lovemore I remember—but the one I alluded to was the letter of Lovemore to Ly. Constant[2]—there is no comedy after all like real life.—We have progressively improved into a less spiritual species of tenderness—but the seal is not yet fixed though the wax is preparing for the impression.—There *ought* to be an excellent *occasion* tomorrow—but who can command circumstances? the most we can do is to avail ourselves of them.———*Publicly* I have been cautious enough—& actually declined a dinner where they went—because I thought something *intelligible* might be seen or suspected—I regretted but regret it less for I hear one of the Fosters[3] was there—& they be cousins & Gossips of our good friends the D[evonshire]'s—Good Night—do *you fear* to write to *me*? are *these* epistles or your answers in any peril *here*—I must remember however the advice of a sage personage to me while abroad—take it in their English—"remember—milor—that delica*ci* ensure every succ*ès*"[4]

yrs. ever
B

[TO LADY MELBOURNE]　　　　*Newstead Abbey—Octr. 17th. 1813*

My dear Ly. M[elbourn]e—The whole party are here—and now to my narrative.—But first I must tell you that I am rather unwell owing to a folly of last night—About midnight after deep and drowsy potations I took it into my head to empty my *skull cup* which holds rather better than a bottle of Claret at *one draught*—and nearly died the death of Alexander—which I shall be content to do when I have achieved his conquests—I had just sense enough left to feel that I was not fit to join the ladies—& went to bed—where my Valet tells me that I was first convulsed & afterwards so motionless that he thought "Good Night

---

[2] See Oct. 8, 1813, to Lady Melbourne, note 3.

[3] The Fosters were closely related to the Devonshire House circle of Lady Caroline Lamb. George Lamb had married the daughter of Lady Elizabeth Foster, who became the second Duchess of Devonshire.

[4] Some years later Byron told the same story, ascribing the saying to a French entremetteuse he had met when he was sowing his first wild oats in London in 1806. See the second letter to Bowles, *LJ*, V, 575.

to Marmion."—I don't know how I came to do so very silly a thing—but I believe my guests were boasting—& "company villainous company hath been the spoil of me" I detest drinking in general—& beg your pardon for this excess—I *can't* do so any more.——To my theme—you were right—I have been a little too sanguine—as to the *conclusion*—but hear.—One day left entirely to ourselves was nearly fatal—another such *victory* & with Pyrrhus we were lost——it came to this—"I am entirely at your *mercy*—I own it—I give myself up to you—I am not *cold*—whatever I seem to others—but I know that I cannot bear the reflection hereafter—do not imagine that these are mere words—I tell you the truth—now act as you will—["] was I wrong?—I spared her.—There was a something so very peculiar in her manner—a kind of mild decision—no scene—not even a struggle—but still I know not what that convinced me she was serious—it was not the mere "*No*" which one has heard forty times before—& always with the same accent—but the *tone*—and the aspect—yet I sacrificed much—the hour *two* in the morning——away—the Devil whispering that it was mere *verbiage* &c.—& yet I know not whether I can regret it—she seems so very thankful for my forbearance—a proof at least that she was not playing merely the usual decorous reluctance which is sometimes so tiresome on these occasions.——You ask if I am prepared to go "all lengths" if you mean by "all lengths" any thing including duel or divorce—I answer *yes*—I love her—if I did not and much too—I should have been more *selfish* on the occasion before mentioned—I have offered to go away with her—& her answer whether sincere or not is "that on *my account* she declines it"—in the mean time we are all as wretched as possible—*he* scolding on *account* of *unaccountable* melancholy—the sister very suspicious but rather amused—the friend very suspicious too but (why I know not) not at all amused—il Marito something like Lord Chesterfield in De Grammont[1]—putting on a martial physignomy—prating with his worthy ally—swearing at servants—sermonizing both sisters—& buying sheep—but never quitting her side now—so that we are in despair—*I* very feverish—restless—and silent—as indeed seems to be the *tacit* agreement of every one else—in short I can foresee nothing—it may end in nothing—but here are half a dozen persons very much occupied—& two if not three in great perplexity—& as far as I can judge—so we must continue.——She *don't* & *won't* live with him—

[1] The 2nd Earl of Chesterfield (1633–1713) is pictured in the *Memoirs* of the Comte de Gramont as being tortured by an insane and ridiculous jealousy of his second wife, whom he married in 1660.

& they have been so far separate for a long time—therefore—I have nothing to answer for on that point—poor thing—she is either the most *artful* or *artless* of her age (20) I ever encountered—she *owns* to so much—and perpetually says—"rather than you should be *angry*"—or—"rather than you should like anyone else I will do whatever you please" ["]I won't speak to this that or the other if you dislike it—["] & throws or seems to throw herself so entirely upon my direction in every respect—that it disarms me quite—but I am really wretched with the perpetual conflict with myself.—Her health is so very delicate —she is so thin & pale—& seems to have lost her appetite so entirely —that I doubt her being much longer—this is also her own opinion— but these fancies are common to all who are not very happy——if she were once my wife or likely to be so—a warm climate should be the first resort nevertheless for her recovery.—The most perplexing—& yet I can't prevail on myself to give it up—is the *caressing* system—in her it appears perfectly childish—and I do think innocent—but it really puzzles all the Scipio about me to confine myself to the laudable portion of these endearments.———What a cursed situation I have thrust myself into—Potiphar (it used to be O[xford]'s name) putting some stupid question to me the other day—I told him that I rather admired the *sister*—& what does he? but tell *her* this & his *wife* too— who a little too hastily asked him "if he was *mad*"? which put him to demonstration that a man ought not to be asked if he was mad—for relating that a friend thought his wife's sister a pretty woman—upon this topic he held forth with great fervour for a customary period—I wish he had a quinsey.———Tell Ly. H[olland] that Clarke is the name—& Craven Street (No. forgotten) the residence—may be heard of at Trin. Coll.—excellent man—able physician—shot a friend in a duel (about his sister) & I believe killed him professionally afterwards— Ly. H[olland] may have him for self or friends—I don't know where I am going—my mind is a chaos—I always am setting all upon single stakes—& this is one—your story of the Frenchman is Matta in Grammont & the Marquis[2]—Heigh ho!—Good Night—address to *Aston.*—

ever yrs.

B

[2] Charles de Bourdeille, Comte de Matta (1614–1674), was a celebrated wit. The story to which Byron refers, as recounted in Gramont's *Memoirs*, concerns the gallantries of Gramont and Matta at the Court of Turin with Mlle. de Saint-Germain and Mme. de Sénantes. The story might have been pertinent to Byron's remarks on Webster because of the brash self-confidence of Matta as a lover and gallant.

P.S.—My stay is quite uncertain—a moment may overturn every thing—but you shall hear—happen what may—nothing or something.

[TO LADY MELBOURNE (*a*)]   *Octr. 19th. 1813*

My dear Ly. M[elbourn]e—In a day or two—probably before you receive this letter I shall be in town—so that if you write let it be to Bennet Street.—This may perhaps surprize you after my yesterday's epistle—but nevertheless nothing particular has occurred—at least sufficient to *alarm* you—or disturb me—everything is nearly as it was —except our hopes & our spirits—many things interrupted—but nothing terminated.——Do you remember Matta's complaint of the court of Turin[1]—where a man could not be in love with the wife— without making love to the husband too—or do you rather recollect Hamilton's expedition to Ld. Chesterfield's[2]—with the result? mine is not exactly the same—for I have incurred no disgrace & encountered no peril—but I have thrown away the best opportunity that ever was wasted upon a spoiled child—& when it may occur again is not in my calculation.——You shall hear more when we meet—at present I shall only say—that Matta & the Marquis de Senantes[3] will furnish you with a lively idea of me & my guest (late host)—I really can bear his humours no longer—no not for —— with her I am ready & willing to fly to the "Green earth's end" but of that anon.——*We* are in despair— & he & I without coming to a downright quarrel—have yet subsided into a mortal coldness—for which he will be the first to be sorry—I hope to see you—

ever yrs.
B

[TO LADY MELBOURNE (*b*)]   *Northampton—Octr. 19th. 1813*

My dear Ly. M[elbourn]e—& I am thus far on my way to town—he [Webster] was seized with a sudden fit of friendship & would accom-

[1] Matta at the court of Turin (in Gramont's *Memoirs*) owed his ill success with Mme. de Sénantes to the fact that he did not pay proper respect to her husband.

[2] Anthony Hamilton, author of the *Memoirs* of Gramont, recounts, supposedly in the words of Gramont, how he (Hamilton) was duped by the Countess of Chesterfield, who induced him to make a long journey to see her in the country while her husband was away. When he arrived he discovered that she had plotted the trick with the connivance of her husband with whom she was then reconciled.

[3] See Oct. 17, 1813, to Lady Melbourne, note 2.

pany me—or rather finding that some business could not conveniently
be done without me—he thought proper to assume ye. appearance of it.
——He is not exactly the companion I wished to take—it is really
laughable when you think of the *other*—a kind of pig in a poke.—
Nothing but squabbles between *them*—for the last three days—and at
last he rose up with a solemn & mysterious air—& spake—"Ly. ——
[Frances] you have at last rendered an explanation necessary between
me & Ld. B[yron] which must take place"—I stared—& knowing that
it is the custom of country gentlemen (if Farquhar is correct) to
apprize their moieties of such intentions—& being also a little out of
humour & conscience—I thought a crisis must ensue—and announced
very quietly that "he would find me in such a room at his leisure ready
to hear & reply" "Oh! says he I shall choose my own time" I wondered
that he did not choose his *own house* too—but walked away—& waited for
him.—All this mighty pickle led only to what he called an explanation
for *my satisfaction* that whatever appearances were—*he* & *she* were on
the very best terms—that she loved him so much—& he her—it was
impossible not to disagree upon *tender* points—& for fear a man who
&c. &c. should suppose that marriage was not the happiest of all
possible estates—he had taken this resolution of never quarrelling
without letting me know that he was the best husband & most fortunate person in existence.———I told him he had fully convinced me—
that it was utterly impossible people who liked each other could behave
with more interesting suavity—and so on—yesterday morning—on
our going—(I pass over the scene which shook me I assure you)
"B—quoth he I owe to you the most unhappy moments of my life" I
begged him to tell me how that I might either sympathize or put him
out of his pain—"Don't you see how the poor girl *doats* on me—(he
replied) when I quit her but for a week as you perceive she is absolutely overwhelmed—& you staid so long & I necessarily for you—
that she is in a worse state than I ever saw her in before—even before
we married!————["] Here we are—I could not return to A[ston]
unless he had asked me—it is true he did—but in such a manner—as I
could not accept—what will be the end—I know not—I have left
every thing to *her*—and would have rendered all further *plots* superfluous by the most conclusive step—but she wavered—& escaped—
perhaps so have I—at least it is as well to think so—yet it is not over.
———Whatever I may feel—you know me too well to think I shall
plague my friends with long faces—or elegies.—

My dear Ly. Me. ever yrs.

B

149

Excuse haste and laconism. I am in town but for a few days, and hurried with a thousand things.

Believe me ever yours most truly,

BYRON.

[TO DR. SAMUEL BUTLER[1]]

4 Bennet Street, St. James's
October 20th, 1813

Sir,—The honour of your letter has laid me under an additional obligation to my friend Hodgson. I am truly proud of your favourable opinion and glad of the opportunity of adding my testimony—my most sincere suffrage—to the acknowledged merits of a man whom I have known intimately for several years. To yourself I can safely say that I never knew a being more warm in heart, more amiable and inoffensive yet independent in spirit, and where not occasionally biassed by feelings which though the kindest are the weakest in our nature, one of sounder judgment than the subject of your letter and of this reply. So much for him as a man—as a man of talents, I trust he is and ever will be far above the necessity of appealing to me or any individual of prouder pretensions in behalf of abilities already neither unknown nor unappreciated. As a translator his Juvenal has placed him in the first rank, and I know nothing wanting to his fame as an original writer, except the more frequent exertion of his own powers, and less diffidence (a rare fault) in his own capacity.

The little that I have seen by stealth and accident of *Charlemagne* quite electrified me. It must be a stupendous work—it seems to be of another age, and, I grieve for the certainty, of another country. Hodgson must make as much of it our own as he has done by Juvenal; and then we shall have less, and the author nothing to regret. M. Lucien will occupy the same space in the annals of poetry which his imperial brother has secured in those of history—except that with posterity the verdict must be in his favour. Once more begging you to accept my best thanks for your communication, I have the honour to be, very sincerely,

Your obliged servant

BIRON

[1] Dr. Samuel Butler, headmaster of Shrewsbury School, was engaged in translating Lucien Buonaparte's poem *Charlemagne*, and had asked Byron's opinion of Hodgson as a collaborator. Butler and Hodgson worked together on the translation which was published in 1815.

P.S.—I have written in great haste and after a long and freezing journey from Yorkshire, which must form my apology for not having said half enough what I ought of Mr. Hodgson. But I console myself with the idea that more would be superfluous.

My dear Ly. M[elbourn]e—You may well be surprised—but I had more reasons than one or two[;] either —— [Webster] had taken it into his notable head or wished to put it into mine—aye & worse still. into ye. girls also—that I was a pretendant to the *hand* of the sister of "the Lady whom I had nearly—but no matter (to continue Archer's speech with the variation of one word) tis a cursed *fortnight's* piece of work—& there's an end."[1]—This brilliant notion besides widening ye. breach between him & me—did not add to the harmony of the two females—at least my idol was not pleased with the prospect of any transfer of incense to another altar.——She was so unguarded— after telling me too fifty times to "take care of Cate" "that she could conceal nothing &c. &c." as to give me a very unequivocal proof of her own imprudence—in a carriage (dusk to be sure) before her face— and yet with all this—& much more—she was the most tenacious personage—either from fear or weakness—or delicate health—or G-d knows what—that with the vigilance of no less than *three* Arguses in addition—it was utterly impossible save once—to be decisive—and then—tears & tremors & prayers—which I am not yet old enough to find piquant in such cases—prevented me from making her wretched—I do detest everything which is not perfectly mutual— and any subsequent reproaches—(as I know by one former long ago bitter experience) would heep coals of fire upon my head.——Do you remember what Rousseau says to somebody—"if you would know that you are beloved—watch your lover when he leaves you—["][2]to me the most pleasing moments have generally been—when there is nothing more to be required—in short the subsequent repose without satiety—which Lewis never dreamed of in that poem of his "Desire &

[1] In Farquhar's *The Beaux Stratagem* Archer says, after the failure of an attempted gallantry, " 'tis a cursed Night's work." (Act. V)
[2] In *La Nouvelle Héloïse* (Première partie, lettre LV) Rousseau says: "Femme trop facile, voulez vous savoir si vous êtes aimée? examinez votre amant sortant de vos bras. O amour! Si je regrette l'âge ou l'on te goûte, ce n'est pas pour l'heure de la jouissance; c'est pour l'heure qui la suit."

Pleasure"[3] when you are secure of the past yet without regret or disappointment—of this there was no prospect with her—she had so much more dread of the D – – –l than gratitude for his kindness—and I am not yet sufficiently in his good graces to indulge my own passions at the certain misery of another.——Perhaps after all—I was her dupe—if so—I am the dupe also of the few good feelings I could ever boast of—but here perhaps I am my own dupe too in attributing to a good motive what may be quite otherwise —— [Webster] is a most extraordinary person—he has just left me & a snuff box with a flaming inscription—after squabbling with me for these last ten days! & I too have been of some real service to *him* which I merely mention to mark the inconsistency of human nature!—I have brought off a variety of foolish trophies (foolish indeed without victory) such as epistles—& lockets—which look as if she were in earnest—but she would not go off *now*—nor render going off unnecessary—am I not candid to own my want of success—when I might have assumed the airs of an "aimable Vainquer" but that is so paltry & so common without cause too—and what I hear & see every day—that I would not—even to gain the point I have missed. I assure you not one knows but you one particle of this business—& you always must know everything concerning me—it is hard if I may not have one friend—believe me none will ever be so valued—& none ever was so trusted by yrs. ever.

B

[TO LADY MELBOURNE]   *Octr. 23rd. 1813*

My dear Ly. M[elbourn]e—C[aroline] again!—will you pray tell her that I was only in town a day before she left it—& that if it were otherwise it must be long ago perfectly understood between her & me & everyone else—that it could have made no difference—I wrote to her a kind & a friendly letter—& regret that it has displeased her—I know no more & can say no further—but do most humbly hope she will leave me to my own reflections—& as a further inducement she may rest assured that they are by no means agreeable enough to make their disturbance a temptation. One of your A[ston] letters has arrived —& the other I doubt not will follow—I wish *he would* open a letter of mine—but he dare not—I am not sorry for this business—were it only

---

[3] Lewis's poem "Pleasure and Desire" (*Poems*, 1812) concludes:
   Desire must still awaken Pleasure,
   And Pleasure lull desire to sleep.

on account of your epistles—which I do think the most amusing—the most *developing*—and tactiques in the world—come what may—I can hardly regret the untoward events which led to an intimacy productive to me of much instruction—& not less *intellectual* pleasure—you have preserved me from *two*—one eventually & the other had been immediately fatal[1]—I cannot repay the obligation but I may at least acknowledge it—& as the world goes it is something not to hate you for having done me so much service.—If —— [Webster] is playing a part—he cannot I know long keep it up—his *marrying* scheme if premeditated had been an excellent way of turning the tables—but it was done too abruptly & awkwardly to succeed—there was no foundation for his edifice—& if there had I would have blown it up about his ears—I prefer—if in the *regular* way—chusing my own moiety though truth to tell he recommended a woman of Virtue—for I heard her say "that she never was in a warm bath in her life" a certain sign—the care of your truly good woman is always confined to her soul.—I don't know if you ever saw her—she is very pretty—but petite—perhaps handsomer than the other—and I think more mechante—but in all other respects like all other young ladies of the market.—My Seaham correspondence has ceased on both sides—& I shall not renew it—I am in great suspence—Marquis Tweedale wants me to go with him to the army[2]—like Corporal Nym "to wink & hold out mine iron" I suppose—Madrid hath charms more than Glory—or mere curiosity—and a fit of ill humour or vanity might or may lead me where "Honour comes unlooked for" but unless when *in* love or *out* of temper—my chivalry is not the most Gothic—though a box on the ear from one sex—or a frown from the other might possibly call it into action.———A more pleasing expedition would be to Middleton—I am asked next month—so are you—shall we go? we—at least *I* shall have nothing to do—but probably something to observe & communicate.—I send you (return it) the only notice *since* my departure—will you judge—& *augur* from it for me? it puzzles me—you have more insight—& are besides impartial—I have just sense enough left to know that I cannot be so myself.—Your approbation of my Ethic on *the* subject gratifies me much—when we are happy we are too much occupied to be aware of its extent—it is only during the subsequent repose—the

[1] Lady Melbourne, he believed, had saved him from an eventual scandalous denouement with Lady Caroline Lamb, and immediate disaster if he had pursued his intention of taking Augusta abroad.

[2] George Hay, 8th Marquis of Tweeddale (1787–1876) succeeded to the title in 1804. He had served in the Peninsular campaigns, and was shortly to leave for the American war.

"abandon" that you can discover even to yourself if you have *really* loved—if your thoughts recur to your own exclusive situation—it is all over—but if still occupied by the other—I do not know whether the *memory* & the *hope* are not worth all the rest.—It is difficult & I have failed in expressing what I mean—no matter—let it go—You will be in town on Wednesday—a great consolation to me—I am in the horrors of a hundred schemes—of which I shall say nothing—till they are accomplished or useless.—Perhaps you will write on Monday—

ever yrs.

B

[TO LADY MELBOURNE]   *Monday—[October 25, 1813?]*

I *had* finished my letter—but tear half of it—today's Post has been hard in bringing me more than I have yet had time to read *twice*—& *your* last Aston Letter *safe*—but your Brocket one is a little savage— you hint at my *presumption*—but after all the "vielle cour" when once people understand each other—is it not as well to come to the point?— yet you see (& I am glad you approved it) I *did* (and it is no trifle) sacrifice the selfish consideration to spare her [Frances's] self reproach. —I am going to be guilty of a breach of confidence in sending you the inclosed—though I cannot consider my *trust* in you as betraying her— if she is serious so am I—and as willing as ever to go through with the business—the letter merely says—what you already know—and all women (except Ly. O[xford] & Mrs. S[pence]r Sm[it]h) in that situation seem to have much the same style—except that my little *white* penitent appears rather more bewildered & uses two words— "effusions" & "soul" rather oftener than befits out of the circulating library.—You are not perhaps so just as usual in prophesying *"not* to the purpose" every thing a woman *writes* must be to the purpose— *no*—as much as *yes*—*once* put a pen into their hands—and then tell me when they will lay it down again?——She mentions C[aroline]—but not one word of *you*—a proof at least—that she knows nothing of my extreme reliance & confidence in you—Perhaps you will think worse of me for sending this—if I were not in *earnest* I should not—but I want your judgement about her—*I* can't be impartial—& I again repeat *but* to *you*—her name is never breathed.—You are with "the illustrious" which makes me tremble—I know she thinks ill of me[1]—& if you betray me she will think worse—I can possibly have no anxiety about

---

[1] Probably Lady Melbourne's daughter Lady Cowper.

her good opinion further than as I am aware of her natural & unbounded influence over your own.—I am wrong—but you really *wrong* me too —if you do not suppose that I would sacrifice every thing for *Ph* [Frances]—I hate sentiment—& in consequence my epistolary levity— makes you believe me as hollow & heartless as my letters are light— Indeed it is not so—and I think my unbounded reliance on you (my *natural* enemy) may prove it—I don't fear you—no—notwithstanding *all*—& yet if I were reduced to the alternative of losing your friend- ship or any other person's love—our Platonics would triumph.—

ever yrs.

B

P.S.—Poor Robinson! it must be very ill-convenient to *you*—this fracture.—In your Aston Letter—you say the Jackall must be in love too—I did not think so—but nevertheless gave W[ebster] a hint about those "Joseph Surface gentlemen" and asked him what he should have thought of *me*—if after our long acquaintance—I had suddenly com- menced *talking* moralist?—W[ebster] at last almost went down on his knees to prevent an explanation between us—and now this odd expression—"if not for *my* sake for that of Ly. F[rances] do not quarrel—I never will forgive you—nor will *she* if there is any scene on what passed at N[ewstead]—these were nearly his last words—but if he renews his tricks or has views of his own—I will revenge or perish in the attempt.—"In love" how came I not to think so before? but he has left A[ston]—if I am not even with him never trust me—a man too whom I did much to conciliate—& who dissembled to *me* with some success.—

[TO LORD HOLLAND] *Octr. 25th. 1813*

My dear Lord—As I was quite convinced before I ever heard you say a syllable on the subject that you had probably been amused with some terrific narrative on the subject—which first led me to a certain composition—I am glad of an opportunity to present you with any- one's testimony rather than my own—although that person's assertion has turned out so unfortunate on his own account that probably it may do little good on mine.[1]—However as he was the only Englishman

---

[1] Byron sent Lord Holland Sligo's letter on the events in Athens that were the basis of the story of *The Giaour*. Sligo was in trouble with the Navy for his treat- ment of some sailors under his command, and his "assertion" on his own account had not extricated him from the difficulty.

who arrived there for a long time after my departure (Hob[hous]e left me a year before) and as these things in a country where tradition is the only record are soon forgotten—or perverted—I wish you to see this such as it is—only begging that unless you hear anything on the subject—it may rest with you & yours.—One part of the letter is expunged—it merely contained some uncouth Turkish patronymics—and some circumstances amusing enough but neither singular nor edyfying—the rest may amuse you as a Portrait of Mussulman Ethics.———

Believe me yrs. ever obliged & sincerely

B

[TO JOHN MURRAY (*a*)]　　　　　　　　　　　　[*Nov. 1813?*]

A correction in the last paragraph of the MS which may as well be attended to
now

　　　　　"May there be marked—*and eye may note*

let it be thus

　　　　　May there be marked—nor far remote
　　　　　A broken torch—an oarless boat[1]

you will easily find the lines they are in the *last sent*—in the last paragraph but one of the 2nd Canto. Send this correction off directly pray

Yrs.

B

[TO JOHN MURRAY (*b*)]　　　　　　　　　　　　[*Nov.? 1813*]

Dear Sir—Pray attend to the *corrections* they are slight but *important* and remember the *Bride*.

yrs. ever

B

---

[1] *The Bride of Abydos*, Canto II, lines 1073–1074. Byron said in his diary of Nov. 16, 1813, that the poem was written "in four nights" But see Nov. 12, to Gifford, where he says it was "the work of a week". But he continued to make revisions for some time before it was published.

Dear Sir—It is very odd that as fast as I correct one thing the Printer either omits or *re*blunders—look at page [*72?*][1] which I now correct for I believe the 30th. time in the same place.—

yrs. ever

B<small>N</small>

P.S.—Don't trouble yourself to answer this—but you must at least acknowledge that this perpetual fooling of Master Davison is very vexatious.—

My dear friend—I lose no time in assuring you that I not only am not—but never have been for an instant—in the least pettish about you—the other night at the play—I was merely *"buffooning"* & I really thought you knew me well enough to perceive this.—Angry— quotha! I am a pretty fellow to be angry with anybody—& least of all with you.—In the last three days I have been quite shut up—my mind has been from *late* and *later* events in such a state of fermentation that as usual I have been obliged to empty it in rhyme—& am in the very heart of another Eastern tale[1]—something of the *Giaour cast*—but not so *sombre* though rather more villainous—this is my usual resource— if it were not for some such occupation to dispel reflection during *inaction*—I verily believe I should very often go mad.—I have heard from *Ph* [Frances]—she is very angry at me for *not* writing—(after telling me it was impossible without *ruining her*) & supposes that I *must have* told *everybody* her adventures—& is particularly afraid that *I I* by myself *I* should confide it to W[edderburn] W[ebster]!!!—Was there ever such a fancy?—tell a man that I wanted —— it is really laughable.—C[aroline] has been playing the devil about some engravings & fooleries—will she never be quiet till she is in the round-house with the Sieur Henri[2]—who it seems is a great villain & her particular protege—at least so you said to me.—Good night—my dear Ly. M[elbourn]e.—Buonaparte has lost all his allies but *me* & the

---

[1] This probably refers to corrections for the 7th edition of *The Giaour* which was published towards the end of November. It contained 75 pages.

[1] *The Bride of Abydos.*

[2] Henry Grattan, Jr. [?]. Byron told Medwin that Lady Caroline Lamb "promised young Grattan her favours if he would call me out." (Medwin, Lovell ed., p. 218.)

King of Wirtemberg—do you remember Wolsey—"*I* & my king" no matter my alliance is quite as useful as that of Bavaria.

ever yrs.

B

Novr. 8th. 1813

My dearest Augusta—I have only time to say that I shall write tomorrow—and that my present & long silence has been occasioned by a thousand things (with which *you* are not concerned) it is not Ly. C[aroline] nor O[xford] but perhaps you may *guess*—& if you do—do *not tell*.—You do not know what mischief your being with me—might have prevented.—You shall hear from me tomorrow—in the mean time dont be alarmed—I am in *no immediate* peril—Believe me

ever yrs.

B

[November 8, 1813]

Dear Sir—If you would like me to see Farleigh—I should wish to pass *2* days there & to bring Mrs. Leigh with me—sometime next week—Mrs. H's *absence* will be of no consequence and I want to *see* the place[1]—

yrs. ever

B

Novr. 10th. 1813

A variety of circumstances & movements from place to place—none of which would be very amusing in detail—nor indeed pleasing to any one who (I may flatter myself) is my friend have hitherto prevented me from answering your two last letters—but if my daily self-reproach for the omission can be any atonement—I hope it may prove as satisfactory an apology to you—as it has been a "compunctious visiting" to

---

[1] This is a strange statement, for Byron had seen Farleigh, Hanson's country place in Hampshire, a number of times in his youth. Perhaps Hanson had acquired a new house there or refurbished the old and Byron wanted to see it in its new state.

myself.————Your opinion of my "reasoning powers" is so exactly my own—that you will not wonder if I avoid a controversy with so skilful a casuist—particularly on a subject where I am certain to get the worst of it in this world—and perhaps incur a warmer confutation in the next.—But I shall be most happy to hear your observations on the subject—or on any subject—if anybody could do me much *good* —probably you might—as by all accounts you are mistress of the practice as well as theory of that benevolent science (which I take to be better than even your *Mathematics*) at all events it is *my* fault if I derive no benefit from your remarks.—I agree with you quite upon Mathematics too—and must be content to admire them at an incomprehensible distance—always adding them to the catalogue of my regrets—I know that two and two make four—& should be glad to prove it too if I could—though I must say if by any sort of process I could convert 2 & 2 into *five* it would give me much greater pleasure.— The only part I remember which gave me much delight were those theorems (is that the word?) in which after ringing the changes upon— A—B—& C—D. &c. I at last came to "which is absurd—which is impossible" and at this point I have always arrived & I fear always shall through life—very fortunate if I can continue to stop there. ———I perceive by part of your last letter—that you are still a little inclined to believe me a very gloomy personage—those who pass so much of their time entirely alone cannot be always in very high spirits —yet I don't know—though I certainly do enjoy society to a certain extent I never passed two hours in mixed company in my life—without wishing myself out of it again—still I look upon myself as a facetious companion—well respected by all the Wits—at whose jests I readily laugh—& whose repartees I take care never to incur by any kind of contest—for which I feel as little qualified as I do for the more solid pursuit of demonstration.—I am happy so far in the *intimate* acquaintance of two or three men with whom for ten years of my life I have never had one word of difference—and what is rather strange—their opinions religious moral & political are diametrically opposite to mine— so that when I say "difference" I mean of course *serious* dispute—coolness—quarrel—or whatever people call it—now for a person who began life with that endless source of squabble—satire—I may in this respect think myself fortunate.—My reflections upon this subject qualify me to sympathize with you very sincerely in the departure of your friend Miss Montgomery—the more so—as notwithstanding many instances of the contrary I believe the friendship of *good* women —more sincere than that of men—& certainly more tender—at least

I never heard of a male intimacy that spoilt a man's dinner—after the age of fifteen—which was that when I began to think myself a mighty fine gentleman & to feel ashamed of liking anybody better than one'-self. I have been scribbling another poem—as it is called—Turkish as before—for I can't empty my head of the East—and horrible enough—though not so sombre quite as ye. Giaour (that unpronounceable name) and for the sake of intelligibility it is *not* a fragment.—The scene is on the Hellespont—a favourite sejour of mine—and if you will accept it—I will send you a copy—there are some Mussulman words in it which I inflict upon you in revenge for your "Mathematical ["] & other superiority.————When shall you be in town?—by the bye—you won't take *fright* when we meet will you? & imagine that I am about to add to your thousand and one pretendants?—I have taken exquisite care to prevent the possibility of that[1]—though less likely than ever to become a Benedick—indeed I have not seen (with one exception) for many years a Beatrice——and she will not be troubled to assume the part.—I think we understand each other perfectly—& may talk to each other occasionally without exciting speculation—the worst that can be said—is—that I *would*—& you *wont*—and in this respect *you* can hardly be the sufferer—and I am very sure I *shant*.—If I find my heart less philosophic on the subject than I at present believe it—I shall keep out of the way—but I *now* think it is well shielded—at least it has got a new suit of armour—and certainly it stood in need of it.—I have heard a rumour of another added to your list of unacceptables—and I am sorry for him—as I know that he has talent—& his pedigree ensures him wit & good humour.[2]—You make sad havock among "us youth" it is lucky that Me. de Staël has published her Anti-suicide at so killing a time—*November* too!—I have not read it—for fear that the love of contradiction might lead me to a practical confutation.—Do you know her? I don't ask if you have *heard* her? her tongue is "the perpetual motion."—

ever yrs.

B

P.S. Nov. 17th.—The enclosed was written a week ago & has lain in my desk ever since—I have had forty thousand plagues to make me

[1] Annabella was probably not much pleased at Byron's hint that he had formed another attachment.

[2] It appears that one of Annabella's suitors was Stratford Canning (later Lord Stratford de Redcliffe). His biographer says: "An additional cause of [his] depression [in 1814] was his failure to win the hand of Annabella Milbanke . . ." (*The Life of Stratford Canning*, by E. F. Malcolm-Smith, London, 1933, p. 49.)

forget not *you* but *it*—and now I might as well burn it—but let it go &
pray forgive ye. scrawl & the Scribe

ever yrs.

B

[in another hand?] If you favour me with an answer—any letter
addressed here will reach me wherever I may be—I have a little cousin
Eliza Byron[4] coming—no—going to some school at Stockton—will
you notice her? it is the prettiest little blackeyed girl of Paradise—&
but 7 years old.—

[TO WILLIAM GIFFORD] *Novr. 12th. 1813*

My dear Sir—I hope you will consider when I venture on any
request that it is the reverse of a certain dedication[1]—and is addressed
not to the "Editor of the Quarterly Review" but to Mr. Gifford.—You
will understand this and on that point I need trouble you no further.—
You have been good enough to look at a thing of mine in M.S.—a
Turkish story—and I should feel gratified if you would do it the same
favour in it's probationary state of printing.—It was written—I
cannot say for amusement nor "obliged by hunger and request of
friends"[2] but in a state of mind from circumstances which occasionally
occur to "us youth" that rendered it necessary for me to apply my mind
to something—any thing but reality—and under this not very brilliant
inspiration it was composed.—Being done—and having at least diverted me from myself—I thought you would not perhaps be offended if
Mr. Murray forwarded it to you—he has done so—& to apologize for
his doing so a second time is the object of my present letter.—I beg
you will *not* send me an answer—I assure you very sincerely—I know
your time to be occupied—and it is enough more than enough if you
read—you ought not to be bored with the fatigue of answers.————A
word to Mr. Murray will be sufficient—and send it—either to the
flames—or

[4] Eliza Byron was the daughter of the Rev. Henry Byron, second son of The
Rev. and Hon. Richard Byron, and nephew of William, 5th Lord Byron. Thus Eliza
was not a first cousin of Byron, for their grandfathers and not their fathers were
brothers. In his journal of November 14, 1813, Byron wrote of Eliza: "She will
grow up a beauty and a plague; but, in the meantime, it is the prettiest child! dark
eyes and eyelashes, black and long as the wing of a raven."
[1] Unidentified.
[2] Pope, *Epistle to Dr. Arbuthnot*, line 44.

> "a hundred hawkers' load
> On wings of winds to fly or fall abroad—[''][3]

it deserves no better than the first, as the work of a week, and scribbled "stans pede in uno" (by the bye the only foot I have to stand on) and I promise never to trouble you again under forty cantos and a voyage between each.—Believe me

ever yr. obliged & affectionate Sert.

BIRON

[TO JOHN MURRAY (*a*)]   [*November 12, 1813*]

Dear Sir—I have looked over—corrected—and added—*all* of which you may do too—at least *certainly* the *two* first—There is more M.S. *within*—let us know tomorrow—at your leisure *how* & *when* we shall proceed? it looks better than I thought at first—*Look over* again—I suspect some omissions on my part—& on the printer's—

yrs. ever

B

Always print *"een" "even"*—I utterly abhor *"een"*—if it must be contracted be it *"ev'n"*.

The lines which rhyme to [each other?] are printed even thus—this applies to the concluding paragraph chiefly.—$\begin{smallmatrix}-A\\-B\end{smallmatrix}$ not $\begin{smallmatrix}-A\\-B\end{smallmatrix}$[at bottom

of page in another hand: "with first proof of Bride of Abydos correct"]

[TO JOHN MURRAY (*b*)]   *Nov. 12th, 1813*

Two friends of mine (Mr. Rogers and Mr. Sharpe)[1] have advised me not to risk at present any single publication separately, for various reasons. As they have not seen the one in question, they can have no bias for or against the merits (if it has any) or the faults of the present

---

[3] Slightly misquoted from Pope, *Epistle to Dr. Arbuthnot*, lines 217–218:
   . . . a hundred hawkers load,
   On wings of winds came flying all abroad.

[1] Probably Richard ("conversation") Sharp, who was a friend of Rogers and whom Byron had met at various gatherings. Byron was shy of separate publication of *The Bride of Abydos*, but Murray assured him that Canning had read the manuscript. "I told him your delicacy as to separate publication, of which he said you should remove every apprehension." (*LJ*, II, 280n.)

subject of our conversation. You say all the last of the "Giaour" are gone—at least out of your hands. Now, if you think of publishing any new edition with the last additions which have not yet been before the reader (I mean distinct from the two-volume publication), we can add the "Bride of Abydos," which will thus steal quietly into the world: if liked, we can then throw off some copies for the purchasers of former "Giaours;" and, if not, I can omit it in any future publication. What think you? I really am no judge of those things, and with all my natural partiality for one's own productions, I would rather follow any one's judgment than my own.

P.S.—Pray let me have the proofs I sent *all* to-night. I have some alterations that I have thought of that I wish to make speedily. I hope the proof will be on separate pages, and not all huddled together on a mile-long ballad-singing sheet, as those of the Giaour sometimes are; for then I can't read them distinctly.

[TO JOHN MURRAY (*a*)]   [*Novr. 13th. 1813*]

Dear Sir—Will you forward the letter to Mr. Gifford—with the proof [*Bride of Abydos*]—there is one alteration I may make in Zuleika's speech in 2d. C[ant]o—(the only one of *hers* in that Canto)—it is now thus—

"And curse—if I could curse—the day"

it must be

"And mourn—I dare not curse—the day
That saw my solitary birth &c.
&c. &c.

in the last M.S. lines sent—instead of "living heart" correct to "quivering heart" it is in line 9th of the M.S. passage—

ever yrs. again

B

Alter in the inscription "the most affectionate respect" to "with every sentiment of Regard & Respect["]¹

[TO JOHN MURRAY (*b*)]   [*November 13? 1813*]

Alteration of a line in Canto 2d.—
Instead of

"And tints tomorrow with a *fancied* ray—

¹ The dedication of *The Bride of Abydos* was to Lord Holland.

163

print

"And tints tomorrow with *prophetic* ray

———————————

"The evening beam that smiles the clouds away
"And tints tomorrow with prophetic ray

or

$\begin{array}{c} gilds \\ tints \end{array}$

"And $\begin{array}{c} gilds \\ tints \end{array}$ the hope of Morning with it's ray—

or

"And gilds tomorrow's hope with heavenly ray—
Dear Sir—I wish you would ask Mr. G[ifford] which of these is best
—or rather *not worst*

ever yrs.

B

You can send the request contained in this at the same time—with
the *revise—after* I have seen the *said revise*—

[TO JOHN MURRAY (*c*)]   [*November 13? 1813*]

Certainly—do you suppose that no one but the Galileans are acquainted with *Adam* & *Eve* & *Cain*[1] & *Noah*—[why] I might have had
Solomon & Abraham & David & even Moses on the other—when you
know that *Zuleika* is the *Persian poetical* name for *Potiphers* wife on
whom & Joseph there is a long poem—in the Persian this will not
surprise you—if you want authority—look at Jones—D'Herbelot—
Vathek—or the Notes to the Arabian N[ight]s—& if you think it
necessary model this into a *note*.—

[TO W. J. BALDWIN[1]]   *Novr. 14th. 1813*

Sir—It is with considerable regret that I repeat—the shortness
of the notice (even if I remained in town which I hardly believe I can
accomplish at present) would not permit me to do more than *present*

[1] Murray had expressed a doubt "as to the propriety of putting the name of
Cain into the mouth of a Mussulman." (Moore, I, 483n.)
[1] W. J. Baldwin was a debtor in King's Bench prison, who sent a number of
pathetic letters to Byron describing the inhuman treatment of the prisoners and
asking for prison reform.

164

the petition.[2] Upon the principle itself—the question at issue on the *confinement* of debtors—as far as regards the rights of humanity and the social compact—my mind is fully made up—but the minor grievances —the various though I doubt not—well grounded subjects of complaint which I conjecture will form a considerable portion of the petition —I have not had leisure to examine—nor opportunity to collect.—I confess to you that I have not the "copia fandi" nor quickness of comprehension sufficient to enable me at a few hours notice to do justice to a subject which I regard as of too much importance to hazard the interests of the petitioners by a premature & precipitate pressure of the question upon the legislature—if I were indifferent to the interests of others—or confident in my own powers—I should hold a different language.—I have read your address—and I have read it with a hope almost for the sake of those to whom it is uttered—that their situation is less grievous than it would lead me to believe—not that I have any reason to doubt the statement—except the wish that in this—or in any country—such oppression had never existed. ————I have the honour to be
very sincerely yr. obedt. & very h[umb]le Sert.
BYRON

[TO JOHN MURRAY (*a*)] [*November 14, 1813*]

Dear Sir—I send you a note for the *ignorant*—but I really wonder at finding *you* among them.—I don't care one lump of Sugar for my *poetry*—but for my *costume*—and my *correctness* on those points (of which I think the *funeral* was a proof) I will combat lustily.—
yrs. ever
B

[TO JOHN MURRAY (*b*)] [*November 14, 1813*]

Let the Revise which I sent just now (and *not* the proof in Mr. G[ifford]'s possession) be returned to the printer as there are several additional corrections & 2 new lines in it.
yrs. &c.
B

[2] Baldwin had asked Byron to present his petition to the House of Lords. Byron gave his reasons for not being able to do so, but he was full of self-reproaches. "Ah, I am as bad as that dog Sterne, who preferred whining over 'a dead ass to relieving a living mother' ", he wrote in his journal (Dec. 1, 1813). He finally got Lord Holland to present the petition.

Dear Sir—Mr. Hodgson has looked over & *stopped* or rather *pointed* this revise which must be the one to print from.—He has also made some suggestions with most of which I have complied—as he has always for these ten years been a very sincere & by no means (at times) flattering critic of mine.—*He* likes it (you will think *flatteringly* in this instance) better than the Giaour—but doubts (and so do I) it being so popular—but contrary to some others—advises a *separate* publication—On this we can easily decide—I confess I like the *double* form better—Hodgson says it is *better versified*—than any of the others—which is odd if true—as it has cost me less time (though more *hours* at a time) than any attempt I ever made.—

yrs. ever
B

P.S.—Do attend to the punctuation—I cant—for I dont know a comma—at least where to place one.———That Tory of a *Printer* has omitted two lines of the opening—and *perhaps more*—which were in the M.S. Will you pray—give him a hint of accuracy.—I have reinserted the *2*—but they were in the Manuscript I can swear.—

My dear Lord—I send you two *proofs* (of my regard if you please)—one the enlarged & yet *unpublished* "Giaour"—in which you may—if you will—find in the last 20 pages about 200 additional lines—The other—eye hath not yet seen (except 2 pair—of Hodgson—& another) it is Turkish too—and will not—both Cantos (of which the *last* is the least bad) take you half an hour's reading—If you could let me have them tomorrow morning again—you would oblige me—and (if you will accept) they shall be sent in a few days in a less questionable shape.—

ever yr. obliged & sincere
BIRON

P.S.—I should not have bored you with this (and never did before) but you told me you liked this same scanning & proving.—

My Dear Sir—That you and I may distinctly understand each other on a subject which like "the dreadful reckoning when men smile no more"[1] makes conversation not very pleasant I think it is as well to *write* a few lines on ye. topic.—Before I left town for Yorkshire—you said that you were ready & willing to give five hundred guineas for ye. copyright of "the Giaour" and my answer was—from which I do not mean to recede—that we would discuss the point at Xmas.—The new story may or may not succeed—the probability under present circumstances seems to be that it may at least pay its expences—but even that remains to be proved—& till it is proved one way or the other we will say nothing about it.—Thus then be it—I will postpone all arrangement about it & the Giaour also till *Easter* 1814—and you shall then according to your own notions of fairness make your own offer for the two—at the same time I do not rate the last in my own estimation at half the Giaour—and according to your own notions of it's worth—and it's success within the time mentioned—be the addition or deduction to or from whatever sum may be your proposal for the first—which has already had it's success.[2]———My account with you since my last payment (which I believe cleared it off within five pounds) I presume has not *much* increased—but whatever it is—have the goodness to send it me—that I may at least meet you on even terms. —The pictures of Phillips I consider as *mine* all three—& the one (not the Arnaut) of the 2 best—is much at *your service* if you will accept it as a present[3] from

> yrs. very truly
> BIRON

P.S.—The expence of engraving from the Miniature send me on my account—as it was destroyed by my desire—& have the goodness to burn that detestable print from it immediately.

[TO LORD HOLLAND]   *Novr. 17th. 1813*

My dear Lord—Many thanks for your troubles & kindness—you don't know how sensible I am to both.—The fact is that I adopt that measure as the Duke of Norfolk takes the oaths there is no voting or

---

[1] John Gay, *The What d'ye call't*, Act. II, Scene 9.

[2] Murray replied on Nov. 18, 1813: "I restore the *Giaour* to your Lordship entirely, and for *it*, the *Bride of Abydos*, and the miscellaneous poems intended to fill up the volumes of the small edition. I beg leave to offer you the sum of One Thousand Guineas, and I shall be happy if you perceive that my estimation of your talents in my character of a man of business is not much under my admiration of them as a man." (*LJ*, II, 285n.)

[3] The Phillips portrait presented to Murray now hangs over the fireplace in the Byron Room at John Murray's.

even franking on Parnass. in these days without.—C[hild]e Harold I could not continue unless on the *spot*—and the first run is perilously against the popularity of the sequal the most I have been able to do is to sprinkle about 15 stanzas here & there in the 2d. C[ant]o principally —which cost me more time & pains & pleasure too than scribbling forty such things as ye. Bride & Giaour—the popularity of which last really surprised—& (you may think it affectation) but certainly did not raise my opinion of the public taste.—My head is full of Oriental names & scenes—and I merely chose that measure as *next* to *prose* to tell a story or describe a place which struck me—I have a thorough & utter contempt for all measures but Spencer's [sic] stanza and *Dryden's couplet*—the whole of the Bride cost me *four nights*—and you may easily suppose that I can have no great esteem for lines that can be strung as fast as minutes.—I have here & there risen to the couplet when I meant to be [*vastly*] *fine*—but it is my story & my *East*—(& here I am venturing with no one to contend against—from having *seen* what my contemporaries must copy from the drawings of others only) that I want to make palpable—and my skull is so crammed from having lived much with them & in their own way (after Hobhouse went home a year before me) with their scenes & manners—that I believe it would lead me to St. Luke's[1] if not disgorged in this manner—particularly as my cursed affairs—and fevers abroad & foolishness at home—won't allow me a chance of seeing them before Spring.—Besides I was a short time ago in a very larmoyante way—and at those moments I generally take refuge in rhyme—and so far imagination is a relief as I have often found it—for as Ly. H[olland] well said yesterday— thinking much of those from whom we are absent is an useless proof of regard and as painful as it is vain.—Hodgson my oldest acquaintance and most rigid critic says it is more *correct* (that is with fewer sins against grammar) than anything of mine before—and likes it better than the G[iaou]r which by the bye he never did like—from its *ferocity*— I have altered *Sunk* to *Cut*—"blench" is to grow pale—to shrink—but is a vile word nevertheless.—The Bride is to be appended to the G[iaou]r and I hope to lay the two at your feet in a short time.—If the public will read things written in that debauched measure—that is their own fault—and if they begin in the present instance—to dislike it—I shall be more happy in curing them—than in adding one to their Philistine Idols—The very *wild* Stanzas are more like Southey or King David—"By the waters of Babylon" &c. than anything English—

---

[1] St. Luke's was a hospital for lunatics established in 1751.

but that is thoroughly Eastern—& partly from the Koran.—Depend upon it the whole *present* generation of Bards are not for the *next*— they will not live 20 years—but how is it *now?*—see how they treated Columbus?[2]—whom I take to be by far the best *regular* left us—and worth *all* us Cossacks in fair fighting.—

ever my dear Lord—yrs. faithfully
BIRON

[TO JOHN MURRAY (*a*)]   [*Nov. 20, 1813*]

Dear Sir—You will cut out the *last half* of the *note* I sent you—& only print down to *"for us both."*—these words will conclude the note.—

yrs. truly
B

P.S.—If I could see you for 5 minutes about 1 or 2—you would oblige me—there is a parcel I cant send—

[TO JOHN MURRAY (*b*)]   [*Nov. 20, 1813*]

More work for the *Row*—I am doing my best to beat the "Giaour" *no* difficult task for anyone but the author.

yrs. truly
B

[TO JOHN MURRAY (*c*)]   [*Nov. 20, 1813*]

To make you some amends for eternally pestering you with altera- tions I send you Cobbett to confirm your orthodoxy.—One more alteration of *a* into *"The"*—in the M.S.
it must be

"The heart whose softness—&c.

Remember—and in the inscription "to the Right Honble. Lord H[olland]" *without* the previous *names* Henry &c.—

yrs. truly
B

---

[2] *Columbus*, a poem by Samuel Rogers, was rather severely criticised in the *Quarterly Review* for March, 1813.

Dear Sir—I have no time to *cross*-investigate but—I believe & hope all is right—I care less than you will believe about it's success—but I can't survive a single mis*print*—it *choaks* me to see words misused by the Printers.—Pray look over in case of some eyesore escaping me.

ever yrs.

B

P.S.—Send the earliest copies—to Mr. Frere—Mr. Canning— Mr. Heber—Mr. Gifford—Ld. Holland—Ly. Melbourne—(Whitehall) Ly. C[aroline] L[amb] Brocket—Mr. Hodgson Cambridge—Mr. Merivale—Mr. Ward—from ye. *Author*.—

My dear Lady M[elbourn]e—C[aroline] has at last done a very good natured thing—she sent me Holmes's picture for a *friend leaving England*—to which friend it is now making the best of its way.—You do not go to M[iddleton] *till* 28th. and I shall procrastinate according-ly.——Yesterday the Lady Ossulstone sent for me to complain of you *all*—we had met at Ld. Holland's the night before—and she asserted that the "extreme gravity of my countenance" made her & Ld. O[ssul-stone] believe that I had some whim about that slip of the pen-*knife* of C[aroline]'s and the consequent rumours &c. &c.—and some resent-ment about *her* in particular—to all which I pleaded ignorance & innocence.—She says Lady Blarney [Bessborough] is a very noxious person & hates her—and that none of you have taken the least notice of her since—that she is the most *discreet* of women—to prove which she produced an epistle of Ly. Somebody's *wondering* (it was but *three* hours after) she had not *already* written a full & true account of it to her!! I thought I should have laughed in her pretty black face—and—in short we are all very repulsive sort of persons and have not behaved well to her nor any body else.—Remember all *this* (like all our *thises*) is *entre Nous*—and so there is an end of the matter.—We had had a kind of squabble at the Argyle—which I could not help tormenting her a little by reminding her not of *that* but that Evening—when we were all wrong-*paired*—*she* wanted to sit by Mildmay at Supper—and I wanted to have been next that Kashmeer Butterfly of the "Blues" Ly. Charlemont[1]—or in short any body but a person who had serious concerns to think of—every body else was coupled much in the same way—in short Noah's Ark *upset* had been but a type of the *pairing* of our supper table.——Ly. Holland & I go on very well—her *unqualified* praises of you proving their *sincerity!*—she is the first woman I ever heard praise another *entirely.*—Ly. B[essborough] had better let us remain undisturbed—for if Ly. H[olland] thinks that it annoys her there will be no end to ye. intimacy.—I have taken the *half weeks* (3 days in each) of Lord Salisbury's[2] box at Covent Garden—and there when C[aroline] is in town we can always talk for an hour on Emergency.—The occasional oddity of Ph's [Frances Webster's] letters have amused me much—the simplicity of her cunning—& her exquisite reasons—she vindicates her treachery to —— [Webster] thus—after condemning deceit in general & hers in particular—she says—"but then remember it is to deceive 'un Marito' and to prevent all the unpleasant consequences["] &c. &c. and she says this in perfect persuasion that she has a full conception of the "fitness of things" & the "beauty of virtue" and "the social compact" as Philosopher Square[3] has it—Again—she desires me to write to *him kindly*—for—she believes he cares for nobody but *me!* besides—she will then hear *of* when she can't *from* me.—Is not all this a comedy?—next to Ly. Ossuls[tone]'s *voucher* for her discretion—it has enlivened my ethical studies on the human mind beyond 50 volumes—how admirably we accommodate our reasons to our wishes!————She concludes by denominating that respectable man *"Argus"* a very irreverent appellation—if we can both hold out till Spring—perhaps he may have occasion for his Optics.—After all—"it is to deceive un Marito" does not this expression convey to you the strangest mixture of right & wrong?—a really guilty person could not have used it—or rather they would *but* in different words—I find she has not the *but* and that makes much difference—if you consider it—the experienced would have said it is *"only* deceiving *him"*—thinking of themselves—she makes a *merit* of it on his account & mine.——The Dutch have taken Holland

---

[1] Lady Charlemont was a famous beauty, daughter of William Bermingham, of Ross Hill, Galway. She married Francis William Caulfield, the 2nd Earl of Charlemont, in 1802. Though Byron spoke slightingly of her intellect, he was not blind to her beauty, for he wrote of her in his first letter on Bowles in 1821: ". . . the head of Lady Charlemont (when I first saw her nine years ago) seemed to possess all that sculpture could require for its ideal." (*LJ*, V, 549.)

[2] James Cecil, Earl of Salisbury (1748–1823).

[3] See *Tom Jones*, Book III, Chapter 3.

& got Bernadotte & Orange—the Stork & King Log at once—in their Froggery.[4]—

ever yrs.

B

I must quote to you correctly—

"—how easily mankind are deceived—*May he be always deceived*! and I—alas—am the base instrument of deception—but in this instance *concealment* is *not* a crime—for it preserves the peace 'd'un marito' the contrary would &c. ["] I have been arguing on wrong premises—but no matter—the *marked* lines are quite as good.—

[TO JAMES WEDDERBURN WEBSTER]   *Novr. 22d. 1813*

My dear W.—I have but time for a few words which shall be to the *purpose*—I have before told you & now repeat very sincerely—that when the time of your bond is up—I shall not enforce it[1]—I consider ye. security as merely nominal—& surely more for your *own* satisfaction than mine—even if my exigencies were pressing—I should not trouble you on the subject—and you know me well enough not to doubt me on such *wordly* matters—I have but one favour to ask you— if you feel any pressure for additional accommodation—always apply in the *first* instance—to *me*—if I can assist you further I will—& if I cannot—I may at least hit on some expedient to prevent you from taking the imprudent step you had otherwise adopted on the present occasion.—So there is an end of the matter—until you revive the subject—I suppose you will at least prefer me to a *Jew.*—I meant to write you a long letter on lighter topics—but talking of money materializes one's thoughts and I must for the present close my dispatch with the satisfaction of having at least set you at rest on that head.—

yrs. ever

BIRON

[TO JOHN MURRAY]   [*November 23, 1813*]

Dear Sir—You wanted some *reflections*—and I send you *per Selim* (in his speech in Canto 2d. page 46) eighteen lines in decent couplets

---

4 See Byron's journal, Nov. 17, 1813.

1 Byron had taken a bond for a loan of £1,000 which he had given to Webster to prevent him from going to the usurers although he was in the hands of usurers himself.

of a pensive if not *ethical* tendency.—One more revise poz [positively?]
the *last* if decently done—at any rate the *pen*ultimate.—Mr. C[an-
ning]'s approbation (*if* he did approve) I need not say makes me
proud[1]—as to printing—print as you will & how you will—by itself
if you like—but let me have a few copies in *duets*.

ever yrs.
B—

[TO JOHN MURRAY]   [*November 24, 1813*]

You must pardon me once more as it is all for your good—it must
be thus—

> "He makes a Solitude—& calls it—Peace.—["]

"*Makes*"—is closer to the passage of Tacitus from which the line is
taken—& is besides a stronger word than "*leaves*"

yrs. ever
B

[TO LADY MELBOURNE]   *Novr. 25th. 1813*

My dear Ly. M[elbourn]e—Thanks by the thousand for yr. letter.—
I have lately been leading a whimsical life—Tuesday I dined with
Ward & met Canning & all the Wits—and yesterday I dined with the
Patrons of Pugilism & some of the professors—who amused me about
as much.———I wrote to C[aroline] a very earnest but not *savage*
letter—I believe the obnoxious sentence was—"if after this you
refuse I hope you will forgive yourself for I fear I cannot["]—all the
rest was merely *entreaty*—The Picture is however—God knows where
—*they* have now that is *four* (the Mussulman *legal* allotment) one
picture apiece—and as many Originals of other people as they please in
the interim.—I had no idea C[aroline] would have restored it but it was
very kind and I am very much obliged to her.—It is strange that Ph's
[Frances Webster's] greatest dread appears to be discovery—& yet
she is perpetually as it were contriving everything to lead to it—she
writes—makes me answer through an address to a 3d. person—whom
she has *not trusted*—of course their curiosity will not be the least
excited by being made an involuntary Post-office!—Then she would
not rest till she had this picture sent—in the same way—and the odds

---

[1] Canning, to whom Murray had sent *The Bride of Abydos*, wrote: "It is very,
very beautiful."

173

are—particularly with such a person as —— [Webster] that he has—
or will in some manner stumble on something incontrovertible—& out
of which she cant *"conceal"* herself (as she calls it) that is in other
words invent an excuse.———To say the truth I am not very unwilling
that this should be the case—as it will hasten a crisis of some kind or
other.—His first impulse will be probably *Martial*—but if I have a
motive I don't mind that—it will at least leave her for the Survivor—&
the *Survived* won't feel the want of her—besides in my case it would be
so *dramatic* a conclusion—all the sex would be enamoured of my
Memory—all the Wits would have their jest—& the Moralists their
sermon—C[aroline] would go wild with *grief* that—*it did not happen*
about *her*—Ly. O[xfor]d would say I deserved it for not coming to
Cagliari—and— —— [Augusta] poor —— [Augusta] she would be
really uncomfortable—do you know? I am much afraid that that per-
verse passion was my deepest after all.—Well—suppose he should not
take the angry road—at least with me—it then comes to a point
between her & him—"Give him up or part with me"—no one wants
spirit—particularly the spirit of contradiction with that they dislike
(she swore to me she never would give me up—but that is nothing—)
yet I don't know that she would not take him at his word—& send to
me; but at all events the superiority this advantage would give him—
and the additional distrust & ill agreement between them must in-
crease *soon* so far that *our* union must be the Event.—The 3d. course is
her getting the better—& his finding (as he has partly found) that my
friendship is not inconvenient—and our all "being happy ever after"—
to one of these conclusions we must come sooner or later—& why not
now?—We shall have forty other things to think of before Spring—
merely from the irritation of Hope deferred—the most annoying of
discordant feelings.—"Have patience" in the mean time—you say—
so I will—if I can have nothing else.———The Duchess [of Devon-
shire]'s verses are beautiful[1]—but I don't like *her* a bit the better—I
send you in return some, *not* of mine as you will see by the hand—but
I am not certain they are *hers* (Ph's) though from the cast of thought—
it is very like her.—I hope I am not doing what Lord Grey did—He
showed some letters of a woman as the most exquisite &c. &c. till
some sagacious person pointed them out either in Rousseau's Eloise—
or the Portuguese letters!—I received these this morning—& think

---

[1] The Duchess of Devonshire was the widow of the 5th Duke of Devonshire.
Lady Elizabeth Hervey, daughter of the 4th Earl of Bristol, married John Thomas
Foster in 1776. After his death Gibbon proposed marriage to her but she refused.
In 1809 she married the Duke of Devonshire, who died two years later.

them pretty—pray tell me if they are—for seriously I am a very erring Critic—one may write—and yet not be able to judge—and the reverse.—return them on your return to town.—My new Turkish tale will be out directly—I shall of course send you a copy—Frere & Canning & the Hollands have seen & like it—the *public* is another question—but it will for some *reasons interest you* more than anybody— these I leave you to discover—(I mean totally independent of Criticism—for you may not like it a bit the better)—you know me better than most people—and are the only person who can trace & I want to see whether you think my *writings* are *me* or not.[2]—

yrs. ever
B

When I speak of this *tale* & the *author*—I merely mean *feelings*— the characters & the costume & the tale itself (at least are very like it I heard) are Mussulman.—This no one but *you* can tell.—

[TO JOHN MURRAY]   [*November 27, 1813*]

Dear Sir—If you look over this carefully by the *last proof* with my corrections it is probably right—this *you* can *do* as well or better—I have not now time.—The copies I mentioned to be sent to different friends last night[1] I should wish to be made up with the new Giaours if it also is ready—if not send the G[iaour]s afterwards.—the M[orning] P[os]t says *I* am the Author of Nourjahad!![2] this comes of lending the drawings for their dresses—but it is not worth a *formal contradiction.*— Besides—the criticisms on the *supposition* will some of them be quite amusing & furious.—The *Orientalism*—which I hear is very splendid of the Melodrame (whos ever it is & I am sure I don't know) is as good as an Advertisement for your Eastern stories—by filling their heads with glitter.—

yrs. ever
B

[2] Byron knew that Lady Melbourne would recognize some of the "feelings" for Augusta and Lady Frances Webster in the poem. The close relationship of Selim and Zuleika (they were brother and sister in the first version, but he changed the relationship to cousins) would have a meaning for her which others might not note.
[1] On Nov. 22 Byron had mentioned the friends to whom he wanted copies of *The Bride of Abydos* sent. This would suggest that the date of this letter should be Nov. 23, but someone, presumably Murray himself, has written "Nov. 27, 1813" at the top of the manuscript.
[2] *Illusion, or the Trances of Nourjahad* was acted at Drury Lane Nov. 23, 1813. It was an anonymous melodrama in three acts. The *Satirist* (Vol. XIII, p. 508) also ascribed the play to Byron, probably because of the Oriental theme.

P.S. You will of course *say* the truth—that I am *not* the Melodramatist if any one charges me in your presence with the performance.——

[TO DR. WILLIAM CLARK]   *Novr. 27th. 1813*

My dear Sir—I hope you will have no objection to keep our engagement—and do me the favour of accompanying me to Holland next week[1]—Fevers—plagues—& everything are against the Mediterranean which we will exchange for the Zuyder Zee—and if affairs go on well—Germany & even Italy are within our range.—Pray let me hear from you—ever dear Sir

yrs. truly
BIRON

[TO JOHN MURRAY (*a*)]   *Novr. 28th. 1813*

Dear Sir—Send another copy (if not too much of a request) to Ly. Holland of the *Journal*[1] in my name when you receive this—it is for *Earl Grey*—and I will relinquish my *own*.—Also to Mr. *Sharpe*—Ly. H[ollan]d and Ly. C[aroline] L[amb] copies of "the Bride" as soon as convenient.

ever yrs.
BIRON

P.S.—Mr. W[ard] & myself still continue our purpose[2]—but I shall not trouble you on any arrangement on the score of "the Giaour & Bride" till our return—or at any rate before *May*—1814—that is six months from hence—and before that time you will be able to ascertain how far your offer may be a losing one—if so—you can deduct proportionally—& if not I shall not at any rate allow you to go higher

1 Byron was planning a trip to Holland with J. W. Ward, and now asked Dr. Clark, who had been waiting to go abroad with him since the middle of the summer, to go along. But this trip too was postponed and finally cancelled because Ward was called suddenly to Scotland.

1 *The Journal of Llewellin Penrose, a Seaman*, edited by the Rev. John Eagles, was published by Murray. It was an anonymous narrative of a Robinson Crusoe-like experience of the author, William Williams (c. 1710-c. 1790) whom Thomas Eagles, the father of the editor, had befriended. Williams bequeathed the manuscript to his benefactor.

2 Their purpose was to go to Holland. See Nov. 27, 1813, to Dr. William Clark, note 1.

than your present proposal which is very handsome & more than fair.[3] ———— I have had but this must be *"entre nous"* a very kind note on the subject of "the Bride" from Sir J[ames] M[ackintosh]—& an invitation to go there this Even[ing] which it is now too late to accept.—

[TO JOHN MURRAY (*b*)]   *Novr. 28th. 1813*

Dr. Sr.—In page 45 of "the *Giaour*" there is an error line second "agel" for *"Angel"* which with a little botching it may not yet be too late to rectify.—I have as yet discovered no other erratum in either—but have not redde ye. notes.—

yrs. ever

B

P.S.—Let this mistake be rectified if possible in *any way.*———

[TO JOHN MURRAY (*c*)]   [*November 28, 1813*]

Alteration of these lines—you will recollect the page (it is 46)

————"Man's warring kind—
"Mark where his carnage & his conquests cease
He makes a Solitude—and calls it—peace![*"*][1]

you will perceive that the sense is now clearer the *"He"* refers to *"Man"* in the preceding couplet.

yrs. &c.

[TO JOHN MURRAY (*d*)]   [*November 28? 1813*]

Page 45 (I believe but having no copy am not certain) after line
            "And tints tomorrow with prophetic ray
read—
            "Sweet as his native song to Exile's ears
            Shall sound each tone thy long-loved voice endears.[*"*][1]

Insert this in its proper place—as also the other insertions & alterations before sent on the first opportunity

B

[3] See Nov. 17, 1813, to Murray, note 2.
[1] *The Bride of Abydos*, Canto II, lines 911–913. See [Nov. 24, 1813] to Murray.
[1] *The Bride of Abydos*, Canto II, lines 888–889.

No one can *a*ssume or *pre*sume less than you do though very few
with whom I am acquainted possess half your claims to that "Superiority" which you are so fearful of affecting—nor can I recollect one
expression since the commencement of our correspondence which has
in any respect diminished my opinion of your talents—my respect for
your virtues.—My only reason for avoiding the discussion of *sacred*
topics—was the sense of my own ignorance & the fear of saying something that might displease—but I *have listened* & will listen to you with
not merely patience but pleasure.—When we meet—if we do meet—
in Spring—you will find me ready to acquiesce in all your notions upon
the point merely personal between ourselves—you will act according
to circumstances—it would be premature in us both to anticipate
reflections which may never be made—& if made at all—are certainly
unfounded.—You wrong yourself very much in supposing that "the
charm" has been broken by our nearer acquaintance—on ye. contrary
—that very intercourse convinces me of the value of what I have lost—
or rather never found—but I will not deny that circumstances have
occurred to render it more supportable.[1]——You will think me very
caprious & apt at sudden fancies—it is true I could not exist without
some object of attachment—but I have shewn that I am not quite a
slave to impulse—no man of tolerable situation in life who was quite
without self command could have reached the age of 26 (which I shall
be—I grieve to speak it—in January) without marrying & in all
probability foolishly.—But however weak—(it may merit a harsher
term) in my disposition to attach myself—(and as society is now much
the same in this as in all other European countries—it were difficult
to avoid it) in my search for the "ideal" the being to whom I would
commit the whole happiness of my future life—I have never yet seen
but two approaching to the likeness—the first I was too young to
have a prospect of obtaining—& subsequent events have proved that
my expectations might not have been fulfilled had I ever proposed to
& secured my early idol[2]—the *second*—the *only* woman to whom I
ever seriously pretended as a wife—had disposed of her heart already
—and I think it too late to look for a third.—I shall take ye. world as I
find it—& I have seen it much the same in most climates—(a little

[1] Thinking that Annabella was attached to another, Byron was again hinting at
an attachment of his own in order to make her more comfortable in their "friendship". (See Nov. 10, 1813, to Annabella, note 2) But Annabella was already
regretting that she had let him think that her heart was engaged elsewhere.
[2] Mary Chaworth.

more fiery perhaps in Greece & Asia—for there they are a strange
mixture of languid habits & stormy passions) but I have no confidence
& look for no constancy in affections founded in caprice—& preserved
(if preserved) by accident—& lucky conformity of disposition without
any fixed principles.—How far this may be my case at present—I
know not—& have not had time to ascertain—I can only say that I
never was cured of loving any one but by the conduct—by the change
—or the violence of the object herself—and till I see reason for
distrust I shall flatter myself as heretofore—& perhaps with as little
cause as ever.———I owe you some apology for this disquisition—
but the singularity of *our* situation led me to dwell on this topic—&
your friendship will excuse it.—I am anxious to be candid with you
though I fear sometimes I am betrayed into impertinence.—They say
that a man never *forgives* a woman who stands in the relation which you
do towards me—but to *forgive*—we must first be offended—& I think
I cannot recall—even a moment of pique at the past to my memory—I
have but *2 friends* of your sex—yourself & Ly. Melbourne—as
different in years as in disposition—& yet I do not know which I prefer
—believe me a better-*hearted* woman does not exist—and in talent I
never saw her excelled & hardly equalled—her kindness to me has
been uniform—and I fear severely & ungratefully tried at times on my
part—but as it cannot be so again—at least in the same manner—I shall
make what atonement I can—if a regard which my own inclination
leads me to cultivate—can make any amends for my trespasses on
her patience.———The word *patience* reminds me of ye. book I am
to send you—it shall be ordered to Seaham tomorrow.—I shall be
most happy to see any thing of your writing—of what I have already
seen you once heard my favourable & sincere opinion.—I by no means
rank poetry or poets high in the scale of intellect—this may look like
Affectation—but it is my real opinion—it is the lava of the imagination
whose eruption prevents an earth-quake—they say Poets never or
rarely go *mad*—Cowper & Collins are instances to the contrary—(but
Cowper was no poet)—it is however to be remarked that they rarely
do—but are generally so near it—that I cannot help thinking rhyme
is so far useful in anticipating & preventing the disorder.—I prefer the
talents of *action*—of war—or the Senate—or even of Science—to all
the speculations of these mere dreamers of another existence (I don't
mean *religiously* but *fancifully*) and spectators of this.———Apathy—
disgust—& perhaps incapacity have rendered me now a mere specta-
tor—but I have occasionally mixed in the active & tumultuous depart-
ments of existence—& on these alone my *recollection* rests with any

179

satisfaction—though not the *best* parts of it.—I wish to know your Joanna[3]—& shall be very glad of the opportunity—never mind *ma cousine*[4] I thought Stockton had been your Post town & nearer Seaham. —Mr. Ward & I have talked (I fear it will be only talk as things look undecided in that quarter) of an excursion to Holland—if so—I shall be able to compare a Dutch canal with the Bosphorus.—I never saw a Revolution transacting[5]—or at least completed—but I arrived just after the last Turkish one—& the *effects* were visible—& had all the grandeur of desolation in their aspect——Streets in ashes—immense barracks (of a very fine construction) in ruins—and above all Sultan Selim's favourite gardens round them in all the wildness of luxurient neglect—his fountains waterless—& his kiosks defaced but still glittering in their decay.—They lie between the city & Buyukderé on the hills above the Bosphorus—& the way to them is through a plain with the prettiest name in the world—"the Valley of Sweet Waters".[6] —But I am sending a volume not a letter.

ever yrs. most truly
B

[TO DR. WILLIAM CLARK]   *Novr. 29th. 1813*

Dear Sir—I have just seen Mr. Ward who tells me that it will be as well we should be *prepared*—but that at present till Gen. Graham is gone & the communication more regulated we must not set off upon Speculation.[1]—All this we shall know in a *week*—and if you will have the goodness to be ready I will send you notice in time for every thing as there is nothing I should regret more than the dissolution of our partnership.—Excuse the hasty letter I sent under the notion that we should embark this week—I trust every thing will be practicable the

[3] Joanna Baillie, who was a friend of Annabella and her family.
[4] See Nov. 10, 1813, to Annabella, note 3.
[5] Holland, which had been a kingdom of France since 1806, was incorporated with the French Empire in 1810. On Nov. 15, 1813, the people of Amsterdam revolted, raised the Orange colours, and expelled the French. They were joined by other provinces, and on Nov. 21 they sent a delegation to London to ask the Prince of Orange to lead the movement for independence. He landed in Holland on Nov. 30. To see "a Revolution transacting" was one of Byron's motives for wanting to go to Holland.
[6] One of Byron's favourite rides while he was in Constantinople was to "the Valley of Sweet Waters". Büyükdere is a village on the Bosphorus, at the head of its largest bay, which gives a first view of the Black Sea.
[1] See Nov. 27, 1813, to Dr. Clark, note 1; and Nov. 29, 1813, to Annabella Milbanke, note 5. Sir Thomas Graham had assisted Wellington in the campaign in Spain, but was sent home after the unsuccessful siege of San Sebastian. In November, 1813, he was sent to Holland to help General Bülow against Antwerp.

next—at all events *I* am decided to go somewhere—& I believe you are Citizen enough of the world to feel as few partialities for particular parts of it—as myself.—If you come to town I shall of course be very glad to see you—but I lose no time in saying that my exceeding hurry was a little premature—an anxiety I trust you will excuse when you know the motive.—I shall write again in a day or two—do not quit C[ambridg]e at any inconvenience to yourself—but still do not be surprised if I send another impatient epistle—as every thing depends upon the news of the next week.—ever my dear Sir.

yr. very faithful St.

BIRON

[TO JOHN MURRAY (*a*)]   [*November 29, 1813*]

Sunday—Monday Morning—3 o'clock
in my doublet & hose—swearing.—

Dear Sir—I send you in time an Errata page containing an omission of mine which must be thus added as it is too late for insertion in the text—the passage is an imitation altogether from Medea in Ovid—& is incomplete without these two lines—pray let this be done & directly —it is necessary—will add one page to your book-(*making*) & can do no harm & is yet in time for the *public*—Answer me—thou Oracle— in the Affirmative—you can send the loose pages to those who have copies already if they like—but certainly to all the *Critical* copy holders.[1]—

ever yrs.

BIRON

P.S.—I have got out of my bed—(in which however I could not sleep whether I had amended this or not) & so Good Morning—I am trying whether De L'Allemagne[2] will act as an opiate—but I doubt it.—

[TO JOHN MURRAY (*b*)]   [*November 29, 1813*]

Dear Sir—"*You have looked at it*![*"*] to much purpose to allow so stupid a blunder to stand—it is *not "courage"* but "*Carnage*" & if you

---

[1] *The Bride of Abydos* was already printed by Nov. 29, 1813, but Byron still sent in corrections. The added lines (Canto II, lines 838–839) were changed before being printed in later editions. In his Journal (Dec. 5) Byron says it was published December 2.

[2] Madame de Staël's *De l'Allemagne* was a book much admired by Byron. His annotated copy is now in the Houghton Library, Harvard University.

don't want me [to] cut my own throat—see it altered.—I am sorry to hear of the fall of Dresden———

ever yrs.

B.

[TO JOHN MURRAY (c)] [*Monday November 29, 1813*]

Dear Sir—You will act as you please upon that point—but whether I go or stay—I shall not say another word on ye. subject till May—nor then unless quite convenient to yourself.[1]—I have many things I wish to leave to your care—principally papers—the *vases* need not be now sent as Mr. W[ard] is gone to Scotland.—You are right about the Er[rata] Page—place it at the beginning.——Mr. Perry is a little premature in his compliments[2]—these may do harm by exciting expectation—& I think *we* ought to be above it—though I see the next paragraph is on the *Journal*[3] which makes me suspect *you* as the author of both.—Would it not have been as well to have said in *2* Cantos in the Advertisement? they will else think of *fragments* a species of composition very well for *once* like *one ruin* in a *view*—but one would not build a town of them—The Bride such as it is is my first *entire* composition of any length—(except Satire & be d————d to it) for the G[iaou]r is but a string of passages—& C[hil]d Ha[rol]d is & I rather think always will be unconcluded.——I return Mr. Hay's note with thanks to him & you.—there have been some epigrams on Mr. W[ar]d one I see today[4]—the first I did not see but heard yesterday—the second seems very bad—and Mr. P[erry] has placed it over *your* puff—I only hope that Mr. W[ard] does not believe that I had any connection with either—the Regent is the only person on whom I ever expectorated an epigram or ever should—& even if I were disposed that way—I like & value Mr. W[ard] too well to allow my politics to contract into spleen—or to admire anything intended to annoy him or his.—You need not take the trouble to answer this—as I shall see you in ye. course of ye. Afternoon—

yrs, very truly

B

1 See Nov. 17, 1813, to Murray, note 2.

2 The *Bride* was printed but not yet distributed to booksellers when Perry's *Morning Chronicle* of Nov. 29, 1813, announced that Byron "has another poem coming out, entitled *The Bride of Abydos*, which is spoken of in terms of the highest encomium."

3 See Nov. 28, 1813, to Murray (*a*), note 1.

4 The epigram was:

"Ward has no heart, they say; but I deny it;—
He has a heart, and gets his speeches by it."

P.S.—I have said this much about the epigrams because I live so much in the *opposite camp*—& from my post as an Engineer—might be suspected as ye. flinger of these hand Grenadoes—but with a worthy foe I am all for open war—& not this bush-fighting—& have [not] had nor will have anything to do with it—I do not know the author.—

[TO JOHN MURRAY (*a*)]   *[November 30, 1813]*

Print this at the end of *All that is of* [*the*] "*Bride of Abydos*" as an Errata page

B<small>N</small>

Omitted Canto 2d.
page 47—after line 449
"So that these arms cling closer round my neck["]
Read
"Then—if my lip once murmurs—it must be.—
No sigh for safety—but a prayer for thee![")

[TO JOHN MURRAY (*b*)]   *Tuesday Even.* [*November 30, 1813*]

Dear Sir—For the sake of correctness particularly in an Er[rata] page—the alteration of the couplet I have just sent (half an hour ago) must take place in spite of delay or cancel—let me see the *proof* early tommorow—I found out "*murmur*' to be a neuter *verb* & have been obliged to alter the line so as to make it a substantive thus

"The deepest murmur of this life shall be
No sigh for Safety but a prayer for thee!

don't send the copies to the *country* till this is all right.—

yrs.
B

[TO THOMAS MOORE]   *November 30th, 1813*

Since I last wrote to you, much has occurred, good, bad, and in-different,—not to make me forget you, but to prevent me from reminding you of one who, nevertheless, has often thought of you, and to whom *your* thoughts, in many a measure, have frequently been a consolation. We were once very near neighbours this autumn; and a good and bad neighborhood it has proved to me. Suffice it to say, that your French quotation was confoundedly to the purpose,[1]—though very *unexpectedly* pertinent, as you may imagine by what I *said* before, and my silence since. * * * * * * * * *

However, "Richard's himself again,"[2] and, except all night and some part of the morning, I don't think very much about the matter.

All convulsions end with me in rhyme; and, to solace my midnights, I have scribbled another Turkish story—not a Fragment—which you will receive soon after this. It does not trench upon your kingdom in the least, and, if it did, you would soon reduce me to my proper boundaries. You will think, and justly, that I run some risk of losing the little I have gained in fame, by this further experiment on public patience; but I have really ceased to care on that head. I have written this, and published it, for the sake of the *employment*,—to wring my thoughts from reality, and take refuge in "imaginings," however "horrible;" and, as to success! those who succeed will console me for a failure—excepting yourself and one or two more, whom luckily I love too well to wish one leaf of their laurels a tint yellower. This is the work of a week, and will be the reading of an hour to you, or even less, —and so, let it go * * * * * * * * * * * * * * *

P.S. Ward and I *talk* of going to Holland. I want to see how a Dutch canal looks, after the Bosphorus. Pray respond.

[TO MADAME DE STAËL]   *Novr. 30th. 1813*

Dear Madam—I shall not apologize for answering your very kind letter in my own language with which you are so well acquainted. I should be fearful of replying to you in yours—even had I been born and educated a native of France.—My knowledge of French is superficial yet sufficient to comprehend the beauty & originality of thoughts which belong to no particular country or quarter of the globe—but must strike to the hearts of all who inhabit it.—In referring to your recent work in the note with which you are obliging enough to be pleased[1]—I was but too happy to avail myself of your authority for a

[1] Moore's French quotation was from Fontenelle: "Si je recommençais ma carrière, je ferais tout ce que j'ai fait."

[2] Colley Cibber's *Richard III*, Act. V, Scene 3:
　　　　"Conscience, avaunt! Richard's himself again."

[1] In a note to a line in *The Bride of Abydos* (Canto I, stanza VI) Byron wrote: "For an eloquent passage in the latest work of the first female writer or this, perhaps of any, age, on the analogy . . . between 'painting and music,' see vol. iii, cap. 10, *De L'Allemagne*." This letter is an answer to Mme. de Staël's "very pretty billet", as he described it in his Journal (Nov. 30, 1813).

real or fancied confirmation of my own opinion on a particular subject. —My praise was only the feeble echo of more powerful voices—to yourself any attempt at eulogy must be merely repetition.—Of the work itself I can only say—that few days have passed since it's publication without my perusal of many of it's pages—& that I should be sorry for my own sake to fix the period when I should not recur to it with pleasure—The tale—which you have honoured by your notice— was written hastily—& published I fear injudiciously—and has moreover the disadvantage of being composed in some of those moments when we are forced by reality to take refuge in Imagination—I am much more obliged to it than I ever can be to the most partial reader— as it wrung my thoughts from selfish & sorrowful contemplation—& recalled them to a part of the world to which I am indebted for some of the brightest and darkest but always the *most living* recollections of my existence.—My time is passed so irregularly that you will not mistake my omissions in the etiquette of visiting—for want of respect for your talents—nor neglect of your society: with all the world at your feet; you can neither miss nor regret the absence of a solitary and sometimes a sullen individual.—My friends—at least my acquaintances—who are most of them your friends—and all your admirers—could or might tell you that this carelessness is habitual— I do not say it is excusable—& certainly is not so in the present instance. But your Goodnature will forgive my negligence & perhaps some of my faults—amongst which however cannot be numbered any deficiency in *real* respect & sincere admiration on the part of

your obliged & very faithful humble servt.

Byron

[TO JOHN MURRAY (a)]   [*Dec.?* *1813*]

"Ecce Homo"—published by Cobbett's man—Eaton[1]—I want to

---

[1] *Ecce Homo*, translated from "Histoire Critique de Jésus-Christ" of Baron d'Holbach, was put out with the imprint of Daniel Isaac Eaton at Ave Maria Lane in 1813. Although it was attributed to him, he was then in Newgate serving an 18-month term imposed by Lord Ellenborough for selling the third and last part of Paine's *Age of Reason*; it was apparently the work of either Joseph Webb (*Notes and Queries*, 3d. ser., X, 297) or Houston (*Newgate Monthly Magazine*, I, 292). Eaton had a long history of publishing and selling "seditious" and "blasphemous" works. He was indicted in 1793 for selling the second part of Paine's *Rights of Man*, but was acquitted. Lord Ellenborough passed sentence on him in 1794 for publishing a periodical called *Politics for the People*. Shelley defended him in 1812 in "A Letter to Lord Ellenborough Occasioned by the Sentence which he passed on Mr. D. I. Eaton".

see this publication—it must be obtained soon—as Eaton is about to be compelled to Suppression.—

[TO JOHN MURRAY (*b*)]   [*Dec. 1813?*]

Will you have the kindness to lend me your Buccaneer's Journal[1] for the Evening?

yrs. &c.
B

[TO JOHN MURRAY (*c*)]   [*December, 1813?*]

I send you some lines which may as well be called a *Song* as anything else—it will do for the latter pages of any new Edition

B

a Song

1

Thou art not false, but thou art fickle
⟨And seekest often⟩
To those thyself so fondly sought;
The tears that thou hast forced to trickle
Are doubly bitter from that thought,
'Tis this which breaks the heart thou grievest,
Too well thou lov'st—*too soon* thou leavest.

2

The wholly false the *heart* despises
And spurns deceiver & deceit,
But *her* who not a thought disguises,
Whose Love is as sincere as sweet,
When *She* can change who loved so truly
It *feels* what mine has *felt* so newly.

3

To dream of joy & wake to sorrow
Is doomed to all who love or live
And if when conscious on the Morrow
We scarce our *Fancy* can forgive
That cheated us in Slumber only
To leave the waking soul more lonely.

---

[1] Byron thus referred to *The Journal of Llewellin Penrose, a Seaman*. See Nov. 28, 1813, to Murray (*a*), note 1.

What must they feel whom no false Vision
But truest tenderest Passion warmed,
Sincere, but swift in sad transition,
As if a Dream alone had charmed,
Ah sure such *Grief* is *Fancy's* scheming,
And all thy *Change* can be but *dreaming*.

[TO FRANCIS HODGSON] *Novr.—Decr. 1st. 1813*

I have just heard that *Knapp*[1] is acquainted with what I was but too happy in being enabled to do for you[2]—now—my dear H[odgso]n—you or Drury must have told this—for upon my own honour—not even to Scrope—nor to one soul—(D[rur]y knew it before) have I said one syllable of the matter—so don't be out of humour with me about it—but you can't be more so than I am.—I am however glad of one thing—if you ever conceived it to be in the least an obligation—this disclosure most fairly & fully releases you from it—
"To John I owe great obligation
                    But John &c.["]
and so there's an end of the matter.—Ward *wavers* a little about the Dutch till matters are more sedative—& the French more sedentary—The Bride will blush upon you in a day or two there is *much* at least a *little* addition—I am happy to say that Frere & Heber and some other "good men & true" have been kind enough to adopt the same opinion that you did.—Pray—write when you like & believe me

ever yrs.
BYRON

P.S. Murray has *offered* me a thousand guineas for the *2* (G[iaou]r & B[rid]e) and told Me. de Stael that he had *paid* them to me!! I should be glad to be able to tell her so too—but the truth is—he would—but I thought the fair way was to decline it till May & at the end of 6 months he can safely say whether he can afford it or not—without running any risk by Speculation[3]—if he paid them now & lost by it—it would be hard—if he gains—it will be time enough when he has

---

[1] Unidentified.
[2] Byron had made another "loan" to Hodgson to enable him to clear his father's debts so that he could marry Miss Tayler, sister-in-law of Henry Drury. In all Byron gave Hodgson £1,500 which he intended as a gift, though he called it a loan.
[3] See Nov. 17, 1813, to Murray.

already funded his profits—but he needed not have told "la Baronne" such a devil of an uncalled for piece of—premature *truth* perhaps—but nevertheless a *lie* in the meantime.—

[TO JOHN MURRAY]   *Decr. 2d. 1813*

Dear Sir—When you can—let the couplet enclosed—be inserted either in the page or in the Errata page[1]—I trust it is in time for some of the copies.—this alteration is in the same part (the page *but one* before) the last insertion sent

yrs. &c.

B

P.S.—I am afraid from all I hear that people are rather inordinate in their expectations which is very unlucky but cannot now be helped—this comes of Mr. Perry[2]—& one's wise friends—but do not *you* wind *your* hopes of success to the same pitch for fear of accidents—and I can assure you that my philosophy will stand the test very fairly—and I have done—everything to ensure you at all events from positive loss—which will be some satisfaction to both.—

[TO LEIGH HUNT[1]]   *4. Bennet Street—Decr. 2d. 1813*

My dear Sir—Few things could be more welcome than your note—& on Saturday morning I will avail myself of your permission to thank you for it in person.—My time has not been passed since we met either profitably or agreeably—a very short period after my last visit an incident occurred with which I fear you are not unacquainted (as report in many mouths & more than one paper was busy with the topic) that naturally gave me much uneasiness.—Then—I nearly incurred a lawsuit on the scale of an estate—but *that* is now arranged—next—but why should I go on with a series of selfish & silly details?—I merely wish to assure you that it was not the frivolous forgetfulness of a mind occupied by what is called pleasure (*not* in the true sense of Epicurus) that kept me away but a perception of my *then* unfitness to share the society of those whom I value & wish not to displease.—I hate being larmoyant—& making a serious face among those who

1 The Errata page was for *The Bride of Abydos.*
2 See Nov. 29, 1813, to Murray (*c*), note 2.
1 For Hunt's relationship with Byron see the biographical sketch in the Appendix to Volume 2.

are cheerful.———It is my wish that our acquaintance or—If you please to accept it—friendship may be permanent—I have been lucky enough to preserve some friends from a very early period—& I hope as I do not (at least now) select them lightly I shall not lose them capriciously. I have a thorough esteem for that independence of spirit which you have maintained with sterling talent and at the expence of some suffering.—You have not I trust abandoned the poem you were composing when Moore & I partook of your hospitality in ye. summer?—I hope a time will come when he & I may be able to repay you in *kind* for the *latter*—for the *rhyme*—at least in *quantity* you are in arrear to both.—Believe me

very truly & affectly. yrs.
BYRON

[TO LORD HOLLAND]   [*Dec. 2, 1813?*]

My dear Lord—In compliance with your suggestion you will find in my *scrawl* 2 lines page 47 that fill up the *Ovidian* hiatus[1]—& if Lady H[olland] will allow me I will copy them out in her vol. also in my decentest handwriting.—The public will have them in an Errata column as it is too [late] for the text.—I have ordered Mr. M[urray] to send Ly. H[olland] another copy of ye. Journal[2]—& he will send or I will bring it this day.—I write to you at 4 in the morning—in my doublet & *hosen*—not at all sleepy—(though I have been in bed) but I soon shall be for I am going to read.—

ever yrs. my dear Lord
BIRON

[TO ZACHARY MACAULAY][1]
4 Bennet Street St. James's—Decr. 3d. 1813

Sir/—I have just finished the perusal of an article in the "Christian Observer" on ye. "Giaour."—*You* perhaps are unacquainted with ye. writer—and at all events I have no business to enquire.—I only wish you would have ye. goodness to thank him very sincerely on my part

---

[1] See [Nov. 29, 1813], to Murray (*a*); and [Nov. 30, 1813]. to Murray.
[2] See Nov. 28, 1813, to Murray (*a*), note 1.
[1] Zachary Macaulay (1768–1828) philanthropist and ardent anti-slavery advocate, edited the *Christian Observer* (1802–1816), a periodical devoted to the abolition of the British slave-trade.

for ye pleasure (I do not say *un*mixed pleasure) which the perusal of a very able and I believe just criticism has afforded me.[2]—Of course *I* cannot be an impartial witness of it's justice—but it is something in it's favour when the author criticised does not complain of his sentence.—This is not *affectation*—if I felt angry I could not conceal it even from others—and contempt can only be bestowed on the weak—amongst whom the writer of this article has certainly no place.—I shall merely add that this is ye. first notice I have for some years taken of any *public* criticism good or bad in the way of either thanks or defence—and I trust that yourself & the Writer will not attribute to any unworthy motive my deviating for once from my usual custom to express myself *obliged* to him.—May I request that this communication may remain *private*.—I have the honour to be

> very sincerely yr. most obedt. very humble Sert.
> BIRON

P.S.—I cannot fold this sheet without congratulating you on the acquisition of a writer in your valuable journal whose style & powers are so far above the generality of writers as the author of the remarks to which I have alluded.—

[TO JOHN MURRAY (*a*)]   [*Dec. 3, 1813*]

I send you a *scratch* or *two*—the which heal—The C[hristian] Observer is very savage but certainly uncommonly well written—[1] & quite uncomfortable at the naughtiness of book & author.—I rather suspect you wont much like the *present* to be more moral—if it is to share also the usual fate of your virtuous volume.—Let me see a proof of the *6* before *incorporation*.

[TO JOHN MURRAY (*b*)]   [*Dec. 3, 1813*]

Look out in the Encyclopedia article *Mecca* whether it is there or at *Medina* the Prophet is entombed—if at Medina the first lines of my alteration must run—

2 The writer of the review of *The Giaour* was a Mr. Cunningham to whom Macaulay relayed Byron's letter (*Life and Letters of Zachary Macaulay*, page 310) It is probable that this was John William Cunningham (1780–1861), an evangelical divine, fellow of St. John's College, Cambridge, and vicar of Harrow. He later became the editor of the *Christian Observer*.

1 See Dec. 3, 1913, to Zachary Macaulay, note 2.

"Blest—as the call which from Medina's dome
Invites Devotion to the Prophet's tomb
&c.

if at "Mecca" the lines may stand as before.—Page 45. C[ant]o 2d.—
Bride of Abydos.

yrs.
B

You will find this out either by Article—*Mecca*—*Medina*—or
Mohammed—I have no book of reference by me.—

[TO JOHN MURRAY (*c*)]   [*Dec. 3, 1813*]

Dear Sir—I send you back the copy—that when the alteration is
printed from page 45 (to which I request you to turn) you may
perceive *another* insertion of 2 lines—tho 4 are in the margin—you
will be good enough to attend to this as soon as possible—either in the
Er[rat]a page—or the leaf itself—as you please

yrs.
B

[TO JOHN MURRAY]   [*Dec. 3–4, 1813?*]

Did you look out? is it *Medina* or *Mecca* that contains the *holy*
sepulchre?—don't make me blaspheme by your negligence—I have
no book of reference or I would save you the trouble I *blush* as a good
Mussulman to have confused the point.

yrs.
B

[TO JOHN MURRAY]   *Decr. 4th. 1813*

Dear Sir—I have redde through your Persian tale[1]—& have taken
ye. liberty of making some remarks on ye. *blank* pages—there are many
beautiful passages and an interesting story—and I cannot give a
stronger proof that such is my opinion than by the *date* of the *hour 2
o'clock.*—till which It has kept me awake *without a yawn.*—The conclusion is not quite correct in *costume*—there is no *Mussulman suicide*
on record—at least for *love.*—But this matters not—the tale must be

---

[1] Prothero (*LJ*, II, 299n.) assumes that this was the manuscript of Henry
Gally Knight's *Ilderim, a Syrian Tale*, but this was not "Persian" in a strict sense,
and it was not published until 1816, and when it appeared Byron spoke slightingly
of it to Moore (March 25, 1817), and to Murray on the same day.

written by some one—who has been on the *spot*—and I wish him—& he deserves success.—Will you apologize to the author for the liberties I have taken with his M.S.—had I been less awake to & interested in his theme—I had been less obtrusive—but you know *I* always take this in good part—& I hope he will. It is difficult to say what *will* succeed—& still more to pronounce what *will not*—I am at this moment in *that uncertainty*—(on our *own* score) & it is no small proof of the author's powers—to be able to *charm* & *fix* a *mind's* attention on similar subjects and climates in such a predicament—that he may have the same effect upon all his readers is very sincerely the wish—& hardly the *doubt* of

yrs. truly
B

[TO JOHN MURRAY]   *[Monday Evening Dec. 6, 1813]*

Dear Sir—It is all very well except that the lines are not numbered properly—and a diabolical mistake page *67* which *must* be corrected with the *pen* if no other way remains—it is the omission of *"not"* before *"disagreeable"* in the *note* on the *amber* rosary.—This is really horrible & nearly as bad as the stumble of mine at the Threshold—I mean the *misnomer* of bride—pray do not let a copy go without the *not*—it is nonsense & worse than nonsense as it now stands—I wish the Printer was saddled with a vampire.—

yrs. ever
B

P.S.—It is still *hath* instead of *have* in page *20*—never was anyone so *misused* as I am by your Devils of printers.—

P.S.—I hope & trust the *not* was inserted in the first Edition—we must have something anything to set it right—it is enough to answer for one's own bulls—without other people's.—

[TO JOHN MURRAY]   *Tuesday Even.—Decr. 7 1813*

Dear Sir—Among the heap of blotted M.S.S. I gave you are some which don't belong to the *mass*—& some left out—I shall be obliged to you to let me have ye. *bundle* early *tomorrow*—& if you would like to have it again it shall be sent—

yrs. truly
B

My dear Lord—Will you have ye. goodness to present ye. petition which accompanies this billet for me[1]—you will think it an odd thing after the impudence with which I supported Cartwright's & the variety of impudencies I have uttered in our august house—but I really have not nerves even to present a pet[itio]n far less say a word upon it—at this moment—I can't tell why but so it is—either indolence—or hippishness—or incapacity—or all three.—Pray pardon me this & all other intrusions (*past* at least) from

yrs. very truly

B

[TO THOMAS MOORE]   *December 8th, 1813*

Your letter, like all the best, and even kindest, things in this world, is both painful and pleasing. But, first, to what sits nearest. Do you know I was actually about to dedicate to you,—not in a formal inscription, as to one's *elders*,—but through a short prefatory letter, in which I boasted myself your intimate, and held forth the prospect of *your* Poem; when, lo, the recollection of your strict injunctions of secrecy as to the said Poem, more than *once* repeated by word and letter, flashed upon me, and marred my intents. I could have no motive for repressing my own desire of alluding to you (and not a day passes that I do not think and talk of you), but an idea that you might, yourself, dislike it. You cannot doubt my sincere admiration, waving personal friendship for the present, which, by the by, is not less sincere and deep-rooted. I have you by rote and by heart; of which "ecce signum!" When I was at * * [Aston], on my first visit, I have a habit, in passing my time a good deal alone, of—I won't call it singing, for that I never attempt except to myself—but of uttering, to what I think tunes, your "Oh breathe not," "When the last glimpse," and "When he who adores thee," with others of the same minstrel;—they are my matins and vespers. I assuredly did not intend them to be overheard, but, one morning, in comes, not La Donna, but Il Marito, with a very grave face, saying, "Byron, I must request you won't sing any more, at least of *those* songs." I stared, and said, "Certainly, but why?"—"To tell you the truth," quoth he, "they make my wife *cry*, and so melancholy, that I wish her to hear no more of them."

---

[1] This was the petition of W. J. Baldwin, who had appealed to Byron from debtor's prison. See Nov. 14, 1813, notes 1 and 2.

Now, my dear M., the effect must have been from your words, and certainly not my music. I merely mention this foolish story, to show you how much I am indebted to you for even your pastimes. A man may praise and praise, but no one recollects but that which pleases—at least, in composition. Though I think no one equal to you in that department, or in satire,—and surely no one was ever so popular in both,—I certainly am of opinion that you have not yet done all *you* can do, though more than enough for any one else. I want, and the world expects, a longer work from you; and I see in you what I never saw in poet before, a strange diffidence of your own powers, which I cannot account for, and which must be unaccountable, when a *Cossac* like me can appal a *cuirassier*. Your story I did not, could not, know,—I thought only of a Peri. I wish you had confided in me, not for your sake, but mine, and to prevent the world from losing a much better poem than my own, but which, I yet hope, this *clashing* will not even now deprive them of.[1] Mine is the work of a week, written, *why* I have partly told you, and partly I cannot tell you by letter—some day I will.

* * * * * * * * * * * * * *

Go on—I shall really be very unhappy if I at all interfere with you. The success of mine is yet problematical; though the public will probably purchase a certain quantity, on the presumption of their own propensity for "the Giaour" and such "horrid mysteries." The only advantage I have is being on the spot; and that merely amounts to saving me the trouble of turning over books, which I had better read again. If *your chamber* was furnished in the same way, you have no need to *go there* to describe—I mean only as to *accuracy*—because I drew it from recollection.

* * * * * * * * * * * * * *

This last thing of mine *may* have the same fate, and I assure you I have great doubts about it. But, even if not, its little day will be over before you are ready and willing. Come out—"screw your courage to the sticking-place." Except the Post Bag (and surely you cannot

---

[1] Moore wrote to Byron that he had planned to include in *Lalla Rookh* a story which was similar to one Byron had used in *The Bride of Abydos*. When he saw that poem he gave up the idea and substituted the episode of the Fire-worshippers. "In my hero (to whom I had given the name of 'Zelim', and who was a descendant of Ali, outlawed, with all his followers, by the reigning Caliph,) it was my intention to shadow out, as I did afterward in another form, the national cause of Ireland." In his letter to Byron he said: "I chose this story because one writes best about what one feels most, and I thought the parallel with Ireland would enable me to infuse some vigour into my hero's character. But to aim at vigour and strong feeling after *you*, is hopeless;—that region 'was made for Cæsar.'" (Moore, I, 433n.)

complain of a want of success there), you have not been *regularly* out for some years. No man stands higher,—whatever you may think on a rainy day, in your provincial retreat. "Aucun homme, dans aucune langue, n'a été, peut-être, plus complètement le poëte du coeur et le poëte des femmes. Les critiques lui reprochent de n'avoir representé le monde ni tel qu'il est ni tel qu'il doit être; *mais les femmes répondent qu'il l'a representé tel qu'elles le désirent.*"—I should have thought Sismondi[2] had written this for you instead of Metastasio.

Write to me, and tell me of *yourself.* Do you remember what Rousseau said to some one—"Have we quarreled? you have talked to me often, and never once mentioned yourself."

P.S. The last sentence is an indirect apology for my own egotism, —but I believe in letters it is allowed. I wish it was *mutual.* I have met with an odd reflection in Grimm; it shall not—at least, the bad part— be applied to you or me, though *one* of us has certainly an indifferent name—but this it is: "Many people have the reputation of being wicked, with whom we should be too happy to pass our lives." I need not add it is a woman's saying—a Mademoiselle de Sommery's,[3]

* * * * * * * * * * * * * * *

[TO JOHN GALT] *Decr. 10th. 1813*

My dear Galt—The coincidence I assure you is a most unintentional & unconscious one nor have I even a guess where or when or in what manner it exists[1]—it is rather odd there is a Mr. Semple who I have since heard wrote a prose story like it—but on it's being pointed out to me the resemblance was so slight as to become almost imperceptible at least in my eyes—further than that there were 2 lovers who died.— Be that as it may I certainly had read no work of his or yours when this story was written that at all contained the likeness—or suggested the idea—I had a living character in my eye for *Zuleika*[2]—but what is still more extraordinary a living poet writes to me—that I have

[2] Sismondi, *De la Littérature du Midi de l'Europe*, ed. 1813, tome II, p. 436.

[3] Grimm recorded this saying of Mlle. de Sommery: "Que de gens ont la réputation d'être méchans, avec lesquels on serait heureux de passer sa vie." (Grimm, *Correspondance Littéraire*, ed. 1813, Part III, Tome ii, p. 126.)

[1] John Galt, who had been in Athens when Byron was there had written to Byron that when he saw *The Bride of Abydos*, "there was a remarkable coincidence in the story, with a matter in which I had been interested." Galt, *Life of Lord Byron*, (1830), Chapter XXVIII.

[2] The model for Zuleika was perhaps a composite of his feelings for Augusta and Lady Frances Webster.

actually *anticipated* a tale he had ready for the press—& which he admits it is impossible I could ever have seen or heard of in its details.[3] —Raymond[4] has heard from me—& has promised an answer—he shall be jogged again—if this wont do.—Anything I can do in accelerating your pursuits shall be done readily & with pleasure, by

> ever yrs.
> B

[TO JOHN GALT] *Dec. 11, 1813*

My dear Galt,—There was no offence—there *could* be none. I thought it by no means impossible that we might have hit on something similar, particularly as you are a dramatist, and was anxious to assure you of the truth, viz., that I had not wittingly seized upon plot, sentiment, or incident; and I am very glad that I have not in any respect trenched upon your subjects.[1] Something still more singular is, that the *first* part, where you have found a coincidence in some events within your observations on *life*, was *drawn* from *observations* of mine also, and I meant to have gone on with the story, but on *second* thoughts, I thought myself *two centuries* at least too late for the subject; which, though admitting of very powerful feeling and description, yet is not adapted for this age, at least this country, though the finest works of the Greeks, one of Schiller's and Alfieri's in modern times, besides several of our *old* (and best) dramatists, have been grounded on incidents of a similar cast.[2] I therefore altered it as you perceive, and in so doing have weakened the whole, by interrupting the train of thought; and in composition I do not think *second* thoughts are the best, though *second* expressions may improve the first ideas.

I do not know how other men feel towards those they have met abroad; but to me there seems a kind of tie established between all who have met together in a foreign country, as if we had met in a state of pre-existence, and were talking over a life that has ceased: but I always look forward to renewing my travels; and though *you*, I think, are now stationary, if I can at all forward your pursuits *there* as well as here, I shall be truly glad in the opportunity.

> Ever yours very sincerely,
> B

[3] See Dec. 8, 1813, to Moore, note 1.
[4] Raymond was stage manager of Drury Lane Theatre.
[1] See Dec. 10, 1813, to Galt, note 1.
[2] Byron refers to the incest theme in those writers. He had first made Selim and Zuleika in *The Bride of Abydos* brother and sister.

196

P.S.—I believe I leave town for a day or two on Monday, but after that I am always at home, and happy to see you till half-past two.

[TO JOHN MURRAY (*a*)]   *Decr. ye. 14th. 1813*

Deare Sir—Send ye. E[dito]r of ye. new R[evie]w a copy as he hath had ye trouble of two walks on yr. acct. As to the man of the Satirist[1]— I hope you have too much spirit to allow a single sheet to be offered as a peace offering to him or any one—If you *do*—expect *never* to be *forgiven* by me—if he is not personal he is quite welcome to his opinion—& if he is—I have my own remedy.———Send a copy *double* to Dr. Clarke (ye traveller) Cambrigge by ye. first opportunitie—& let me see you in ye. morninge yt. I may mention certain thinges ye. wh. require sundrie though slight alterations.—Sir—

yr. Servitor
BIRON

[TO JOHN MURRAY (*b*)]   [*Dec.* ⟨*18*⟩ *14 1813*]

Send a double copy to *Dr. Clarke Cambridge—Trumpington—* Cawthorne is sending to Mr. *Hobhouse Vienna*[1] & it is a good opportunity for a number of the Quarterly—Send it it will please him.—

B

[TO THOMAS ASHE[1]]   *4 Bennet Street St. James's Decr. 14th. 1813*

Sir,—I leave town for a few days tomorrow on my return I will answer your letter more at length.—Whatever may be your situa-

[1] The Satirist for July 1, 1813, had reviewed *The Giaour* rather mercilessly, accusing Byron of carelessness, grammatical errors, and obscurity in his rambling and fragmented tale. It is understandable that he would not want Murray to grant the editor the favour of an advance copy of his new poem, *The Bride of Abydos.*

[1] Hobhouse had left England on May 25 on a continental tour lasting eight months. During that time he visited most of the European capitals not in the hands of Napoleon.

[1] Thomas Ashe (1770–1835) had written some travel books and two novels, one of which had a *succès de scandale*. It was called *The Spirit of "The Book"* and purported to give the substance of a book written by Spencer Perceval defending the Princess of Wales against the charges of Lady Douglas in 1806–7. The full title of Ashe's book which was published in 1811, was: *The Spirit of "The Book"; or Memoirs of Caroline, Princess of Hasburgh, a Political and Amatory Romance.* It contains letters supposedly written from Caroline to Charlotte and attacking Lady Jersey. Ashe's *Memoirs and Confessions* (1815) was dedicated to the Duke of Northumberland and to Byron, and expressed "transcendent obligations" to the latter.

tion——I cannot but commend your resolution to abjure & abandon the publication & composition of works such as those to which you have alluded.—Depend upon it—they amuse *few*—disgrace both *reader* & *writer*—& benefit *none*.—It will be my wish to assist you as far as my limited means will admit—to break such a bondage—In your answer—inform me what sum you think would enable you to extricate yourself from the hands of your employers—& to regain at least temporary independence—& I shall be glad to contribute my mite towards it—At present I must conclude—your name is not unknown to me—& I regret for your own sake that you have ever lent it to the works you mention.——In saying this I merely repeat our *own words* in your letter to me & have no wish whatever to say a single syllable that may appear to insult your misfortunes—If I have—excuse me—it is unintentional.—

yrs. &c.

BYRON

[TO J.? ASHAM ESQRE. CORNHILL[1]]   *Decr. 14th. 1813*

Sir/—I regret very much that I have not time for the purpose of sitting to Mr. D.[2] of whose talents I think very highly.—Mr. Westall's objection seems to me very strange—but there *are 2* also at Mr. Phillips's from either of these or from Mr. Westall's the engraving you require can be obtained but it is not in my power to devote the proper time to Mr. D. at present & I should regret very much that his talents should be thrown away on a restless & impatient subject—as a *hurried* sitter must naturally be.—I cannot but be sorry for the trouble you are taking on so trifling an occasion—but remember it was not *my* seeking though I must feel obliged by your anxiety—& certainly wish to relieve it.—

yr. obliged & obedt. Sert.

B

---

1 It is tempting to think that this is the same person as Thomas Ashe, to whom Byron had written on the same day, but the name as here is distinct in the manuscript.

2 Unidentified. There were several portrait painters then flourishing whose names began with D: George Dawe (1781–1829), Arthur W. Devis (1763–1822), J. P. Drew (fl. London, 1800–1829), and George Dance (1741–1825).

My dear Sir—Your very kind letter is the more agreeable because—
setting aside talents—judgment—& ye. "laudari a laudato" &c. *you*
have been on ye spot—*you* have seen & described more of the East
than any of your predecessors—I need not say how ably & success-
fully—and (excuse the *Bathos*) *you* are one of ye. very few who can
pronounce how far my *costume* (to use an affected but expressive word)
is correct.—As to poesy—*that* is—as "Men Gods & Columns" please
to decide upon it—but I am sure that I am anxious to have an observer's—particularly a *famous* observer's testimony on ye. fidelity of my
manners & *dresses*—and as far as Memory and an Oriental twist in my
imagination have permitted—it has been my endeavour to present to
the Franks—a sketch of that with which you *have* & will present them a
complete picture.—It was with this notion that I felt compelled to
make my hero & heroine relatives—as you well know that none else
could there obtain that degree of intercourse leading to genuine
affection—I had nearly made them rather too much akin to each other
—& though the wild passions of the East—& some great examples in
Alfieri—Ford—& Schiller (to stop short of Antiquity) might have
pleaded in favour of a copyist—yet the times & the *North* (*not
Frederic*[2] but our *Climate*) induced me to alter their consanguinity &
confine them to cousinship.—I also wished to try my hand on a female
character in Zuleika—& have endeavoured as far as ye. grossness of
our masculine ideas will allow—to preserve her purity without im-
pairing the ardour of her attachment.—As to *Criticism*—I have been
reviewed about 150 times—praised & abused—I will not say that I
am become indifferent to either eulogy or condemnation—but for some
years at least I have felt grateful for the former—and have never
attempted to answer the latter.—For success equal to the first efforts—
I had & have no hope—ye novelty was over—& ye. "Bride"—like all
other brides—must suffer or rejoice for & with her husband.—By the
bye—I have used Bride *Turkishly* as *affianced* not married—& so far it
is an English *bull*—which I trust will be at least a comfort—to all
Hibernians not bigotted to Monopoly.—You are good enough to

---

[1] Prothero (*LJ*, II, 308n.) confuses Professor E. D. Clarke, the Eastern
traveller, whom Byron is addressing here, and Dr. William Clark, who had
planned to go abroad with Byron, and whom Byron voted for at Cambridge when
he was a candidate for the Professorship of Anatomy in 1814. E. D. Clarke was
Professor of Mineralogy at Cambridge.

[2] Frederick North (1766–1827), later the 5th Earl of Guilford, had met Byron
in Athens in 1810. He was an ardent Grecophile who later founded the Ionian
University on Corfu.

mention your *quotations* in your 3d. vol.—I shall not only be indebted to it for a renewal of the high gratification received from ye. 2 first—but for preserving my relics embalmed in your own spices—& ensuring me readers to whom I could not otherwise have aspired.——I called on you as bounden by duty & inclination when last in your neighbourhood—but I shall always take my *chance*—you surely would not have me inflict upon you a formal annunciation—I am proud of your friendship—but not so proud of *myself* as to break in upon your better avocations.——I trust that Mrs. Clarke is well—I have never had ye. honour of presentation—but I have heard so much of her in many quarters—that any notice she is pleased to take of my productions is not less gratifying than my thanks are sincere both to her & you—by all accounts I may safely congratulate you on ye. possession of a "Bride" whose personal & mental accomplishments are more than poetical.—

ever yrs. most truly
BYRON

P.S. Murray has sent—or will send a double copy of the Bride & Giaour—in ye. last one some *lengthy* additions—pray accept them according to old custom "from ye. Author" to one of his better brethren.—Your *Persian* or any memorial will be a most agreeable—& it is my fault—if not an useful present.[3]—I trust your third will be out before I sail next month; can I say or do anything for you in the Levant? I am now in all the agonies of equipment, and full of schemes, some impracticable, and most of them improbable; but I mean to fly "freely to the green earth's end," though not quite so fast as Milton's sprite.[4]

P.S. 2d.—I have so many things to say.—I want to show you Lord Sligo's letter to me detailing, as he heard them on the spot, the Athenian account of our adventure (a personal one) which certainly first suggested to me the story of *The Giaour*. It was a strange and not a very long story, and his report of the reports (he arrived just after my departure, and I did not know till last summer that he knew anything of the matter) is not very far from the truth. Don't be alarmed. There was nothing that led further than to the water's edge; but one part (as is often the case in life) was more singular than any of the *Giaour's* adventures. I never have, and never should have, alluded to it on my own authority, from respect to the ancient proverb on Travellers.

[3] The manuscript ends here; the remainder is from *LJ, II*, 310–311.
[4] See June 17, 1813, to E. D. Clarke, note 2.

Insert page 57 Canto 2d. after line 633
"What quenched it's ray—the blood that thou hast shed"
Insert
"Hark to the hurried question of Despair!
Where is my child?—an Echo answers—'Where?'"
Note
"I came to the place of my birth and cried 'the friends of my Youth,
where are they?' and an Echo answered 'Where are they'["]
"From an Arabic M.S.["]

The above quotation (from which the idea in the text is taken) must
be already familiar to every reader—it is given in the first annotation
page 67 of "the Pleasures of Memory."

[TO JOHN MURRAY]   [*Dec. 17, 1813*]

Dear Sir—There is a line in Canto 2d.
"A thousand swords—thy Selim's heart—["] &c.
let it be
"A thousand swords—with Selim's heart & hand ["] &c.
it is in page *45*.—
I shall see Mr. Dallas today at *5*—& for particular reasons think &
hope that I shall be able notwithstanding your *feud* to settle what you
wish—at any rate I will do my best.[1]

yrs. truly
Bn

[TO JOHN MURRAY]   *Decr. 18—1813*

Dr. Sr.—Can you send me ye. J[ourne]y[1] or at least Mr. Hobhouse's
[work?] of it tonight & also ye. proof of C[Hilde] H[arold]e[2] as [I] am
anxious to see the one—[&] correct ye other before tomorrow
morning

yrs.
B

[1] See Dec. 18, 1813, to Dallas, note 1.
[1] The reference here is obscure. Byron can scarcely be asking to see Hobhouse's
Journey through Albania . . . which was published in May, 1813, and which he had
seen long before.
[2] Byron was probably preparing for the publication of the seventh edition of
Childe Harold, to which he had prefixed the stanzas "To Ianthe" (Lady Charlotte
Harley).

My dear Drury—"But why *Bitch* Mr. Wild?"[1] but why *"Lord"*
Mr. Drury?—I wish when you write you would not call names—
unless you think to use a pugilistic phrase that "the conceit has not
been taken out of me."—Take care that you don't find a *"false* con-
cord" in or about other *brides*—I use the word in a foreign sense as
affianced not actually spliced—& refer of course to our friend H[odg-
son] who talks about *hope* as if it meant despair.[2]— Every day confirms
my opinion on the superiority of a vicious life—and if Virtue is not
it's own reward I don't know any other stipend annexed to it—but I
fear H[odgson]'s impatience savours rather cardinally—curtail him of
his meals—or of anything else that may cool his pulsations—look
you——I shall send the *order* or reserve it for Thursday next——but
it grieves me that I cannot dine with you tomorrow as I leave town
(for a day only)—the *order* you may depend upon.—Burns's nauseous-
ness shall be kept for our next after-dinner[3]—or for *you* & *I* on the eve
of Hodgson's *happiness* (as people call it delicately) that we may have
both ethics & practics at the same time.—Pray make my respects
acceptable to your friend Mr. Heber who is a patron of mine for whom
I have great reverence—remember me in one cup of "Canaries" and
believe me ever my dear *Revd. Mr. Drury*

ever yours

B

[TO ROBERT CHARLES DALLAS] *December 18th, 1813*

My dear Sir—If you wish to do me the greatest favour possible,
which I am soliciting for another, you will let Mr. Murray (who is in
despair about it) have the publication of the S. F.[1] if not absolutely
impracticable. By so doing you will return *good* for evil; and, in the
true gospel spirit, "heap coals of fire upon his head"—pray do. I am
sure he will now *deal* liberally by you, and I see him so anxious on this
subject, that I quite feel for him, and *so* will you. You shall have it all

---

[1] Fielding's *Life of Mr. Jonathan Wild*, Book III, Chap. 8.
[2] Hodgson was engaged to Miss Tayler, Drury's sister-in-law.
[3] See Byron's reference to Burns's "unpublishable" letters, Journal, Dec. 1813.
[1] According to Dallas, Murray was so anxious to get the publication of an American poem that Dallas's son had brought to England, that he engaged Byron to use
his influence with Dallas, who had already committed it to Cawthorn. The poem
was a burlesque of the *Lay of the Last Minstrel*. (Dallas, *Correspondence*, III, 55.)

your own way. I have really no other motive whatever than to assist Murray, and certainly *not* to injure you. This will not only be a *triumph* to yourself, but will set all right between you and him, and I hope be of eventual service to both. Pray pardon my importunity, and, if you can, comply with it.

Ever most truly yours,
BYRON.

P.S.—You can easily dispose of Cawthorn, if he has already arranged with you; don't be *embarrassed* about that. I will settle it, or ensure your doing so.[2]

[TO LEIGH HUNT]   *Decr. 22d. 1813—*

My dear Sir/—I am indeed "in your debt—" and what is still worse am obliged to follow *royal* example (he has just apprized *his* Creditors that they must wait till ye. [next] meeting) and entreat your indulgence for I hope a very short time.—The nearest relation and almost ye. only friend I possess—has been in London for a week & leaves it tomorrow with me for her own residence—I return immediately— but we meet so seldom—& are so *minuted* when we meet at all—that I give up all engagements—till *now*—without reluctance.—On my return I must see you to console myself for my past disappointments— I should feel highly honoured in Mr. Brougham's[1] permission to make his acquaintance—& *there* you are in *my* debt—for it is a promise of last summer which I still hope to see performed.—Yesterday I had a letter from Moore—you have probably heard from him lately—but if not— you will be glad to learn that he is the same in heart—head—& health.

[TO JOHN MURRAY]   *London   Decr. 27th. 1813*

Dear Sir—Ld. Holland is laid up with ye gout & would feel very much obliged if you could obtain & send as soon as possible Me.

---

[2] Cawthorn had the poem in press, however, and Byron's effort was unsuccessful. See Dallas, *Correspondence*, III, 57.

[1] Henry Brougham, the liberal politician and contributor to the *Edinburgh Review*. He had defended and secured an acquittal for Hunt when the latter was prosecuted for writing an article on the savagery of military floggings. Byron was then unaware that Brougham was the sarcastic reviewer of his *Hours of Idleness* in the *Edinburgh Review* in 1808.

D'Arblay's[1] (or even Miss Edgeworth's thing)[2] new work.—I know they are not out but it is perhaps possible for your *Majesty* to command what we cannot with much sueing purchase as yet.—I need not say that when you are able or willing to confer the same favour on me I shall be obliged—I would almost fall sick myself to get at Me. D'Arblay's writings.—

yrs. ever

B

P.S.—⟨My interest in [d'Arblay?] started with you⟩ You were talking today of ye. American E[ditio]n of a certain unquenchable memorial of my younger days[3]—as it can't be helped now—I own I have some curiosity to see a copy of transatlantic typography—this you will perhaps obtain—& *one* for yourself but I must beg that you will not *import more*—because *seriously*—I *do wish* to have that thing forgotten—as much as it has been forgiven.————If you send to ye *Globe* E[dito]r say that I want neither excuse nor contradiction but merely a discontinuance of a most ill grounded charge—I never was consistent in anything but my politics—& as my redemption depends on that solitary virtue—it is murder to carry away my last anchor.—

JOURNAL

November 14, 1813—April 19, 1814

[Moore's transcription: see Special Note, page xii]

If this had been begun ten years ago, and faithfully kept!!!—heigho! there are too many things I wish never to have remembered, as it is. Well,—I have had my share of what are called the pleasures of this life, and have seen more of the European and Asiatic world than I have made a good use of. They say "virtue is its own reward,"—it certainly should be paid well for its trouble. At five-and-twenty, when the better part of life is over, one should be *something*;—and what am I? nothing but five-and-twenty—and the odd months. What have I seen? the same man all over the world,—ay, and woman too. Give *me* a Mussulman who never asks questions, and a she of the same race who saves

---

[1] Madame d'Arblay's fourth and last novel, *The Wanderer, or Female Difficulties*, was published in 1814.

[2] Miss Edgeworth's novel *Patronage* was published at the end of 1813 or the beginning of 1814.

[3] *English Bards and Scotch Reviewers.*

one the trouble of putting them. But for this same plague—yellow fever—and Newstead delay, I should have been by this time a second time close to the Euxine. If I can overcome the last, I don't so much mind your pestilence; and, at any rate, the spring shall see me there,— provided I neither marry myself nor unmarry any one else in the interval. I wish one was—I don't know what I wish. It is odd I never set myself seriously to wishing without attaining it—and repenting. I begin to believe with the good old Magi, that one should only pray for the nation and not for the individual;—but, on my principle, this would not be very patriotic.

No more reflections.—Let me see—last night I finished "Zuleika,"[1] my second Turkish Tale. I believe the composition of it kept me alive —for it was written to drive my thoughts from the recollection of—

"Dear sacred name, rest ever unreveal'd"[2]

At least, even here, my hand would tremble to write it. This afternoon I have burnt the scenes of my commenced comedy. I have some idea of expectorating a romance, or rather a tale in prose;—but what romance could equal the events—

"quæque ipse . . . . . . vidi,
Et quorum pars magna fui."[3]

Today Henry Byron called on me with my little cousin Eliza.[1] She will grow up a beauty and a plague; but, in the mean time, it is the prettiest child! dark eyes and eyelashes, black and long as the wing of a raven. I think she is prettier even than my niece, Georgina,—yet I don't like to think so neither; and, though older, she is not so clever.

Dallas called before I was up, so we did not meet. Lewis,[2] too,— who seems out of humour with every thing. What can be the matter? he is not married—has he lost his own mistress, or any other person's

[1] This was Byron's first title for The Bride of Abydos, taken from the name of the heroine.
[2] Zuleika seems to have evolved from two emotional impasses, one with his sister Augusta and the other with Lady Frances Webster. The fact that he had first made Selim and Zuleika brother and sister (they were cousins in the published poem) indicates his preoccupation with that relationship. The quotation is from Pope's Eloisa to Abelard, lines 9–10: "Dear fatal name, rest ever unrevealed."
[3] Virgil, Æneid, II, 5. "I myself saw these things in all their horror, and I bore great part in them."
[1] The Rev. Henry Byron was the second son of the Rev. and Hon. Richard Byron, younger brother of Byron's grandfather. Henry was thus a first cousin of Byron's father.
[2] Matthew Gregory Lewis had gained the nickname of "Monk" from his popular Gothic tale, Ambrosio, or the Monk, which on its publication in 1795 made him famous.

wife? Hodgson, too, came. He is going to be married, and he is the kind of man who will be the happier. He has talent, cheerfulness, every thing that can make him a pleasing companion; and his intended is handsome and young, and all that. But I never see any one much improved by matrimony. All my coupled contemporaries are bald and discontented. W[ordsworth] and S[outhey] have both lost their hair and good humour; and the last of the two had a good deal to lose. But it don't much signify what falls *off* a man's temples in that state.

Mem. I must get a toy to-morrow for Eliza, and send the device for the seal of myself and * * * * * [Augusta?] Mem. too, to call on the Staël and Lady Holland to-morrow, and on * * [Dallas?], who has advised me (without seeing it, by the by) not to publish "Zuleika"; I believe he is right, but experience might have taught him that not to print is *physically* impossible. No one has seen it but Hodgson and Mr. Gifford. I never in my life *read* a composition, save to Hodgson, as he pays me in kind. It is a horrible thing to do too frequently;— better print, and they who like may read, and if they don't like, you have the satisfaction of knowing that they have, at least, *purchased* the right of saying so.

I have declined presenting the Debtor's Petition,[1] being sick of parliamentary mummeries. I have spoken thrice; but I doubt my ever becoming an orator. My first was liked; the second and third—I don't know whether they succeeded or not. I have never yet set to it *con amore*;—one must have some excuse to oneself for laziness, or inability, or both, and this is mine. "Company, villanous company, hath been the spoil of me;"[2]—and then, I "have drunk medicines," not to make me love others, but certainly enough to hate myself.

Two nights ago I saw the tigers sup at Exeter 'Change. Except Veli Pacha's lion in the Morea,—who followed the Arab keeper like a dog,—the fondness of the hyæna for her keeper amused me most. Such a conversazione!—There was a "hippopotamus," like Lord L[iverpoo]l in the face; and the "Ursine Sloth" hath [had] the very voice and manner of my valet—but the tiger talked too much. The elephant took and gave me my money again—took off my hat—opened a door— *trunked* a whip—and behaved so well, that I wish he was my butler. The handsomest animal on earth is one of the panthers; but the poor antelopes were dead. I should hate to see one *here*:—the sight of

---

[1] The petition, which Byron had been urged to present by W. J. Baldwin, a debtor in the King's Bench prison (see Nov. 14, 1813, to Baldwin), was directed against Lord Redesdale's Insolvent Debtors Act. Byron finally got Lord Holland to present the petition in the House of Lords.

[2] *Henry IV*, Part I, Act. III, Scene 3.

the *camel* made me pine again for Asia Minor. "Oh quando te aspiciam?"

* * * * * * * * * * * * * * *

Nov. 16th

Went last night with Lewis to see the first of Antony and Cleopatra.[3] It was admirably got up and well acted—a salad of Shakespeare and Dryden. Cleopatra strikes me as the epitome of her sex—fond, lively, sad, tender, teasing, humble, haughty, beautiful, the devil!—coquettish to the last, as well with the "asp" as with Anthony. After doing all she can to persuade him that—but why do they abuse him for cutting off that poltroon Cicero's head? Did not Tully tell Brutus it was a pity to have spared Antony? and did he not speak the Philippics? and are not *"word things?"*[4] and such *"words"* very pestilent *"things"* too? If he had had a hundred heads, they deserved (from Antony) a rostrum (his was stuck up there) apiece—though, after all, he might as well have pardoned him, for the credit of the thing. But to resume— Cleopatra, after securing him, says, "yet go"—"it is your interest," etc.—how like the sex! and the questions about Octavia—it is woman all over.

To-day received Lord Jersey's invitation to Middleton—to travel sixty miles to meet Madame * * [De Staël]! I once travelled three thousand to get among silent people; and this same lady writes octavos, and *talks* folios. I have read her books—like most of them, and delight in the last; so I won't hear it, as well as read.

* * * * * * * * * * * * * * *

Read Burns to-day. What would he have been, if a patrician? We should have had more polish—less force—just as much verse, but no immortality—a divorce and a duel or two, the which had he survived, as his potations must have been less spirituous, he might have lived as long as Sheridan, and outlived as much as poor Brinsley. What a wreck is that man! and all from bad pilotage; for no one had ever better gales, though now and then a little too squally. Poor dear Sherry! [Sheridan] I shall never forget the day he and Rogers and

---

[3] In the revival of *Antony and Cleopatra* at Covent Garden, Nov. 15, 1813, additions were made from Dryden's *All for Love or the World Well Lost.*

[4] It is interesting to see how phrases stored in Byron's memory found their way into his poetry:

> But words are things, and a small drop of ink,
> Falling like dew, upon a thought, produces
> That which makes thousands, perhaps millions, think.
> *Don Juan*, 3, 88.

Moore and I passed together; when *he* talked, and *we* listened, without one yawn, from six till one in the morning.

Got my seals * * * * * *. Have again forgot a plaything for *ma petite cousine* Eliza; but I must send for it to-morrow. I hope Harry will bring her to me. I sent Lord Holland the proofs of the last *"Giaour,"* and *"The Bride of Abydos."* He won't like the latter, and I don't think that I shall long. It was written in four nights to distract my dreams from * *. Were it not thus, it had never been composed; and had I not done something at that time, I must have gone mad, by eating my own heart,—bitter diet!—Hodgson likes it better than the Giaour, but nobody else will,—and he never liked the Fragment. I am sure, had it not been for Murray, *that* would never have been published, though the circumstances which are the groundwork make it * * * heigho!

Tonight I saw both the sisters of * * [Frances Webster?]; my God! the youngest so like! I thought I should have sprung across the house, and am so glad no one was with me in Lady H.'s box. I hate those likenesses—the mock-bird, but not the nightingale—so like as to remind, so different as to be painful. One quarrels equally with the points of resemblance and of distinction.

Nov. 17th

No letter from * *; but I must not complain. The respectable Job says, "Why should a *living man* complain?"[1] I really don't know, except it be that a *dead man* can't; and he, the said patriarch, *did* complain, nevertheless, till his friends were tired, and his wife recommended that pious prologue. "Curse—and die;" the only time, I suppose, when but little relief is to be found in swearing. I have had a most kind letter from Lord Holland on "The Bride of Abydos," which he likes, and so does Lady H. This is very good-natured in both, from whom I don't deserve any quarter. Yet I *did* think, at the time, that my cause of enmity proceeded from Holland-house, and am glad I was wrong, and wish I had not been in such a hurry with that confounded satire, of which I would suppress even the memory;—but people, now they can't get it, make a fuss, I verily believe, out of contradiction.

George Ellis[2] and Murray have been talking something about Scott and me, George pro Scoto,—and very right too. If they want to

---

[1] The question was Jeremiah's: "Wherefore doth a living man complain . . ." (*Lamentations*, III, 39)

[2] George Ellis (1753–1815), a contributor to the *Rolliad* and the *Anti-Jacobin*, also reviewed frequently for the *Quarterly Review*. He had reviewed *Childe Harold* in the *Quarterly* (March, 1812, Vol. VII, pp. 180–200).

depose him, I only wish they would not set me up as a competitor. Even if I had my choice, I would rather be the Earl of Warwick[3] than all the *kings* he ever made! Jeffrey and Gifford I take to be the monarch-makers in poetry and prose. The British Critic, in their Rokeby Review,[4] have presupposed a comparison, which I am sure my friends never thought of, and W. Scott's subjects are injudicious in descending to. I like the man—and admire his works to what Mr. Braham calls *Entusymusy*.[5] All such stuff can only vex him, and do me no good. Many hate his politics—(I hate all politics); and, here, a man's politics are like the Greek *soul*—an $\varepsilon\acute{\iota}\delta\omega\lambda o\nu$,[1] besides God knows what *other soul*; but their estimate of the two generally go together.

Harry has not brought *ma petite cousine.* I want us to go to the play together;—she has been but once. Another short note from Jersey, inviting Rogers and me on the 23d. I must see my agent to-night. I wonder when that Newstead business will be finished. It cost me more than words to part with it—and to *have* parted with it! What matters it what I do? or what becomes of me?—but let me remember Job's saying, and console myself with being "a living man."

I wish I could settle to reading again,—my life is monotonous, and yet desultory. I take up books, and fling them down again. I began a comedy and burnt it because the scene ran into *reality*;—a novel, for the same reason. In rhyme, I can keep more away from facts; but the thought always runs through, through . . . yes, yes, through. I have had a·letter from Lady Melbourne—the best friend I ever had in my life, and the cleverest of women.

Not a word from * * [Lady F. W. Webster]. Have they set out from * *? or has my last precious epistle fallen into the Lion's jaws? If so—and this silence looks suspicious—I must clap on "my musty morion" and "hold out my iron".[2] I am out of practice—but I won't begin again at Manton's now. Besides, I would not return his shot. I was once a famous wafer-splitter; but then the bullies of society made

---

[3] Richard Neville, Earl of Warwick (1428–1471), known as the "king-maker", was instrumental in putting Edward IV on the throne, and later Henry VI.

[4] The *British Critic* in its review of Scott's *Rokeby* compared Scott with Byron and Southey: "Let us subtract from them [Byron and Southey] their affectations—their obscurities—their mysterious sublimities; and let us see what may remain unaffected, simple and natural. ; . . . This then is the pure poetry, which, in Scott, has no peculiarities characteristic of an Old or of a New School. . . ." (*British Critic*, Oct., 1813, Vol. 42, pp. 110–125)

[5] John Braham, a famous tenor, assisted Isaac Nathan in the arrangement of the music for Byron's *Hebrew Melodies*.

[1] The Greek word means an image in the mind, or a vision or fancy.

[2] *Henry V*, Act. II, Scene 1.

it necessary. Ever since I began to feel that I had a bad cause to support, I have left off the exercise.

What strange tidings from the Anakim[3] of anarchy—Buonaparte! Ever since I defended my bust of him at Harrow against the rascally time-servers, when the war broke out in 1803, he has been a "Héros de Roman" of mine—on the continent; I don't want him here. But I don't like those same flights—leaving of armies, &c. &c. I am sure when I fought for his bust at school, I did not think he would run away from himself. But I should not wonder if he banged them yet. To be beat by men would be something; but by three stupid, legitimate-old-dynasty boobies of regular-bred sovereigns—O-hone-a-rie!—O-hone-a-rie! It must be, as Cobbett says, his marriage with the thick-lipped and thick-headed *Autrichienne* brood. He had better have kept to her who was kept by Barras.[1] I never knew any good come of your young wife, and legal espousals, to any but your "sober-blooded boy" who "eats fish" and drinketh "no sack."[2] Had he not the whole opera? all Paris? all France? But a mistress is just as perplexing—that is, *one*—two or more are manageable by division.

I have begun, or had begun, a song, and flung it into the fire. It was in remembrance of Mary Duff, my first of flames, before most people begin to burn. I wonder what the devil is the matter with me! I can do nothing, and—fortunately there is nothing to do. It has lately been in my power to make two persons (and their connexions) comfortable, *pro tempore*, and one happy, *ex tempore*,[3]—I rejoice in the last particularly, as it is an excellent man. I wish there had been more inconvenience and less gratification to my self-love in it, for then there had been more merit. We are all selfish—and I believe, ye gods of Epicurus! I believe in Rochefoucault about *men*, and in Lucretius (not Busby's translation)[4] about yourselves. Your bard has made you very *nonchalent* and blest; but as he has excused *us* from damnation, I don't envy you your blessedness *much*—a little, to be sure. I remember, last year, * * [Lady Oxford] said to me, at * * [Eywood]. "Have we not passed our last month like the gods of Lucretius?" And so we had. She is an adept in the text of the original (which I like too); and when that

---

[3] The plural of Anak, an Old Testament race of giants.
[1] Barras had fostered the match between the young Napoleon and Josephine de Beauharnais.
[2] *Henry IV*, Part II, Act IV, Scene 3.
[3] Byron had given £3,000 to Augusta to extricate her from the debts of her husband, and had given enough to Hodgson to clear him of his father's debts so that he could marry.
[4] For Dr. Busby see Oct. [17?], 1812, to Murray (a).

booby Bus[by] sent his translating prospectus, she subscribed. But, the devil prompting him to add a specimen, she transmitted him a subsequent answer, saying, that, "after perusing it, her conscience would not permit her to allow her name to remain on the list of subscribers." * * * * * *. Last night, at Lord H[olland]'s—Mackintosh, the Ossulstones, Puységur,5 &c., there—I was trying to recollect a quotation (as *I* think) of Staël's, from some Teutonic sophist about architecture. "Architecture," says this Macoronico Tedescho, reminds me of frozen music."6 It is somewhere—but where?—the demon of perplexity must know and won't tell. I asked M[ackintosh], and he said it was not in her; but P[uységu]r said it must be *hers*, it was so *like*. * * * * * *. H. laughed, as he does at all "De l'Allemagne"—in which, however, I think he goes a little too far. B., I hear, contemns it too. But there are fine passages;—and, after all, what is a work—any —or every work—but a desert with fountains and, perhaps, a grove or two, every day's journey? To be sure, in Madame, what we often mistake, and "pant for," as the "cooling stream," turns out to be the *"mirage"* (criticé *verbiage*); but we do, at last, get to something like the temple of Jove Ammon, and then the waste we have passed is only remembered to gladden the contrast.

* * * * * * * * * * * * * * * * *

Called on C * * to explain * * *. She is very beautiful, to my taste, at least; for on coming home from abroad, I recollect being unable to look at any woman but her—they were so fair, and unmeaning, and *blonde*. The darkness and regularity of her features reminded me of my "Jannat al Aden." But this impression wore off; and now I can look at a fair woman, without longing for a Houri. She was very good tempered, and every thing was explained.

To-day, great news—"the Dutch have taken Holland,"—which, I suppose, will be succeeded by the actual explosion of the Thames. Five provinces have declared for young Stadt, and there will be inundation, conflagration, constupration, consternation, and every sort of nation and nations, fighting away, up to their knees, in the damnable quags of this will-o'-the-wisp abode of Boors. It is said Bernadotte is amongst them, too; and, as Orange will be there soon, they will have (Crown) Prince Stork and King Log in their Loggery at the same time. Two to one on the new dynasty!

5 Monsieur de Puységur was described by Lady H. Leveson-Gower as "the oldest, gayest, thinnest, most withered, and most brilliant thing one can meet with." (*Letters of Harriet, Countess of Granville*, Vol. I, p. 23.)
6 The phrase was Goethe's, "*eine erstarrte Musik*". See A. Stevens, *Madame de Staël; A Study* (1881) Vol. II, p. 195.

Mr. Murray has offered me one thousand guineas for the "Giaour" and the "Bride of Abydos." I won't—it is too much, though I am strongly tempted, merely for the *say* of it. No bad price for a fortnight's (a week each) what?—the gods know—it was intended to be called Poetry.

I have dined regularly to-day, for the first time since Sunday last—this being Sabbath, too. All the rest, tea and dry biscuits—six *per diem*. I wish to God I had not dined now!—It kills me with heaviness, stupor, and horrible dreams;—and yet it was but a pint of bucellas, and fish. Meat I never touch,—nor much vegetable diet. I wish I were in the country, to take exercise,—instead of being obliged to *cool* by absinence, in lieu of it. I should not so much mind a little accession of flesh,—my bones can well bear it. But the worst is, the devil always came with it,—till I starve him out,—and I will *not* be the slave of *any* appetite. If I do err, it shall be my heart, at least, that heralds the way. Oh my head—how it aches?—the horrors of digestion! I wonder how Buonaparte's dinner agrees with him?

Mem. I must write to-morrow to "Master Shallow, * * [Webster], who owes me a thousand pounds," and seems, in his letter, afraid I should ask him for it;—as if I would!—I don't want it (just now, at least,) to begin with; and though I have often wanted that sum, I never asked for the repayment of £10 in my life—from a friend. His bond is not due this year, and I told him when it was, I should not enforce it. How often must he make me say the same thing?

I am wrong—I did once ask * * * [Hobhouse] to repay me. But it was under circumstances that excused me *to him*, and would to any one. I took no interest, nor required security. He paid me soon,—at least, his *padre*. My head! I believe it was given me to ache with. Good even.

Nov. 22d. 1813

"Orange Boven!" So the bees have expelled the bear that broke open their hive. Well,—if we are to have new De Witts and De Ruyters,[1] God speed the little republic! I should like to see the Hague and the village of Brock, where they have such primitive habits. Yet, I don't know,—their canals would cut a poor figure by the memory of the Bosphorus; and the Zuyder Zee look awkwardly after "Ak-

[1] For the revolution in Holland, see Nov. 29, 1813, to Annabella Milbanke. De Witt and De [van] Ruyter were fighters for Dutch freedom in the 17th century. Two brothers, Corneille and Jean de Witt were executed, victims of calumny and popular furore, for having attempted to oppose the establishment of absolute power in their country. Michel-Adriaanzoon van Ruyter (1607–1676) was accused of complicity in their plot, but he continued his battles for freedom and became enshrined as a popular hero.

Degnity [Denizi]."[2] No matter,—the bluff burghers, puffing freedom out of their short tobacco-pipes, might be worth seeing; though I prefer a cigar, or a hooka, with the rose-leaf mixed with the milder herb of the Levant. I don't know what liberty means,—never having seen it,—but wealth is power all over the world; and as a shilling performs the duty of a pound (besides sun and sky and beauty for nothing) in the East,—*that* is the country. How I envy Herodes Atticus!—more than Pomponius.[3] And yet a little *tumult*, now and then, is an agreeable quickener of sensation; such as a revolution, a battle, or an *aventure* of any lively description. I think I rather would have been Bonneval, Ripperda, Alberoni, Hayreddin, or Horuc Barbarossa, or even Wortley Montague [*sic*],[4] than Mahomet himself.

Rogers will be in town soon?—the 23d is fixed for our Middleton visit. Shall I go? umph!—In this island, where one can't ride out without overtaking the sea, it don't much matter where one goes.

* * * * * * * * * * * * * * *

I remember the effect of the *first* Edinburgh Review on me. I heard of it six weeks before,—read it the day of its denunciation,—dined and drank three bottles of claret, (with S. B. Davies, I think,) neither ate nor slept the less, but, nevertheless, was not easy till I had vented my wrath and my rhyme, in the same pages against every thing and every body. Like George, in the *Vicar of Wakefield*, "the fate of my paradoxes" would allow me to perceive no merit in another.[5] I remembered only the maxim of my boxing-master, which, in my youth, was found useful in all general riots,—"Whoever is not for you is against you—*mill* away right and left," and so I did;—like Ishmael, my hand was against all men, and all men's anent me. I did wonder, to be sure, at my own success—

"And marvels so much wit is all his own."[1]

2 The Lake of Ak-Deniz, northeast of Antioch.
3 A typically wealthy Greek and Roman.
4 Prothero gives the following summary account of these adventurers: "Bonneval (1675–1747) was a French soldier of fortune, who served successively in the Austrian, Russian, and Turkish armies. Ripperda (died 1737), a Dutch adventurer, became Prime Minister of Spain under Philip V, and after his fall turned Mohammedan. Alberoni (1664–1752) was an Italian adventurer, who became Prime Minister of Spain in 1714. Hayreddin (died 1547) and Horuc Barbarossa (died 1518) were Algerine pirates. Edward Wortley Montague [*sic*] (1713–1776), son of Lady Mary, saw the inside of several prisons, served at Fontenoy, sat in the British Parliament, was received into the Roman Catholic Church at Jerusalem (1764), lived at Rosetta as a Mohammedan with his mistress, Caroline Dormer, till 1772, and died at Padua, from swallowing a fish-bone." (*LJ*, II, 329–330n.)
5 *Vicar of Wakefield*, Chapter 20.
1 "From Boileau", Hobhouse, *Imitations and Translations*, p. 233.

as Hobhouse sarcastically says of somebody (not unlikely myself, as we are old friends);—but were it to come over again, I would *not*. I have since redde the cause of my couplets, and it is not adequate to the effect. C[aroline?] told me that it was believed I alluded to poor Lord Carlisle's nervous disorder in one of the lines. I thank Heaven I did not know it—and would not, could not, if I had. I must naturally be the last person to be pointed on defects or maladies.

Rogers is silent,—and, it is said, severe. When he does talk, he talks well; and, on all subjects of taste, his delicacy of expression is pure as his poetry. If you enter his house—his drawing-room—his library—you of yourself say, this is not the dwelling of a common mind. There is not a gem, a coin, a book thrown aside on his chimney-piece, his sofa, his table, that does not bespeak an almost fastidious elegance in the possessor. But this very delicacy must be the misery of his existence. Oh the jarrings his disposition must have encountered through life!

Southey, I have not seen much of. His appearance is *Epic*; and he is the only existing entire man of letters. All the others have some pursuits annexed to their authorship. His manners are mild, but not those of a man of the world, and his talents of the first order. His prose is perfect. Of his poetry there are various opinions: there is, perhaps, too much of it for the present generation; posterity will probably select. He has *passages* equal to any thing. At present, he has a *party*, but no *public*—except for his prose writings. The life of Nelson is beautiful.

* * [Sotheby] is a *Littérateur*, the Oracle of the Coteries, of the * *s[2] L[ydia] W[hite] (Sydney Smith's "Tory Virgin"),[3] Mrs. Wilmot[4] (she, at least, is a swan, and might frequent a purer stream,) Lady B[eaumont,][5] and all the Blues, with Lady C[harlemont][6] at their head—but I say nothing of her—"look in her face and you forget

---

[2] Possibly the Berry sisters.

[3] Miss Lydia White was a wealthy Irish "blue-stocking" well known for her dinners and conversation parties. At one of her dinners, the desperate prospects of the Whig party was being discussed and Sydney Smith, one of the founders of the *Edinburgh Review* and a brilliant wit, said: "we are in a most deplorable condition; we must do something to help ourselves. I think," he said, looking at Lydia White, "we had better sacrifice a Tory Virgin." (Lady Morgan's *Memoirs*, Vol. II, p. 236.) Lydia White, was the "Miss Diddle" of Byron's *The Blues*.

[4] Mrs. Wilmot (née Barberina Ogle) was the widow of Valentia Wilmot. She later wrote a number of dramas, translations, and poems.

[5] Lady Beaumont was the wife of Sir George Beaumont, painter, collector, and founder of the National Gallery, and a friend of Sir Joshua Reynolds, Dr. Johnson, and Wordsworth.

[6] Lady Charlemont was an Irish beauty, wife of the 2nd Earl of Charlemont.

them all,"[7] and every thing else. Oh that face!—by "te Diva potens Cypri"[8] I would, to be beloved by that woman, build and burn another Troy.

M[oor]e has a peculiarity of talent, or rather talents,—poetry, music, voice, all his own; and an expression in each, which never was, nor will be, possessed by another. But he is capable of still higher flights in poetry. By the by, what humour, what—every thing, in the "Post-Bag!" There is nothing M[oor]e may not do, if he will but seriously set about it. In society, he is gentlemanly, gentle, and, altogether more pleasing than any individual with whom I am acquainted. For his honour, principle, and independence, his conduct to * * * * speaks "trumpet-tongued." He has but one fault—and that one I daily regret —he is not *here*.

Nov. 23d

Ward—I like Ward. By Mahomet! I begin to think I like every body;—a disposition, not to be encouraged;—a sort of social gluttony, that swallows every thing set before it. But I like Ward. He is *piquant;* and, in my opinion, will stand *very* high in the House, and every where else, if he applies *regularly.* By the by, I dine with him to-morrow, which may have some influence on my opinion. It is as well not to trust one's gratitude *after* dinner. I have heard many a host libelled by his guests, with his burgundy yet reeking on their rascally lips.

* * * * * * * * * * * * * * *

I have taken Lord Salisbury's box at Covent Garden for the season; —and now I must go and prepare to join Lady Holland and party, in theirs, at Drury Lane, *questa sera.*

Holland doesn't think the man *is Junius*; but that the yet unpublished journal throws great light on the obscurities of that part of George the Second's reign.—What is this to George the Third's? I don't know what to think. Why should Junius be yet dead? If suddenly apoplexed, would he rest in his grave without sending his εἰδωλον to shout in the ears of posterity, "Junius was X.Y.Z., Esq., buried in the parish of * * *. Repair his monument, ye churchwardens! Print a new edition of his Letters, ye booksellers!" Impossible,—the man must be alive, and will never die without disclosure. I like him;—he was a good hater.

Came home unwell and went to bed,—not so sleepy as might be desirable.

[7] Pope, *Rape of the Lock,* II, 18.
[8] Horace, *Odes,* I, iii, 1.

I awoke from a dream!—well! and have not others dreamed?—Such
a dream!—but she did not overtake me. I wish the dead would rest,
however. Ugh! how my blood chilled,—and I could not wake—and—
and—heigho!

"Shadows to-night
Have struck more terror to the soul of Richard,
Than could the substance of ten thousand * * s,
Arm'd all in proof, and led by shallow * *."[1]

I do not like this dream,—I hate its "foregone conclusion." And am I
to be shaken by shadows? Ay, when they remind us of—no matter—
but, if I dream thus again, I will try whether *all* sleep has the like
visions. Since I rose, I've been in considerable bodily pain also; but
it is gone, and now, like Lord Ogleby[2], I am wound up for the
day.

A note from Mountnorris[3]—I dine with Ward;—Canning is to be
there, Frere[4] and Sharpe,[5]—perhaps Gifford. I am to be one of "the
five" (or rather six), as Lady * * said a little sneeringly yesterday.
They are all good to meet, particularly Canning, and—Ward, when
he likes. I wish I may be well enough to listen to these intellectuals.

No letters to-day;—so much the better,—there are no answers. I
must not dream again;—it spoils even reality. I will go out of doors,
and see what the fog will do for me. Jackson has been here: the boxing
world much as usual;—but the Club[6] increases. I shall dine at Crib's[7]
to-morrow. I like energy—even animal energy—of all kinds; and I

[1] *Richard III*, Act V, Scene 3.

[2] Lord Ogleby is a character in Colman and Garrick's *The Clandestine Marriage*.
His valet says of him (Act II): "What with qualms, age, rheumatism, and a few
surfeits in his youth, he must have a great deal of brushing, oyling, screwing, and
winding up, to set him a-going for the day."

[3] George Annesley, Viscount Valentia (1769–1844) became Earl of Mountnorris in 1793. He was the father of Byron's friend Viscount Valentia and of Lady
Frances Webster.

[4] John Hookham Frere (1769–1846) was a school friend of Canning, who joined
with him in the *Anti-Jacobin*. He later wrote *Whistlecraft*, a mock-heroic poem in
ottava rima, which gave Byron his model for *Beppo*.

[5] Richard Sharp (1759–1835), a wealthy hat-manufacturer, was prominent in
Whig political and literary circles. He was a friend of all the eminent political and
literary figures of half a century, from Burke on down. His anecdotes and his
entertaining talk won him the nickname of "Conversation Sharp".

[6] This was Jackson's Pugilistic Club, which met in his rooms at 13 Bond Street.

[7] Thomas Cribb (1781–1848) had been a coal porter before he established
himself as a pugilist. With his victory over Bob Gregson on Oct. 25, 1808, he
became champion of England. In 1813, he was landlord of the King's Arms, Duke
Street, St. James's.

have need of both mental and corporeal. I have not dined out, nor, indeed, *at all*, lately: have heard no music—have seen nobody. Now for a *plunge*—high life and low life. "Amant *alterna* Camœnae!"[8]

I have burnt my *Roman*—as I did the first scenes and sketch of my comedy—and, for aught I see, the pleasure of burning is quite as great as that of printing. These two last would not have done. I ran into *realities* more than ever; and some would have been recognized and others guessed at.

Redde the Ruminator—a collection of Essays, by a strange, but able, old man (Sir E[gerton] B[rydges]),[1] and a half-wild young one, author of a Poem on the Highlands, called *Childe Alarique*.[2] The word "sensibility" (always my aversion) occurs a thousand times in these Essays; and, it seems, is to be an excuse for all kinds of discontent. This young man can know nothing of life; and, if he cherishes the disposition which runs through his papers, will become useless, and, perhaps, not even a poet, after all, which he seems determined to be. God help him! no one should be a rhymer who could be any thing better. And this is what annoys one, to see Scott and Moore, and Campbell and Rogers, who might have all been agents and leaders, now mere spectators. For, though they may have other ostensible avocations, these last are reduced to a secondary consideration. * *, too, frittering away his time among dowagers and unmarried girls. If it advanced any *serious* affair, it were some excuse; but, with the unmarried, that is a hazardous speculation, and tiresome enough, too: and, with the veterans, it is not much worth trying, unless, perhaps, one in a thousand.

If I had any views in this country, they would probably be parliamentary. But I have no ambition; at least, if any, it would be "aut Caesar aut nihil." My hopes are limited to the arrangement of my affairs, and settling either in Italy or the East (rather the last), and drinking deep of the languages and literature of both. Past events have unnerved me; and all I can now do is to make life an amusement, and

[8] Virgil, Eclogue, III, 59: ". . . you shall sing turn by turn as the Muses love."

[1] Sir Samuel Egerton Brydges (1762–1837), bibliographer and genealogist, also wrote poems and novels. In 1813 he published *The Ruminator: containing a series of moral, critical, and sentimental Essays*. Of the 104 essays, 72 had appeared in his *Censura Literaria, Titles and Opinions of Old English Books*. Just after Byron's death in 1824 he published *Letters on the Character and Poetical Genius of Lord Byron*.

[2] Robert Pearse Gillies (1788–1858) published *Childe Alarique, a Poet's Reverie, with other Poems* in 1813. He was a friend of Scott and Wordsworth and contributed to Christopher North's "Noctes Ambrosianae" in *Blackwood's Magazine*. He was the founder and first editor of the *Foreign Quarterly Review* (1827).

look on, while others play. After all—even the highest game of crowns and sceptres, what is it? *Vide* Napoleon's last twelvemonth. It has completely upset my system of fatalism. I thought, if crushed, he would have fallen, when *"fractus illabitur orbis,"* [3] and not have been pared away to gradual insignificance;—that all this was not a mere *jeu* of the gods, but a prelude to greater changes and mightier events. But Men never advance beyond a certain point;—and here we are, retrograding to the dull, stupid old system,—balance of Europe— poising straws upon king's noses, instead of wringing them off! Give me a republic, or a despotism of one, rather than the mixed government of one, two, three. A republic!—look in the history of the Earth— Rome, Greece, Venice, France, Holland, America, our short (*eheu!*) Commonwealth, and compare it with what they did under masters. The Asiatics are not qualified to be republicans, but they have the liberty of demolishing despots, which is the next thing to it. To be the first man—not the Dictator—not the Sylla, but the Washington or the Aristides—the leader in talent and truth—is next to the Divinity! Franklin, Penn, and, next to these, either Brutus or Cassius —even Mirabeau—or St. Just. I shall never be any thing, or rather always be nothing. The most I can hope is, that some will say, "He might, perhaps, if he would."

12, midnight

Here are two confounded proofs from the printer. I have looked at the one, but, for the soul of me, I can't look over that "Giaour" again,—at least, just now, and at this hour—and yet there is no moon.

Ward talks of going to Holland, and we have partly discussed an *ensemble* expedition. It must be in ten days, if at all, if we wish to be in at the Revolution. And why not? * * is distant, and will be at * *, still more distant, till spring. No one else, except Augusta, cares for me—no ties—no trammels—*andiamo dunque—se torniamo, bene—se non, ch' importa?* Old William of Orange talked of dying in "the last ditch" of his dingy country. It is lucky I can swim, or I suppose I should not well weather the first. But let us see. I have heard hyænas and jackalls in the ruins of Asia; and bull-frogs in the marshes,—besides wolves and angry Mussulmans. Now, I should like to listen to the shout of a free Dutchman.

Alla! Viva! For ever! Hourra! Huzza!—which is the most rational or musical of these cries? "Orange Boven," according to the *Morning Post*.

---

[3] Horace, *Odes*, III, iii, 7: "If wide Creation broke".

No dreams last night of the dead nor the living—so—I am "firm as the marble, founded as the rock"[1]—till the next earthquake. Ward's dinner went off well. There was not a disagreeable person there—unless *I* offended any body, which I am sure I could not by contradiction, for I said little, and opposed nothing. Sharpe[1] (a man of elegant mind, and who has lived much with the best—Fox, Horne Tooke, Windham, Fitzpatrick, and all the agitators of other times and tongues,) told us the particulars of his last interview with Windham,[2] a few days before the fatal operation which sent "that gallant spirit to aspire the skies."[3] Windham,—the first in one department of oratory and talent, whose only fault was his refinement beyond the intellect of half his hearers,—Windham, half his life an active participator in the events of the earth, and one of those who governed nations,—*he* regretted,—and dwelt much on that regret, that "he had not entirely devoted himself to literature and science!!!" His mind certainly would have carried him to eminence there, as elsewhere;—but I cannot comprehend what debility of that mind could suggest such a wish. I, who have heard him, cannot regret any thing but that I shall never hear him again. What! would he have been a plodder? a metaphysician? —perhaps a rhymer? a scribbler? Such an exchange must have been suggested by illness. But he is gone, and Time "shall not look upon his like again."[4]

I am tremendously in arrear with my letters,—except to * *, and to her my thoughts overpower me,—my words never compass them. To Lady Melbourne I write with most pleasure—and her answers, so sensible, so *tactique*—I never met with half her talent. If she had been a few years younger, what a fool she would have made of me, had she thought it worth her while,—and I should have lost a valuable and most agreeable *friend.* Mem. a mistress never is nor can be a friend. While you agree, you are lovers; and, when it is over, any thing but friends.

I have not answered W. Scott's last letter,—but I will. I regret to hear from others, that he has lately been unfortunate in pecuniary involvements. He is undoubtedly the Monarch of Parnassus, and the

---

[1] *Macbeth,* Act III, Scene 4: "Whole as the marble, founded as the rock."
[1] "Conversation Sharp".
[2] William Windham (1750–1810), an M.P. for Norwich from 1784, held various Cabinet posts and was one of the managers of the impeachment of Warren Hastings. He was an effective speaker.
[3] *Romeo and Juliet,* Act III, Scene 1.
[4] *Hamlet,* Act I, Scene 2.

most *English* of bards. I should place Rogers next in the living list—
(I value him more as the last of the *best* school)—Moore and Campbell
both *third*—Southey and Wordsworth and Coleridge—the rest δι πολλοι
—thus:—

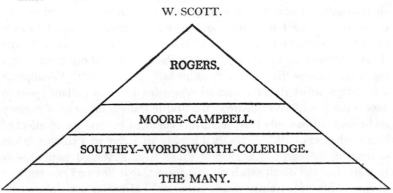

W. SCOTT.

ROGERS.

MOORE.-CAMPBELL.

SOUTHEY.-WORDSWORTH.-COLERIDGE.

THE MANY.

There is a triangular "Gradus ad Parnassum!"—the names are too
numerous for the base of the triangle. Poor Thurlow has gone wild
about the poetry of Queen Bess's reign—*c'est dommage*. I have ranked
the names upon my triangle more upon what I believe popular opinion,
than any decided opinion of my own. For, to me, some of M[oor]e's
last *Erin* sparks—"As a beam o'er the face of the waters"—"When
he who adores thee"—"Oh blame not"—and "Oh breath not his
name"—are worth all the Epics that ever were composed.

＊ ＊ [Rogers] thinks the *Quarterly* will attack me next. Let them. I
have been "peppered so highly" in my time, *both* ways, that it must
be cayenne or aloes to make me taste. I can sincerely say that I am not
very much alive *now* to criticism. But—in tracing this—I rather believe
that it proceeds from my not attaching that importance to authorship
which many do, and which, when young, I did also. "One gets tired
of every thing, my angel," says Valmont.[1] The "angels" are the only
things of which I am not a little sick—but I do think the preference
of *writers* to *agents*—the mighty stir made about scribbling and scribes,
by themselves and others—a sign of effeminacy, degeneracy, and
weakness. Who would write, who had any thing better to do? "Action
—action—action"—said Demosthenes: "Actions—actions," I say,
and not writing,—least of all, rhyme. Look at the querulous and

---

[1] Valmont is the hero of *Les Laisons Dangereuses*. The passage Byron quoted,
however, is not a saying of Valmont, but is quoted by the Marquise de Merteuil:
"On s'ennuie de tout, mon ange, c'est une loi de la Nature; ce n'est pas ma faute."
(Letter CXLI).

monotonous lives of the "genus;"—except Cervantes, Tasso, Dante, Ariosto, Kleist (who were brave and active citizens), Æschylus, Sophocles, and some other of the antiques also—what a worthless, idle brood it is!

12, Mezza Notte.

Just returned from dinner with Jackson (the Emperor of Pugilism) and another of the select, at Crib's the champion's. I drank more than I like, and have brought away some three bottles of very fair claret—for I have no headache. We had Tom [Crib] up after dinner;—very facetious, though somewhat prolix. He don't like his situation—wants to fight again—pray Pollux (or Castor, if he was the *miller*) he may! Tom has been a sailor—a coal-heaver—and some other genteel profession, before he took to the cestus. Tom has been in action at sea, and is now only three-and-thirty. A great man! has a wife and a mistress, and conversations well—bating some sad omissions and misapplications of the aspirate. Tom is an old friend of mine; I have seen some of his best battles in my nonage. He is now a publican, and, I fear, a sinner;—for Mrs. [Crib] is on alimony, and * *'s daughter lives with the champion. This * * told me,—Tom, having an opinion of my morals, passed her off as a legal spouse. Talking of her, he said, "she was the truest of women"—from which I immediately inferred she could *not* be his wife, and so it turned out.

These panegyrics don't belong to matrimony;—for, if "true," a man don't think it necessary to say so; and if not, the less he says the better. [Crib] is the only man except * * * * [Webster?], I ever heard harangue upon his wife's virtue; and I listened to both with great credence and patience, and stuffed my handkerchief into my mouth, when I found yawning irresistible—By the by, I am yawning now— so, good night to thee.—Μπαιρων.

Thursday, 26th November

Awoke a little feverish, but no headache—no dreams neither, thanks to stupor! Two letters, one from * * * [Lady Frances Webster], the other from Lady Melbourne—both excellent in their respective styles. * * * * [Lady Frances]'s contained also a very pretty lyric on "concealed griefs"—if not her own, yet very like her. Why did she not say that the stanzas were, or were not, of her composition? I do not know whether to wish them *hers* or not. I have no great esteem for poetical persons, particularly women; they have so much of the "ideal" in *practics*, as well as *ethics*.

I have been thinking lately a good deal of Mary Duff. How very odd that I should have been so utterly, devotedly fond of that girl, at an age when I could neither feel passion, nor know the meaning of the word. And the effect! My mother used always to rally me about this childish amour; and, at last, many years after, when I was sixteen, she told me one day, "Oh, Byron, I have had a letter from Edinburgh, from Miss Abercromby, and your old sweetheart Mary Duff is married to a Mr. Coe."[1] And what was my answer? I really cannot explain or account for my feelings at that moment; but they nearly threw me into convulsions, and alarmed my mother so much, that after I grew better, she generally avoided the subject—to *me*—and contented herself with telling it to all her acquaintance. Now, what could this be? I had never seen her since her mother's faux pas at Aberdeen had been the cause of her removal to her grandmother's at Banff; we were both the merest children. I had and have been attached fifty times since that period; yet I recollect all we said to each other, all our caresses, her features, my restlessness, sleeplessness, my tormenting my mother's maid to write for me to her, which she at last did, to quiet me. Poor Nancy thought I was wild, and, as I could not write for myself, became my secretary. I remember, too, our walks, and the happiness of sitting by Mary, in the children's apartment, at their house not far from Plainstones at Aberdeen, while her lesser sister Helen played with the doll, and we sat gravely making love, in our way.

How the deuce did all this occur so early? where could it originate? I certainly had no sexual ideas for years afterwards; and yet my misery, my love for that girl were so violent, that I sometimes doubt if I have ever been really attached since. Be that as it may, hearing of her marriage several years after was like a thunder-stroke—it nearly choked me—to the horror of my mother and the astonishment and almost incredulity of every body. And it is a phenomenon in my existence (for I was not eight years old) which has puzzled, and will puzzle me to the latest hour of it; and lately, I know not why, the *recollection* (*not* the attachment) has recurred as forcibly as ever. I wonder if she can have the least remembrance of it or me? or remember her pitying sister Helen for not having an admirer too? How very pretty is the perfect image of her in my memory—her brown, dark hair, and hazel eyes; her very dress! I should be quite grieved to see *her now*; the reality, however beautiful, would destroy, or at least confuse, the features of the lovely Peri which then existed in her, and still lives in my imagination, at the distance of more than sixteen years. I am now twenty-five and odd months . . . .

[1] Mary Duff married Robert Cockburn, a wine merchant of Edinburgh and London.

I think my mother told the circumstances (on my hearing of her marriage) to the Parkynses, and certainly to the Pigot family, and probably mentioned it in her answer to Miss A[bercromby], who was well acquainted with my childish *penchant*, and had sent the news on purpose for *me*,—and thanks to her!

Next to the beginning, the conclusion has often occupied my reflections, in the way of investigation. That the facts are thus, others know as well as I, and my memory yet tells me so, in more than a whisper. But, the more I reflect, the more I am bewildered to assign any cause for this precocity of affection. [See page 258 for additional passage.]

Lord Holland invited me to dinner to-day; but three days' dining would destroy me. So, without eating at all since yesterday, I went to my box at Covent Garden.

* * * * * * * * * * * * * * *

Saw * * * * [Lady Frances Webster's younger sister?] looking very pretty, though quite a different style of beauty from the other two. She has the finest eyes in the world, out of which she pretends *not* to see, and the longest eyelashes I ever saw, since Leila's and Phannio's Moslem curtains of the light. She has much beauty,—just enough,— but is, I think, *méchante*.

* * * * * * * * * * * * * * *

I have been pondering on the miseries of separation, that—oh how seldom we see those we love! yet we live ages in moments, *when met*. The only thing that consoles me during absence is the reflection that no mental or personal estrangement, from ennui or disagreement, can take place; and when people meet hereafter, even though many changes may have taken place in the mean time, still—unless they are *tired* of each other—they are ready to re-unite, and do not blame each other for the circumstances that severed them. * * * * * * * * * * *

Saturday, 27th (I believe—or rather am in *doubt*, which is the ne plus ultra of mortal faith.)

I have missed a day; and, as the Irishman said, or Joe Miller[1] says for him, "have gained a loss," or *by* the loss. Every thing is settled for Holland, and nothing but a cough, or a caprice of my fellow-traveller's, can stop us. Carriage ordered—funds prepared—and, probably, a gale of wind into the bargain. *N'importe*—I believe with Clym o' the Clow,

---

[1] Joseph or Joe Miller (1684–1738) was an actor and humorist, who joined the Drury Lane Company in 1709. He was reputed as a natural comedian. After his death a collection (actually by John Mottley) was published with the title *Joe Miller's Jests* (1789), which became a popular book.

or Robin Hood, "By our Mary, (dear name!) thou art both Mother and May, I think it never was a man's lot to die before his day."[2] Heigh for Helvoetsluys, and so forth!

To-night I went with young Henry Fox to see "Nourjahad,"[3]—a drama, which the Morning Post hath laid to my charge, but of which I cannot even guess the author. I wonder what they will next inflict upon me. They cannot well sink below a Melodrama; but that is better than a Satire, (at least, a personal one,) with which I stand truly arraigned, and in atonement of which I am resolved to bear silently all criticisms, abuses, and even praises, for bad pantomimes never composed by me, without even a contradictory aspect. I suppose the root of this report is my loan to the manager of my Turkish drawings for his dresses, to which he was more welcome than to my name. I suppose the real author will soon own it, as it has succeeded; if not, Job be my model, and Lethe my beverage!

* * * * [Lady Frances Webster] has received the portrait safe; and, in answer, the only remark she makes upon it is, "indeed it is like"— and again, "indeed it is like." * * * * With her the likeness "covered a multitude of sins;" for I happen to know that this portrait was not a flatterer, but dark and stern,—even black as the mood in which my mind was scorching last July, when I sat for it.[1] All the others of me— like most portraits whatsoever—are, of course, more agreeable than nature.

Redde the Edinburgh Review of Rogers.[2] He is ranked highly—but where he should be. There is a summary view of us all—*Moore* and *me* among the rest; and both (the *first* justly) praised—though, by implication (justly again) placed beneath our memorable friend. Mackintosh is the writer, and also of the critique on the Staël.[3] His

---

[2] "Ballad of Robin Hood."

[3] *Illusion, or the Trances of Nourjahad* was acted at Drury Lane, Nov. 25, 1813. It was an anonymous melodrama in three acts, which the *Morning Post* and the *Satirist* both ascribed to Byron.

[1] This was probably the portrait by Holmes, mentioned in Byron's letter to Lady Melbourne, Nov. 22, 1813.

[2] The review of Rogers's *Poems* including Fragments of a Poem called the *Voyage of Columbus* in the *Edinburgh Review* of October, 1813, paid some compliments to Byron and Moore without naming them. Commenting on the stanzas in *Childe Harold* inspired by Greece, the critic wrote: "Full of enthusiasm for those perfect forms of heroism and liberty, which his imagination had placed in the recesses of antiquity, he gave vent to his impatience of the imperfections of living men and real institutions, in an original strain of sublime satire, which clothes moral anger in imagery of an almost horrible grandeur . . . ."

[3] The critique on De Staël followed the one on Rogers in the *Edinburgh Review*, of October, 1813.

grand essay on Burke, I hear, is for the next number. But I know nothing of the Edinburgh, or of any other Review, but from rumour; and I have long ceased—indeed, I could not, in justice, complain of any, even though I were to rate poetry, in general, and my rhymes in particular, more highly than I really do. To withdraw *myself* from *myself* (oh that cursed selfishness!) has ever been my sole, my entire, my sincere motive in scribbling at all; and publishing is also the continuance of the same object, by the action it affords to the mind, which else recoils upon itself. If I valued fame, I should flatter received opinions, which have gathered strength by time, and will yet wear longer than any living works to the contrary. But, for the soul of me, I cannot and will not give the lie to my own thoughts and doubts, come what may. If I am a fool, it is, at least, a doubting one; and I envy no one the certainty of his self-approved wisdom.

All are inclined to believe what they covet, from a lottery-ticket up to a passport to Paradise,—in which, from description, I see nothing very tempting. My restlessness tells me I have something within that "passeth show." It is for Him, who made it, to prolong that spark of celestial fire which illuminates, yet burns, this frail tenement; but I see no such horror in a "dreamless sleep," and I have no conception of any existence which duration would not render tiresome. How else "fell the angels," even according to your creed? They were immortal, heavenly, and happy, as their *apostate Abdiel* is now by his treachery. Time must decide; and eternity won't be the less agreeable or more horrible because one did not expect it. In the mean time, I am grateful for some good, and tolerably patient under certain evils—grace à Dieu et mon bon tempérament.

Sunday, 28th. Monday, 29th. Tuesday, 30th.

Two days missed in my log-book;—hiatus *haud* deflendus. They were as little worth recollection as the rest; and luckily, laziness or society prevented me from *notching* them.

Sunday, I dined with the Lord Holland in St. James's Square. Large party—among them Sir S. Romilly and Lady Ry.[1]—General Sir Somebody Bentham,[2] a man of science and talent, I am told—Horner—

[1] Sir Samuel Romilly (1757–1818) was a follower of Rousseau and a law reformer. He effected great reforms in the criminal code, favoured Catholic emancipation, and the abolition of slavery. His liberal stance in Parliament and elsewhere should have impressed Byron favourably, but when he gave advice to Lady Byron in the separation proceedings in 1816, Byron developed an undying hatred for him. On the death of his wife in 1818, Romilly committed suicide.

[2] Sir Samuel Bentham (1757–1831), naval architect and engineer, was, like his brother Jeremy Bentham, a reformer.

the Horner, an Edinburgh Reviewer,[3] an excellent speaker in the "Honourable House," very pleasing, too, and gentlemanly in company, as far as I have seen—Sharpe[4]—Philips of Lancashire[5]—Lord John Russell,[6] and others, "good men and true." Holland's society is very good; you always see some one or other in it worth knowing. Stuffed myself with sturgeon, and exceeded in champagne and wine in general, but not to confusion of head. When I *do* dine, I gorge like an Arab or a Boa snake, on fish and vegetables, but no meat. I am always better, however, on my tea and biscuit than any other regimen, and even *that* sparingly.

Why does Lady H. always have that damned screen between the whole room and the fire? I, who bear cold no better than an antelope, and never yet found a sun quite *done* to my taste, was absolutely petrified, and could not even shiver. All the rest, too, looked as if they were just unpacked, like salmon from an ice-basket, and set down to table for that day only. When she retired, I, watched their looks as I dismissed the screen, and every cheek thawed, and every nose reddened with the anticipated glow.

Saturday, I went with Harry Fox to Nourjahad; and, I believe, convinced him, by incessant yawning, that it was not mine. I wish the precious author would own it, and release me from his fame. The dresses are pretty, but not in costume;—Mrs. Horne's,[1] all but the turban, and the want of a small dagger (if she is a sultana), *perfect.* I never saw a Turkish woman with a turban in my life—nor did any one else. The sultanas have a small poniard at the waist. The dialogue is drowsy—the action heavy—the scenery fine—the actors tolerable. I can't say much for their seraglio—Teresa, Phannio, or * * * *, were worth them all.

Sunday, a very handsome note from Mackintosh, who is a rare instance of the union of very transcendent talent and great good-nature. To-day (Tuesday) a very pretty billet from M. la Baronne de

---

[3] Francis Horner (1778–1817), a Scottish lawyer who was one of the founders of the *Edinburgh Review* and a frequent contributor, was an impressive speaker in the House of Commons.

[4] "Conversation Sharp."

[5] George Philips was the son of Thomas Philips of Sedgley, Lancashire. He later represented South Warwickshire in the reformed House of Commons.

[6] Lord John Russell (1792–1878), a reformer who was one of the most active movers of the Reform Bill of 1832, held numerous government posts and was several times Prime Minister. He was the literary executor of Thomas Moore, and after Moore's death edited his journal. He was the grandfather of the philosopher Bertrand Russell. He became the 1st Earl Russell in 1861.

[1] Mrs. Horn took the part of Nourjahad's wife in the Drury Lane production.

Staël Holstein. She is pleased to be much pleased with my mention of her and her last work in my notes.[2] I spoke as I thought. Her works are my delight, and so is she herself, for—half an hour. I don't like her politics—at least, her *having changed* them; had she been *qualis ab incepto*, it were nothing. But she is a woman by herself, and has done more than all the rest of them together, intellectually;—she ought to have been a man. She *flatters* me very prettily in her note;—but I *know* it. The reason that adulation is not displeasing is, that, though untrue, it shows one to be of consequence enough, in one way or other, to induce people to lie, to make us their friend:—that is their concern.

* * is, I hear, thriving on the repute of a *pun* (which was *mine* at Mackintosh's dinner some time back), on Ward, who was asking, "how much it would take to *re-whig* him?" I answered that, probably, he "must first, before he was *re-whigged*, be re-*warded*." This foolish quibble, before the Staël and Mackintosh, and a number of conversationers, has been mouthed about, and at last settled on the head of * *, where long may it remain!

George[3] is returned from afloat to get a new ship. He looks thin, but better than I expected. I like George much more than most people like their heirs. He is a fine fellow, and every inch a sailor. I would do any thing, *but apostatize*, to get him on in his profession.

Lewis[4] called. It is a good and good-humoured man, but pestilently prolix and paradoxical and *personal*. If he would but talk half, and reduce his visits to an hour, he would add to his popularity. As an author he is very good, and his vanity is *ouverte*, like Erskine's, and yet not offending.

Yesterday, a very pretty letter from Annabella, which I answered. What an odd situation and friendship is ours!—without one spark of love on either side, and produced by circumstances which in general lead to coldness on one side, and aversion on the other. She is a very superior woman, and very little spoiled, which is strange in an heiress —a girl of twenty—a peeress that is to be, in her own right—an only child, and a *savante*, who has always had her own way. She is a poetess—a mathematician—a metaphysician, and yet, withal, very kind, generous, and gentle, with very little pretension. Any other head would be turned with half her acquisitions, and a tenth of her advantages.

[2] See Nov. 30, 1813, to Mme. de Staël, Note 1.
[3] George Anson Byron, Byron's first cousin and successor to the title.
[4] Monk Lewis.

Wednesday, December 1st, 1813.

To-day responded to La Baronne de Staël Holstein, and sent to Leigh Hunt (an acquisition to my acquaintance—through Moore—of last summer) a copy of the two Turkish tales. Hunt is an extraordinary character, and not exactly of the present age. He reminds me more of the Pym and Hampden times—much talent, great independence of spirit, and an austere, yet not repulsive, aspect. If he goes on *qualis ab incepto,* I know few men who will deserve more praise or obtain it. I must go and see him again;—the rapid succession of adventure, since last summer, added to some serious uneasiness and business, have interrupted our acquaintance; but he is a man worth knowing; and though, for his own sake, I wish him out of prison, I like to study character in such situations. He has been unshaken, and will continue so. I don't think him deeply versed in life;—he is the bigot of virtue (not religion), and enamoured of the beauty of that "empty name", as the last breath of Brutus pronounced, and every day proves it. He is, perhaps, a little opinionated, as all men who are the *centre* of *circles,* wide or narrow—the Sir Oracles, in whose name two or three are gathered together—must be, and as even Johnson was; but, withal, a valuable man, and less vain than success and even the consciousness of preferring "the right to the expedient" might excuse.

To-morrow there is a party of *purple* at the "blue" Miss ✳ ✳ ✳ [Berry]'s. Shall I go? um!—I don't much affect your blue-bottles;—but one ought to be civil. There will be, "I guess now" (as the Americans say), the Staëls and Mackintoshes—good—the ✳ ✳ ✳ s and ✳ ✳ ✳ s—not so good—the ✳ ✳ ✳ s, &c., &c.—good for nothing. Perhaps that blue-winged Kashmirian butterfly[1] of book-learning, Lady ✳ ✳ ✳ ✳ [Charlemont,] will be there. I hope so; it is a pleasure to look upon that most beautiful of faces.

Wrote to H[odgson]—he has been telling that I—. I am sure, at least, *I* did not mention it, and I wish he had not. He is a good fellow, and I obliged myself ten times more by being of use than I did him,—and there's an end on't.[2]

Baldwin is boring me to present their King's Bench petition.[3] I

---

[1] *The Giaour* (lines 388–392):
> As rising on its purple wing
> The insect-queen of Eastern spring,
> O'er emerald meadows of Kashmeer
> Invites the young pursuer near

[2] Byron was embarrassed that his "loan" meant as a gift to Hodgson had become known.

[3] See Journal, Nov. 14, 1813.

presented Cartwright's last year; and Stanhope and I stood against the whole House, and mouthed it valiantly—and had some fun and a little abuse for our opposition. But "I am not i' th' vein"[4] for this business. Now, had * * [Lady Oxford] been here, she would have *made* me do it. *There* is a woman, who, amid all her fascination, always urged a man to usefulness or glory. Had she remained, she had been my tutelar genius. * * *

Baldwin is very importunate—but, poor fellow, "I can't get out, I can't get out—said the starling." Ah, I am as bad as that dog Sterne, who preferred whining over "a dead ass to relieving a living mother"[5] —villain—hypocrite—slave—sycophant! but *I* am no better. Here I cannot stimulate myself to a speech for the sake of these unfortunates, and three words and half a smile of * * [Lady Oxford] had she been here to urge it (and urge it she infallibly would—at least, she always pressed me on senatorial duties, and particularly in the cause of weakness) would have made me an advocate, if not an orator. Curse on Rochefoucault for being always right! In him a lie were virtue,— or, at least, a comfort to his readers.

George Byron has not called to-day; I hope he will be an admiral, and, perhaps, Lord Byron into the bargain. If he would but marry, I would engage never to marry myself, or cut him out of the heirship. He would be happier, and I should like nephews better than sons.

I shall soon be six-and-twenty (January 22d, 1814). Is there any thing in the future that can possibly console us for not being always *twenty-five*?

"Oh Gioventu!
Oh Primavera! gioventu dell' anno.
Oh Gioventu! primavera della vita."

* * * * * * * * * * * * * * *

Sunday, December 5th.

Dallas's nephew (son to the American Attorney-general) is arrived in this country, and tells Dallas that my rhymes are very popular in the United States. These are the first tidings that have ever sounded like *Fame* to my ears—to be redde on the banks of the Ohio! The greatest pleasure I ever derived, of this kind, was from an extract, in Cooke the actor's life, from his journal, stating that in the reading-room of Albany, near Washington, he perused English Bards and

---

[4] *Richard III*, Act IV, Scene 2.
[5] Sterne, *A Sentimental Journey.*

Scotch Reviewers.[1] To be popular in a rising and far country has a kind of *posthumous feel*, very different from the ephemeral *éclat* and fête-ing, buzzing and party-ing compliments of the well-dressed multitude. I can safely say that, during my *reign* in the spring of 1812, I regretted nothing but its duration of six weeks instead of a fortnight, and was heartily glad to resign.

Last night I supped with Lewis;—and, as usual, though I neither exceeded in solids nor fluids, have been half dead ever since. My stomach is entirely destroyed by long abstinence, and the rest will probably follow. Let it—I only wish the *pain* over. The "leap in the dark" is the least to be dreaded.

The Duke of * * called. I have told them forty times that, except to half-a-dozen old and specified acquaintances, I am invisible. His grace is a good, noble, ducal person; but I am content to think so at a distance, and so—I was not at home.

Galt called.—Mem.—to ask some one to speak to Raymond[1] in favour of his play. We are old fellow-travellers, and, with all his eccentricities, he has much strong sense, experience of the world, and is, as far as I have seen, a good-natured philosophical fellow. I showed him Sligo's letter on the reports of the Turkish girl's *aventure* at Athens soon after it happened. He and Lord Holland, Lewis, and Moore, and Rogers, and Lady Melbourne have seen it. Murray has a copy. I thought it had been *unknown*, and wish it were; but Sligo arrived only some days after, and the *rumours* are the subject of his letter. That I shall preserve,—*it is as well.* Lewis and Galt were both *horrified*; and L. wondered I did not introduce the situation into "the Giaour". He *may* wonder;—he might wonder more at that production's being written at all. But to describe the *feelings* of *that situation* were impossible—it is *icy* even to recollect them.

The Bride of Abydos was published on Thursday the second of December; but how it is liked or disliked, I know not. Whether it succeeds or not is no fault of the public, against whom I can have no complaint. But I am much more indebted to the tale than I can ever be to the most partial reader; as it wrung my thoughts from reality to imagination—from selfish regrets to vivid recollections—and recalled me to a country replete with the *brightest* and *darkest*, but always most

[1] See Dunlap's *Memoirs of George Frederick Cooke*, Vol. II, p. 313: "Read *English Bards and Scotch Reviewers*, by Lord Byron. It is well written. His Lordship is rather severe, perhaps justly so, on Walter Scott, and most assuredly justly severe upon Monk Lewis."

[1] Raymond was the stage manager at Drury Lane Theatre. He played the ghost when Drury Lane reopened with *Hamlet*.

lively colours of my memory. Sharpe called, but was not let in,—which I regret.

* * * * * * * * * * * * * * *

Saw * * [Rogers] yesterday. I have not kept my appointment at Middleton, which has not pleased him, perhaps; and my projected voyage with * * [Ward] will, perhaps, please him less. But I wish to keep well with both. They are instruments that don't do in concert; but, surely, their separate tones are very musical, and I won't give up either.

It is well if I don't jar between these great discords. At present I stand tolerably well with all, but I cannot adopt their *dislikes*;—so many *sets*. Holland's is the first;—every thing *distingué* is welcome there, and certainly the *ton* of his society is the best. Then there is Mde. de Staël's—there I never go, though I might, had I courted it. It is composed of the * * s and the * * family with a strange sprinkling,—orators, dandies, and all kinds of *Blue*, from the regular Grub-street uniform, down to the azure jacket of the *Littérateur*. To see * * and * * sitting together, at dinner, always reminds me of the grave, where all distinctions of friend and foe are levelled; and they—the Reviewer and the Reviewée—the Rhinoceros and Elephant—the Mammoth and Megalonyx—all will lie quietly together. They now *sit* together, as silent, but not so quiet, as if they were already immured.

* * * * * * * * * * * * * * *

I did not go to the Berrys' the other night. The elder is a woman of much talent, and both are handsome, and must have been beautiful. To-night asked to Lord H.'s—shall I go? um!—perhaps.

Morning, two o'clock.

Went to Lord H.'s—party numerous—*mi*lady in perfect good-humour, and consequently *perfect*. No one more agreeable, or perhaps so much so, when she will. Asked for Wednesday to dine and meet the Staël—asked particularly, I believe, out of mischief to see the first interview after the *note*, with which Corinne professes herself to be so much taken. I don't much like it;—she always talks of *my*self or *her*self, and I am not (except in soliloquy, as now,) much enamoured of either subject—especially one's Works. What the devil shall I say about "De l'Allemagne?" I like it prodigiously; but unless I can twist my admiration into some fantastical expression, she won't believe me; and I know, by experience, I shall be overwhelmed with fine things about rhyme, &c., &c. The lover, Mr. * * [Rocca], was there to-night, and C * * said "it was the only proof *he* had seen of her good taste."

Monsieur L'Amant is remarkably handsome; but *I* don't think more so than her book.

C * * [Campbell] looks well,—seems pleased, and dressed to *sprucery*. A blue coat becomes him,—so does his new wig. He really looked as if Apollo had sent him a birthday suit, or a wedding-garment, and was witty and lively. * * * He abused Corinne's book, which I regret; because, firstly, he understands German, and is consequently a fair judge; and, secondly, he is *first-rate*, and, consequently, the best of judges. I reverence and admire him; but I won't give up my opinion —why should I? I read *her* again and again, and there can be no affectation in this. I cannot be mistaken (except in taste) in a book I read and lay down, and take up again; and no book can be totally bad which finds *one*, even *one* reader, who can say as much sincerely.

C[ampbell] talks of lecturing next spring; his last lectures were eminently successful. Moore thought of it, but gave it up,—I don't know why. * * had been prating *dignity* to him, and such stuff; as if a man disgraced himself by instructing and pleasing at the same time.

Introduced to Marquis Buckingham[1]—saw Lord Gower[2]—he is going to Holland;—Sir J. and Lady Mackintosh and Horner, G. Lamb,[3] with I know not how many (R[ichard] Wellesley,[4] one—a clever man), grouped about the room. Little Henry Fox, a very fine boy, and very promising in mind and manner,—he went away to bed, before I had time to talk to him. I am sure I had rather hear him than all the *savans*.

Monday, Dec. 6th.

Murray tells me that C[roke]r asked him why the thing was called

[1] George Nugent-Temple Grenville, 1st Marquis of Buckingham (1753–1813) had been Lord-Lieutenant of Ireland, and acted for George III in procuring the defeat in the House of Lords of Fox's India Bill in 1783.

[2] Lord Granville Leveson-Gower (1773–1846), youngest son of Granville Leveson-Gower, 1st Marquis of Stafford, was created Viscount Granville in 1815, and Earl Granville in 1833. He had been a Privy Councillor and Ambassador Extraordinary at St. Petersburg (1804–5) and was later Minister at Brussels and Ambassador at Paris.

[3] George Lamb (1784–1834) was the fourth son of the first Lord Melbourne. He was one of the early contributors to the *Edinburgh Review*, an amateur actor and a playwright. He was later associated with Byron on the sub-committee of management of Drury Lane Theatre.

[4] Richard Colley Wellesley, Marquis Wellesley (1760–1842), eldest son of Garrett Wellesley, 1st Earl of Mornington, and brother of Arthur Wellesley, Duke of Wellington, was Governor-General of India from 1797 to 1805. He was Ambassador to Spain in 1809 when Byron passed through on his way to the East. He was Foreign Secretary in Perceval's Cabinet (1809–1812). He favoured free trade and Catholic emancipation. He was later Lord-Lieutenant of Ireland.

the *Bride* of Abydos? It is a cursed awkward question, being unanswerable. *She* is not a *bride*, only about to be one; but for, &c., &c., &c.

I don't wonder at his finding out the *Bull*; but the detection * * * is too late to do any good. I was a great fool to make it, and am ashamed of not being an Irishman. * * * * * * * * *

C[ampbel]l last night seemed a little nettled at something or other—I know not what. We were standing in the ante-saloon, when Lord H. brought out of the other room a vessel of some composition similar to that which is used in catholic churches, and, seeing us, he exclaimed, "Here is some *incense* for you." C[ampbel]l answered—"Carry it to Lord Byron, *he is used to it.*" * * * * * * *

Now, this comes of "bearing no brother near the throne."[1] I, who have no throne, nor wish to have one *now*—whatever I may have done —am at perfect peace with all the poetical fraternity; or, at least, if I dislike any, it is not *poetically* but *personally*. Surely the field of thought is infinite;—what does it signify who is before or behind in a race where there is no *goal*? The temple of Fame is like that of the Persians, the Universe;—our altar, the tops of mountains. I should be equally content with Mount Caucasus, or Mount anything; and those who like it, may have Mount Blanc or Chimborazo, without my envy of their elevation.

I think I may *now* speak thus; for I have just published a Poem, and am quite ignorant whether it is *likely* to be *liked* or not. I have hitherto heard little in its commendation, and no one can *downright* abuse it to one's face, except in print. It can't be good, or I should not have stumbled over the threshold, and blundered in my very title. But I beg[a]n it with my heart full of * * *, and my head of oriental*ities* (I can't call them *isms*), and wrote on rapidly.

This journal is a relief. When I am tired—as I generally am—out comes this, and down goes every thing. But I can't read it over; —and God knows what contradictions it may contain. If I am sincere with myself (but I fear one lies more to one's self than to any one else), every page should confute, refute, and utterly abjure its predecessor.

Another scribble from Martin Baldwin the petitioner: I have neither head nor nerves to present it. That confounded supper at Lewis's has spoiled my digestion and my philanthropy. I have no more charity than a cruet of vinegar. Would I were an ostrich, and dieted on fire-irons,—or any thing that my gizzard could get the better of.

[1] Pope, *Epistle to Dr. Arbuthnot*, line 198.

To-day saw W[ard]. His uncle is dying, and W. don't much affect our Dutch determinations. I dine with him on Thursday, provided *l'oncle* is not dined upon, or peremptorily bespoke by the posthumous epicures, before that day. I wish he may recover—not for *our* dinner's sake, but to disappoint the undertaker, and the rascally reptiles that may well wait, since they *will* dine at last.

Gell[1] called—he of Troy—after I was out. Mem.—to return his visit. But my Mems. are the very landmarks of forgetfulness;—something like a lighthouse, with a ship wrecked under the nose of its lantern. I never look at a Mem. without seeing that I have remembered to forget. Mem.—I have forgotten to pay Pitt's taxes, and suppose I shall be surcharged. "An I do not turn rebel when thou art king"—oons! I believe my very biscuit is leavened with that imposter's imposts.

Lady M[elbourn]e returns from Jersey's to-morrow;—I must call. A Mr. Thomson has sent a song, which I must applaud.[2] I hate annoying them with censure or silence;—and yet I hate *lettering*.

Saw Lord Glenbervie[3] and his Prospectus, at Murray's, of a new Treatise on Timber. Now here is a man more useful than all the historians and rhymers ever planted. For by preserving our woods and forests, he furnishes materials for all the history of Britain worth reading, and all the odes worth nothing.

Redde a good deal, but desultorily. My head is crammed with the most useless lumber. It is odd that when I do read, I can only bear the chicken broth of—*any thing* but Novels. It is many a year since I looked into one, (though they are sometimes ordered, by way of experiment, but never taken) till I looked yesterday at the worst parts of the Monk. These descriptions ought to have been written by Tiberius at Caprea—they are forced—the *philtred* ideas of a jaded voluptuary. It is to me inconceivable how they could have been composed by a man of only twenty—his age when he wrote them. They have no nature—all the sour cream of cantharides. I should have suspected Buffon of writing them on the deathbed of his detestable dotage. I had never redde this edition and merely looked at them from curiosity and recollection of the noise they made, and the name they have left to Lewis. But they could do no harm, except * * * *.

[1] Sir William Gell, archaeologist and traveller, who published his *Topography of Troy* in 1804. Byron called him "rapid Gell" because he spent only three days on the site of Troy (*English Bards and Scotch Reviewers*, line 1034).

[2] See Sept. 27, 1813, to J. Thomson, note 1.

[3] Sylvester Douglas (1743–1823), created in 1800 Baron Glenbervie, was chief commissioner of the united land and forest department, 1810–1814.

Called this evening on my agent—my business as usual. Our strange adventures are the only inheritances of our family that have not diminished. * * * *

I shall now smoke two cigars, and get me to bed. The cigars don't keep well here. They get as old as a *donna di quaranti anni* in the sun of Africa. The Havannah are the best;—but neither are so pleasant as a hooka or chibouque. The Turkish tobacco is mild, and their horses entire—two things as they should be. I am so far obliged to this Journal, that it preserves me from verse,—at least from keeping it. I have just thrown a Poem into the fire (which it has relighted to my great comfort), and have smoked out of my head the plan of another. I wish I could as easily get rid of thinking, or, at least, the confusion of thought.

Tuesday, December 7.

Went to bed, and slept dreamlessly, but not refreshingly. Awoke, and up an hour before being called; but dawdled three hours in dressing. When one subtracts from life infancy (which is vegetation),—sleep, eating, and swilling—buttoning and unbuttoning—how much remains of downright existence? The summer of a dormouse. * * * * *

Redde the papers and *tea*-ed and soda-watered, and found out that the fire was badly lighted. Lord Glenbervie wants me to go to Brighton—um!

This morning, a very pretty billet from the Staël about meeting her at Ld. H's to-morrow. She has written, I dare say, twenty such this morning to different people, all equally flattering to each. So much the better for her and those who believe all she wishes them, or they wish to believe. She has been pleased to be pleased with my slight eulogy in the note annexed to the "Bride". This is to be accounted for in several ways:—firstly, all women like all, or any, praise; secondly, this was unexpected, because I have never courted her; and thirdly, as Scrub says,[1] those who have been all their lives regularly praised, by regular critics, like a little variety, and are glad when any one goes out of his way to say a civil thing; and fourthly, she is a very good-natured creature, which is the best reason, after all, and, perhaps, the only one.

A knock—knocks single and double. Bland called.—He says Dutch society (he has been in Holland) is second-hand French; but the women are like women every where else. This is a bore: I should like to see them a little *un*like; but that can't be expected.

[1] Scrub in *The Beaux' Stratagem* (Act IV, Scene 2) speaks in a similar series, though the subject is not the same, except for the statement "there's a woman in't."

235

Went out—came home—this, that, and the other—and "all is vanity, saith the preacher," and so say I, as part of his congregation. Talking of vanity—whose praise do I prefer? Why, Mrs. Inchbald's,[2] and that of the Americans. The first, because her "Simple Story" and "Nature and Art" are, to me, *true* to their *titles*; and consequently, her short note to Rogers about the "Giaour" delighted me more than any thing, except the Edinburgh Review. I like the Americans, because *I* happened to be in *Asia*, while the English Bards and Scotch Reviewers were redde in *America*. If I could have had a speech against the *Slave Trade, in Africa*, and an Epitaph on a Dog, in *Europe*, (i.e. in the Morning Post), my *vertex sublimis*[3] would certainly have displaced stars enough to overthrow the Newtonian system.

Friday, December 10th, 1813.

I am *ennuyé* beyond my usual tense of that yawning verb, which I am always conjugating; and I don't find that society much mends the matter. I am too lazy to shoot myself—and it would annoy Augusta, and perhaps * *; but it would be a good thing for George, on the other side, and no bad one for me; but I won't be tempted.

I have had the kindest letter from M[oor]e. I *do* think that man is the best-hearted, the only *hearted* being I ever encountered; and then, his talents are equal to his feelings.

Dined on Wednesday at Lord H.'s—the Staffords, Staëls, Cowpers, Ossulstones, Melbournes, Mackintoshes, &c., &c.—and was introduced to the Marquis and Marchioness of Stafford,—an unexpected event. My quarrel with Lord Carlisle (their or his brother-in-law) having rendered it improper, I suppose, brought it about.[1] But, if it was to happen at all, I wonder it did not occur before. She is handsome, and must have been beautiful—and her manners are *princessly*. * * * * * *

The Staël was at the other end of the table, and less loquacious than heretofore. We are now very good friends; though she asked Lady Melbourne whether I had really any *bonhommie*. She might as well

<hr>

[2] Mrs. Elizabeth Inchbald, née Simpson (1753–1821), was an actress, dramatist, and novelist. She had married Joseph Inchbald, an actor, and appeared on the stage with him, but retired after his death and devoted herself to writing. She was extremely popular in society because of her attractiveness, her wit, and her facility in telling stories. She wrote a number of comedies and farces and two popular novels, *A Simple Story* (1791) and *Nature and Art* (1796).

[3] Horace, *Odes*, I, i, 36. The reference is to the lines:
But if by thee place 'mid the bards I'm given,/With soaring head I'll strike the stars of heaven.

[1] George Granville Leveson-Gower (1758–1833) became the 2nd Marquis of Stafford in 1803. He had married in 1785 Elizabeth, Countess of Sutherland. Lord Carlisle married in 1770 Margaret Caroline, sister of the 2nd Marquis of Stafford.

have asked that question before she told C. L. "c'est un démon." True enough, but rather premature, for *she* could not have found it out, and so—she wants me to dine there next Sunday.

Murray prospers, as far as circulation. For my part, I adhere (in liking) to my Fragment. It is no wonder that I wrote one—my mind is a fragment.

Saw Lord Gower,[2] Tierney,[3] &c., in the square. Took leave of Lord G[owe]r, who is going to Holland and Germany. He tells me, that he carries with him a parcel of "Harolds" and "Giaours," &c., for the readers of Berlin, who, it seems, read English, and have taken a caprice for mine. Um!—have I been *German* all this time, when I thought myself *oriental?* * * * * *

Lent Tierney my box for to-morrow; and received a new Comedy sent by Lady C. A.[1]—but *not hers*. I must read it, and endeavour not to displease the author. I hate annoying them with cavil; but a comedy I take to be the most difficult of compositions, more so than tragedy.

G[al]t says there is a coincidence between the first part of "the Bride" and some story of his[2]—whether published or not, I know not, never having seen it. He is almost the last person on whom any one would commit literary larceny, and I am not conscious of any *witting* thefts on any of the genus. As to originality, all pretensions are ludicrous,— "there is nothing new under the sun".

Went last night to the play. * * * * Invited out to a party, but did not go;—right. Refused to go to Lady * *'s on Monday;—right again. If I must fritter away my life, I would rather do it alone. I was much tempted;—C * * looked so Turkish with her red turban, and her regular dark and clear features. Not that *she* and *I* ever were, or could be, any thing; but I love any aspect that reminds me of the "children of the sun".

To dine to-day with Rogers and Sharpe, for which I have some appetite, not having tasted food for the preceding forty-eight hours. I wish I could leave off eating altogether.

Saturday, December 11.

---

[2] Lord Granville Leveson-Gower (1773–1846) was a younger brother of the 2nd Marquis of Stafford.

[3] George Tierney (1761–1830) was a statesman who held posts in the administration of Addington and in that of "All the Talents". He had fought a duel with Pitt in 1798. In 1817 he became a leader in the Opposition and drafted a petition of the "Society of Friends of the People".

[1] Possibly Lady Catherine Annesley, Lady Frances Webster's sister.

[2] See Dec. 10, 1813, to Galt, note 1.

Sunday, December 12.

By G[al]t's answer, I find it is some story in *real life*, and not any work with which my late composition coincides.[3] It is still more singular, for mine is drawn from *existence* also.

I have sent an excuse to Madame de Staël. I do not feel sociable enough for dinner to-day;—and I will not go to Sheridan's on Wednesday. Not that I do not admire and prefer his unequalled conversation; but—that *"but"* must only be intelligible to thoughts I cannot write. Sheridan was in good talk at Rogers's the other night, but I only staid till *nine*. All the world are to be at the Staël's to-night, and I am not sorry to escape any part of it. I only go out to get me a fresh appetite for being alone. Went out—did not go to the Staël's but to Ld. Holland's. Party numerous—conversation general. Staid late—made a blunder—got over it—came home and went to bed, not having eaten. Rather empty, but *fresco*, which is the great point with me.

Monday, December 13, 1813.

Called at three places—read, and got ready to leave town to-morrow. Murray has had a letter from his brother Bibliopole of Edinburgh,[1] who says "he is lucky in having such a *poet"*—something as if one was a pack-horse, or "ass, or any thing that is his;" or, like Mrs. Packwood,[2] who replied to some inquiry after the Odes on Razors,—"Laws, sir, we keeps a Poet." The same illustrious Edinburgh bookseller once sent an order for books, poesy, and cookery, with this agreeable postscript—".The *Harold* and *Cookery*[3] are much wanted." Such is fame, and, after all, quite as good as any other "life in others' breath." 'Tis much the same to divide purchasers with Hannah Glasse[4] or Hannah More.

Some editor of some Magazine has *announced* to Murray his intention of abusing the thing *"without reading it."* So much the better; if he redde it first, he would abuse it more.

---

[3] See Dec. 11, 1813, to Galt.

[1] William Blackwood was the bookseller who distributed Murray's books in Scotland at this time.

[2] Mrs. Packwood was the wife of George Packwood, a razor strop maker who published *Packwood's Whim: The Goldfinch's Nest, or the Way to get Money and be Happy* (1796; 2nd edition 1807), a collection of his advertisements in prose and verse. Apparently a Soho poet wrote the verses for him.

[3] One of Murray's most successful books was Mrs. Rundell's *Domestic Cookery*.

[4] A popular eighteenth-century cookbook, *The Art of Cookery Made Plain and Easy*, was published under the name of H. Glasse.

Allen (Lord Holland's Allen[5]—the best informed and one of the ablest men I know—a perfect Magliabecchi[6]—a devourer, a Helluo of books, and an observer of men,) has lent me a quantity of Burns's unpublished, and never-to-be-published, Letters. They are full of oaths and obscene songs. What an antithetical mind!—tenderness, roughness—delicacy, coarseness—sentiment, sensuality—soaring and grovelling, dirt and deity—all mixed up in that one compound of inspired clay!

It seems strange; a true voluptuary will never abandon his mind to the grossness of reality. It is by exalting the earthly, the material, the *physique* of our pleasures, by veiling these ideas, by forgetting them altogether, or, at least, never naming them hardly to one's self, that we alone can prevent them from disgusting.

* * * * * * * * * * * * * * *

December 14, 15, 16.

Much done, but nothing to record. It is quite enough to set down my thoughts,—my actions will rarely bear retrospection.

December 17, 18.

Lord Holland told me a curious piece of sentimentality in Sheridan. The other night we were all delivering our respective and various opinions on him and other *hommes marquans*, and mine was this. "Whatever Sheridan has done or chosen to do has been, *par excellence*, always the *best* of its kind. He has written the *best* comedy (School for Scandal) the *best* drama (in my mind, far before that St. Giles's lampoon, the Beggar's Opera), the best farce (the *Critic*—it is only too good for a farce), and the best Address (Monologue on Garrick), and, to crown all, delivered the very best Oration (the famous Begum Speech) ever conceived or heard in this country." Somebody told S. this the next day, and on hearing it he burst into tears!

Poor Brinsley! if they were tears of pleasure, I would rather have said these few, but most sincere, words than have written the Iliad or made his own celebrated Philippic. Nay, his own comedy never gratified me more than to hear that he had derived a moment's gratification from any praise of mine, humble as it must appear to "my elders and my betters".

---

[5] John Allen, M.D. (1771–1843) accompanied Lord Holland to Spain and later lived at Holland House, where he contributed to the brilliance of the Holland House circle. He wrote numerous articles for the *Edinburgh Review* and the one on Fox in the *Encyclopaedia Britannica*.

[6] Antonio Magliabecchi (1633–1714), Librarian to the Grand Duke of Tuscany, to whom he bequeathed his collection of 30,000 volumes. He had a reputation for learning and was said to be able to direct an enquirer to any book in the world.

239

Went to my box at Covent-garden to-night; and my delicacy felt a little shocked at seeing S * * *'s mistress (who, to my certain knowledge, was actually educated, from her birth, for her profession) sitting with her mother, "a three-piled b — — d, b — — d-Major to the army," in a private box opposite. I felt rather indignant; but, casting my eyes round the house, in the next box to me, and the next, and the next, were the most distinguished old and young Babylonians of quality;— so I burst out a laughing. It was really odd; Lady * * *divorced*—Lady * * and her daughter, Lady * *, both *divorceable*—Mrs. * *, in the next, the *like*, and still nearer * * * * * *! What an assemblage to *me*, who know all their histories. It was as if the house had been divided between your public and your *understood* courteseans;—but the Intriguantes much outnumbered the regular mercenaries. On the other side were only Pauline and *her* mother, and, next box to her, three of inferior note. Now, where lay the difference between *her* and *mamma*, and Lady * *[1] and daughter? except that the two last may enter Carleton and any *other house*, and the two first are limited to the opera and b — — -house. How I do delight in observing life as it really is!— and myself, after all, the worst of any. But no matter—I must avoid egotism, which, just now, would be no vanity.

I have lately written a wild, rambling, unfinished rhapsody, called "The Devil's Drive," the notion of which I took from Porson's "Devil's Walk."[2]

Redde some Italian, and wrote two Sonnets on * * *.[3] I never wrote but one sonnet before, and that was not in earnest, and many years ago, as an exercise—and I will never write another. They are the most puling, petrifying, stupidly platonic compositions. I detest the Petrarch so much, that I would not be the man even to have obtained his Laura, which the metaphysical, whining dotard never could.

* * * * * * * * * * * * * * *

January 16, 1814.

Tomorrow I leave town for a few days. I saw Lewis to-day, who is just returned from Oatlands,[1] where he has been squabbling with

---

[1] Moore's note says these names indicated by asterisks were left blank in the original manuscript of the journal.

[2] Coleridge and Southey were the joint authors of a poem called "The Devil's Thoughts", published in the *Morning Post*, Sept. 6, 1799. It was printed separately as *The Devil's Walk*, a Poem, By Professor Porson, London, Marsh and Miller, 1830. But Byron must have heard of its ascription to Porson much earlier. Southey later expanded it to 57 stanzas and published it as *The Devil's Walk*.

[3] These were the sonnets "To Genevra" [Lady Frances Webster].

[1] The estate, near Weybridge, Surrey, bought by the Duke of York in 1794.

Mad. de Staël about himself, Clarissa Harlowe, Mackintosh, and me. My homage has never been paid in that quarter, or we would have agreed still worse. I don't talk—I can't flatter, and won't listen, except to a pretty or a foolish woman. She bored Lewis with praises of himself till he sickened—found out that Clarissa was perfection, and Mackintosh the first man in England. There I agree, at least *one* of the first—but Lewis did not. As to Clarissa, I leave to those who can read it to judge and dispute. I could not do the one, and am, consequently, not qualified for the other. She told Lewis wisely, he being my friend, that I was affected, in the first place, and that, in the next place, I committed the heinous offence of sitting at dinner with my *eyes* shut, or half shut. * * * * I wonder if I really have this trick. I must cure myself of it, if true. One insensibly acquires awkward habits, which should be broken in time. If this is one, I wish I had been told of it before. It would not so much signify if one was always to be checkmated by a plain woman, but one may as well see some of one's neighbours, as well as the plate upon the table.

I should like, of all things, to have heard the Amabæan eclogue between her and Lewis—both obstinate, clever, odd, garrulous, and shrill. In fact, one could have heard nothing else. But they fell out, alas!—and now they will never quarrel again. Could not one reconcile them for the "nonce?" Poor Corinne—she will find that some of her fine sayings won't suit our fine ladies and gentleman.

I am getting rather into admiration of [Lady Juliana Annesley?] the youngest sister of [Lady F. Webster]. A wife would be my salvation. I am sure the wives of my acquaintances have hitherto done me little good. [Juliana?] is beautiful, but very young, and, I think, a fool. But I have not seen enough to judge; besides, I hate an *esprit* in petticoats. That she won't love me is very probable, nor shall I love her. But, on my system, and the modern system in general, that don't signify. The business (if it came to business) would probably be arranged between papa and me. She would have her own way; I am good-humoured to women, and docile; and, if I did not fall in love with her, which I should try to prevent, we should be a very comfortable couple. As to conduct, *that* she must look to. * * * * * * * But *if* I love, I shall be jealous;—and for that reason I will not be in love. Though, after all, I doubt my temper, and fear I should not be so patient as becomes the *bienséance* of a married man in my station. * * * * * Divorce ruins the poor *femme*, and damages are a paltry compensation. I do fear my temper would lead me into some oriental tricks of vengeance, or, at any rate, into a summary appeal to the court of twelve paces. So "I'll none on't," but e'en remain single and solitary;—though I should like to have somebody now and then to yawn with one.

W[ard], and, after him, * *, has stolen one of my buffooneries about Mde. de Staël's Metaphysics and the Fog, and passed it, by speech and letter, as their own. As Gibbet says, "they are the most of a gentleman of any on the road."[1] W. is in sad enmity with the Whigs about this Review of Fox (if he *did* review him);[2]—all the epigrammatists and essayists are at him. I hate *odds*, and wish he may beat them. As for me, by the blessing of indifference, I have simplified my politics into an utter detestation of all existing governments; and, as it is the shortest and most agreeable and summary feeling imaginable, the first moment of an universal republic would convert me into an advocate for single and uncontradicted despotism. The fact is, riches are power, and poverty is slavery all over the earth, and one sort of establishment is no better, nor worse, for a *people* than another. I shall adhere to my party, because it would not be honourable to act otherwise; but, as to *opinions*, I don't think politics *worth* an *opinion*. *Conduct* is another thing:—if you begin with a party, go one with them. I have no consistency, except in politics; and *that* probably arises from my indifference on the subject altogether.

Feb. 18.

Better than a month since I last journalised:—most of it out of London, and at Notts., but a busy one and a pleasant, at least three weeks of it. On my return, I find all the newspapers in hysterics, and town in an uproar, on the avowal and republication of two stanzas on Princess Charlotte's weeping at Regency's speech to Lauderdale in 1812.[1] They are daily at it still;—some of the abuse good, all of it hearty. They talk of a motion in our House upon it— be it so.

Got up—redde the Morning Post containing the battle of Buonaparte, the destruction of the Custom-house, and a paragraph on me as long as my pedigree, and vituperative, as usual. * * * * *

---

[1] Farquhar, *The Beaux' Stratagem*, Act IV, Scene 3.
[2] Ward was the author of the article on *The Correspondence of Gilbert Wakefield with Mr. Fox*, in the *Quarterly Review* for July, 1813. Like most numbers of the *Quarterly* it was late in appearing. In it Ward voiced some criticisms of Fox that irritated his admirers.
[1] Byron's "Sympathetic *Address* to a Young Lady" had appeared anonymously in the *Morning Chronicle* for March 7, 1812, and when he reprinted it at the end of *The Corsair* in January, 1814, the authorship was revealed and he was attacked by the Tory press.

Hobhouse is returned to England.[2] He is my best friend, the most lively, and a man of the most sterling talents extant. "The Corsair" has been conceived, written, published, &c., since I last took up this Journal. They tell me it has great success;—it was written *con amore*, and much from *existence*. Murray is satisfied with its progress; and if the public are equally so with the perusal, there's an end of the matter.

Nine o'clock.

Been to Hanson's on business. Saw Rogers, and had a note from Lady Melbourne, who says, it is said I am "much out of spirits." I wonder if I really am or not? I have certainly enough of "that perilous stuff which weighs upon the heart,"[3] and it is better they should believe it to be result of these attacks than of the real cause; but—ay, ay, always *but*, to the end of the chapter. * * * * * *

Hobhouse has told me ten thousand anecdotes of Napoleon, all good and true. My friend H. is the most entertaining of companions, and a fine fellow to boot.

Redde a little—wrote notes and letters, and am alone, which, Locke says, is bad company. "Be not solitary, be not idle."[1]—Um!— the idleness is troublesome; but I can't see so much to regret in the solitude. The more I see of men, the less I like them. If I could but say so of women too, all would be well. Why can't I? I am now six-and-twenty; my passions have had enough to cool them; my affections more than enough to wither them,—and yet—and yet—always *yet* and *but*—"Excellent well, you are a fishmonger—get thee to a nunnery."—"They fool me to the top of my bent."[2]

Midnight.

Began a letter, which I threw into the fire. Redde—but to little purpose. Did not visit Hobhouse, as I promised and ought. No matter, the loss is mine. Smoked cigars.

Napoleon!—this week will decide his fate. All seems against him; but I believe and hope he will win—at least, beat back the Invaders. What right have we to prescribe sovereigns to France? Oh for a Republic! "Brutus, thou sleepest."[3] Hobhouse abounds in continental anecdotes of this extraordinary man; all in favour of his intellect and

[2] Hobhouse returned from his Continental tour on Feb. 8.
[3] *Macbeth*, Act V, Scene 3.
[1] These words come at the end of the penultimate paragraph of Burton's *Anatomy of Melancholy*.
[2] *Hamlet*, Act II, Scene 2; Act III, Scenes 1 and 2.
[3] *Julius Caesar*, Act II, Scene 1.

courage, but against his *bonhommie*. No wonder;—how should he, who knows mankind well, do other than despise and abhor them? The greater the equality, the more impartially evil is distributed, and becomes lighter by the division among so many—therefore, a Republic!

More notes from Madame de [Staël] unanswered—and so they shall remain. I admire her abilities, but really her society is overwhelming— an avalanche that buries one in glittering nonsense—all snow and sophistry.

Shall I go to Mackintosh's on Tuesday? um!—I did not go to Marquis Lansdowne's, nor to Miss Berry's, though both are pleasant. So is Sir James's,—but I don't know—I believe one is not the better for parties; at least, unless some *regnante* is there.

I wonder how the deuce any body could make such a world; for what purpose dandies, for instance, were ordained—and kings—and fellows of colleges—and women of "a certain age"—and many men of any age—and myself, most of all!

> "Divesne prisco et natus ab Inacho
> Nil interest, an pauper et infimâ
> De gente, sub dio [sic] moreris,
> Victima nil miserantis Orci.
>
> * * * * * * * * * * * * * *
>
> Omnes eodem cogimur,"[1]

Is there any thing beyond?—*who* knows? *He* that can't tell. Who tells that there *is*? He who don't know. And when shall he know? perhaps, when he don't expect, and, generally when he don't wish it. In this last respect, however, all are not alike: it depends a good deal upon education,—something upon nerves and habits—but most upon digestion.

Saturday, Feb. 19th.

Just returned from seeing Kean in Richard. By Jove, he is a soul! Life—nature—truth—without exaggeration or diminution. Kemble's Hamlet is perfect;—but Hamlet is not Nature. Richard is a man; and Kean is Richard. Now to my own concerns.

* * * * * * * * * * * * * *

---

[1] Horace, *Odes*, II, iii, 21 ff.:
> Whether from ancient blood, to wealth and fame
> Thou'rt born, or whether poor and base of birth
> Thou lingerest stretched on pauper earth,
> Grim Death strikes just the same.
> To the same bourne we're driven. . . .

Went to Waite's. Teeth are all right and white; but he says that I grind them in my sleep and chip the edges. That same sleep is no friend of mine, though I court him sometimes for half the 24.

February 20th.

Got up and tore out two leaves of this Journal—I don't know why. Hodgson just called and gone. He has much *bonhommie* with his other good qualities, and more talent than he has yet had credit for beyond his circle.

An invitation to dine at Holland-house to meet Kean. He is worth meeting; and I hope by getting into good society, he will be prevented from falling like Cooke. He is greater now on the stage, and off he should never be less. There is a stupid and under-rating criticism upon him in one of the newspapers. I thought that, last night, though great, he rather under-acted more than the first time. This may be the effect of these cavils; but I hope he has more sense than to mind them. He cannot expect to maintain his present eminence, or to advance still higher, without the envy of his green-room fellows, and the nibbling of their admirers. But, if he don't beat them all, why, then—merit hath no purchase in "these coster-monger days."[1]

I wish that I had a talent for the drama; I would write a tragedy *now.* But no,—it is gone. Hodgson talks of one,—he will do it well;—and I think M[oor]e should try. He has wonderful powers, and much variety; besides, he has lived and felt. To write so as to bring home to the heart, the heart must have been tried,—but, perhaps, ceased to be so. While you are under the influence of passions, you only feel, but cannot describe them,—any more than, when in action, you could turn round and tell the story to your next neighbour! When all is over, —all, all, and irrevocable,—trust to memory—she is then but too faithful.

Went out, and answered some letters, yawned now and then, and redde the Robbers. Fine,—but Fiesco[2] is better; and Alfieri, and Monti's Aristodemo *best.*[3] They are more equal than the Tedeschi dramatists.

Answered—or, rather, acknowledged—the receipt of young Reynolds's Poem, Safie.[4] The lad is clever, but much of his thoughts

---

[1] *Henry IV*, Part II, Act I, Scene 2.
[2] Schiller's *Fiesco* was published in 1783, the year after his *Robbers* was produced.
[3] Vincenzo Monti, in Byron's view, rivalled Alfieri in tragedy. Byron met Monti in Milan in October, 1816.
[4] See Feb. 20, 1814, to Reynolds, note 1.

are borrowed,—*whence*, the Reviewers may find out. I hate discouraging a young one; and I think,—though wild, and more oriental than he would be, had he seen the scenes where he has placed his tale,—that he has much talent, and, certainly, fire enough.

Received a very singular epistle; and the mode of its conveyance, through Lord H.'s hands, as curious as the letter itself. But it was gratifying and pretty.

Sunday, February 27th.

Here I am, alone, instead of dining at Lord H.'s, where I was asked,—but not inclined to go any where. Hobhouse says I am growing a *loup garou*,—a solitary hobgoblin. True;—"I am myself alone."[1] The last week has passed in reading—seeing plays—now and then, visitors—sometimes yawning and sometimes sighing, but no writing,—save of letters. If I could always read, I should never feel the want of society. Do I regret it?—um!—"Man delights not me,"[2] and only one woman—at a time.

There is something to me very softening in the presence of a woman,—some strange influence, even if one is not in love with them,—which I cannot at all account for, having no very high opinion of the sex. But yet,—I always feel in better humour with myself and every thing else, if there is a woman within ken. Even Mrs. Mule, my firelighter,—the most ancient and withered of her kind,—and (except to myself) not the best-tempered—always makes me laugh,—no difficult task when I am "i' the vein."

Heigho! I would I were in mine island!—I am not well; and yet I look in good health. At times, I fear, "I am not in my perfect mind;"[3] —and yet my heart and head have stood many a crash, and what should ail them now? They prey upon themselves, and I am sick—sick—"prithee, undo this button—why should a cat, a rat, a dog have life—and *thou* no life at all?"[4] Six-and-twenty years, as they call them,—why, I might and should have been a Pasha by this time. "I 'gin to be a-weary of the sun."[5]

Buonaparte is not yet beaten; but has rebutted Blucher, and repiqued S[ch]wartzenburg. This it is to have a head. If he again wins, "vae victis!"

---

[1] *Henry VI*, Part III, Act V, Scene 6.
[2] *Hanlet*, Act II, Scene 2.
[3] *King Lear*, Act IV, Scene 7.
[4] *King Lear*, Act V, Scene 3.
[5] *Macbeth*, Act V, Scene 5.

On Tuesday last dined with Rogers,—Mad[am]e de Staël, Mackintosh, Sheridan, Erskine,[1] and Payne Knight,[2] Lady Donegall,[3] and Miss R. there. Sheridan told a very good story of himself and M[adam]e de Recamier's handkerchief; Erskine a few stories of himself only. *She* is going to write a big book about England, she says;—I believe her. Asked by her how I liked Miss [Edgeworth]'s thing called [*Patronage*], and answered (very sincerely) that I thought it very bad for *her*, and worse than any of the others. Afterwards thought it possible Lady Donegall, being Irish, might be a patroness of [Miss Edgeworth,] and was rather sorry for my opinion, as I hate putting people into fusses, either with themselves, or their favourites; it looks as if one did it on purpose. The party went off very well, and the fish was very much to my gusto. But we got up too soon after the women; and Mrs. Corinne always lingers so long after dinner that we wish her in—the drawing-room.

Today C[ampbell] called, and, while sitting here, in came Merivale. During our colloquy, C. (ignorant that M[erivale] was the writer) abused the "mawkishness of the Quarterly Review of Grimm's Correspondence."[4] I (knowing the secret) changed the conversation as soon as I could; and C. went away, quite convinced of having made the most favourable impression on his new acquaintance. Merivale is luckily a very good-natured fellow, or, God he knows what might have been engendered from such a malaprop. I did not look at him while this was going on, but I felt like a coal—for I like Merivale, as well as the article in question. * * * * * *

Asked to Lady Keith's[5] to-morrow evening—I think I will go; but it is the first party invitation I have accepted this "season," as the learned Fletcher called it, when that youngest brat of Lady * *[Oxford]'s cut my eye and cheek open with a misdirected pebble—

[1] Thomas, Lord Erskine (1750–1823), a Whig with sympathy for the doctrines of the French Revolution, defended Tom Paine and other radicals. He was an intimate friend of Sheridan and Fox. He was appointed Lord Chancellor in 1806, but his staunch defense of constitutional liberty made office under the Tories untenable and he retired to private life. He was a good conversationalist but, as Byron intimates, a notorious egoist.

[2] Richard Payne Knight (1750–1824), numismatist and antiquary, wrote on ancient art and later bequeathed to the British Museum his collection of bronzes and other objects.

[3] Anna, daughter of Sir Edward May, married in 1795 the Marquis of Donegal.

[4] The review of Grimm's *Correspondance Littéraire, Philosophique, et Critique* appeared in the *Quarterly Review* of March, 1813, pp. 89–117.

[5] Hester Maria, eldest daughter of Henry Thrale, the friend of Dr. Johnson, married in 1808 Viscount Keith.

"Never mind, my Lord, the scar will be gone before the *season*"; as if one's eye was of no importance in the mean time.

Lord Erskine called, and gave me his famous pamphlet,[1] with a marginal note and corrections in his handwriting. Sent it to be bound superbly, and shall treasure it.

Sent my fine print of Napoleon to be framed.[2] It *is* framed; and the Emperor becomes his robes as if he had been hatched in them.

March 7th.

Rose at seven—ready by half-past eight—went to Mr. Hanson's, Berkeley Square [Bloomsbury Square][3]—went to church with his eldest daughter, Mary Anne (a good girl), and gave her away to the Earl of Portsmouth.[4] Saw her fairly a countess—congratulated the family and groom (bride)—drank a bumper of wine (wholesome sherris) to their felicity, and all that—and came home. Asked to stay to dinner, but could not. At three sat to Phillips for faces. Called on Lady M. [Melbourne]—I like her so well, that I always stay too long. (Mem. to mend of that.)

Passed the evening with Hobhouse, who has begun a Poem, which promises highly;—wish he would go on with it. Heard some curious extracts from a life of Morosini, the blundering Venetian, who blew up the Acropolis at Athens with a bomb, and be d[amne]d to him! Waxed sleepy—just come home—must go to bed, and am engaged to meet Sheridan to-morrow at Rogers's.

Queer ceremony that same of marriage—saw many abroad, Greek and Catholic—one, at *home*, many years ago. There be some strange phrases in the prologue (the exhortation) which made me turn away, not to laugh in the face of the surpliceman. Made one blunder, when I joined the hands of the happy—rammed their left hands, by mistake into one another. Corrected it—bustled back to the altar-rail, and said "Amen." Portsmouth responded as if he had got the whole by heart; and, if any thing, was rather before the priest. It is now midnight and * * * * * * * * * * * * *

March 10th, Thor's Day.

On Tuesday dined with Rogers,—Mackintosh, Sheridan, Sharpe,—much talk, and good,—all, except my own little prattlement. Much

[1] Erskine's "famous pamphlet" was "On the Causes and Consequences of the War with France" (1797).

[2] This print was described in the Evans sale catalogue, April 5, 1816: "Portrait of Bonaparte, engraved by Morghen, *very fine impression, in a gilt frame.*"

[3] Moore has printed "Berkeley Square", but in Byron's deposition on the Portsmouth marriage he wrote "Bloomsbury Square."

[4] See Byron's deposition on the Portsmouth marriage, [Dec.? 1814].

of old times—Horne Tooke—the Trials—evidence of Sheridan, and anecdotes of those times when *I*, alas! was an infant. If I had been a man, I would have made an English Lord Edward Fitzgerald.[1]

Set down Sheridan at Brookes's,—where, by the by, he could not have well set down himself, as he and I were the only drinkers. Sherry means to stand for Westminster, as Cochrane[2] (the stock-jobbing hoaxer) must vacate. Brougham[3] is a candidate. I fear for poor dear Sherry. Both have talents of the highest order, but the youngster has *yet* a character. We shall see, if he lives to Sherry's age, how he will pass over the redhot ploughshares of public life, I don't know why, but I hate to see the *old* ones lose; particularly Sheridan, notwithstanding all his *méchanceté*.

Received many, and the kindest, thanks from Lady Portsmouth, *père* and *mère*, for my match-making. I don't regret it, as she looks the countess well, and is a very good girl. It is odd how well she carries her new honours. She looks a different woman, and high-bred, too. I had no idea that I could make so good a peeress.

Went to the play with Hobhouse. Mrs. Jordan superlative in Hoyden, and Jones well enough in Foppington.[4] *What plays!* what wit!—helas! Congreve and Vanbrugh are your only comedy. Our society is too insipid now for the like copy. Would *not* go to Lady Keith's. Hobhouse thought it odd. I wonder *he* should like parties. If one is in love, and wants to break a commandment and covet any thing that is there, they do very well. But to go out amongst the

[1] Lord Edward Fitzgerald (1763–1798), son of the 1st Duke of Leinster, was an adventurous Irish rebel. He served in the American war and was wounded, was an M.P. in the Irish parliament, and later travelled in America and was admitted to the Bear tribe of Indians. But he was cashiered for attending a revolutionary banquet in Paris in 1792. He later joined the United Irishmen and with Arthur O'Connor negotiated with the French to aid in their intended invasion of England. He died of wounds received while resisting arrest by the British.

[2] Thomas, Lord Cochrane (1775–1860), admiral, and later 10th Earl of Dundonald, entered the House of Commons and became a strong advocate of Parliamentary Reform and a critic of naval administration. In 1814 he was convicted of conspiracy to profit from stock manipulation following a false report of the death of Napoleon, and he was expelled from the House of Commons, deprived of his naval command, and stripped of the Order of the Bath. The circumstances were suspicious, but many believed he had been "framed" because of his liberal views, and after a year in prison he was elected M.P. for Westminster. He accepted command of the Chilean navy in 1817, and helped in the liberation of Chile and Peru. After Byron's death he was admiral of the Greek navy (1827–28).

[3] Henry Brougham lost his seat in the House of Commons in 1812; in 1815 he was elected to represent Winchelsea.

[4] The play Byron saw was Sheridan's *Trip to Scarborough*, a close adaptation of Vanbrugh's *The Relapse*. Mrs. Jordan, the mistress of the Duke of Clarence, played the part of Miss Hoyden in the performance at Covent Garden, March 10, 1814.

mere herd, without a motive, pleasure, or pursuit—'sdeath! "I'll none of it." He told me an odd report,—that *I* am the actual Conrad, the veritable Corsair, and that part of my travels are supposed to have passed in privacy [piracy?]. Um!—people sometimes hit near the truth; but never the whole truth. H. don't know what I was about the year after he left the Levant; nor does any one—nor—nor—nor—however, it is a lie—but, "I doubt the equivocation of the fiend that lies like truth!"[1]

I shall have letters of importance to-morrow. Which, * *, * *, or * *? heigho!—* * is in my heart, * * in my head, * * in my eye, and the *single* one, Heaven knows where. All write, and will be answered. "Since I have crept in favour with myself, I must maintain it;" but *I* never "mistook my person,"[2] though I think others have.

* * called to-day in great despair about his mistress, who has taken a freak of * * *. He began a letter to her, but was obliged to stop short—I finished it for him, and he copied and sent it. If *he* holds out, and keeps to my instructions of affected indifference, she will lower her colours. If she don't, he will, at least, get rid of her, and she don't seem much worth keeping. But the poor lad is in love—if that is the case, she will win. When they once discover their power, *finita è la musica.*

Sleepy, and must go to bed.

Tuesday, March 15th

Dined yesterday with R[ogers], Mackintosh, and Sharpe. Sheridan could not come. Sharpe told several very amusing anecdotes of Henderson,[3] the actor. Stayed till late, and came home, having drunk so much *tea*, that I did not get to sleep till six this morning. R. says I am to be in *this* Quarterly—cut up, I presume, as they "hate us youth." *N'importe.* As Sharpe was passing by the doors of some Debating Society (the Westminster Forum), in his way to dinner, he saw rubricked on the walls *Scott's* name and *mine*—"Which was the best poet?" being the question of the evening; and I suppose all the Templars and *would-bes* took our rhymes in vain in the course of the controversy. Which had the greater show of hands, I neither know nor care; but I feel the coupling of the names as a compliment,—though I think Scott deserves better company.

* * * * * * * * * * * * * * *

[1] *Macbeth*, Act. V, Scene 5.
[2] *Richard III*, Act I, Scene 2, lines 259 and 253.
[3] John Henderson, known as "the Bath Roscius" was praised by Mrs. Siddons and others for his success in Shakespearean productions.

W[edderburn] W[ebster] called—Lord Erskine, Lord Holland, &c., &c. Wrote to * * The Corsair report. She says she don't wonder, since "Conrad is so *like*." It is odd that one, who knows me so thoroughly, should tell me this to my face. However, if she don't know, nobody can.

Mackintosh is, it seems, the writer of the defensive letter in the Morning Chronicle. If so, it is very kind, and more than I did for myself.

* * * * * * * * * * * * * * *

Told Murray to secure for me Bandello's Italian Novels[1] at the sale to-morrow. To me they will be *nuts*. Redde a satire on myself, called "Anti-Byron," and told Murray to publish it if he liked.[2] The object of the author is to prove me an Atheist and a systematic conspirator against law and government. Some of the verse is good; the prose I don't quite understand. He asserts that my "deleterious works" have had "an effect upon civil society, which requires, &c., &c., &c." and his own poetry. It is a lengthy poem, and a long preface, with a harmonious title-page. Like the fly in the fable, I seem to have got upon a wheel which makes much dust; but, unlike the said fly, I do not take it all for my own raising.

A letter from *Bella*,[3] which I answered. I shall be in love with her again, if I don't take care.

* * * * * * * * * * * * * * *

I shall begin a more regular system of reading soon.

Thursday, March 17th.

I have been sparring with Jackson for exercise this morning; and mean to continue and renew my acquaintance with the muffles. My chest, and arms, and wind are in very good plight, and I am not in flesh. I used to be a hard hitter, and my arms are very long for my height (5 feet 8½ inches.) At any rate, exercise is good and this the severest of all; fencing and the broadsword never fatigued me half so much.

Redde the "Quarrels of Authors" (another sort of *sparring*)—a new work, by that most entertaining and researching writer, Israeli.[1] They seem to be an irritable set, and I wish myself well out of it.

[1] Matteo Bandello (1480–1562) became Bishop of Agen in 1550. He wrote 214 tales in the manner of Boccaccio (published 1554–1573). Byron's set of Bandello's *Novelle* was that published in 9 volumes in Leghorn in 1791.
[2] See March 12, 1814, to Murray.
[3] Anne Isabella Milbanke (Annabella).
[1] Isaac D'Israeli's *Quarrels of Authors* appeared in 3 volumes in 1814.

"I'll not march through Coventry with them, that's flat."[2] What the devil had I to do with scribbling? It is too late to inquire, and all regret is useless. But, an' it were to do again,—I should write again, I suppose. Such is human nature, at least my share of it;—though I shall think better of myself, if I have sense to stop now. If I have a wife, and that wife has a son—by any body—I will bring up mine heir in the most anti-poetical way—make him a lawyer, or a pirate, or—any thing. But if he writes too, I shall be sure he is none of mine, and cut him off with a Bank token. Must write a letter—three o'clock.

> *Sunday, March 20th.*

I intended to go to Lady Hardwicke's,[3] but won't. I always begin the day with a bias towards going to parties; but, as the evening advances, my stimulus fails, and I hardly ever go out—and, when I do, always regret it. This might have been a pleasant one;—at least, the hostess is a very superior woman. Lady Lansdowne's to-morrow —Lady Heathcote's, Wednesday. Um!—I must spur myself into going to some of them, or it will look like rudeness, and it is better to do as other people do—confound them!

Redde Machiavel, parts of Chardin, and Sismondi,[4] and Bandello— by starts. Redde the Edinburgh, 44, just come out. In the beginning of the article on "Edgeworth's Patronage," I have gotten a high compliment, I perceive.[5] Whether this is creditable to me, I know not; but it does honour to the editor, because he once abused me. Many a man will retract praise; none but a high-spirited mind will revoke its censure, or *can* praise the man it has once attacked. I have often, since my return to England, heard Jeffrey most highly commended by those who know him for things independent of his talents. I admire him for *this*—not because he has *praised me* (I have been so praised elsewhere and abused, alternately, that mere habit has rendered me as indifferent to both as a man at twenty-six can be to any thing), but because he is, perhaps, the *only man* who, under the relations in which he and I stand, or stood, with regard to each other,

---

[2] *Henry IV*, Part I, Act IV, Scene 2.

[3] Elizabeth, daughter of the 5th Earl of Balcarres, married in 1782 Philip Yorke, 3rd Earl of Hardwicke.

[4] Machiavelli, *Opere*, 13 vols., Milan (1804); Chardin's *Voyages en Perse*, 10 vols. (1811); and Sismondi's *De la Littérature du Midi*, 4 vols., Paris (1813) were among Byron's books sold at auction on April 5, 1816.

[5] The sentence to which Byron refers in the *Edinburgh* review of *Patronage* was: "Our alleged severity upon a youthful production has not prevented the noble author from becoming the first poet of his time." (*Edinburgh Review*, Vol. XXII, page 416.)

would have had the liberality to act thus; none but a great soul dared hazard it. The height on which he stands has not made him giddy;—a little scribbler would have gone on cavilling to the end of the chapter. As to the justice of his panegyric, that is a matter of taste. There are plenty to question it, and glad, too, of the opportunity. Lord Erskine called to-day. He means to carry down his reflections on the war—or rather wars—to the present day. I trust that he will. Must send to Mr. Murray to get the binding of my copy of his pamphlet finished, as Lord E. has promised me to correct it, and add some marginal notes to it. Any thing in his handwriting will be a treasure, which will gather compound interest from years. Erskine has high expectations of Mackintosh's promised History.[1] Undoubtedly it must be a classic, when finished.

Sparred with Jackson again yesterday morning, and shall to-morrow. I feel all the better for it, in spirits, though my arms and shoulders are very stiff from it. Mem. to attend the pugilistic dinner—Marquis [Marquess of] Huntley is in the chair.

* * * * * * * * * * * * * *

Lord Erskine thinks that ministers must be in peril of going out. So much the better for him. To me it is the same who are in or out;—we want something more than a change of ministers, and some day we will have it.

I remember, in riding from Chrisso to Castri (Delphos), along the sides of Parnassus, I saw six eagles in the air. It is uncommon to see so many together; and it was the number—not the species, which is common enough—that excited my attention.

The last bird I ever fired at was an *eaglet*, on the shore of the Gulf of Lepanto, near Vostitza. It was only wounded, and I tried to save it, the eye was so bright; but it pined, and died in a few days; and I never did since, and never will, attempt the death of another bird. I wonder what put these two things into my head just now? I have been reading Sismondi, and there is nothing there that could induce the recollection.

I am mightily taken with Braccio di Montone, Giovanni Galeazzo, and Eccelino.[1] But the last is *not* Bracciaferro (of the same name), Count of Ravenna, whose history I want to trace. There is a fine engraving in Lavater, from a picture by Fuseli, of *that* Ezzelin, over

[1] Sir James Mackintosh did not publish his *History of the Revolution in England in 1688* until 1834. His *History of England* for Lardner's *Cabinet Cyclopaedia* appeared in 1830.
[1] See Aug. 25, 1814, to Annabella Milbanke, note 2.

the body of Meduna, punished by him for a *hitch* in her constancy
during his absence in the Crusades. He was right—but I want to
know the story.

****

Tuesday, March 22d.

Last night, *party* at Lansdowne-house. To-night, *party* at Lady
Charlotte Greville's[2]—deplorable waste of time, and something of
temper. Nothing imparted—nothing acquired—talking without ideas
—if any thing like *thought* in my mind, it was not on the subjects on
which we were gabbling. Heigho!—and in this way half London pass
what is called life. To-morrow there is Lady Heathcote's—shall I go?
yes—to punish myself for not having a pursuit.

Let me see—what did I see? The only person who much struck me
was Lady S * * d's [Stafford's] eldest daughter, Lady C. L. [Charlotte
Leveson].[3] They say she is *not* pretty. I don't know—everything is
pretty that pleases; but there is an air of *soul* about her—and her
colour changes—and there is that shyness of the antelope (which I
delight in) in her manner so much, that I observed her more than I
did any other woman in the rooms, and only looked at any thing else
when I thought she might perceive and feel embarrassed by my
scrutiny. After all, there may be something of association in this.
She is a friend of Augusta's, and whatever she loves I can't help
liking.

Her mother, the Marchioness, talked to me a little; and I was
twenty times on the point of asking her to introduce me to *sa fille*,
but I stopped short. This comes of that affray with the Carlisles.[1]

Earl Grey told me laughingly of a paragraph in the last *Moniteur*,
which has stated, among other symptoms of rebellion, some particulars
of the *sensation* occasioned in all our government gazettes by the
"tear" lines,—*only* amplifying, in its re-statement, an epigram (by the
by, no epigram except in the *Greek* acceptation of the word) into a
roman.[2] I wonder the *Couriers*, &c., &c., have not translated that part
of the Moniteur, with additional comments.

---

[2] Charlotte, the daughter of William Henry Cavendish Bentinck, 3rd Duke of
Portland, married Charles Greville in 1793.

[3] See June 18, 1814, to Augusta Leigh, note 2.

[1] Lord Carlisle had married the sister of Lord Granville Leveson-Gower,
Marquis of Stafford, the father of Lady Charlotte Leveson.

[2] The *Moniteur*, 17 Mars, 1814, said that Byron had made a romance of Princess
Charlotte's detestation of her future husband. This was a distortion of his "Lines
to a Lady Weeping".

The Princess of Wales has requested Fuseli to paint from "the Corsair"—leaving to him the choice of any passage for the subject: so Mr. Locke tells me. Tired—jaded—selfish and supine—must go to bed.

Roman, at least Romance, means a song sometimes, as in the Spanish. I suppose this is the Moniteur's meaning, unless he has confused it with "the Corsair."

Albany, March 28.

This night got into my new apartments, rented of Lord Althorpe,[3] on a lease of seven years. Spacious, and room for my books and sabres. In the house, too, another advantage. The last few days, or whole week, have been very abstemious, regular in exercise, and yet very unwell.

Yesterday, dined *tête-a-tête* at the Cocoa with Scrope Davies—sat from six till midnight—drank between us one bottle of champagne and six of claret, neither of which wines ever affect me. Offered to take Scrope home in my carriage; but he was tipsy and pious, and I was obliged to leave him on his knees praying to I know not what purpose or pagod. No headache, nor sickness, that night nor to-day. Got up, if any thing, earlier than usual—sparred with Jackson *ad sudorem*, and have been much better in health than for many days. I have heard nothing more from Scrope. Yesterday paid him four thousand eight hundred pounds, a debt of some standing, and which I wished to have paid before. My mind is much relieved by the removal of that *debit*.[1]

Augusta wants me to make it up with Carlisle. I have refused *every* body else, but I can't deny her any thing;—so I must e'en do it, though I had as lief "drink up Eisel—eat a crocodile."[2] Let me see— Ward, the Hollands, the Lambs, Rogers, &c. &c.—every body, more or less, have been trying for the last two years to accommodate this *couplet* quarrel[3] to no purpose. I shall laugh if Augusta succeeds.

Redde a little of many things—shall get in all my books to-morrow.

---

[3] In 1804 Albany House, which had been the residence of the Duke of York and Albany, was converted into bachelor chambers. Byron took over the lease of number 2 in the original building that had been occupied by John Charles Spencer, Viscount Althorp (later 3rd Earl Spencer), who was getting married.

[1] Byron had paid the remainder of his debt to Scrope Davies, who apparently had borrowed from usurers to furnish cash for Byron's first trip abroad in 1809.

[2] *Hamlet*, Act V, Scene 1.

[3] Byron's lines on Lord Carlisle in *English Bards and Scotch Reviewers* (lines 725–740) were written in the belief that Lord Carlisle, his guardian and kinsman, had deliberately refrained from easing his way into the House of Lords.

Luckily this room will hold them—with "ample room and verge, &c. the characters of hell to trace."[4] I must set about some employment soon; my heart begins to eat *itself* again.

April 8th.

Out of town six days. On my return, found my poor little pagod, Napoleon, pushed off his pedestal;—the thieves are in Paris. It is his own fault. Like Milo, he would rend the oak; but it closed again, wedged his hands, and now the beasts—lion, bear, down to the dirtiest jackall—may all tear him. That Muscovite winter *wedged* his arms;—ever since, he has fought with his feet and teeth. The last may still leave their marks; and "I guess now" (as the Yankees say) that he will yet play them a pass. He is in their rear—between them and their homes. Query—will they ever reach them?

Saturday, April 9th, 1814.

I mark this day!

Napoleon Buonaparte has abdicated the throne of the world. "Excellent well." Methinks Sylla did better; for he revenged and resigned in the height of his sway, red with the slaughter of his foes —the finest instance of glorious contempt of the rascals upon record. Dioclesian did well too—Amurath[1] not amis, had he become aught except a dervise—Charles the Fifth but so so—but Napoleon, worst of all. What! wait till they were in his capital, and then talk of his readiness to give up what is already gone!! "What whining monk art thou—what holy cheat?"[2] 'Sdeath!—Dionysius at Corinth was yet a king to this. The "Isle of Elba" to retire to!—Well—if it had been Caprea, I should have marvelled less. "I see men's minds are but a parcel of their fortunes."[3] I am utterly bewildered and confounded.

I don't know—but I think *I*, even *I* (an insect compared with this creature), have set my life on casts not a millionth part of this man's. But, after all, a crown may be not worth dying for. Yet to outlive *Lodi* for this!!! Oh that Juvenal or Johnson could rise from the dead! "Expende—quot libras in duce summo invenies?"[4] I knew they were light in the balance of mortality; but I thought their living dust weighed more *carats*. Alas! this imperial diamond hath a flaw in it,

[4] Gray, *The Bard*, lines 51–52.
[1] Ottoman Sultan known as Murad IV (1611–1640).
[2] Otway, *Venice Preserved*, Act IV, Scene 2.
[3] *Antony and Cleopatra*, Act III, Scene 2.
[4] Juvenal, *Satire* X, 147: Expende Hannibalem; quot libras in duce summo invenies? (Weigh Hannibal; how many pounds' weight will you find in that greatest of commanders?)

and is now hardly fit to stick in a glazier's pencil:—the pen of the historian won't rate it worth a ducat.

Psha! "something too much of this."[5] But I won't give him up even now; though all his admirers have, "like the Thanes, fallen from him."[6]

April 10th.

I do not know that I am happiest when alone; but this I am sure of, that I never am long in the society even of *her* I love, (God knows too well, and the Devil probably too,) without a yearning for the company of my lamp and my utterly confused and tumbled-over library. Even in the day, I send away my carriage oftener than I use or abuse it. *Per esempio,*—I have not stirred out of these rooms for these four days past: but I have sparred for exercise (windows open) with Jackson an hour daily, to attenuate and keep up the ethereal part of me. The more violent the fatigue, the better my spirits for the rest of the day; and then, my evenings have that calm nothingness of languor, which I most delight in. To-day I have boxed one hour—written an ode to Napoleon Buonaparte—copied it—eaten six biscuits—drunk four bottles of soda water—redde away the rest of my time—besides giving poor ＊ ＊ a world of advice about this mistress of his, who is plaguing him into a phthisic and intolerable tediousness. I am a pretty fellow truly to lecture about "the sect." No matter, my counsels are all thrown away.

April 19th, 1814.

There is ice at both poles, north and south—all extremes are the same—misery belongs to the highest and the lowest only,—to the emperor and the beggar, when unsixpenced and unthroned. There is, to be sure, a damned insipid medium—an equinoctial line—no one knows where, except upon maps and measurement.

"And all our *yesterdays* have lighted fools
The way to dusty death."[1]

I will keep no further journal of that same hesternal torch-light; and, to prevent me from returning, like a dog, to the vomit of memory, I tear out the remaining leaves of this volume, and write, in *Ipecacuanha,*—"that the Bourbons are restored!!!"—"Hang up philosophy."[2] To be sure, I have long despised myself and man, but I never spat in the face of my species before—"O fool! I shall go mad."[3]

[5] *Hamlet,* Act III, Scene 2.
[6] *Macbeth,* Act V, Scene 3: "Doctor, the thanes fly from me!"
[1] *Macbeth,* Act V, Scene 5.
[2] *Romeo and Juliet,* Act III, Scene 3.
[3] *King Lear,* Act II, Scene 4.

[The following passage from the 1813–1814 Journal was not printed by Prothero. Moore extracted it from an earlier period and says (Moore, I, 68) that it should come just after the Mary Duff reminiscence (p. 223).]

In all other respects, I differed not at all from other children, being neither tall nor short, dull nor witty, of my age, but rather lively— except in my sullen moods, and then I was always a Devil. They once (in one of my silent rages) wrenched a knife from me, which I had snatched from table at Mrs. B.'s dinner (I always dined earlier), and applied to my breast;—but this was three or four years after, just before the late Lord B.'s decease.

My *ostensible* temper has certainly improved in later years; but I shudder, and must, to my latest hour, regret the consequence of it and my passions combined. One event—but no matter—there are others not much better to think of also—and to them I give the preference. . . .

But I hate dwelling upon incidents. My temper is now under management—rarely *loud*, and *when* loud, never deadly. It is when silent, and I feel my forehead and my cheek *paling*, that I cannot control it; and then . . . . but unless there is a woman (and not any or every woman) in the way, I have sunk into tolerable apathy.

Date	Recipient	Source of Text	Page
		1813 (continued)	
Apr. 11	John Hanson	MS. Murray	38
Apr. 15	John Hanson	MS. Murray	39
Apr. 17	John Hanson	MS. Murray	39
Apr. 19	Lady Melbourne	MS. Murray	40
Apr. 21	John Murray	MS. Murray	41
Apr. 22	Lady Melbourne	MS. Murray	42
Apr. 29	Lady Caroline Lamb	MS. Murray	43
[May]	Lady Davy	MS. Waverly B. Cameron	44
[May?]	Samuel Rogers	MS. Bodleian Library (MS. Autog. C. 24)	44
Apr.-May 2	Lady Melbourne	MS. Murray	44
May 7	Lady Melbourne	MS. Murray	46
May 9	Lady Melbourne	MS. Murray	47
May 14	Lady Melbourne	MS. Murray	47
May 15	Lady Davy	MS. Stark Library, University of Texas	48
May 16	John Murray	MS. Murray	48
May 17	John Murray	MS. Murray	49
May 19	Thomas Moore	Text: Moore, I, 401	49
[May 20?]	John Herman Merivale	Text: Sotheby Catalogue, July 6, 1937	50
May 21	Lady Melbourne	MS. Murray	50
May 22	John Murray	MS. Murray	50
May 23	John Murray	MS. Murray	51
May 24	Lady Melbourne	MS. Murray	51
May 26	Lady Melbourne	MS. Murray	53
[June?]	John Murray (a)	MS. British Museum (Eg. 2075)	54
[June?]	John Murray (b)	MS. Beinecke Library, Yale University	54
[June?]	Thomas Moore	Text: Moore, I, 395-96	54
June 2	John Murray	MS. Murray	55
June 3	John Hanson (a)	MS. Murray	55
June 3	John Hanson (b)	MS. Murray	56
June 6	Francis Hodgson	Text: Hodgson, Memoir, I, 275-76	57
June 8	John Galt	MS. Robert H. Taylor Coll., Princeton University Library	57

261

Date	Recipient	Source of Text	Page
		1813 (continued)	
June 8	Francis Hodgson	MS. British Museum (Ashley 2623)	59
June 8	Lady Melbourne	MS. Murray	59
June 9	John Murray	MS. Murray	60
June 12	John Murray	MS. Murray	60
June 13	John Murray	MS. Murray	61
June 17	E. D. Clarke	MS. Stark Library, University of Texas	62
June 18	William Gifford	MS. Murray	62
June 18	John Murray	MS. Murray	64
June 19	John Murray	MS. Carl H. Pforzheimer Library	65
June 21	Lady Melbourne	MS. Murray	65
June 22	John Murray	MS. Murray	66
June 22	Thomas Moore	Text: Moore, I, 409	66
June 23	Countess of Westmorland	Text: Sotheby, Wilkinson & Hodge Catalogue, June 12, 1899	67
June 26	Augusta Leigh	MS. The Earl of Lytton	67
June 26	John Murray	MS. Meyer Davis Coll., University of Pennsylvania Library	68
[June 26-27?]	Augusta Leigh	MS. The Earl of Lytton	68
June 27	Augusta Leigh	MS. The Earl of Lytton	68
June 29	Lady Melbourne	MS. Murray	69
July 1	John Murray	MS. Murray	69
July 1	Lady Melbourne	MS. Murray	70
July 6	Lady Melbourne (a)	MS. Murray	71
July 6	Lady Melbourne (b)	MS. Murray	72
July 8	Thomas Moore	Text: Moore, 1, 410-11	72
July 9	Lady Melbourne	MS. Murray	74
July 11	Dr. William Clark	MS. Trinity College Library, Cambridge	74
July 13	Thomas Moore	Text: Moore, I, 411-12	75
July 13	John Wilson Croker	MS. Houghton Library, Harvard University	76
July 15	T[J?] Clarke	Text: Parke-Bernet Catalogue, No. 318, Nov. 26, 1941	76

Date	Recipient	Source of Text	Page
		1813 (continued)	
July 18	John Hanson	MS. Murray	76
July 18	Lady Melbourne	MS. Murray	77
July 22	John Murray	MS. Murray	78
July 22	Henry Fox	MS. Henry E. Huntington Library	78
July 25	Thomas Moore	Text: Moore, I, 412-13	78
July 25	J. W. Webster	MS. Facsimile, Literaturnoe Nasledstvo No. 58, Academy of Sciences, U.S.S.R., Moscow, 1952	81
July 27	Thomas Moore	Text: Moore, I, 414	81
July 28	Thomas Moore	Text: Moore, I, 414-15	82
July 29	Henry C. Fox	MS. Henry E. Huntington Library	82
July 30	[John Murray]	Text: Myers & Co. Catalogue, 336, 1941	83
July 30	Lady Melbourne	MS. Murray	83
July 31	Dr. William Clark	MS. Trinity College Library, Cambridge	83
[July 31]	John Murray	MS. Murray	84
Aug. 2	John Wilson Croker	Text: Moore, I, 415	84
[Aug. 21]	Dr. William Clark	Text: MS. copy, Trinity College Library, Cambridge	84
Aug. 5	Lady Melbourne	MS. Murray	85
Aug. 6	Henry Fox	MS. Henry E. Huntington Library	85
Aug. 8	Lady Melbourne	MS. Murray	86
Aug. 10	John Murray	MS. Murray	87
Aug. 11	Lady Melbourne	MS. Murray	87
Aug. 12	J. Wedderburn Webster	MS. Murray	88
Aug. 15	Samuel Jackson Pratt	MS. Gordon N. Ray	89
Aug. 18	Lady Melbourne	MS. Murray	90
Aug. 20	Lady Melbourne	MS. Murray	91
Aug. 21	Lady Melbourne	MS. Murray	92
Aug. 22	Thomas Moore	Text: Moore, I, 419-22	94
Aug. 23	Lady Melbourne	MS. Murray	97

Date	Recipient	Source of Text	Page
		1813 (continued)	
Aug. 25	Annabella Milbanke	MS. The Earl of Lytton	98
Aug. 26	John Murray	MS. Mrs. C. Earle Miller	100
Aug. 28	Thomas Moore	Text: Moore, I, 422-24	100
Aug. 31	Lady Melbourne	MS. Murray	102
Aug. 31	Annabella Milbanke	MS. The Earl of Lytton	103
Sept. 1	Thomas Moore	Text: Moore, I, 424-26	104
Sept. 2	J. Wedderburn Webster	MS. Murray	105
Sept. 5	Thomas Moore	Text: Moore, I, 426-27	106
Sept. 5	Lady Melbourne	MS. Murray	108
Sept. 6	Annabella Milbanke	MS. The Earl of Lytton	108
Sept. 6	J. Wedderburn Webster	MS. Robert H. Taylor Coll., Princeton University Library	110
Sept. 7	Lady Melbourne	MS. Murray	110
Sept. 8	Thomas Moore	Text: Moore, I, 427-28	111
Sept. 8	Lady Melbourne	MS. Murray	112
Sept. 9	Thomas Moore	Text: Moore, I, 428	112
Sept. 9	Lady Melbourne	MS. Murray	112
Sept. 9	Thomas Phillips	MS. Henry E. Huntington Library	113
Sept. 10	George Thomson	MS. Stark Library, University of Texas	113
Sept. 15	Augusta Leigh	MS. The Earl of Lytton	114
Sept. 15	John Murray	MS. Murray	115
Sept. 15	J. Wedderburn Webster	MS. Murray	115
Sept. 21	Lady Melbourne	MS. Murray	115
Sept. 23	Annabella Milbanke	MS. The Earl of Lytton	118
Sept. 25	J. Wedderburn Webster	MS. Royal College of Surgeons Library	118
Sept. 26	Annabella Milbanke	MS. The Earl of Lytton	119
Sept. 27	J. Thomson	MS. Morgan Library	121
Sept. 27	Sir James Mackintosh	Text: *Life of the Right Hon. Sir James Mackintosh*, 1835, II, 268	121
Sept. 27	Thomas Moore	Text: Moore, I, 428-29	122
Sept. 28	Lady Melbourne	MS. Murray	123

Date	Recipient	Source of Text	Page
		1813 (continued)	
Sept. 29	John Murray	MS. Robert H. Taylor Coll. Princeton University Library	125
Sept. 29	Lady Melbourne	MS. Murray	125
Sept. 30	J. Wedderburn Webster	MS. Murray	126
Oct. 1	Lady Melbourne	MS. Murray	127
Oct. 1	Francis Hodgson	Text: Hodgson, *Memoir*, I, 277-78	130
Oct. [1]-2	Thomas Moore	Text: Moore, I, 430-31	130
Oct. 2	John Murray	MS. Berg Coll., New York Public Library	131
Oct. 3	John Murray	MS. Murray	132
Oct. 4	John Murray	Text: J. Pearson & Company Catalogue, 83 (n.d.)	132
Oct. 5	Lady Melbourne	MS. Murray	132
Oct. 8	Lady Melbourne	MS. Murray	133
Oct. 10	Lady Melbourne	MS. Murray	136
Oct. 10	Augusta Leigh	MS. The Earl of Lytton	138
Oct. 10	John Hanson (*a*)	MS. Murray	138
Oct. 10	John Hanson (*b*)	MS. Murray	138
Oct. 11	Lady Melbourne	MS. Murray	139
Oct. 12	John Murray	MS. Murray	141
Oct. 13	Lady Melbourne	MS. Murray	141
Oct. 14	Lady Melbourne	MS. Murray	144
Oct. 17	Lady Melbourne	MS. Murray	145
Oct. 19	Lady Melbourne (*a*)	MS. Murray	148
Oct. 19	Lady Melbourne (*b*)	MS. Murray	148
[Oct. 20?]	Francis Hodgson	Text: Hodgson, *Memoir*, I, 278	150
Oct. 20	Samuel Butler	Text: *Life and Letters of Dr. Samuel Butler*, by his grandson, Samuel Butler, 1896, I, 89-90	150
Oct. 21	Lady Melbourne	MS. Murray	151
Oct. 23	Lady Melbourne	MS. Murray	152
[Oct. 25?]	Lady Melbourne	MS. Murray	154
Oct. 25	Lord Holland	MS. British Museum, (Add. 51639)	155

Date	Recipient	Source of Text	Page
	1813 (continued)		
[Nov.?]	John Murray (a)	Text: copy in Murray MS.	156
[Nov.]	John Murray (b)	MS. Stark Library, University of Texas	156
[Nov.?]	John Murray (c)	MS. Berg Coll., New York Public Library	157
Nov. 4	Lady Melbourne	MS. Murray	157
Nov. 8	Augusta Leigh	MS. The Earl of Lytton	158
[Nov. 8]	John Hanson	MS. Murray	158
Nov. 10-17	Annabella Milbanke	MS. The Earl of Lytton	158
Nov. 12	William Gifford	MS. Murray	161
[Nov. 12]	John Murray (a)	MS. Murray	162
Nov. 12	John Murray (b)	Text: Moore, I, 481-82	162
[Nov. 13]	John Murray (a)	MS. Murray	163
[Nov. 13]	John Murray (b)	MS. Murray	163
[Nov. 13]	John Murray (c)	MS. Murray	164
Nov. 14	W. Baldwin	MS. Morgan Library	164
[Nov. 14]	John Murray (a)	MS. Murray	165
[Nov. 14]	John Murray (b)	MS. Murray	165
[Nov. 15]	John Murray	MS. Murray	166
Nov. 16	Lord Holland	MS. British Museum (Add. 51639)	166
Nov. 17	John Murray	MS. Murray	166
Nov. 17	Lord Holland	MS. British Museum (Add. 51639)	167
[Nov. 20]	John Murray (a)	MS. Robert H. Taylor Coll., Princeton University Library	169
[Nov. 20]	John Murray (b)	MS. Murray	169
[Nov. 20]	John Murray (c)	MS. Murray	169
[Nov. 22]	John Murray	MS. Murray	170
Nov. 22	Lady Melbourne	MS. Murray	170
Nov. 22	J. Wedderburn Webster	MS. National Library of Scotland	172
[Nov. 23]	John Murray	MS. Murray	172
[Nov. 24]	John Murray	MS. Murray	173
Nov. 25	Lady Melbourne	MS. Murray	173
[Nov. 27]	John Murray	MS. Murray	175
Nov. 27	Dr. William Clark	MS. Trinity College Library, Cambridge	176

Date	Recipient	Source of Text	Page
		1813 (continued)	
Nov. 28	John Murray (*a*)	MS. Murray	176
Nov. 28	John Murray (*b*)	MS. Robert H. Taylor Coll., Princeton University Library	177
[Nov. 28]	John Murray (*c*)	MS. Murray	177
[Nov. 28]	John Murray (*d*)	MS. Carl H. Pforzheimer Library	177
Nov. 29	Annabella Milbanke	MS. The Earl of Lytton	178
Nov. 29	Dr. William Clark	Trinity College Library, Cambridge	180
[Nov. 29]	John Murray (*a*)	MS. Murray	181
[Nov. 29]	John Murray (*b*)	MS. Murray	181
[Nov. 29]	John Murray (*c*)	MS. Murray	182
[Nov. 30]	John Murray (*a*)	MS. Murray	183
[Nov. 30]	John Murray (*b*)	MS. Murray	183
Nov. 30	Thomas Moore	Text: Moore, I, 431-32	183
Nov. 30	Mme. de Staël	MS. Facsimile, V. T. De Pange, Madame de Staël and her English Correspondents, II, 412–14. Bodleian Library MS. D. Phil. d. 1441–2	184
[Dec.?]	John Murray (*a*)	MS. Murray	185
[Dec.?]	John Murray (*b*)	MS. Murray	186
[Dec.?]	John Murray (*c*)	MS. Murray	186
Dec. 1	Francis Hodgson	MS. Murray	187
Dec. 2	John Murray	MS. Murray	188
Dec. 2	Leigh Hunt	MS. Victoria and Albert Museum (John Forster Coll.)	188
[Dec. 2?]	Lord Holland	MS. British Museum (Add. 51639)	189
Dec. 3	Zachary Macaulay	MS. Robert H. Taylor Coll., Princeton University Library	189
[Dec. 3]	John Murray (*a*)	MS. Murray	190
[Dec. 3]	John Murray (*b*)	MS. Murray	190
[Dec. 3]	John Murray (*c*)	MS. Morgan Library	191

Date	Recipient	Source of Text	Page
		1813 (continued)	
[Dec. 3-4]	John Murray	MS. Murray	191
Dec. 4	John Murray	MS. Murray	191
[Dec. 6]	John Murray	MS. Murray	192
Dec. 7	John Murray	MS. Beinecke Library, Yale University	192
Dec. 7	Lord Holland	MS. British Museum (Add. 51639)	193
Dec. 8	Thomas Moore	Text: Moore, I, 432-34	193
Dec. 10	John Galt	MS. Stark Library, University of Texas	195
Dec. 11	John Galt	Text: Galt, *Life of Lord Byron*, pp. 179-80	196
Dec. 14	John Murray (*a*)	MS. Murray	197
[Dec. 14]	John Murray (*b*)	MS. Stark Library, University of Texas	197
Dec. 14	Thomas Ashe	MS. Murray	197
Dec. 14	[J?] Asham	MS. Roe-Byron Coll., Newstead Abbey	198
Dec. 15	E. D. Clarke	MS. British Museum (Eg. 2869); *LJ*, II, 310-11	199
[Dec. 16]	John Murray	MS. Murray	201
[Dec. 17]	John Murray	MS. Murray	201
Dec. 18	John Murray	MS. Murray	201
Dec. 18	Henry Drury	MS. Trinity College Library, Cambridge	202
Dec. 18	R. C. Dallas	Text: Dallas, *Correspondence*, III, 55	202
Dec. 22	Leigh Hunt	MS. Victoria and Albert Museum (John Forster Coll.)	203
Dec. 27	John Murray	MS. Murray	203
Nov. 14, 1813– April 19, 1814		Journal: Text: Moore, I, 435–475, 18–19, 491–514	204

FORGERIES OF BYRON'S LETTERS

[1813?]: To Webster. Myers, Catalogue 4, Summer, 1962.

April 3, 1813: To "Dear Sir" MS. Facsimile of whole letter, *The Sphere*, Aug., 1900.

April 29, 1813: To John Parry. Schultess-Young, II, pp. 156–158.

June 12, 1813: To John Murray. Bodleian Library, MS. Montagu d. 17. 25447, f. 28.

June 12, 1813: To Douglas Kinnaird. Schultess-Young, pp. 133–135.

Aug. 23, 1813: To Wedderburn Webster. MS. Stark Library, University of Texas.

Appendix III

BIBLIOGRAPHY FOR VOLUME 3

(*Principal short title or abbreviated references*)

Dallas, R. C.: *Correspondence of Lord Byron with a Friend*, 3 vols., Paris, 1825.

Dictionary of National Biography.

Elwin, Malcolm: *Lord Byron's Wife*, New York, 1963.

[Hodgson, Rev. Francis]: *Memoir of the Rev. Francis Hodgson, B. D.*, by his son, the Rev. James T. Hodgson, 2 vols., London, 1878.

LBC—Lord Byron's Correspondence, ed. John Murray, 2 vols., London, 1922.

LJ—The Works of Lord Byron. A New, Revised and Enlarged Edition. Letters and Journals, ed. Rowland E. Prothero, 6 vols., London, 1898–1901.

Marchand, Leslie A.: *Byron: A Biography*, 3 vols., New York, 1957.

Mayne, Ethel Colburn: *The Life and Letters of Anne Isabella Lady Noel Byron*, New York, 1929.

Medwin, Thomas: *Medwin's Conversations of Lord Byron* . . . . ed. Ernest J. Lovell, Jr., Princeton, N.J. 1966.

Moore, Thomas: *Letters and Journals of Lord Byron: with Notices of His Life*, 2 vols., London, 1830.

Poetry—The Works of Lord Byron. A New, Revised and Enlarged Edition. Poetry, ed. Ernest Hartley Coleridge, 7 vols., London, 1898–1904.

BIOGRAPHICAL SKETCHES

OF PRINCIPAL CORRESPONDENTS AND PERSONS FREQUENTLY MENTIONED

(See also Sketches in Volumes 1 and 2)

WILLIAM GIFFORD

William Gifford (1756-1826), first editor of the *Quarterly Review*, had become John Murray's literary adviser and it was mainly on his recommendation that Murray published *Childe Harold*. Byron had from his Cambridge days been a great admirer of Gifford's satires the "Baviad" (1794) "Maeviad" (1795) as well as his work in the *Anti-Jacobin* and later his edition of Juvenal. The "Baviad" and "Maeviad" were Byron's chief models for his first satire, *English Bards and Scotch Reviewers*. The deferential tone of Byron's references to Gifford in his letters to Murray and in the few letters he wrote to the critic and editor himself was not mere flattery. His admiration and respect was genuine, despite the differences in their political and moral outlooks. But while he bowed to Gifford's literary judgment and often asked Murray to get his opinion of particular lines or poems, he sometimes omitted but never altered his opinions for Gifford. On his side Gifford was extremely indulgent and admiring of some of Byron's romantic poems that by his own strict standards of the classical school he should have condemned. He praised and recommended Byron's oriental tales, and was so affected by the third canto of *Childe Harold* that even when ill he sat up until he had read every line, although it agitated him into a fever. Byron's idolizing of Gifford is a strange but characteristic trait such as his uncritical regard for the novels of Walter Scott.

LADY JERSEY

Lady Jersey was a reigning beauty and arbiter of fashion when Byron first saw her at Melbourne House just after the success of *Childe Harold* had made him famous. He was a frequent guest at her enormous parties and also at Middleton, the Jerseys' country house. Lady Sarah Sophia Fane, daughter of the 10th Earl of Westmorland, married in

1804 George Child-Villiers who succeeded his father in 1805 as the 5th Earl of Jersey. Though she had been a favourite of the Prince of Wales, she fell out of his favour shortly after Byron met her. She was a leading patroness of the fashionable balls at Almack's. Byron said, with admiration rather than critical cynicism, that she was "the veriest tyrant that ever governed Fashion's fools, and compelled them to shake their caps and bells as she willed it". Her wit and kindness toward him made her his favourite among the fashionable ladies after Lady Melbourne. It was at her salon that he first met Madame de Staël and many other people of distinction, and even at a time when he shunned society, as he did when he was emotionally involved during much of 1813 and 1814, he nevertheless went to Lady Jersey's more than anywhere else except Holland House. He was always grateful to Lady Jersey for standing by him during the public scandal of the separation in 1816.

RICHARD BRINSLEY SHERIDAN

Byron first met Sheridan, probably in 1813, through Rogers and Moore. He had long been an admirer of Sheridan's comedies and of his eloquence as a parliamentary orator, and quoted him frequently in his letters. When he met him personally he was much impressed with Sheridan's wit and conversation, though the dramatist's productive work was behind him and his great talents were sunk in alcoholism and he was rather a pathetic figure. In his letters and journals Byron has a considerable number of anecdotes and much admiring comment on Sheridan. And Sheridan had a very great liking for the younger man who paid him so much deference. Byron recalled a dinner at the home of Rogers in the spring of 1813, "when *he* [Sheridan] talked, and *we* listened, without one yawn, from six till one in the morning". When told of Byron's praise of his superior talents in oratory and drama at a party at Holland House, Sheridan burst into tears. Byron saw his faults but was tolerant of them. "Poor fellow! he got drunk thoroughly and very soon. It occasionally fell to my lot to convey him home—no sinecure, for he was so tipsy that I was obliged to put on his cock'd hat for him; to be sure it tumbled off again, and I was not myself so sober as to be able to pick it up again."

MADAME DE STAËL

Madame Germaine de Staël-Holstein was already famous when she came to England in June, 1813. The only daughter of Necker, the

French minister, she had married the Swedish Ambassador Baron de Staël-Holstein, who died in 1802. She had wielded considerable political influence before she fell out of favour with Napoleon, but she was chiefly noted for her literary work. Byron met her at Lady Jersey's and elsewhere soon after her arrival. She made a decided impression in social and literary circles in London. Her *De l'Allemagne* appeared and was reviewed in the *Quarterly* and the *Edinburgh* during her stay. Byron was impressed by her writing but rather appalled initially by her overpowering personality and conversation. At first he was inclined to banter and quiz her as did Sheridan, but he came to respect her superior intelligence, although he was somewhat embarrassed by her penchant for discussing his literary work and her own in public. He later told Lady Blessington that "Madame de Staël was certainly the cleverest, though not the most agreeable woman he had ever known." But he long remembered her kindness to him at Coppet. Among other things she volunteered to make an attempt (though it was fruitless) to effect a reconciliation between Byron and his wife. When he heard of her death in 1817, he told Murray "she will leave a great gap in Society and literature." But in his recollections of his years of fame in his "Detached Thoughts" he recalled many of the ridiculous aspects of her assertive personality in English society.

INDEX OF PROPER NAMES

Page numbers in italics indicate main references and Biographical Sketches in the Appendix. Such main biographical references in Volumes 1 and 2 are included in this index and are in square brackets.

Abercrombie, Miss, 222, 223
Aberdeen, George Hamilton Gordon, fourth Earl of, [*Vol. 1, 254 and n*], 91 and n
Aeschylus, 221
Agar, Mr., unidentified, 133
Albemarle, William Charles, fourth Earl of, 116n
Alberoni, Giulio, 213 and n
Alfieri, Count Vittorio, 133, 245; incest theme, 196 and n, 199
Ali Pasha, [*Vol. 1, 226n*], 110–11, 111–112
Allen, John, associate of Lord Holland, *239 and n*
Althorp, John Charles Spencer, Viscount (later third Earl Spencer), in Albany House, 255 and n
Annesley, Lady Catherine (sister of Lady Webster), 127 and n, 133, 142, 208, 237 and n; B. alleged pretendant to her hand, 151
Annesley, Lady Juliana (sister of Lady Webster), 208, 223, 241
Ariosto, Ludovico, 221
Asham, T., 198 and n
Ashe, Thomas, *Memoirs and Confessions, The Spirit of 'The Book'*, 197n
Athens, 27
Ay, Lady (Aylesford?), 86 and n

Bagdad, 27
Baillie, Joanna, 109, 180 and n
Bairaktar, Pasha of Rouschouk, 58n
Baldwin, W. J., King's Bench prisoner, 164 and n, 165 and n, 193n, 206n, 228–9, 233
Bandello, Matteo, Italian novels, 251 and n, 252
Bankes, William John, [*Vol. 1, 110 and n*], 15 and n, 103
Barbarossa, Horuc, 213 and n
Barras, Paul-Jean, vicomte de, 210 and n

Barrow, Anna Maria and John, 5n
Beaumont, Sir George and Lady, 214 and n
Bentham, Sir Samuel, 225 and n
Bernadotte, Count, 107 and n, 172, 211
Berrys, the Miss, 97n, 214 and n, 228, 231
Berry, Mary, *Journal and Correspondence*, 44 and n
Bessborough, Lady (neé Lady Henrietta Frances Spencer) (nicknamed 'Lady Blarney'), m. of Caroline Lamb, 23, 42n, 69, 90, 170; B.'s antipathy, 23, 27, 31, 40–1, 53, 126
Blacket, Joseph, 89n, 110 and nn
Blackwood, William, 238 and n
Blake, barber, 3 and n
Bland, Rev. Robert, 7 and n, 130 and n
Blinkensop, unidentified, 73
Bonneval, C. A., comte, 213 and n
Boringdon, Lord, B.'s debt to, 29 and n, 30
Braccio di Montone, 253
Braham, John, 209 and n
Brooke, Fulke Greville, first Baron, 62 and n
Brougham, Henry (later Baron Brougham and Vaux), obtains Hunt's acquittal, 203n; loses his seat, 249 and n; reviews *Hours of Idleness* (in *Edinburgh Review*), 203n
Brydges, Sir Samuel Egerton, *Letters on . . . Lord Byron*, 217n; *The Ruminator*, 217 and n
Bucke, Charles, *Philosophy of Nature*, 41 and n
Buckingham, George Nugent-Temple Grenville, first Marquis of, *232 and n*
Buffon, George Louis, comte de, 234
Bülow, General, 180n
Buonaparte, Lucien, 130 and n; *Charlemagne*, 97, 101n, translations, 78 and n, 97n, 130n, 150 and n

Buonaparte, Napoleon, 107, 157–8, 210
  and n, 218, 243–4, 246, 256;
  Mamaluke Guard, 28; portrait
  print, 248 and n; abdication, 256;
  and de Staël, 273
Burdett, Sir Francis, 18 and n
Burney, Fanny, 203–4; *The Wanderer,*
  or Female Difficulties, 204n
Burns, Robert, 114; 'unpublishable'
  letters, 202 and n, 239; B. on, 207
Burton, Robert, *Anatomy of Melan-*
  choly, 243 and n
Bury, Viscount, s. of fourth Lord Albe-
  marle, 116 and n, 133
Busby, Dr. Thomas, 210 and n, 211
Butler, Samuel, *Hudibras*, 52 and n
Butler, Dr Samuel, 130; translates
  Charlemagne, 97n, 130n, 150 and n
Buyukderé, 180
Byron, Eliza, 161 and n, 205, 208
Byron, George Anson (later seventh
  Baron), [*Vol. I, 41 and n*], 228
  and n, 229
Byron, George Gordon, sixth Baron;
  Works:
  Beppo, 80n, 216n
  The Blues, 214n
  The Bride of Abydos, composition,
    156 and n, 157, 160, 161, 168, 208;
    sent to Gifford, 161–2, 163; publi-
    cation questions, 162, 163, 166,
    168, 181n, 230; dedication, 163
    and n, 169; alterations and cor-
    rections, 163–4, 183, 188, 190–1,
    192, 201; payment for, 166–7,
    167n, 176–7, 187–8, 212; recipi-
    ents, 170, 175 and n, 176, 184,
    187, 200; printing, 170, 173, 175,
    177, 181n, 182n; Selim-Zuleika
    relationship, 175n, 196n, 199, 205,
    230; title, 205 and n, 232–3; B.
    advised not to publish, 206; de
    Staël, 235
  Childe Harold, 8, 34 and n, 60n, 106,
    182, 238; parodied in *Cui Bono*, 7
    and n, 11 and n; seventh edition,
    201 and n; makes B. famous, 271;
    'To Ianthe', 33n, 201n; reviewed
    in *Edinburgh Review*, 224n, *Quar-*
    terly Review, 224n
  The Corsair, 242n, 243, 255; identi-
    fied with B., 250
  The Curse of Minerva, 132 and n
  'Detached Thoughts', 48n; J. P.
    Curran, 128n; de Staël, 273

  The Devil's Drive, 240
  Don Juan, 122n, 123n, 207n;
    St. Ursula, 124 and n
  English Bards and Scotch Reviewers,
    61, 101, 107n; Edinburgh review-
    ers, 60n; American ed. 204 and n;
    in an Albany (US) reading-room,
    229–30, 236; Gell, 235n, Gifford,
    271, Carlisle, 255 and n
  'To Genevra' (sonnets), 240 and n
  The Giaour, 126n, 131 and n, 228
    and n, 236; first draft, 28 and n;
    private circulation, 33n, 34, 57
    and n, 88; publication and dedica-
    tion, 44 and n, 45, 59, 63, 69;
    revisions and additions, 51 and n,
    54 and n, 57n, 59, 87n, 88n, 111,
    124, 125, 141, 157 and n; written
    in 'fragments', 62 and n, 105;
    subsequent editions, 65 and n, 66n,
    100 and n, 163, 166, 208; origin,
    102n, 155n, 156, 200; payment for,
    167 and n, 212; reviewed by
    Christian Observer, 189n, *Edin-*
    burgh Review, 94 and n, *The Satirist*
    84 and n, 69 and n, 197 and n
  Heaven and Earth (in *The Liberal*),
    102n
  Hebrew Melodies, 205n
  Hints from Horace, 3n
  Hours of Idleness, reviewed by *Edin-*
    burgh Review, 203n
  Journal, 185n, 204ff
  'Lines to a Lady Weeping' (dis-
    torted in *Moniteur*), 254n
  Occasional verses, to T. Moore, 49–
    50; on Thurlow's poem, 55; a
    Song, 186–7
  Poetry VII, Charles I and Henry
    VIII, 38 and n
  'She Walks in Beauty like the Night',
    140n
  'Sympathetic *Address* to a Young
    Lady', 242 and n
  The Waltz, 94n
Byron, Rev. Henry, 161n, 205 and n
Byron, Capt. John, father of B., 81n
Byron, Julia (later Mrs Robert Heath),
  45 and n
Byron, Rev. and Hon. Richard, 161n,
  205n
Byron, William Byron, fifth Lord, 161n

Cagliari, Sardinia, 29, 174

Campbell, Thomas, 217; B. evaluates, 220, 232; and Merivale's review of Grimm, 247 and n; *The Pleasures of Hope*, 107 and n

Canning, George, 80; *Anti-Jacobin*, 66n, 144, 208n, 216n, 271; and *The Bride of Abydos*, 162n, 170, 173 and n, 175

Canning, Stratford (later Lord Stratford de Redcliffe), [*Vol. I, 242n*]; suitor of Annabella, 160n

Carey, Henry ('Sig. Carini'), *The Dragon of Wantley*, 79n

Carhampton, Henry Luttrell, second Earl of, 97n

Carlisle, Frederick Howard, fifth Earl of, [*Vol. I, 76n*], 214, marriage, 236n, 254n

Carlyle, Thomas, 16n

Carmarthen, Lady, 81n, 122, 140

Caroline, Princess of Wales, 44n; asks B.'s advice, 18 and n; and his relations with Annabella, 19 and n; alleged adultery, 25 and n, 197n; and 'The Corsair', 255

Caroline, Queen, becomes 'thin and gracious', 127

Carrington, Robert Smith, first Baron, 116n

Cartwright, Major John, supported by B. in Lords, 55 and n, 193, 229

Castellan, A. L., *Moeurs, usages costumes des Othomans*, 102 and n, 104

Catullus, 50 and n

Cawthorn, James, 202n, 203 and n

Cazotte, Jaques, *Le Diable Amoureux*, 101 and n

Cervantes Saavedra, Miguel de, 220

Chardin, Jean, *Voyages en Perse*, 252 and n

Charlemont, Francis William Caulfield, second Earl of, 171n, 214n

Charlemont, Lady (née Bermingham), w. of above, 171 and n, 214 and n, 228 and n

Charlotte, Princess, 242, 254n

Chaworth, Mary, 99n, 178 and n

Chesterfield, Philip Stanhope, second Earl of, 146 and n

Chrisso, Bishop of, 61n

Cibber, Colley, *Richard III*, 184 and n

Cicero, 207

Clare, John Fitzgibbon, second Earl of, 5

Clark, Dr. William, 147, 197; invited

abroad with B., 74, 84, 115 and n, 176 and n, 181, 199n

Clarke, Prof. Edward Daniel, 84, 199 and n

Clarke, James Stanier, *Naufragia*, 62 and n

Clarke, Samuel, 63 and n

Claughton, Thomas, purchase of Newstead, 6, 22, 24, 28 and n, 29, 32, 38, 76–7, 138

Cochrane, Thomas, Lord (later tenth Earl of Dundonald), 249 *and n*

Coke, Rev. Richard, 7 and n

Coleridge, Samuel T., 220; with Southey 'The Devil's Thoughts', 240n

Collins, William, 179

Congreve, William, 249

Constantinople, 27, 180 and n

Cooke, George Frederick, *Memoirs*, 95 and n, 229–30, 230n

Corbet, Mr., and Lord Falkland's widow, 17 and n, 24 and n

Cowper, Lady (Emily Mary Lamb), d. of Lady Melbourne, 22, 125n, 154n; nicknamed Countess of Panshanger, 92 and n

Cowper, William, 179

Crabbe, George, *Resentment*, 141n

Cribb, Thomas, pugilist, 216 and n, 221

Croker, John William, 5n, 76; and B.'s passage abroad, 84 and n

Cunegonde, Miss, 111

Cunningham, John William, reviews *The Giaour*, 190 and n

Curran, John Philpot, 128 *and n*, 130–1; on the Prince's corpulence, 128

D., Mr., possible identity, 198 and n

Dallas, Robert Charles, [*Vol. I, 274–5*], 15, 89, 202 and n; arrival of his nephew, 229

Dalton, Edward T., *79 and n*

Dante, 133, 221

D'Arblay, Mme, *see* Burney, Fanny

Davies, Scrope Berdmore, [*Vol. I, 184n*], quarrel with Lord Foley, 85–6, 86n, 93, 95; B.'s debt to, 255 and n

Davison, T., printer, 132n, 156

Davy, Lady (Jane Apreece, née Kerr), w. of Sir Humphry, 44 *and n*; and Maria Edgeworth, 48 and n

Day, *The*, 21 and n

Defoe, Daniel, *Robinson Crusoe*, 62 and n
De Gramont, see Gramont
Delawarr, George John, fifth Earl, 106
Demosthenes, 220
De Quincey, Thomas, *Autobiographical Sketches*, 102n
De Ruyter, see Ruyter.
Devonshire, Elizabeth, second Duchess of, 145n, 174n
Devonshire, Georgiana, Duchess of, 42 and n, 97n, 174 and n
De Witt, see Witt
Diocletian, 256
Disraeli, Benjamin, Earl of Beaconsfield, 79; *Coningsby*, 71n, 94n
D'Israeli, Isaac, *Curiosities of Literature*, 50 and n; *Quarrels of Authors*, 251 and n
Donegal, Lady (née Anna May), 247 and n
Douglas, Sir John and Lady, accusation against Princess of Wales, 25 and n, 26, 197n
Drury, Henry Joseph, [*Vol. I, 144n*], 50 and n, 187 and n
Drury Lane Address competition, 20n, 54n, 121
Dryden, John, 168; *All for Love*, 207n
Duff, Helen, s. of Mary, 222
Duff, Mary, marriage to Robert Cockburn, 222 and n; B.'s early passion, 210, 221–2
Dunlap, W., *Memoirs of George Frederick Cooke*, 95 and n, 230n

Eagles, Rev. John, ed. *The Journal of Llewellin Penrose*, 176 and n
Eardley, Sampson (formerly Gideon) (later Baron Eardley of Spalding), 69 and n
Eardley Wilmot, Sir John, 69n
Eaton, Daniel Isaac, imprisonment, 184n; *Ecce Homo*, 184 and n; *Politics for the People*, 184n
Eccelino da Romano, 253
Edgeworth, Maria, 44, 204; to meet B., 48; *The Absentee*, 48n; *Belinda*, 48n; *Ennui*, 48n; *The Modern Griselda*, 48n; *Patronage*, 204n, 247, reviewed by *Edinburgh Review*, 252 and n
Egremont, 3rd Earl of, 4 and n
Eldon, John Scott, first Earl of, 90n
Elgin, Thomas Bruce, eighth Earl of, 58; in *Horace in London*, 20 and n

Ellenborough, Edward Law, first Baron, 31; sentences Eaton, 184n
Ellis, George, contributor to the *Rolliad* and *Anti-Jacobin*, 208 and n; reviews *Childe Harold*, 208n
Epicurus, 210
Erskine, Thomas Erskine, first Baron, 227, 247n; 'On the Causes and Consequences of the War with France', 248 and n, 253
Eustace, John Chetwode, *Tour through Italy*, 51 and n

Falkland, Charles John, ninth Lord, killed in a duel, 17n
Falkland, Christina, Lady, 17 and n, 24 and n
Farquhar, George, 149; *The Beaux' Stratagem*, 151 and n, 235 and n, 242
Fielding, Henry, *Amelia*, 8; *Jonathan Wild*, 7 and n, 202 and n; *Joseph Andrews*, 13 and n; *Tom Jones*, 134 and n
Firdausí, Abdul Kásim, *The Sháh Námeh*, 101 and n
Fitzgerald, Lord Edward, 249 *and n*
Fitzpatrick, Richard, 219
Fletcher, William, 120
Foley, Lord, 86n, 93, 95
Fontenelle, Bernard le Bouvier, Sieur de, 184 and n
Foote, Samuel, *Mayor of Garratt*, 100n
Forbes, Lady Adelaide, B.'s attachment to, 75 *and n*
Ford, Jack, pugilist, 94n
Ford, John, 199
Foster, Lady Elizabeth, 145n
Foster, John Thomas, 174n
Fox, Charles James, 219, 239n; India Bill, 232n; criticized in *Quarterly*, 242 and n
Fox, Henry (Harry), s. of Lord Holland, 15, 78 and n; his Toledo swords, 82 and n; goes to *Nourjahad* with B., 224 and n, 226, 232
Frere, John Hookham, 170, 175, 216 and n; 'Whistlecraft', 80 and n, 216n
Fuseli, Henry, 253–4, 255

Galt, John, present to B., 57; describes Romaika, 58 and n; and *Bride of Abydos*, 195 and n, 237; and *Giaour*, 230; *Letters from the Levant*, 57n

Garrick, David, *The Country Girl*, 42 and n; with George Colman, *The Clandestine Marriage*, 137 and n, 216 and n

Gay, John, *Beggar's Opera*, 8, 239; *The What d'ye call't*, 167 and n

Gell, Sir William, 234 and n; *Topography of Troy*, 234n

George IV (Prince Regent), 38n, 71n, 182, 273; libelled by Hunt, 49n; sponsors Grand National Fête, 75 and n; at Brighton, 94

Gifford, William, 97, 100n, 156n, 170, 271; adviser to B., 62n, 63–4, 271; ed. *Quarterly Review*, 161, 271; contributor to *Anti-Jacobin*, 271

Gillies, Robert Pearse, *Childe Alarique*, 217 and n; ed. *Foreign Quarterly Review*, 217n

Giovanni Galeazzo, 253

Glasse, Hannah, *The Art of Cookery*, 238 and n

Glenbervie, Sylvester Douglas, Baron, 234 and n

Goethe, Johan Wolfgang von, definition of architecture, 211 and n

Goldsmith, Oliver, 79 and n; *She Stoops to Conquer*, 123 and n; *Vicar of Wakefield*, 10 and n, 15 and n, 213 and n

Graham, Sir Thomas, 180 and n

Gramont, Comte de, *Memoirs*, 146 and n, 148n; Mlle de Saint-Germain and Mme de Sénantes episode, 147n

Granard, George Forbes, sixth Earl of, 71n, 75n

Grattan, Henry (? Jr.), 157 and n

Gray, Thomas, 141; *The Bard*, 256 and n

Gregson, Bob, 216n

Greville, Lady Charlotte (née Cavendish), 254 and n

Grey, Earl, on *Moniteur*, 254 and n

Grimaldi, Joseph, clown, 9

Grimm, Friedrich Melchoir, epitaph on Voltaire, 117–18; *Correspondance Littéraire et Philosophique*, 195 and n; reviews of, 96 and n, 118n, 247 and n

Haddington, Thomas Hamilton, sixth Earl of, 61 and n

Hamilton, author of Gramont's *Memoirs*, 148 and n

Hanson, Charles, 29

Hanson, John, [*Vol. I, 275*], and Newstead, 22, 29, 39, 56; at Farleigh, 158 and n

Hanson, Mary Ann, marriage to Earl of Portsmouth, 248 and n, 249

Hardwicke, Elizabeth, Countess of (née Lindsay), 252 and n

Hardwicke, Philip Yorke, third Earl of, 252n

Harley, Lady Charlotte, 36, 42 and n; 'To Ianthe', 33n; portrait by Westhall, 33 and n

Harmer, Harry, 'the Coppersmith', 94n

Harrington, Barnaby, Drunken Barnaby's Journal, 95 and n

Harrowby, Earl and Countess of, 80

Hayreddin, 213 and n

Heath, Robert, 45n

Heathcote, Lady (Katherine Sophia Manners), 36, 50, 252; B.—Caroline incident, 71–2, 74, 84n

Heber, Richard, 170, 202; to review Lord Brooke's book, 62 and n

Henderson, John ('Bath Roscius'), 250 and n

Herodes Atticus, 213 and n

Hervey, Lady Elizabeth (later Duchess of Devonshire qv.), 174n

Hobhouse, John Cam (later first Baron Broughton de Gyfford), [*Vol. I, 275–6*], 28, 47, 212; continental tour, 51, 97, 197 and n, 243; *Imitations and Translations*, 213 and n; *Journey through Albania*, 41 and n, 51 and n, 201n

Hodgson, Rev. Francis, [*Vol. I, 276–7*], 7 and n, 58, 59; and *The Giaour*, 100, 168; aided financially by B., 130n, 187n, 210n, 228 and n; recommended to Dr. Butler, 150 and n; likes *Bride of Abydos*, 166, 168; engagement, 187n, 202n, 206; translation of *Charlemagne*, 97 and n; Juvenal, 150

Holbach, Paul Heinrich, Baron d', *Histoire critique de Jésus-Christ*, 185 and n

Holland, 171–2, 176 and n, 180, 235; expulsion of French, 180n, 211, 212 and n; B.'s planned visit, 212–13

Holland, Lady, 90, 128, 171, 226, 231; *Journal*, 97n

Holland, Dr. (afterwards Sir) Henry, 111; *Travels in the Ionian Islands*, 110 and n

279

Holland, Henry Fox, third Lord, [*Vol. II, 281*], 34, 130, 155n; to receive *Bride of Abydos*, 163 and n, 166, 208; presents Baldwin's petition, 165n, 193 and n, 206n; and Junius, 215; on Sheridan, 240
Holmes, James, portrait of B., 170, 224 and n
Home, John, *109 and n*; *Douglas*, 109n
Hope, Thomas, 27 and n; *Anastasius*, 27n
Horace, *Odes and Epodes*, 101n, 215 and n, 218 and n, 236 and n, 244 and n
Horn, Mrs., in *Nourjahad*, 226 and n
Horner, Francis, 225–6, *226n*
Hunt, James Henry Leigh, [*Vol. II, 281–2*], 79, 188–9; imprisonment, 49n; B. on, 228
Howard, Lady Gertrude, 68 and n
Huntley, George Gordon, Marquess of, 253

Illusion, or the Trances of Nourjahad, attributed to B., 175 and n, 224n; Drury Lane performance, 175n, 224n, 226 and n
Inchbald, Mrs. Elizabeth (née Simpson), *236 and n*; *Nature and Art, A Simple Story*, 236 and n
Ireland, W. H., *Neglected Genius*, 7n

Jackson, John ('Gentleman'), 94, 221, 251, 253, 255, 257; portrait, 115 and n; Pugilistic Club, 216 and n
Jeffrey, Francis, Lord Jeffrey, 94, 252–3
Jersey, Lady (née Lady Sarah Sophia Fane), 67, 70, 90, 197n, *271–2*
Jersey, George Child-Villiers, fifth Earl of, 271–2; invites B. to Middleton, 207, 209
Jocelyn, Lord, Harrow, friend of B., 106 and n
Johnson, Samuel, 67n, 214n, 228, 247n, 256
Jones, Richard (?), actor, 249
Jordan, Mrs. Dorothea, as Miss Hoyden, 249 and n
Junius (Sir Philip Francis), 215
Juvenal, 150; *Satires*, 256 and n

Kean, Edmund, to meet B., 244; *Richard III*, 244
Keith, Lady (née Hester Maria Thrale), 247 and n

Kleist, Heinrich von, 220
Knapp, unidentified, 187
Knight, Henry Gally, *Ilderim, a Syrian Tale*, 191 and n
Knight, Richard Payne, 247 and n
Kozlovsky, Prince, *45 and n*, 69, 76, 83

Laclos, Pierre Choderlos de, *Les Liaisons Dangereuses*, 220 and n
Lamb, Lady Caroline, [*Vol. II, 283*], 32, 43, 67, 91, 145n, 170; continuing relations with B., 3 and n, 4, 7, 8, 16, 21–2, 23, 26, 27, 35–6, 37, 42, 43, 46, 83, 87, 139, 157; signs herself 'Phryne', 8 and n, 23, 'Your Agnus', 46 and n; inscribes her livery buttons, 9; affair of the necklace, 16; affair of B.'s picture, 10–11, 12, 14, 15, 26, 31, 36–7, 42 and n, 46, 173; requests a lock of his hair, 37 and n, 40; *The Giaour*, 40, 102 and n; incident at Lady Heathcote's, 71, 72, 74, 170; guesses at B.'s new attachment, 125 and n, 126
Lamb, Frederick, s. of Lady Melbourne, 70 and n, 86 and n
Lamb, George, s. of Lady Melbourne, 65, 126, 145n, *232 and n*
Lamb, Mrs George (née Rosalie St. Jules), 31, 37, 90
Lamb, Sir Peniston (later Lord Melbourne), 46n
Landor, Walter Savage, *Count Julian* (credited to B.), 36 and n
Lansdowne, Sir Henry Petty-Fitzmaurice, third Marquis of, 244
Lardner, Dionysius, *Cabinet Cyclopaedia*, 253n
La Rochefoucauld, Francis, duc de, 210, 229; *Maximes*, 102 and n
Learmont of Ercildoune, Thomas ('the Rhymer'), 122 and n
Le Despenser, Lady, self-described 'Baroness', 102 and n
Leigh, Hon. Augusta (née Byron), [*Vol. 1, 273*], 68, 70, 73, 158; in financial trouble, 32 and n, 210n; at Six Mile Bottom, 83 and n, 112 and n; liaison with B., 87 and n, 96 and n, 102 and n, 113 and n; to go abroad with him, 85, 89, 93, 114–15, 153n; legatee, 126 and n; and Carlisle-B. quarrel, 255 and n
Leigh, Georgi[a]na, 205

Leigh, Mr. Chandos, supposed buyer of Newstead, 77
Levant, the, 29, 60, 90
Leveson-Gower, Lady Charlotte, 254
Leveson-Gower, Lord Granville (later Earl of Granville), *232 and n*, 237 *and n*
Leveson-Gower, Harriet, Countess of Granville, *Letters*, 211n
Lewis, Matthew Gregory, 4n, 227, 230 and n; and de Staël, 240–1; *Ambrosio, or the Monk*, 205 and n; 'Pleasure and Desire', 151–2
Liverpool, Lord, 206
Locke, John, 243
Longman, publisher of Moore's *Lalla Rookh*, 112n
Luttrell, Henry, 85n, 97 *and n*; 'Advice to Julia', 97n
Lucretius, 7, 73, 210

Macaulay, Zachary, ed. *Christian Observer*, 189 and n
Machiavelli, Niccoló, *Opere*, 252 and n
Mackintosh, Sir James, 80, 111, 130, 177, 226, 251; Recorder of Bombay, 104 and n; reviews *Germany*, 96n, 224 and n; essay on Burke, 80n, 224–5; *History of England*, 253n; *History of the Revolution in 1688*, 253n
Magliabecchi, Antonio, *239 and n*
Malone, Edmund, ed. of Shakespeare, 80 and n
Manchester, Duchess of, elopement, 37 and n
Manchester, William Montagu, fifth Duke of, 37n
Massinger, Philip, 61, 64
Matta, Charles de Bourdeille, compte de, 147 and n, 148 and n
Medwin, Thomas, 157n
Mee, Mrs., 6, 14
Melbourne, Lady, [*Vol. II, 283–4*], 93, 219; intermediary between B. and Caroline, 8–9, 16, 23, 52, 143, 152, 153n; early marriage, 46n; and Caroline–B. incident at Lady Heathcote's, 72 and n, 74; and his liaison with Augusta, 87 and n, 102 and n, 113n, 124n, 150n; and Annabella, 98, 103; and *Bride of Abydos*, 170, 175n; B.'s regard for, 179, 209
Meletius of Janina, 61 and n

Merivale, John Herman, 7n, 50, 170; reviews Grimm's *Correspondance Littéraire*, 247 and n; *see also*, Bland, Robert
Metastasio, 110, 195
Milbanke, Annabella (later Lady Byron), [*Vol. II, 284*], 48n, 123n, 124n, 136n, 251; B.'s marriage intentions, 18–19, 53, 98–9, 103; requirements in a husband, 108 and n; to retain him as a friend, 178n, 179, 227; a mathematician, 159, 160; other suitors, 160 and n, 178n; separation proceedings, 225n
Miller, Joseph (Joe), 223 and n
Milo, Greek athlete, 256
Milton, John, 37, 141, 100; *Comus*, 63 and n
Moira, John Hastings, first Earl of, 71n, 75n
Montagu, Edward Wortley, *213 and n*
Montgomery, Hugh, 136n
Montgomery, Mary Millicent, 136 and n, 159
Monti, Vincenzo, 245 and n; *Aristodemo*, 245
Moore, Thomas, [*Vol. II, 284–5*], 54n, 217, 226n; and Gifford, 66–7; in Derbyshire, 73 and n; his patron, 75n; attacks Prince Regent, 75n; music for his songs, 79n; at Ashbourne, 81 and n; underrates himself, 111, 194; his many talents, 215, 220, 237, 245; referred to in *Edinburgh Review*, 224 and n; *Irish Melodies*, 113n, 131n, 193–4, 220; *Lalla Rookh*, 101n, 104, 112n, 194n; *Letters and Journals of Lord Byron*, 112n; *Loves of the Angels*, 102n; *Memoirs of the Life of . . . Sheridan*, 54n; *Poems of the Late Thomas Little*, 96n; *Twopenny Post-Bag*, 49 and n, 50–1, 73, 75n, 194–5
More, Hannah, 238
Moreau, Jean Victor Marie, at Dresden, 125 and n
Morghen, engraver, 248n
Morosini, 248
Morris, Charles, laureate, *79 and n*; 'The Old Whig Poet and his Old Buff Waistcoat', 79n
Mottley, John, *Joe Miller's Jests*, 223n
Mountnorris, George Annesley, Viscount Valentia, Earl of, 216 and n

281

Mule, Mrs., B.'s firelighter, 246
Murad IV, 256 and n
Murphy, Arthur, *The Way to Keep Him*,
136 and n, 145
Murray, Joe, 21, 105–6
Murray, John, II, [*Vol.
II, 285–6*], 7,
10–11, 20n, 271; publisher to Hob-
house, 15, to Moore, 112n; and
The Waltz, 41 and n; *The Giaour*,
44n, 51n, 59, 62; publisher of
Quarterly Review, 5n, 7 and n, 11n,
51n, 62 and n

Nathan, Isaac, music for *Hebrew Melo-
dies*, 209n
Nettle, B.'s poodle, 118 and n, 122,
126, 127
Norfolk, Duke of, 167–8
North, Christopher, 'Noctes Ambrosi-
anae'(*Blackwood's Magazine*), 217n
North, Frederick (later fifth Earl of
Guilford), 199 and n
Nourjahad, see *Illusion*
Nugent, —, friend of Luttrell, 85 and n

O'Connor, Arthur, 249n
Ossulstone, Lady (née Corisande Ar-
mandine), d. of duc de Gramont,
4, 70; and Caroline Lamb, 71, 170
Otway, Thomas, 109; *Venice Preserved*,
256 and n
Ovid, 181, 189
Oxford, Edward Harley, fifth Earl of,
10, 59, 65, 147
Oxford, Robert, first Earl of, alleged
author of *Robinson Crusoe*, 62 and n
Oxford, Countess of (née Jane Elizabeth Scott), w. of fifth Earl,
[*Vol. II, 286*], 47, 58, 154;
mistress of B., 3 and n, 4, 27, 32,
65–6, 142n, 210, 229; denounced
by Caroline, 8, 9; lock of hair
incident, 37 and n, 40, 140 and n;
'Harleian Miscellany', 40 and n;
to go abroad, 56, 59, 65, 69

Packwood, Mr. and Mrs. George,
Packwood's Whim, 238 and n
Paine, Thomas, 247n; *Age of Reason*,
Rights of Man, 184n
Parkyns family, 223
Perry, James, and *Bride of Abydos*, 182
and n, 188
Petersham, 'Lord', 117 and n, 126, 128,
133

Petrarch, 240
Philips, George, 226 and n
Phillips, Thomas, 113; portraits of B.,
68 and n, 70, 167 and n, 198
Pigot family, 223
Plunket, William Conyngham (later
Baron), *22 and n*
Pomponius, 213 and n
Pope, Alexander, 20, 58; *Eloise and
Abelard*, 205 and n; *Epistle to Dr.
Arbuthnot*, 36 and n, 161 and n,
162 and n, 233; *Imitations of
Horace*, 96 and n; *Moral Essays*,
91 and n, 109–10; *Rape of the
Lock*, 214–15
Porson, Professor Richard, at Cider
Cellars, 107n; *The Devil's Walk*,
240 and n
Portland, William Henry Cavendish
Bentinck, third Duke of, 254n
Portsmouth, Countess of (née Mary
Ann Hanson), 248 and n, 249
Powerscourt, Richard Wingfield, Lord,
106 and n
Pratt, Samuel Jackson, 89n, 110 and n
Puységur, Mons. de, 211 and n

Quatremèr(e), Antoine, questions sex
of Mme de Staël, 66n

Rancliffe, George Parkyns, second
Baron, 71n
Rancliffe, Lady (née Forbes), w. of
above, 71 and n, 72
Rawdon, Lady C., death, 13
Rawdon, Lady Selina, 75n
Raymond, stage manager, 196 and n,
230 and n
Redesdale, John Mitford, first Baron,
Insolvent Debtors Act, 206n
Regent, Prince, see George IV
Reynolds, John Hamilton, 214n; *Safie*,
245–6
Reynolds, Sir Joshua, 'Lady Melbourne
and Child', 46 and n
Rich, John, and Covent Garden theatre,
79n
Richardson, John, *Persian Dictionary*,
101nn
Richardson, Samuel, *Clarissa Harlowe*,
108, 241; *Sir Charles Grandison*,
106
Ripperda, Johan, Baron d', 213 and n
Rocca, Mr., lover of Mme de Staël,
231–2

282

Rogers, Samuel, [*Vol. II, 286–7*], 29 and n, 44 and n, 70, 217; abused by women, 47; Thurlow's poem to, 54 and n, 55; out of town with Mme de Staël, 73; B.'s jealousy, 81, 82; B. on, 220; *Columbus*, 34, 62 and n, 169 and n, 224n; *The Pleasures of Memory*, 62 and n, 107 and n; *Poems*, reviewed by *Quarterly Review*, 107 and n, by *Edinburgh Review*, 224 and n

Romilly, Sir Samuel, *225 and n*; and B.'s separation from Annabella, 225n

Rousseau, Jean-Jacques, 151, 195, 225n; *La Nouvelle Héloïse*, 151n

Rundell, Maria Eliza, *Domestic Cookery*, 238 and n

Rushton, Robert, 20–1; to be employed by Webster, 81, 88 and n, 89

Russell, Bertrand, 226n

Russell, Lord John (later first Earl Russell), *228 and n*

Ruyter, Michel Adriaanzoon van de, 212 and n

Salisbury, James Cecil, Earl of, 171 and n, 215

Sanders, George, 10, 33 and n, 41

Schiller, Johan Christoph von, incest theme, 196 and n, 199; *Fiesco*, *Robbers*, 245 and n

Scott, Sir Walter, 217n, 230n; B. accused of imitating, 141 and n; compared with him, 209n, 250; admiration for, 209, 271; pecuniary misfortunes, 219–20; burlesque of *Lay of the Last Minstrel*, 202n; *Marmion*, 145–6; *Rokeby*, 209 and n

Scott, Sir William, *90 and n*, 97

Selim III, Sultan, 58n

Shakespeare, William, *Antony and Cleopatra*, 207 and n, 256; *Cymbeline*, 25n; *Hamlet*, 75, 219 and n, 230n, 243 and n, 246, 255; *Henry IV, Pt. I*, 146, 206 and n, 252, *Pt. II*, 210 and n, 212, 245; *Henry V*, 131, 153, 209; *Henry VI, Pt. III*, 107 and n, 246; *Henry VIII*, 225; *Julius Caesar*, 243 and n; *King Lear*, 246 and nn, 257; *Macbeth*, 25n, 38, 219 and n, 243 and n, 246, 250, 257; *Much Ado About Nothing*, 11, 12, 160; *Othello*, 82 and n, 145; *Richard III*, 216, 229, 244, 250; *Romeo and Juliet*, 219 and n, 257

Shannon, Lady Sarah, 51 and n

Sharp(e), Richard ('Conversation'), 162 and n, 216 and n, 226; last interview with Windham, 219 and n

Shelley, Percy Bysshe, defends Eaton, 184n

Sheridan, Richard Brinsley, 129, 249, 272; on Whitbread, 54 and n; conversation, 207–8, 238, 247, 272; sentimentality, 239; relationship with B., 272; Begum Speech, 239; *The Critic*, 239; Monologue on Garrick, 239; *School for Scandal*, 155, 239, 249 and n; *Trip to Scarborough*, 104

Sherwood, Neely and Jones (publishers), *The Waltz*, 41 and n

Sismondi, Léonard Simonde de, 195 and n; *De la Littérature du Midi de l'Europe*, 252 and n

Sitwell, Sir Sitwell, 140n

Sitwell, Lady Sarah Caroline (née Stovin), w. of above, 140 and n, 141

Sligo, second Marquis of (formerly Lord Altamont), travel plans, 27, 82, 90, 230; and origin of *The Giaour*, 102 and n, 155n, 200; in trouble with the Navy, 155n

Smart, Christopher, *Universal Visitor*, 67 and n

Smith, Catherine Lucy (later Lady Stanhope), 116n

Smith, Horace, *First Impressions*, 20 and n

Smith, James and Horace, *Cui Bono* (parody of *Childe Harold*), 7n, 11n; *Horace in London*, 20 and n; *Rejected Addresses*, 7 and n, 11 and n

Smith, Sir Sidney, alleged liaison with Princess of Wales, 25n, 26

Smith, Mrs Constance Spencer [*Vol. I, 224 and n*], 154

Smith, Sydney, his 'Tory Virgin' story, 214 and n

Smollett, Tobias, *Humphry Clinker*, 94 and n

Smyth, Prof. William, 63 and n

Soliman Pasha of Baghdad, 58 and n

Sommery, Mlle de, 195 and n

Sophocles, 220

Southey, Robert, 16n, 60 and n, 168, 206; 'unsaleable' works, 101; appearance, 122, 127, 214; compared with Scott, 209n; B. on, 220; *Life of Nelson*, 214; with Coleridge, 'The Devil's Thoughts', 240n

Spencer, Lady, w. of second Earl, 31 and n, 46–7

Spenser, Edmund, 168

Staël, Albert de, killed in a duel, 86 and n, 94

Staël-Holstein, Mme Germaine de (née Necker), 73, 131, 272–3; called the 'Epicene', 66 and n; and her son's death, 86, 94; relationship with B., 66 and n, 76, 85, 207, 226–7, 228, 235–6, 237, 242, 273; character of her society, 231, 241, 244, 247; Essay against Suicide, 73, 160; *De l'Allemagne*, 96 and n, 181 and n, 184–5, 211, 224 and n, 231, 273

Stafford, Marchioness of, 236 and n, 254

Stafford, Granville Leveson-Gower, first Marquis of, 232n

Stafford, George Granville Leveson-Gower, second Marquis of, 236 and n, 237n

Stair, John W. Dalrymple, seventh Earl of, 85; marriages, 85n

Stanhope, Charles (later fourth Earl of Harrington), styled Lord Petersham, 117 and n, 126, 128, 133

Stanhope, Charles Stanhope, third Earl, 'Jacobin', 55n

Stanhope, Phillip Henry Stanhope, fourth Earl, 106 and n, 116 and n, 229

Staremberg, Count (Prince), 97 and n

Sterne, Laurence, *A Sentimental Journey*, 229 and n; *Tristram Shandy*, 87 and n, 134 and n

Stevenson, Sir John, 79n

Street, Thomas G., ed. *The Courier*, 90n

Stuart, Daniel, owner of *Morning Post* and *Courier*, 90n

Sutherland, Elizabeth, Countess of, 236n

Sylla, 256

Tacitus, 81, 173

Tasso, 97, 221

Tayler, Ann Caroline, 187n, 202n

Thackeray, William Makepeace, *Vanity Fair*, 71n, 94n

Thomson, George, and Moore's *Irish Melodies*, 113 and n

Thomson, T., unidentified, sends B. his poetry, 121 and n, 234

Thrale, Henry, 247n

Thurlow, Edward Thurlow, second Baron, 220; poem to Rogers, 54 and n, 55

Tierney, George, 237 *and n*

Toderini, Giovanni Battista, *Della Litteratura Turchesca*, 104n, 106–7, 111

Tomline, Sir George Pretyman, Bishop of Winchester, 22 *and n*; *A Refutation of Calvinism*, 22n

Tooke, Horne, 219

Turkey, 110–11, 119

Turner, J. W. M., 4n

Tweeddale, George Hay, eighth Marquis of, 153 *and n*

Valentia, Viscount, 216n

Vanbrugh, Sir John, 249; *The Relapse*, 104n, 249n

Veli Pasha, [*Vol. I, 226 and n*], 206

Virgil, *Aeneid*, 205 and n; *Eclogues*, 217 and n

Voltaire, 45n; epitaph on, 117–18

Wadd, William, *Modern Poets*, 60 and n; *Practical Observations on . . . curing Strictures*, 60 and n

Waldegrave, Lady Charlotte Maria, 4n

Walpole, Horace, 4n

Ward, J. W., 170, 173, 219; to go abroad with B., 176 and n, 180, 187, 218; epigram on, 182 and n; B.'s liking for, 215; his pun on, 227; reviews Rogers' works, 62 and n, 107n; and Wakefield-Fox Correspondence, 126 and n, 242 and n

Warwick, Richard Neville, Earl of, 209 and n

Waterpark, Richard Cavendish, second Baron, 123 and n

Webster, Lady Francis (née Valentia), 124n, 137–8, 147, 151; invites Augusta to Aston Hall, 127 and n, 128 and n; character, 142–3; relations with B., 142–3, 146–57 *passim*, 171, 173–4, 221; and his portrait, 224

Webster, James Wedderburn, [*Vol. II*, *287*], leases Aston Hall, 81 and n, 114, 122 and n; death of his son, 106n; treatment of his wife, 116–117, 129, 142, 144, 149, 221; affair with the Countess, 123–4, 127, 128, 129; aided financially by B., 138–9, 144 and n, 172, 212

Wellesley, Richard Colley Wellesley, Marquis, *232 and n*

Wellington, Arthur Wellesley, Duke of, 232n; victory at Vittoria, 73n, 75n, 90n

Westcombe, Mr., unidentified, 133

Westall, Richard, 33 and n; proposed portrait of B., 41, 198

Westmorland, Lady, 65, 71

Whitbread, Samuel, Drury Lane address contestant, 67

White, Lydia, 214 and n

Williams, William, *Journal of Llewellin Penrose*, 176 and n, 186 and n, 189

Wilmot, Mrs. (née Barberina Ogle), 140n, 214 and n

Windham, William, *219 and n*

Wingfield, John, [*Vol. I*, *101 and n*], 34n, 106n

Witt brothers, Corneille and Jean de, 212 and n

Wordsworth, William, 206, 214n, 217n, 220

Wycherley, William, *The Country Wife*, 42n

Yarmouth, Earl of (later Earl of Hertford and Yarmouth), 71n; patron of pugilists, 94 and n

Yorke and Albany, Duke of, 255n